Banishment
in the Early
Atlantic World

Banishment in the Early Atlantic World

Convicts, Rebels and Slaves

*Gwenda Morgan and
Peter Rushton*

BLOOMSBURY
LONDON • NEW DELHI • NEW YORK • SYDNEY

Bloomsbury Academic

An imprint of Bloomsbury Publishing Plc

50 Bedford Square	1385 Broadway
London	New York
WC1B 3DP	NY 10018
UK	USA

www.bloomsbury.com

Bloomsbury is a registered trade mark of Bloomsbury Publishing Plc

First published 2013
Reprinted 2013 (twice)

British Library Cataloguing-in-Publication Data
A catalogue record for this book is available from the British Library.

ISBN:	HB:	978-1-4411-3011-2
	PB:	978-1-4411-0654-4
	ePDF:	978-1-4411-5501-6
	ePUB:	978-1-4411-5498-9

Typeset by Deanta Global Publishing Services, Chennai, India
Printed and bound in Great Britain

CONTENTS

LIST OF MAPS

ACKNOWLEDGEMENTS

We have incurred a great many obligations to many people and places during this project. First, the British Academy, for a small grant on the theme 'Threatening the State' in the British Atlantic. With that funding, we were able to do some work in the United States, as a consequence of which, we must thank Boston Public Library; the Massachusetts Historical Society; The American Antiquarian Society; The South Carolina Historical Society; The Charleston Library Society; Colonial Williamsburg; The Omohundro Institute of Early American History and Culture; The Historical Society of Pennsylvania; the Library Company of Philadelphia. We must also thank the Cultural and Regional Studies Research Beacon, University of Sunderland, for financial assistance at various times, and for support from colleagues in the Beacon, and the University of Newcastle for academic support and insurance cover.

Libraries and archives in the United Kingdom have again offered superb service – our local libraries at the Universities of Sunderland, Durham and Newcastle; the Institute of Historical Research (University of London), The National Archives at Kew, and the British Library, both at St Pancras and Boston Spa. The staff everywhere have been magnificently helpful, as usual.

We would particularly like to thank the Eccles Centre for American Studies based at The British Library, and the British Association for American Studies (B.A.S.S.) for the grant of a Visiting Fellowship in 2010 to Gwenda Morgan to assist with this project.

The United States Library of Congress map collection has provided most of the eighteenth-century maps used to illustrate the book.

People who have helped, sometimes without knowing it, by simply being themselves, include – Prof Chris Brooks; Richard Maber and the Seventeenth-century Conference; Karen Kupperman; Ron Hoffman; colleagues at the British Group for Early American History (BGEAH), particularly Ben Marsh, Matthew Ward and Colin Nicholson; the Low Countries researchers at the European Social Science History Conference; Clive Emsley; Colin Younger and Lauren Clark for asking Peter to give a paper on texts of exile and identity at the 9th Annual Conference of the North-East Irish Culture Network in 2011; Andrea Knox; Warren Hofstra; Judith Rowbotham and the SOLON group; Don and Elizabeth Homsey; Irene Lewis; and Jack P. Greene.

INTRODUCTION

Between 1600 and 1800 CE, people were on the move across the worldwide European empires. This book is about some of the processes by which people were forcibly moved and what happened to them within the wide scope of the British Empire. It is, in this period, largely a story of the Atlantic. For Britain, particularly, an Atlantic perspective is fundamental to the study of the early modern period, and by the eighteenth-century, the country's eighteenth-century history can only be understood within a context of global rivalry with the French. The result of this relatively new approach has been particularly seen in studies of migration, especially of what has been termed 'forced migration'. The dominance of indentured servitude and slavery in the British North American colonies, as Aaron Fogleman has pointed out, meant that for three quarters of the arrivals in the eighteenth-century before the American Revolution, freedom was not an option.[1] This book considers the uses of forms of banishment and criminal transportation in Britain and Ireland, as well as in colonial, revolutionary and early republican North America. In the British-created jurisdictions, legal authorities developed parallel practices of expelling those who were deemed troublesome or threatening. In England, from the late sixteenth and early seventeenth centuries, 'gypsies' and vagrants, rebels and criminals were transported to the growing empire across the Atlantic. In the seventeenth and eighteenth centuries, transportation became fundamental to the application of the criminal law and to the disposal of the survivors of unsuccessful rebellions in Ireland, England and Scotland. In the colonies, however, new traditions were also developing at the same time. Seventeenth-century New England expelled religious dissenters, and in Dutch New York, the 'custom of our fatherland' led to the judicial process of banishing petty offenders from the colony.[2] In addition, a growing body of law specifically concerning African slaves relied on forms of banishment. Both European and American experiences combined and culminated in the formal expulsion of Native Americans in the seventeenth and eighteenth centuries.

'Banishment' serves here as a catch-all word for all these diverse official actions. Legitimate in the eyes of those who carried them out, if not, in fact, created or supported by judicial processes, these expulsions were typical of the way that British authorities, or those under British rule (however nominal and distant) dealt with problematic peoples of many different kinds. There was a long tradition of banning deviants and troublemakers from European cities, and from royal courts. Perhaps only in the latter were people ejected from the country. The urban variant of this kind of expulsion was practised in a number of European countries such as Germany and the Netherlands, and in Britain, remained a fundamental aspect of law enforcement in Scotland until the nineteenth century. There, though, the county or the region was sometimes the unit to be protected, reflecting an understandable adaptation of the technique to a more rural society. These were usually untargetted banishments, the equivalent of showing someone the door and asking them to leave. In many ways, these customs were also related to medieval laws of outlawry and exile, whereby offenders were often allowed to 'abjure' the kingdom without standing trial.[3] Increasingly, though, European societies made use of the need for labour in remote places, domestic and overseas, to send their banished populations there, and this was the invention of the colonial empires, such as those of the Portuguese, the Dutch and particularly the British. The banished were given a destination, and increasingly a legally enforcible social role in the developing economy of the territory, usually as 'unfree labour', and this highly organized form of expulsion reached its zenith in the forms of criminal transportation to the British colonies. Other forms of banishment, though, need to be included. The clearing of whole populations, an entire people or a territory, was unusual in early modern Europe, though Oliver Cromwell's 'settlement' of Ireland in the 1650s came closest to it. In the colonies, the reduction in native populations and the occasional removal of whole peoples was a common practice. It is as though an entire nation, loosely defined, had been criminalized, judged inherently dangerous or deviant. It is hard to use the word 'race' or 'racist' in this period, but native Americans, French speakers or religious groups might all acquire this undeserved reputation for danger.

Together with the practices of banishment, we are concerned with the *law*, that is, the legal or political framework that made such actions lawful or, even if in retrospect, legitimate. The proliferation of legal systems in the British Atlantic in the seventeenth century makes this surprisingly complicated. There was no standard law code that everyone followed everywhere. English, Scottish and Irish laws were speedily supplemented by colonial legislatures passing new laws and establishing new legal institutions to deal with new situations. Innovation in law was required to deal with new social structures such as slavery, and new situations where, for example, civil disputes over land or debts needed speedy local resolution. But this was not only a process going on in the colonies. England, Scotland and Ireland too were generating new social practices that needed new legal frameworks. The unification of Scotland and England in 1707, for example, which abolished the Scottish Parliament and brought lawmaking for the two kingdoms under the same roof, nevertheless produced a very slow and awkward process of harmonization of the two sets of laws. Perhaps it was significant that the first 'English' Act to be passed for Scotland in 1708 was the Treason Law of 1696, thus making sure that the same legal rights, but also the same definitions of the various crimes of treason, were found in both kingdoms in the face of all-too-likely rebellions. In an entirely different area of policy, new forms of welfare in the seventeenth century reduced the English urge to banish the poor, as the local welfare state of the old poor law came to care for most with a rightful place in the parish. But rights to settlement remained contentious, and *in extremis*, those with no rights to live anywhere could be sent to the colonies. More directly, minor criminals, particularly the young, were given a second chance there.[4] As bodies of law grew up on both sides of the Atlantic, they had a natural tendency to grow apart. In this increasing diversity of laws and legal rights, there was always a potential clash between laws and legal cultures.

The situation in the colonies is therefore a further major focus of this chapter, making up most of Part Two. The use of banishment in Britain's American colonies suggests continuity with the European past but, in fact, in North America and the Caribbean, banishment for political, racial or religious purposes was the norm rather than a penalty for criminal offences. Whereas Britain could send those felons who had been condemned and pardoned and, after the Transportation Act of 1718, those convicted of minor offences, to the American colonies, where were the colonists to send their criminals? For colonial courts, therefore, this punishment was not a practical one for the mass of ordinary criminals. Consequently, criminal transportation could not be used in the colonies as it was in England as an intermediate punishment between the finality of the death penalty and the bodily punishments of whipping and branding. Seventeenth-century colonists, however, made good use of banishment to rid themselves of hostile natives, rebellious settlers, religious dissidents and fractious individuals. The authorities were not particularly choosy as to where the banished went (there were even notions of banishment to the wilderness in New England, characterized as a place without white settlers). However, as order and stability came to characterize most colonies in the following century, banishment as well as transportation as a criminal punishment became increasingly associated with race and was largely inflicted on troublesome slaves. There were still small bodies of Native Americans to be dealt with in some places, but mass expulsions were rare in the 70 years up to the American Revolution, with the singular exception of the Arcadians expelled from Nova Scotia in the 1750s. This was the largest ethnic (or cultural) group displaced by the British Empire since Oliver Cromwell's regime in Ireland, a century earlier. As we shall see, one of the places the wretched Acadian diaspora reached was England itself, as hundreds landed in Bristol, Liverpool and elsewhere.

Migration and movement form a vital backdrop to this research. As the Acadian example indicates, traffic in the British Atlantic was not entirely one way, which is why the old language of the 'expansion of Europe' is so misleading for this period. From the first, people moved in both directions. Quakers went from England to the West Indies and thence northwards, to cause alarm in the hearts of devout New Englanders, who promptly banished them – sometimes back to England. Puritans went in both directions as well, some going to England to fight in the civil wars of the 1640s and

1650s, while others afraid for themselves, such as several regicides who had signed Charles I's execution warrant, left for America when his son was restored to the monarchy in 1660. Everywhere, such movements proved unsettling for the receiving society. Neat categories of social structure could suffer disruption in this process. Some of the 'white' servants coming from England were, in fact, brown since their origins were in India, a problem which swarthy British 'gypsies' also posed for the neat tri racial system of the colonies such as Virginia. Colonial racial practices caused equal confusion in London, where the authorities could not understand why freed blacks were forbidden from voting. To men for whom property was everything, a man who met the property qualification not only had a right but a duty to vote, since he had a 'fixed interest in the kingdom', as Cromwell's son-in-law Ireton expressed it in the Putney debates of 1647. Colour was not mentioned in English law, though religion was, as men outside the Church of England were disenfranchised until 1829. But race was beyond their understanding, at least to start with.[5]

This indicates an area where we are treading only with great trepidation – the problem of identities in this Atlantic world. It is not clear how many of the people whose displacement forms the core of this chapter created or sustained a collective identity in their 'exile', that is, a diasporic community whose central common experience was one of expulsion. Some long-lasting identities were already in existence before the banishment, and were reinforced by it. Quakers were part of an international community, a people without a country. The Acadians and Jacobites lost their countries, but perhaps only the former were able to construct a cohesive community with a collective identity in their exile. African slaves, British convicts or Scots and Irish rebels exported to the colonies, all became part of the social relations of their new societies, in different ways, but in ways where their transportation alone was not the sole, or even an important, factor in their self-fashioning. Yet, identity matters, however faintly it is reported in the historical record, and however fleetingly it existed in a particular time and place. It is expressed in the protests and petitions, the legal challenges and political debates, and therefore cannot be avoided. It is part of the language of the victims of the processes of expulsion studied here, and has to be acknowledged. In effect, the nation state and its legitimacy was under question whenever the banished organized their legal and political challenge to their experiences.[6]

In what follows, we start with a largely Eurocentric view in Part One, examining the foundations of English, Scots and Irish banishment in the seventeenth and eighteenth centuries, before moving, in Part Two, across the Atlantic for case studies of the different policies developed in British North America and the Caribbean. The scope could, of course, have been even greater, and we have had to neglect some people and some processes to concentrate on what we feel are a representative selection from the spectrum of judicial, political and military banishments in the British Atlantic.

MAP 1 *Britain and Ireland*

PART ONE

Diverse Patterns of Banishment in Britain and Ireland

1

The origins of English judicial banishment

The focus of this chapter is banishment through a legal process, even if that is an edict by a monarch or their subordinates in the legal system rather than prosecution and sentence. It is, admittedly, hard to distinguish banishment from involuntary exile which, among the rich and powerful, often derived from political conflicts, and among the poor from the social and economic pressures that drove unwanted minorities or individuals out of the community. Powerful exiles came under greater judicial scrutiny under Henry VIII's laws when plots hatched outside England were defined as treasonable crimes that could be tried in English courts. Political refugees were to some degree regarded as always subjects of the kingdom, wherever they were. Yet, they often fled without the force of any judicial sentence, perhaps wisely anticipating moves against them.[1] Differentiating flight from expulsion is therefore difficult, but with this conceptual misgiving in mind, it is clear that formal judicial banishment became part of English law in the final stage of the development of Elizabethan vagrancy laws – the outcome of a long process of Tudor legislation on the general problems of 'rogues' and vagabonds. From vagabonds and rogues, in effect, the targeted poor, the penalty was then extended to include criminals in the Jacobean period.

The Tudor and Stuart periods were not the first to take measures against the wandering poor, but they had their own particular anxieties. There had been laws against various kinds of vagabondage in the fourteenth century, and a system of outlawry drove people away from their usual places of residence. Towns such as Ipswich, moreover, relied on some local ordinances, such as one in 1474 enjoining 'all harlots and bawds' to leave the town within a few days under threat of being put in the pillory. But the town also received exiles, such as one citizen of London who had been outlawed, and fled to Ipswich, where he died (the town's authorities seized his goods and sold them to his widow). Communities at all levels, from parish to city, felt the need to defend themselves against needy outsiders coming to settle, and sought to limit the rights of strangers or 'foreigners'.[2] Tudor legislation focused on the problems of poverty, mobility and, above all, crime, and historians have generally located these efforts within the context of both a changing and increasingly unstable economy, and post-Reformation uncertainties in government circles about solutions to these problems. Undoubtedly, the poor became an object of political anxiety and legislative effort as never before. The first Tudor law was in 1495, and like all its successors directed at this social problem, tried to distinguish the workless from the workshy, and it can be observed that this has echoes in many subsequent policies up to and including the present day. Victorian notions of the 'undeserving poor', or twentieth-century denunciations of the welfare 'scroungers' reflect this continuing obsession with drawing the boundaries between need and greed.[3] The Henry VII law also distinguished 'vagabonds, idle and suspected Persons' from 'every Beggar not able to work' – the former were to be set in the stocks for three days on bread and water, before being put out of town. The second group was to be sent to the place where they had last dwelled, or were 'best known', and there to remain on pain of similar punishment. Subsequent laws under Henry VIII and Edward VI were much more savage, as seemingly the problem of vagrancy worsened, or perhaps was seen to be worse. These laws involved branding and even slavery as penalties for vagabondage.[4]

Under Elizabeth I, there were major efforts at general legislation against rogues and vagabonds in 1572 and 1597, together with more caring experiments in what eventually became a national system of parish-based poor law in 1601. In 1572, it was conceded that some people might have legitimate reasons to be wandering abroad – harvesters, 'cockers' (cockle-pickers, presumably), men from the armed services returning home, and those honest servants who had either been turned away by their masters or become unemployed at their death, and were therefore homeless through no fault of their own. The last was one of the first acknowledgements that poverty and mobility might occur unavoidably. It was finally in 1597 that banishment achieved its first explicit role as a judicial punishment for repeated offences of vagabondage, in *An Act for Punishment of Rogues, Vagabonds and Sturdy Beggars.*[5] The 1597 law may never have been applied in Elizabeth's reign, for when it was renewed under James I in 1603, his proclamation complained of 'the remissenesse, negligence, and connivence of some Justices of the Peace' that had permitted rogues, vagabonds, 'idle and dissolute persons' to spread so they 'swarmed and abounded every where than in times past, which will grow to the great and imminent danger of the whole Realme'. The Privy Council simultaneously noted that there had been no 'suite [suit] for assigning some place beyond the seas, to which such incorrigible or dangerous rogues might bee banished', and designated a range of places to send them to, namely 'The New-Found Land, the East and West Indies, France, Germanie, Spaine and the low-Countries, or any of them'. The 1597 legislation was continually renewed under James I and Charles I, with the Privy Council providing the specific destinations. Yet, in the 1660s, one justification for the new laws of settlement was that there were too many inducements for the poor to turn vagabond, among them the 'neglect of the faithful execution' of the laws for apprehending rogues and vagabonds.[6] The concept of rogue was also subject to legal modification that threw a widening net with broader definitions of the kinds of people who could be included in it. Early in James I's reign, under plague regulations, anyone who left an infected area, whether or not they themselves showed signs of disease, could be punished as vagabonds, and in 1609, the same could be done to those who abandoned their families to the mercies of the parish poor law.[7]

It is important to note that, although much of the official anxiety centred on 'masterless men', the legislation carefully uses 'he or she' at every point to emphasize that deviant mobility was not seen as committed only by men. The mid-Tudor laws began to add the word 'rogue' to the list of identities to be repressed, apparently a new coinage that was speedily incorporated in the legislation by Elizabeth's reign.[8] Culturally, as well as legally, 'rogues' and their way of life acquired widespread currency in England through their growing representation in print, with both supposedly factual accounts and theatrical characters reinforcing the image of an underground culture of mobility and deviance. This has also resounded through the centuries since, with the idea of rogue cultures and, today, 'rogue states' operating as an image of the exact opposite of civilization and order. From the picaresque characters in the underworld settings of Jacobean plays, to the printed guides to criminal cant and techniques, the rogue had become a permanent feature of English society by the early 1600s. Wanderers in society were therefore constantly subject to interrogation by the authorities to determine their character, compared with the image, though quite what the magistrates in Southampton made of a bricklayer in 1639 who reported that he was unemployed in winter, during which time 'he doth go abroad to see fashions', is unclear. The 'rogue' had become a part of the law, literary conceit and print culture.[9]

Another significant development was the recognition of wanderers of ethnically different origin from the English, often known initially as 'Egyptians' and later, in shortened form, as 'gypsies' – both terms reflecting their eastern derivation, if not any accurate geographic knowledge of their origins. Here, as with 'rogues', there was a cultural dimension that aroused official anxiety.[10] There seems to have been almost more attention given to fake or fraudulent gypsies than real ones, with a few exceptional instances of mass prosecution of 'Egyptians' themselves. Language specialists generally agree that there were real Romani speakers in the sixteenth and seventeenth centuries in England and Wales. Some of their words became part of a travellers' underground culture. 'Cant' and canting language show Romani influence in various periods, including the sixteenth century, when the terms were first used and associated with 'gypsies', and in the seventeenth and eighteenth centuries when dictionaries of underground jargon and sayings were published. Telling the real from their imitators, however, is as difficult for historians in retrospect as it was at the time. The apparently exotic character of underground culture exercised fascination on the literary imagination throughout the period to the rise of nineteenth-century Romanticism.[11] Political responses, however, were less sympathetic.

On occasions, the legal repression of either gypsies or those who associated with them could be severe. The first laws were under Henry VIII in 1530, allowing the authorities to order the removal from the kingdom of illegal gypsy immigrants within fifteen days of their being discovered. If any of those remaining committed a serious felony, then all the rest could be expelled. In fact, there are records of several mass expulsions in Henry VIII's reign – in 1544, groups were deported to France through the port of Calais from Huntingdon, and to Norway from Boston, Hull and Newcastle. Details are scanty, but it seems that prosecutions of various kinds had preceded these decisions.[12] The legislation in the mid-Tudor period became more intense under Edward VI, Mary and Elizabeth I. As before, it was illegal to import 'Egyptians', and they could be expelled if found or if serious offences had been proved to be their responsibility. Much of the force of the law was against non-gypsies associating with them and assuming their culture and appearance – the Elizabethan law of 1562, 'for further punishment of vagabonds calling themselves Egyptians', made it a capital felony without benefit of clergy to associate with them for one month, or 'counterfeiting, transforming or disguising themselves by their Apparel, Speech or other Behaviour, like unto such Vagabonds'.[13]

Expulsions from the country of gypsies themselves, however, seem to have been abandoned because, by the middle of Elizabeth's time, an increasing number were native-born, and appearing in parish records as baptized like any other inhabitant. In a famous case of 196 gypsies tried at York in 1596, 106 were sentenced to death. In the end, however, all but nine were reprieved and sent to their home parishes. Evidence elsewhere is slim – A. L. Beier found few gypsies among his large sample of those arrested for vagrancy and, when they were identified, concluded that they were not in the large menacing groups the authorities feared so much. When arrested, their groups were rarely more than a dozen strong, and consisted of several families. They were usually treated as vagabonds.[14] Things were decidedly different with regard to those who 'consorted' with gypsies, and appeared like them. In several Middlesex cases in the Elizabethan period, for example, death sentences are recorded for groups of men and women who 'were seen and found in the consort or society of vagabonds called Egipcians' – five men in 1595 and one of two women (the other was reprieved because she was pregnant) in 1601. These cases involved people from London, since the fairs and markets attracted travellers of all kinds, and others elsewhere in the country on the same charges claimed to have joined up with gypsies there. One of the most comprehensive lists of Romani words derives from a Hampshire confession provided by a man who had met gypsies in London.[15]

Whatever the judicial strategy, 'gypsies' remained a permanent feature of British society. Gypsies, rogues, vagabonds and other apparently uncontrollable travellers have remained both a presence and a flashpoint for local conflicts and legal disputes up to the twenty-first-century – they are, as in Ireland, an 'indigenous other', simultaneously native and alien. We have little evidence of gypsies transported from England under Elizabethan

or Stuart laws, though there are occasionally identified among the criminals
sent to the colonies in the eighteenth century. In the colonies themselves,
'Egyptians' are occasionally mentioned, for example in late seventeenth-
century Virginia, usually when it was decided that the law against fornication
could not apply to people who were not Christian. But it is not known how
they arrived there. Others, recorded as running away from their indentured
service, were clearly convicts from England.[16] One undoubted incident of
English gypsies transported to the colonies was from Northumberland in the
early eighteenth century. Significantly, there is no use of the words 'Egyptian'
or 'gypsy' in this series of Border events, which had its own language of
vagrancy. In the autumn of 1711, the magistrates pronounced that:

> Whereas severall notorious sturdy vagrants calling themselves by the
> names of Baleys, Shaws, Falls or ffawes have of late come into this county
> and keepe themselves together in severall parts thereof – threatning
> to burne houses and are suspected of burglarys thefts and other evill
> practices and ride armed to the great terror of her maj. [esty's] subjects.
> It is therefore ordered by this court that a warrant under the seale of this
> court issue forth to take and apprehend the said vagrants.

In addition, six pounds were to be paid for the apprehension of each one
above the age of 16 years, by way of 'incouragement'.[17] They were uncertain
about the strategy they should adopt, and were perhaps unfortunate that
they began to take action just as the law was being changed. Richard Burn
notes that the vagrancy law of Queen Anne repealed all previous legislation,
and this occurred right in the middle of the campaign against the Faws or
Baileys in Northumberland. The justices therefore first tried the Elizabethan
method of applying for an order 'of Councell' that is, from the Privy Council,
under the 1597 law, and, since they had not made sufficient arrests, had
to renew their efforts under more recent laws against incorrigible rogues.
Though they managed to arrest a large number in 1712, it seems that most
of the men broke out of the prison, leaving four women and a large number
of their children in custody. The women were whipped, and the children
maintained, initially at great expense, and then more cheaply, by being
apprenticed to various trades. Although a large number of men and women,
involving at least six married couples, were named in a 1713 indictment
for being incorrigible vagabonds, attempts to arrest them were still being
made early in 1717, and it was then, almost six years after the initial panic,
that many were rounded up. In March 1717, they were deemed 'indicted
and convicted' of being vagabonds, and more expense was incurred when
putting them on board ship to be 'transported beyond seas'. The children
were still being maintained by the county, and it seems that a total of more
than £179 had been spent in searching for, arresting and keeping the gang.
The children were receiving payments for years after the expulsion of their
parents.[18] A parallel effort was made on the Scottish side of the border
simultaneously (see Chapter 2). Elsewhere in Europe, there may have been

more assiduous efforts to banish them – 'perhaps the most severe repression occurred in Portugal where the crown attempted to systematically round up and banish gypsy (*cigano*) families to overseas colonies in Africa and America'. Certainly, there was nothing like the situation in the Netherlands, where gypsies 'appear to have been literally chased out of the country by the mid-eighteenth century'. In England, there were occasional individuals and groups of 'incorrigible rogues' who, like Bamfylde Moore Carew in 1739 (the self-styled 'king of the gypsies'), were sent to serve seven years in the colonies for vagrancy.[19]

Another group targeted for removal from the late Tudor period were the Irish, fleeing from poverty, the chaos of the Elizabethan nine-year war from 1594 to 1603, and, in the early seventeenth century, intermittent famine. They provided a specific focus of anxiety in late-Elizabethan and early Jacobean England – and also in France, whose towns and cities witnessed an influx of rich and, particularly, poor refugees in the first decade of the seventeenth century. There were many parallels in the ways the two countries, scarcely allies in other regards, responded to the threat. Policies of concentration, expulsion and transportation back to Ireland were, in various measures, adopted at different times. In France, these centred on the wave of refugees arriving in large numbers by 1605. In England, the government responded in a similar way to what were deemed emergencies. In 1633, for example, as famine produced large numbers fleeing from Ireland, Charles I's 1633 *Proclamation for the speedie sending away of the Irish Beggars out of this Kingdome into their owne Countrey and for the Suppressing of English Rogues and Vagabonds according to Our Lawes* gave Irish beggars 40 days to leave the country or be punished as rogues and vagabonds, after which they would be sent to Ireland from the ports of Bristol, Minehead, Barnstaple, Chester, Liverpool, Milford Haven or Workington.[20] Paul Slack observes that apart from the professional rogues and 'wandering pedlars', there were two main groups identifiable in the early seventeenth century – runaway apprentices and servants, and the Irish. Of the latter, he notes:

> Nineteen of them were punished as vagrants in Salisbury, between 1629 and 1633 when Irish famine pushed hundreds of emigrants into the western counties. They were more conspicuous than their numbers suggest, since they often moved in bands of a dozen or more.

They were found in places as far apart as Colchester in Essex and Colyton, the groups consisting of a small number of adults with much more numerous children.[21] A few years later, when fighting started in Ireland in 1640–1, with the rebellion and alleged massacres that provoked vengeful anger in England and, in effect, started the civil wars, there were other forms of Irish found wandering – refugees. Parishes on this occasion took sympathy with their fellow Protestants and tried to maintain them if they could afford it – in North-East England, Gateshead helped a number of families at this time. This was in marked contrast to the treatment of the Catholic poor in previous decades. There were others in subsequent years, such as in April 1648, when the town gave two shillings each to two women, 'Elizabeth Hendson that came from Ireland' and 'Elizabeth young that was robbed in Ireland', but in 1650, it gave five shillings to 'an Irish gentleman, his wife and four children'.[22]

There is little comprehensive statistical evidence of the consequences of all this legislative effort and political action, as Abbot E. Smith pointed out many years ago, but there is some indication that, for southern authorities under James I, in England at least, sending vagabonds to Virginia was a great deal cheaper than some alternatives. In Middlesex in September 1619, four vagabonds (two of them women) were convicted as 'incorrigible rogues' and branded with the letter 'R' on their left shoulders, while a man who had already been branded was condemned to 'perpetual imprisonment in the House of Correction'. Yet, the previous month in a similar case, a man had been reprieved by the sheriff and sent to Virginia. This was chosen as an alternative to branding and release back into the community.[23] By the 1620s and 1630s, it seems to have been almost routine to try and empty the London Bridewell by transporting some of the poor to the colonies, probably without any official process of accusing them of more than vagabondage, let alone 'incorrigible' roguery – poverty was sufficient proof. Some had little choice, as they were virtually children. In 1619, nearly 100 young people – who, it was said, laid 'in the streets . . . having no place of abode nor friends to relieve them', were gathered together and shipped to Virginia by the combined efforts of the Virginia Company and the Common Council of the City of London. From 1622, despite the Indian massacres of that year, a programme was undertaken that sent more than 500 young people to the colony over the next five years.[24] As A. L. Beier notes, concerning the poor in London and particularly the inmates of the Bridewell, the recruitment of the children has become a familiar story:

> What is not well known is that transportation of London vagrants continued on a large scale after 1622. Bridewell's Court Books are peppered with references to vagrants sent to Bermuda, Barbados, Virginia, and 'to sea'. Questions remain to be answered about transportation in seventeenth-century London – how many were sent, who was sent, and to which colonies – but a more thorough analysis of the records will be required than heretofore and than is possible here.[25]

In 1631, for example, the Mayor and Aldermen of London reported that:

> Great sums of money were last year raised for relief of the poor and setting them to work. Fifty vagrants were bound apprentices to merchants to serve in the Islands of Barbadoes and Virginia; 70 were taken as apprentices

into Bridewell; 773 poor children were maintained by Christ's hospital, 40 had been put apprentices to trades since Easter last, and 4,000 and odd vagrants conveyed according to the statute.[26]

After the Restoration, the categorization was far more casual, with convicted criminals and those of 'loose and idle conversation' held in various London lock-ups gathered together indiscriminately for transportation to the West Indies. As before, this was largely an effort at clearing out the unwanted from London institutions and jails. In 1661, it was reported:

> This day severall Lists of the Names of Prisoners remaining in the Prisons of Newgate, White Lyon in South-warke, Gate house at Westminster, New Bridewell (otherwise called the house of Correction) at St James Clerkenwell, Bridewell in London, House of Correction at Westminster in Tuttlefeilds, and the Prison of the Marshalsey, being presented to this Board, together with the humble petition of Jeremy Boimell, Edward Bernerd and Company of London Merchants Shewing,
> That whereas his Majestic hath been graciously pleased to favour them with his Shipp the Great Charity for the better setling the Island of Jamaica, and to that purpose have putt themselves in good forwardness to proceed in their Voyage for Advance of that Plantation. And having notice of many convicted persons, and others of loose and idle Conversation who remayn in the said Prisons, which being transported thither, might do his Majestic good Service, And prayed his Majestie to graunt Warrant to the Lord Maior of London for delivery of the said convicted persons into the petitioners possession to bee transported to the Island aforesaid: [the petition and lists] are Referred to the Lord Cheife Justice of the Kings Bench and to the Recorder of the Citty of London, to consider which and how many of the said Prisoners are fitt to bee sent to Jamaica; and to give Warrant . . . for delivery of them to the said Merchants . . . in such manner as his Lordshipp and Mr. Recorder shall conceive best and safest for the more certain putting them on Ship board, and acquitting this Nation from them.[27]

These were only a part of the larger traffic across the Atlantic, as many were induced to sign up as indentured service. From the first shipments of servants, paupers and convicts, 'free' and unfree, to the colonies, there were accusations of coercion. The surviving records suggest that the royal authorities were willing to take action against those responsible – for example, in 1634, it was reported before the High Commission that a man was under arrest – 'Henry Deane, of Greenwich, fisherman. Receiving men and young women to be transported beyond seas, without leave; committed to Newgate'. A few years later, in 1638, it was reported that 'two men are apprehended [in] Westminster, upon information given by this bearer John Bradstreet, of misdemeanours usually committed by them and their associates, as, namely, the taking up of men and selling them like cattle to be transported beyond seas by such as have no Licence to levy. Mr. Secretary desires you to examine them upon interrogatories, that according to the nature of their offences they may be remitted to the Lords or otherwise ordered'.[28] These accusations against those using coercion would recur throughout the history of the servant trade, from 'spiriters' in Restoration Bristol and London to the 'soul-drivers' in Ulster in the middle of the eighteenth century. Few were subject to any legal accountability, though from the middle of the seventeenth century, many were brought to court in Middlesex, following a 1645 ordinance against those who were trying to 'steal away many little children'. It might be going too far to say that 'the dark underside of servant recruitment was kidnapping', but it is clear that the rumours of violent seizure and colonial oppression made young people reluctant to sign up for servitude in the colonies in the 1670s. One Jamaica planter was told that 'soe many storys [were] being told from the Bristoll men of their Hard usage and Want of provisions' that it was impossible to recruit servants, and another reported that all he could get as a result were 'poore prisoners' and the 'spirited', the latter of which he thought 'neither honest nor Christian'.[29]

As in other examples, the line between free choice and coercion is here so thin as to be almost invisible. If poverty did not drive people abroad, then the law might; if they were not deceived, they were forced. The structures at home and overseas combined to blur these distinctions and provide the means for supplying the colonies with workers. Internal and external colonialism coincided and overlapped, as mobility at home and abroad dovetailed neatly to provide the means of pacifying the wild people in England and the savage places abroad.[30]

Before the civil wars: The first colonies and the development of criminal transportation

According to John Beattie, two parallel developments led to the adoption of transportation as a means of punishment, particularly of those pardoned from execution, in the seventeenth century. First, the way that the 'capital provisions of the English criminal law were strengthened and extended, very largely by Parliament', which removed the benefit of clergy from many offences – this meant that it was not possible for those accused of many serious offences to escape the full punishment by passing a simple reading test (though, in practice, it was rarely performed). This process, beginning in the sixteenth century and resumed after the Glorious Revolution of 1688, greatly increased the chances of death for many convicted criminals. However, in a counter-process, benefit of clergy was extended to women in several stages in the seventeenth century, in 1624 and 1692, and eventually in 1706 to all accused, whether they were literate or not. 'In the course of two centuries, beginning in the sixteenth, the nature of clergy was changed entirely, for it was increasingly withdrawn from more and more offences, but at the same time extended to more people'. 1706 also saw the first Act suggesting imprisonment as the normal punishment for those convicted under these conditions of grand larceny.[31] This reflects the second key policy being pursued at this time – the search for a secondary punishment for those who, in various ways, had been let off the death penalty. The use of the Atlantic colonies as the location for the punishment was an obvious choice. However, to quote Beattie, before the 1718 Transportation Act, there was great enthusiasm but a 'decidedly mixed legislative record' of laws to underpin what seems to have been an increasingly popular form of punishment in government circles.[32]

What Radzinowicz once called the 'Doctrine of Maximum Severity', derived from the record of repeated creation of new hanging offences and punitive discussions in public prints, such as the 1701 pamphlet *Hanging Not Punishment Enough*, contained a signal paradox – as William Paley put it towards the end of the eighteenth century, 'the charge of cruelty is answered by observing that these laws were never meant to be carried into indiscriminate execution'. This reflects that fact that all new severity continually proved unworkable, and other means of punishment were sought.[33] The coincidence of increased legal penalties being followed almost immediately by a search for milder alternatives to the death penalty cannot be accidental, if only because it seems to have occurred twice, at the beginning of both the seventeenth and eighteenth centuries.[34] Severity needed to be balanced by mechanisms of mercy. According to A. E. Smith, 'the initiative was taken by James I who in 1615 gave judges discretion to reprieve felons on condition that they were employed "in foreign discoveries or other services beyond the seas"', leading Barbara Shapiro to comment that while no one could argue that 'Jacobean interest in the criminal code was as intense as that of later years, it was not negligible'.[35] As we have seen, under the 1603 decree on vagabondage the designated destinations were Newfoundland, East and West Indies, France, Germany, Spain and the Low Countries, but this was followed soon after by the foundation of the North American and Caribbean colonies – Virginia in 1607, St Christopher (St Kitts) in 1624, Barbados in 1627, Nevis in 1628 and Montserrat and Antigua in the 1630s. Jamaica was seized in 1655. This produced a more extensive and continually expanding range of destinations for banishment.[36] It seems that severity and mercy had to go hand in hand, and that every time the severity of punishment was increased towards certain execution, the British state had to seek less savage alternatives. In this way, the government and the monarchy could tread an ill-defined line between severity and mercy, between being justly severe and selectively forgiving. Calibrating the punishment to the person, the circumstances and the crime was not a matter of scientific judgement or accurate measurement of the seriousness of the crime or the culpability of the offender. If the need for greater harshness was induced by fear of crime, then the establishment of transatlantic colonies provided the opportunity for selective acts of royal mercy. These were judicious, if not precisely judicial.

Therefore, the idea of banishment, which began as a way of disposing of the vagrant and uncontainable poor, was quickly adapted and developed into an integral part of criminal justice. There appears to have been an experiment in individual cases under James I, as criminals were assigned to Virginia and elsewhere, and this expanded into a much larger system of pardon under his son, Charles I. A. E. Smith appears to have been right when he detected a shift in the procedure in the mid-1630s, by which time the full implementation seems to have been in evidence, with pardoning and transporting condemned criminals becoming almost routine. At first, the process seems to have involved petitions on behalf of the condemned, which were sent to a special commission for consideration. This group had to be renewed at regular intervals with the appointment of new members. At the start, the chair authorized to convene it was the Archbishop of Canterbury, and he continued to receive this commission among others into Charles I's reign. The instructions were to 'repryve and staye from execution such persons as stand convicted or hereafter shall be convicted for small offences, who for strength of body or other abilitye shall be thought to be ymployed in forraigne discoveries of other services beyond the seas'. The Archbishop was also charged with the duty of expelling from England and Ireland Catholic priests – in fact, 'all Jesuits and seminary preists as are indicted, convicted or attaynted'.[37] The information is not plentiful, but it seems this was an adjunct to the general procedure that had seen pardons being authorized through the king's authority for centuries. The change, however, is perhaps significant. Whereas in the thirteenth century, a pardon allowed a person to resume their place in society after a period of outlawry, in the early seventeenth century, a pardon was a granted on the condition that the convicted felons would leave the country.[38] One of the earliest criminal cases led to a decision 'that Ambrose Smithe, convicted of a felony on the goods of the Earl of Arundel and reprieved, is of able body to be employed in any service in Virginia, or in the East Indies'. The following year, 1619, a highway robber in Newgate jail was assisted by Lord Francis Russell, who begged a reprieve from the Privy Council, only to be told 'there was an Order from the Board for that purpose for some offences of that kind and that robbery by the highway was a thing the Lords would be sparing in to grant'. Perhaps because this was a crime not *specifically* ruled out of the exercise of mercy, the plea was allowed, but it is unclear if it was successful.[39]

There are several features of this system, which laid down precedents for the future. There were certain crimes for which pardons were not considered – in the original royal proclamation, James I had excluded those condemned for 'wilful murther, rape, witchcraft or burglary'.[40] Though petitions came through for pardoning such criminals, there were likely to be refused. Highway robbers and those guilty of repeated offences, such as pickpocketing, were also regarded sceptically, while there are several others convicted of horse stealing who received mercy. In the case of a repeated offender as a pickpocket, it was reported:

> Wallis taken in the Star Chamber this day for picking a pocket, sent to the King's Bench and arraigned there: he had been often in such offences before. His Majesty was to be moved to grant [him] no more pardons, nor to give way to his sending abroad.[41]

Prisoners had to be fit or have 'strength of bodye' to serve abroad, particularly in the tropics or the military. This was defined at the outset, and remained a criterion that was carefully applied before the mid-seventeenth century. Exceptionally, such criteria of fitness were based on the convict's occupation. In the Middlesex county records, for example, the magistrates suggested that a man convicted of manslaughter (for which he would normally be branded on the hand, except if it involved a stabbing, which was exempt from the usual benefit of clergy) was recommended for Virginia, because he was a carpenter, a skill which the colony desperately needed.[42]

Destinations were sometimes left vague – convicts were 'to be transported into the parts beyond the seas, either to serve in the wars, or in some of his Majesty's plantations', or 'into foreign parts', or to the 'English plantations beyond the seas'. As more colonies were established, so they could be specified, and the sentences became quite diverse – 'Virginia or the Bermudas' (1622), Barbados and Virginia (1631, the only one mentioning Barbados, and significantly affecting vagrants rather than criminals); Guyana, St Christopher and, by the 1660s, Jamaica.[43] In one exceptional case, from London in 1637, 'Clare Corneline, a Dutch woman, convicted of stealing 33 ells of sarsnet, [was] reprieved in regard the Court was informed that the elders of the Dutch Church would cause her to be transported into her own country'.[44] Rather more obscure was a petition from the French authorities that resulted in the deportation of one man – 'Certificate of the Under-keeper of the Clink, that Richard Salum removed prisoner from the King's Bench to the Clink, and from thence to be transported over sea with others; had ever since suffered from an infirmity, in which he had no ease'. Later, it was ordered by 'The King to the Keeper of the prison of the Clink. Warrant Westminster, to enlarge Richard Salum, and deliver him to Du Moulin, a French gentleman, to be transported beyond seas'.[45] The penalty for returning was the execution of the original death sentence. Those who returned without 'warrant' or 'licence' from the king in effect condemned themselves to death.[46]

This process of reprieve became almost institutionalized as the king personally signed the pardons, after about 1634. After then, both the process of selection, involving royal pardon, and the threat of the death penalty if the transportees returned without permission, had taken the form that was to be picked up and extended even further at the Restoration and in legislation in the eighteenth century. Even the language of the penalty for returning was carefully repeated during the Interregnum in certain legal measures, though the licence required was then issued by Parliament. The evidence of pre-Civil War transportation of criminals derives from the royal orders sent to a number of county authorities and jailers, usually, as discussed above, in response to a plea for mercy. The numbers revealed in the sources are not large compared with later shipments. In 1635 and 1636, for example, at least 24 people were ordered to the colonies, nine of them women. The counties where they were convicted were largely around London and in the cities of London and Westminster themselves – Kent, Sussex, Essex, Hertfordshire and Surrey are mentioned.[47] In all cases, Virginia was the intended destination. Most of the orders named ship captains who were to carry out the transportation (or, sometimes, a couple, one of whom would do so). On one occasion, the arrangement was left to the felon's family:

> The King to the Sheriffs of London and the Keeper of Belvoir Castle. Newgate. The King having received certificate from Edward Littleton, Recorder, touching the King's mercy to Tho[ma]s Brice, a condemned prisoner in Newgate, they are required to deliver him to Capt. Thomas Ketelby, or to any other Captain whom Ralph Brice, father to the delinquent, shall appoint, the body of said Thomas Brice, to be Transported to the King's plantation in Virginia.[48]

The orders of royal mercy authorizing their transportation consistently involved the threat that the original death sentence would be carried out if the felons returned 'without the King's special license'. The issue of whether the condemned had a license from the King to be in the kingdom could be a matter of discussion by the Privy Council if a convict came before them later on – in the case of Surrey criminal Richard Ingram, who was found at large in 1635, there was his previous record of stealing two 'kine' or cows two years before, when he had been ordered for transportation, as well as his taking two horses in 1635 itself. 'Ingram confesses he had not been in Virginia nor had license to stay in this kingdom. The sheriff is commanded to stay execution till his Majesty's further direction'. It is unlikely that he escaped death a second time.[49] All the extant cases involved convictions for crimes where there was no benefit of clergy. It is striking that no period of transportation was specified at this time, which suggests that, at this period, the penalty was intended to be for life. The definition of being 'at large' after order for transportation, as it was later called, seems at this period to have been subject to individual definitions, perhaps varying with a particular order. In 1639, with regard to seven Surrey convicts, the order ran:

> Warrant to the Sheriff of Surrey and the Keeper of the Gaol of White Lion, Southwark. To deliver to William Flemmen of London, gent., the bodies of Francis Osborne, alias Stillinge, Alice Williams, and five others

> condemned prisoners in the said gaol, to be transported to Virginia, with
> proviso that if they remain here above 20 days after their enlargement, or
> return without license, then to be executed.[50]

It is not clear why this was specified – it is possible that it was a device to
induce a speedy disposal of the criminals abroad.

It is unclear who initiated the process of reprieve, but it seems to have
taken force from the reports of the judges to the King or his commissioners.
In at least one case, the Recorder of London, Edward Littleton, sent the king
a 'certificate . . . touching the King's mercy to Thomas Brice, a condemned
prisoner in Newgate'. This suggests that either Littleton had already
offered Brice mercy at the trial, or it was subsequent to conviction and
condemnation petitioning on his behalf.[51] One case was closer to voluntary
exile – significantly headed, 'Acts of the Court of High Commission', a
court invented in the Elizabethan time for enforcing orthodoxy on deviating
ministers and punishing other deviant practices inside the Church; the order
went:

> A petition read from John Haydon, prisoner in Bridewell, wherein he
> voluntarily acknowledges his manifold contempts against the authority
> of the Court, as well in preaching abroad since his degradation, as also
> in making sundry escapes out of prison, and offers voluntarily to leave
> this kingdom and go to Virginia, if order were given for his enlargement;
> which the Court ordered on his giving bond with sufficient sureties.[52]

It is likely that this rogue preacher chose Virginia in preference to an equally
disease-ridden jail.

The civil wars and the Interregnum

The Cromwellian Interregnum was a crucial period both for legislative
invention and the development of the practices of banishment and
transportation. Yet, the debates and policies of the 1640s and 1650s were
inconsistent and, in many ways, contradictory. In one way, Parliament and
the Cromwellian government continued the policies of Charles I's despised
regime. Religious persecution and political trials had led in 1637 to the
banishment of several men, the ferociously punished Puritan 'martyrs',
Dr John Bastwick, Henry Burton and William Prynne, who were subjected
to a kind of internal exile for sedition. After being put in the pillory
and losing their ears, Prynne was sent, via Caernarvon in North Wales,
to Jersey in the Channel Islands, and Burton to Guernsey; Bastwick was
imprisoned in the Scilly Isles. Despite this background, the Cromwellian
regime treated 'Freeborn' John Lilburne in a similar way, also sending

him to imprisonment in the Channel Islands. He was, in fact, banished twice, once by Act of Parliament in 1651 after a jury had acquitted him of treason through his writings, including a petition to Parliament. After returning from the Continent in 1653, he was again acquitted by a London jury – possibly the first trial of a returned exile – and imprisoned, first in the Tower of London, and then eventually in Jersey. His first exile was a simple expulsion from 'England, Scotland, Ireland and the islands, territories and dominions thereof', return from which was to be judged 'felony after the fact'.[53]

The Interregnum nevertheless saw the first widespread critique of the criminal law and systems of punishment, which presaged many of the debates in the late eighteenth century. Oliver Cromwell himself is recorded in 1656 as commenting to Parliament that:

The truth of it is, there are wicked and abominable laws which it will be in your power to alter. To hang a man for six and eight pence and I know know not what: to hang for a trifle and acquit murder, is in the ministration of the law through the ill framing of it. I have known in my experience abominable murderers acquitted and to see men lose their lives for petty matters: this is a thing God will reckon for.

There had been longstanding and general puritan dissatisfaction with the law, its complexity and expense, which had broken open into substantial criticism of the severity of the criminal law in the 1640s. One aspect, the use of the death penalty to protect property from thefts, attracted particular criticism from the Levellers. There was also the supporting evidence from Biblical literalists that the Bible tended to sanction compensation as a punishment for theft, rather than severe corporal punishment. Despite these debates, there was little substantial alteration to the criminal statutes.[54]

Legislation during the Interregnum authorizing more widespread banishment was largely confined to the repression of the Irish after 1649 (see Chapter 4). However, there was some deployment of transportation in England, and some debate in Parliament about it. The first involved *An Act against several Atheistical and Execrable Opinions, derogatory to the Honor of God, and destructive to Human Society*, in 1650, which, asserting that propagating the Gospel was a parliamentary duty, expressed great 'grief and astonishment, that there are divers men and women who have lately discovered themselves to be most monstrous in the their Opinions and loose in all wicked and abominable Practices . . . not onely [sic] to the notorious corrupting and disordering, but even to the dissolution of all Humane Society, who rejecting the use of any Gospel Ordinances, do deny the necessity of Civil and Moral Righteousness among men'. The Act made it law that first offenders should be imprisoned for six months without bail. Conviction was in front of a magistrate or equivalent, by the evidence of two or more witnesses, resembling the practice in treason trials. Second offenders, convicted at trial at the assizes or gaol delivery, were to be sentenced to 'Banishment . . . out of the Commonwealth of England and all Dominions thereof', their departure to be timed as could be reasonably arranged. As was by now traditional, returning from transportation 'without special licence of Parliament' was to be treated as a felony, without benefit of clergy, ensuring a death sentence.[55]

The same year, Parliament was exercised by the actions of the royalist authorities in the colonies, which, it was claimed, had committed 'divers acts of rebellion', whereby they 'have most Trayterously, by Force and Subtilty, usurped a Power of Government, and seized the Estates of many well-affected persons into their hands, and banished others'. In order to restore the victims of these actions 'to the freedom of their persons and possession of their own Lands and goods', the perpetrators were declared 'robbers and Traitors, and such as by the Law of Nations are not to be permitted any maner of Commerce or Traffique with any people whatsoever'. This affected trade with Virginia, Barbados, Antigua and Bermuda.[56] The displacement of huge numbers of people, however, was the policy adopted by the Cromwellian authorities after the brutal conquest and forcible resettlement of Ireland, from 1649 onwards. Legal formalities were few before 1657, by which time most of the damage had been done, and thousands had been exported to foreign service or servitude in the colonies. The legal framework was set up by *An Act for the Attainder of the Rebels in Ireland*. In essence, the fighting was over in 1653, and yet, there were many rebels and ex-rebels at large, so by forcibly removing them to Connaught, the Cromwellian government wanted to make the identification of potential enemies simpler – if they were found in Leinster, Ulster and Munster (excepting County Clare), such people could be tried and convicted of being at large and sentenced to 'perpetual banishment', and be sent 'into America or some other parts beyond the Seas'. The offence was that, by being there, they contradicted the 1652 *Act for the Setling [sic] of Ireland*.[57] Thomas Burton's notes suggest that a general Act was contemplated the same year in England, making returning from transportation a statutory felony for the first time – on 28 May 1657, he records, 'Mr Bond moved, that it might be felony for any person banished to return; which was resolved'. In a footnote, the formula was 'That the [blank], not to return, after transported to some of the plantations, be filled up with the word "seven", and the blank for the penalty with the word "felony"' – this suggests that seven years had entered official thinking as the minimum sentence of transportation. However, it seems that this was incorporated in the Irish legislation, but not applied specifically to England.[58]

Yet, the proposed transportation of James Nayler during his 1656 arraignment before Parliament for blasphemy (imitating Christ by riding into town on an ass), discussed as one of the options for punishing him for blasphemy, was regarded sceptically by several speakers as being illegal if not ordered by Parliament, and even then, in danger of setting a bad precedent. The lack of any legal framework for general transportation of felons may have been at question here. One moderate commentator, Major General Disbrowe suggested, 'I shall offer an expedient, though haply foolishly: that this fellow may be banished; for life is precious, and you have matter enough, already, to ground such a sentence upon'. A few days later, there was serious consideration given to the idea. Lord Strickland, who had commented 'it is a hard case that we should have no law in force to try this gentleman, but you must have recourse to your legislative power', took up the problem further:

> There may be a Bill for banishment; for, by the law, no Englishman ought to be banished but by Act of Parliament. Nor can you properly pass any sentence upon him but you must do it by Bill. I am not satisfied in your judicial way of proceeding. I would have every Englishman be careful in this case. It has been our happiness to be governed by a known law. The Earl of Strafford's case is particularly excepted, not to be drawn into precedent.
>
> Heresies are like leaden pipes under ground. They run on still, though we do not see them, in a commonwealth where they are restrained. Where liberty is, they will discover themselves, and come to punishment. There is no such need of drawing you out to such punishment as death. Restrain him, rather, to some country or place; banish him, &c. This House is a living law, but make as little use of the legislative power as you can. It is a dangerous precedent to posterity. It is against the *Instrument of Government* to proceed to further punishment upon this business. Confine him, banish him, or do what you will.

Major General Jephson responded:

> I wonder such a doctrine should be broached in this House, that it is against the liberty of the people to have recourse to the legislative power. I think rather, the contrary. The case of the Earl of Strafford only limits the judges not to proceed upon that law; but surely the gentlemen are mistaken, who say the Parliament is restrained thereby. I know no such clause in that Bill. Doubtless you may resume that power when you please. I would, to choose, leave a precedent in this case, to posterity. There is no danger at all in it.
>
> I hope God will stir up your zeal in a matter that so eminently concerns the cause of God. We ought to vindicate his honour. For my part, I am clearly satisfied that, upon the whole matter, this person deserves to die.

In their discussions, they were aware of recent cases of banishment to nearby islands, such as that of the radical John Liburne and, when it came to Nayler, one suggestion was 'send him to Biddle in the Isle of Scilly'.[59]

Pardon and criminal transportation
after the restoration

Banishment underwent renewed emphasis in the Restoration period, in a number of legal contexts. In addition to the punishment of criminals, it became one of the key features of judicial repression of Quakers and other people whose forms of worship were defined as 'seditious conventicles' in the 1660s (see Chapter 3). More importantly, transportation was also embodied, for the first time, in some of the criminal laws. Beattie notes that the Restoration 'enthusiasm for transportation was embodied in a number of statutes', notably *An Act for the Better prevention of Theft and Rapine on the Borders*, which allowed judges to substitute transportation for life for execution, while removing the benefit of clergy from a variety of thefts committed in Northumberland and Cumberland. Also, new legislation made stealing cloth from tenters at night a capital offence, but one for which an Act of 1670 allowed transportation.[60]

In addition to the legislative framework, there was a much more widespread policy of reprieve, particularly during the trial process, as judges, in effect, negotiated with the accused. Beattie distinguishes these 'administrative' pardons performed by the judges at the trials from the 'more personal pardons' that resulted from appeal to the Secretary of State for royal consideration, which also remained important, at least while royalty took a personal interest. What might be described as the traditional methods of pardoning and transporting – approval by royal signature – were turned into a system after 1660. At times, it seems that Charles II was also deciding between a complete pardon and one conditional on transportation. In a letter to the Lord Chief Justice, he commented on the reprieve of two convicted criminals who were, he said, 'designed to be put into the Transportation Pardon', but he had decided that they 'shall receive the benefit of the pardon without the necessity of transportation'. In many instances, a free pardon was allowed if the convicts 'transported themselves'. For much of the time, the judges were negotiating in open court before sentencing, as Beattie notes, 'The men and women who found themselves manipulated into transportation in the decades after 1660 were perhaps grateful to opt for this lesser evil since the alternative they faced was the death penalty. But manipulated they were; and their agreement to be transported – an agreement that was essential if their removal was to be legal – was in effect extorted from them'.[61]

The consequences are clear in the widespread use of pardon for those condemned to death. In London, among the Old Bailey sentences for non-clergyable offences between 1663 and 1689, 114 of 116 women were reprieved before or after sentence, and only 34 of the 74 men – in all, 14 women and 33 men were hanged. At least 191 people were transported – or sentenced to it – from London in this quarter century, 112 from those accused of crimes without benefit of clergy, and 79 from crimes with benefit.

More than 70 per cent of women on the most serious (non-clergyable) charges, were transported. Beattie comments that, for women, this may represent an *increased* severity of punishment compared with the pardons of the previous era.[62] The wider national picture has not been studied in detail, and the paucity of records makes it difficult to generalize. From available lists of the reprieved and transported, though, some data emerge. On the Northern Circuit, with probably incomplete records of pardons from the assizes, there were at least 31 reprieves from North-East England (County Durham, Newcastle-upon-Tyne and Northumberland). Unlike in London, or indeed in the north-east in the eighteenth century, few of these were women (only three, one of them condemned for newborn child murder) between 1673 and 1710. Though not numerous, these transportation sentences indicate that even counties remote from the usual transatlantic sea lanes were accustomed to shipping criminals to the American colonies by 1700. Nationally, the picture seems to indicate that thousands were pardoned for transportation between the 1650s and the 1690s – A. E. Smith calculated a total of 4,451, on the basis of imperfectly surviving records.[63]

Although convicts were now leaving the country, one way or another, in larger numbers than ever before, there were few returned convicts in the courts in London and the Home Counties in the last 40 years of the seventeenth century, and none were specifically tried as such. There was, perhaps, little statutory support for such prosecutions. Returned convicts were convicted of further crimes at home, and the fact of having returned was then used to justify execution. Best known, perhaps, and famous for many years afterwards, was Mary Carleton, the 'German Princess', who figured in the popular imagination as well as in the many editions of the *Newgate Calendar*. She was executed in London in 1673.[64] In 1676, Elizabeth Longman and two men were executed in a session that saw most let off:

> Mercy so far interposed after the Sentence of Justice, that only Five of them actually suffered: Among whom was Elizabeth Longman, an old Offendor, having been above a Dozen several times in Newgate: Some time since she was convicted, and obtained the benefit and favour of Transportation, and was accordingly carried into Virginia . . . She had not been there above Fourteen Moneths, before she procured Monies remitted from some of the Brotherhood here, wherewith she bought off her Servitude, and ever she comes again into England, long before the term of her Sentence was expired. Nor was she content to violate the Law only in that point, but returned to her old Trade (for so these people call stealing) as well as to her Countrey.

She was asked by the judge why she should not be executed, 'To which she still pleaded, that she was quick with Child. But being searched by a Jury of Matrons, they found no such thing; so that she was carried with the rest into the Hole, and ordered for Execution'. It was alleged that she induced two men, in the middle of calling on a gentleman to help them with an appeal for pardon for a wife of one of them ('that passed for one of their wives'), to steal a silver plate from the house instead. They, too, went to the gallows. In other cases, the accused were known to have returned, but it seems it was not illegally, according to the scanty records.[65]

As the numbers being sent abroad grew, so did the misgivings of the colonies about receiving them. In a movement that presaged similar attempts in the eighteenth century, Virginia highlighted the danger and tried to prevent further imports of convicts.

> Order of the General Court held at James City. Setting forth the danger to the Colony caused by the great numbers of Virginia felons and other desperate villains being sent over from the prisons in England, the horror yet remaining of the barbarous designs of those villains, in September 1663, who attempted at once the subversion of our religion, laws, liberties, rights, and privileges, and prohibiting the landing of any jail birds from and after 20th January next upon pain of being forced to carry them to some other country.

The London authorities responded a few months later:

> His Majestie being this day Informed in Councill by Letters from Virginia of the great danger and disrepute is brought vpon that his Majestys Plantation by the frequent sending thither of ffellons and other Condemned Persons, for prevention whereof the Court there haue made an Order Prohibiting the Importation of any such People after the 20th of January next.

For which they received thanks from the colony:

> Thomas Ludwell to Secretary Lord Arlington, Thanks in his country's behalf for his assistance in the confirmation of the order of the Governor and Council prohibiting the importation of Newgateers. The safety of this country depends upon the continuance of it, so many insolent villanies having been committed by men of that sort, that greater numbers would hazard the peace of it.[66]

This kind of conflict between priorities, metropolitan and colonial, or even between different groups of colonists, would recur in the eighteenth century as the numbers of convicts rose, and it seemed to respectable Americans that whole counties were populated by them. This was never the case, and the ban on importing convicts was never successful. Up until the American Revolution, the convict business remained convenient for both the British government and the significant numbers of plantation owners and farmers in the Chesapeake.[67]

2

The distinctive character of Scottish banishment

Scottish banishment deserves separate treatment in this chapter because, although the kingdom shared a monarch and, substantially, a framework of government with England after 1603, its judicial policies of banishment were well established before this, and highly distinctive. Legal banishment had a long history in Scotland, and went on in much the same way until the nineteenth century. Although there was some use of new destinations as colonies opened up, most Scottish banishment was most often *banishment from*, rather than *transportation to*. An offender could be banished from a town or county, a region or the whole kingdom itself. As with some of the Continental parallels, such as practices in the Netherlands, *where* the criminals went was of less interest than the fact that they had left. As has been observed in the case of Dutch practices, the danger of this policy is that it just leads to 'exchange of individuals from one urban subculture to another' or, as the authorities of Leiden said, 'we banish such people upon each other's necks'.[1] The essence was expulsion from the community. This produced some protests from the places where these people wandered to, but despite this, the practice continued until finally brought to an end after 1800. In the early nineteenth century it produced protests from England – mainly from Northumberland – that criminals were simply crossing over into England, and had to be abandoned. The interaction with English practices, and the way that they influenced Scottish policies, is one theme throughout the period. The two kingdoms had an uneasy relationship in the Tudor period, and even later. The tradition of political exile was also strong, with England and France at different times receiving bands of political refugees. In the sixteenth century, many were found in England, plotting their return – in 1584–5, a party of Scottish nobles who were hoping to take control of the young James VI were reported as wandering from one university town to another.[2] Later, Jacobites were found in France, Spain and even Russia, in various forms of refuge, many serving loyally in the armed forces of those countries. As ever, there is a thin line between those driven abroad and those actively expelled.

The Kirk and the local state

The legal context in Scotland differed fundamentally from that in England in the way that the law and the courts developed after the Reformation. In England, the church courts inherited from the medieval period retained their independence and continued to deal with many sexual offenders and those who broke the rules of Christian conduct, without being able to inflict much by way of punishment, apart from a humiliating penance in front of the congregation for fornication or adultery. In Scotland, by contrast, their equivalent – the Kirk Sessions – worked closely with the town magistrates to inflict more severe punishments. As David M. Walker points out, the distinction between ecclesiastical and civil laws was maintained, but the Kirk Sessions often referred cases to the magistrates for punishment, which could include banishment by putting offenders out of town – in many cases, therefore, the elders of the Kirk and the 'bailies' of the burgh 'were overlapping groups'. In this, Scotland resembled New England rather than England in its deep mutual collaboration between religious and secular law – almost seamlessly deployed, though there has not been a chapter of 'kirk-based social discipline' for the whole of the country. Certainly, the Kirk Session in St Andrews was continually demanding the imprisonment of fornicators and adulterers, with mixed results. As well as assisting in the enforcement of religious values, the magistrates, under the *Leges Burgorum*, were permitted to deal with secular crimes, such as assault, theft and damage, and inflict punishments, such as fines, whipping, imprisonment or banishment from the burgh.[3] The result was that a common sentence by the burgh court was 'banishment out of the town and or beyond the county', while the judges at higher courts sentenced criminals for theft 'furth of Scotland'. The usual threat was that offenders would be whipped, branded or even hanged if they returned.[4] The records of the Justiciary Court in Edinburgh at the Restoration suggest that 'banishment was frequently the penalty, and this might be from the country or only from a district, as in one case we find, from the three Lothians'.[5]

Targets of Scottish banishment

Whatever the differences in legal structures and religious beliefs, Scotland's targets selected for banishment resembled those in England, and similar solutions were offered for the same problems. Some late-sixteenth-century Scottish laws, particularly those of the 1570s, were modelled on English laws, such as that of 1572.[6] In both countries, vagabondage of many different kinds was regarded as potentially dangerous. Scots, too, toyed with the idea of imposing slavery for beggars and vagabonds, and in the seventeenth century, this was inflicted on beggars and those who had 'escaped hanging for thefts' – they were sent to work in mines for the rest of their lives, with collars around their necks proclaiming their name, crime and owner. In addition, popish priests, and 'sorners and thiggers' (sturdy beggars and thieves) could all be banished from Scotland.[7] Other groups, particularly minstrels and storytellers, seem to have been unique to Scotland and Ireland, and reflect the fraught relations between Gaelic and non-Gaelic cultures. Travelling groups of musicians and other entertainers – often named as a band of people of common descent, such as the 'Cliar Sheanchain', 'Senchan's Company' and so on, were traditional storytellers and bards, who claimed a tradition going back centuries. They were often from the Highlands, and regarded as dangerous, partly because they were difficult to distinguish from other uncontrollably mobile groups. The problem was common to both Ireland and Scotland. An Act of 1567 banned Irish or Highland beggars or bards from the Lowlands on pain of imprisonment, while in 1579, another measure rendered 'all menstrallis, sangstares and tailtellaris not avouit in speciall service be sum of the lordis of parliament or greit barronis, or be the heid burrowis for the commoun menstralis', in danger of being whipped, branded on the cheek 'or even hanged'. In effect, this aimed to control unlicensed or freelance performers.[8]

'Ethnic cleansing' before the name: Scottish policies towards gypsies, vagabonds and others

A great deal of the history of Scottish relations with gypsies is buried within romantic and legendary traditions and stories, and the historian has difficulty seeking and finding the dull facts of their treatment. Despite the overlay of legends and nineteenth-century antiquarian storytelling, travellers and gypsies have had an uneasy Scottish history. Even today, when they are an acknowledged ethnic group in English law, gypsies have had an uncertain public identity in Scotland.[9] Like the Gaelic travellers, they are first mentioned in the fifteenth century (as immigrants from Ireland), and included under the same 1407 legislation. Under later laws, perpetual servitude in mines could be inflicted on 'gypsies', a word first used in 1598. 1603 saw a proclamation, ratified in 1609, that gypsies could choose between banishment or death. The 1609 Act ordered them from the kingdom, 'never to returne . . . on paine of death'.[10]

As in England, much of the legislation proved too severe to be enforceable, but at times, the full force of the law fell on groups defined as a threat. In late 1714, a group on the border near Jedburgh were rounded up and prosecuted at the Justiciary Court, which ordered Peter and Mary Faas, Mabile Stirling, Janet Yorstoun, John Finnick, Elizabeth Lindsay, Jean Ross and Mary Robertson, 'to be transported to the plantations, for being habite and repute gypsies, sorners etc'. Jedburgh, unable to organize this, handed them to the City of Glasgow which, in January 1715, arranged 'with the first conveniencie to sett them aboard of any ship going to the plantations', the contract going to three men, Robert Buntrine of Airdoch, James Lees and Charles Crawford, who used their ship *Greenock* (master James Watson) for the purpose. The city authorities also complained to the judges of the Justiciary about the expense of keeping them in jail for months and then transporting them all, which, they claimed, they had never done before. This was connected with a series of prosecutions early in 1714 in Jedburgh for vagabondage and arson, resulting in a number of people, notably one 'Patrick Faa' being put in the local pillory and having his ears cut off. This, at least, is the tale, but it may be local myth rather than proven fact – Faa was supposed to have been married to one Jean Gordon, who had a long and vigorous local career in the Borders, and stories about her formed the origins of Meg Merrilies, the gypsy character in Walter Scott's *Guy Mannering* who also inspired a poem by John Keats. To evaluate what was really happening at that time is difficult to disentangle from the local legends. There may be genuine facts hidden away behind the stories, at least in the court cases, but the names have seemingly become confused (Peter Faas, above, was one of the two men sent out from Glasgow, not Patrick Faa). It is notable that allegations of serious threats to life, and consequent local fears, led to the transportations. In other individual cases, a milder policy was adopted.[11] So, in Argyll in 1729, Ewan McDonald, a 'vagrant person', who pretended to be dumb, and travelled through 'all the shires of Scotland, England and part of Ireland as a fortune teller', was proceeded against as a 'sworner and Egyptian', and was whipped through the streets of Campelltown and banished from the jurisdiction on pain of imprisonment.[12]

The newness of transatlantic transportation in 1715 for Glasgow's authorities deserves note, here, as does the identity of the married couple called 'Faa' or 'Faas' – this was a traditional gypsy name in Scotland, and on the English side of the Border, 'faw' or 'faws' were the generic terms for gypsies and travellers. The early 1710s saw a parallel repression by Northumberland of 'faws', also transported to the colonies, and the Scottish move against them may have been a reflection of a coordinated effort (see Chapter 1). Nevertheless, even at this late stage, 'banishment' did not automatically mean transportation to the colonies, for many local Scottish authorities.

Highlanders

Another category to come under scrutiny for ethnic cleansing were the perpetual internal aliens in early modern Scotland, the Highlanders. 'Judicial' would be the wrong word to apply to James VI/I's policies towards the Highlands and Ulster, but a combination of plantations of virtuous (and trustworthy) Protestants with banishment formed the core of his thinking about the problems they posed. He had first contemplated instigating the policy as a means of integrating the Highlands and Islands into his kingdom. In 1598, in advice to his son Henry in *Basilicon Doron*, he described his intention for the Highlands was to insert 'colonies among them of answerable Inlands subjects that within a shorte time may reforme and civilize the best inclined among them; rooting out or transporting the barbarous and stubborne sort, and planting civilitie in their rooms'. He despaired of their leaders. By contrast, he had hopes of being able to strike a deal with the Ulster lords, and 'removal of the Irish elite had not been part of his original plan'.[13] Following the 'Flight of the Earls' in 1607, he was forced to rethink. Ironically, in his overall scheme to break the link between the western Isles and Ulster Catholic rebellion, it was in Ireland that he finally carried out his policy while accepting the submission and compliance of the Highland lords. The strategy of selective banishment recurred in the Jacobite rebellions in the eighteenth century (see Chapter 5), but the repeated problems of lawlessness and rebellion often evoked the policy of transportation as one solution in the seventeenth century. In the 1680s, a special commission on the Highlands suggested to the Privy Council 'that, instead of outlawing thieves, protections might be issued for them to "come in and inact themselves" to "banish themselves forever out of the kingdome", an idea to which the Council acquiesced', and they made widespread use of amnesties at the same time, largely because they 'wished to isolate the most incorrigibly lawless elements by bringing more peaceable individuals back into the fold'.[14]

The Burghs and the Justiciary: Levels of banishment in Scotland

Banishment figured as a penalty for a wide range of crimes and misdemeanours in Scottish courts at different levels, and was deployed in flexible and adaptable ways, depending on the crime and the criminal. Not only were Scottish courts flexible as to the area from which people were banned, they also varied sentences according to the length of time for the banishment. It was not unusual, even in the eighteenth century, for offenders to be taken out of prison and drummed out of town, from which they were expelled for the rest of their natural lives. Such people were ordered 'never to be seen again in the burgh'. This was tantamount to outlawry, which was also an official punishment, sometimes indicating banishment from the whole kingdom of Scotland. In the early 1800s, when there many prosecutions for seditious speaking and writing, and some for blasphemy, Scottish courts carefully distinguished transportation to the colonies from outlawry – the majority of those convicted of these offences were simply 'outlawed'.[15] In less political cases, the banishment was often for a specific term, and the impression is that once this had been served, the offenders were accepted back into the community. In sixteenth-century Aberdeen, for example, one woman, who committed perjury and disobeyed the magistrates (and had a reputation for many other 'odious' crimes) was banished for a year and a day on penalty of being branded on the cheek. More than a third of those convicted of petty thefts were banished in this way at this time.[16]

The moral discipline of the Kirk produced many cases for banishment. In part, the Kirk Sessions acted to refer cases to the magistrates for punishment, but it is also clear that when they threatened reprobates with a penalty, they could be sure of the civil authorities' support. In many cases, the refusal to show penitence – and perform it in public, was a factor, as was repeated offending.[17] For example, in 1581, St Andrews' Session presented a single mother before them, and ordered her to 'depart of this parroche within 15 days', and indicated that they were applying to the magistrates to get agreement from them for that penalty. In other cases, the sessions were less confident – the Inverness Session in 1720 recorded that they were entreating the magistrates to an exemplary punishment for a single mother, such as banishment, 'not thinking it to Edification to proceed longer with her in [the] usual course of Church Discipline'. In a more complex case a few years later, the same sessions dealt with a woman who followed the soldiers, but who had been banished from the regiment. They recommended the magistrates to banish her from the town. Single women, particularly those living on their own, had long been disproportionately subject to investigation by the authorities and placed in danger of banishment.[18] More direct punishments are asserted in many cases, however, suggesting that the sessions assumed a right to inflict civil penalties. In a couple of cases of defamation in St Andrews, a man who had made sexual allegations against a woman was ordered to avoid her company, and keep the peace with her, under pain of banishment from Fyfe 'all the dayes of his lyfetym'. A woman of 'evil tung' confessed to the sin, and was ordered to be banished from the town by order of the magistrates. In Aberdeen, there are several cases where the distinction between church and civil powers is ignored completely. Several women presented to the Kirk Sessions for varieties of 'harlotrie'; one for being 'ane pandarous and seducer of her sister', was sentenced to multiple public punishments. One was to stand in the session house with a paper on her head (presumably announcing her sin), before being banished. Two others were subject to more forceful corporal punishment – one was to be ducked in the ducking stool before being banished, while the other was to be whipped. In cases where the magistrates had taken the initiative, the sessions provided support for the orders of banishment, for example, by adding excommunication to the punishment, or using the pronouncements from the pulpit on Sunday to exhort people not to give lodging or refuge to the banished. In exceptional cases, the Kirk had to deal with the consequences of such a policy. One elderly man in St Andrews in 1559 had seen his wife and mother-in-law banished from the realm many years earlier for suspected adultery. Pleading before the Kirk Session for the right to marry again – he had met a 'chaste virgane' of 40, he reported – he argued that by this time, his wife must surely be dead. The social consequences of policies of banishment for the personal relationships of those left behind are scarcely mentioned in the records, but it is worth noting that, by definition, many banished for suspected adultery would have been married, as were many of those penalized for fornication. It was possible to gain a divorce after one partner had been convicted for adultery and on the grounds of desertion – in this case, there is no clear mention of a formal divorce application, the husband going for the safer grounds of the probable death of his wife.[19]

Many of those banished by local magistrates were simply poor and mobile, and here, the law acted to expel them, as vagrancy laws did in England at the same time. In 1660, for example, it was reported from Glasgow, one 'Douglas',

> formerlie appoyntit to remove himself aft the toune, quhilk he hes not obeyed . . . and is brunt on the cheek, and is known to be ane idle vagabounde, without ony lawfull calling: he is, therfoir, ordained to remove aff the toune, and all his, and that within ten days, and not to returne therto heirafter, under the paine of scurgeing him throw the towne, and banishing the burghe.

This was common elsewhere in Scotland, but some local authorities took further steps to ensure that such troublesome people did not settle in the first place. In the regality (a town or area under control of a baron) of Falkirk and Callender, for example, one early seventeenth-century local statute threatened any 'indweller' who took in any sturdy beggars or any other 'unlawful persons' with banishment themselves and a fine of 10 pounds. In this jurisdiction, the court tried to distinguish relatively minor offenders from the more serious, such as thieves and robbers, by varying the penalties for returning. Beggars, vagabonds and sexual offenders such as fornicators were threatened with whipping and branding on the cheek, while thieves and adulterers were in danger of being executed. This reflected the differences in the original crimes, where certain thefts and adultery were capital felonies, but with different methods of execution. Elspeth Monteithe, who confessed to adultery in 1641, for example, was in danger of being drowned (according to the statute of 1563) if she was found in the jurisdiction at any time thereafter. Fornication, by contrast, committed by a widow, was treated like vagabondage, as something only deserving public corporal punishment on returning. All these sentences seem to be for perpetual banishment.[20]

In Aberdeenshire, most of the offences for which banishment 'from the sheriffdom' was imposed by the civil courts were various sorts of theft, as in the case of Andrew Hay, who broke into a house in Aberdeen in 1603, and stole two pecks of meal and a pair of shoes. More unusual was another sentence for theft the same year, in which Meriorie Burne, daughter to the late John Burne in Fechill, was convicted of the theft of 10 pounds in April, and sentenced to scourging through the town, banishment from the county and drowning without trial if she returned. There was a similar case of a woman convicted of theft in 1620, banished from the county and threatened with drowning.[21] Later cases suggest a nuanced use of banishment as a sanction, as in one 1649 case of a sheepstealer, William Lindsay who, convicted on one of four charges, was bound under penalty of 500 'merks'(marks) to be of good behaviour, or in case of failure, to be banished, significantly from the 'country'. This and other Aberdeenshire cases suggest that the Interregnum saw a major shift in local Scottish custom, as English practices of transportation were imported into Scotland for the first time. For example, when in 1652, Alexander Ferguson was convicted of robbery, the court persuaded him to consent to leave the Sheriffdom within 24 hours, and Britain within six weeks, under pain of death by hanging. The reference to Britain is new, for earlier banishments from Aberdeenshire meant (as the editors of the records comment) 'that he or she was packed off by way of the Bridge of Dee into the neighbouring County of Kincardine'. Clearly, things changed under the Commonwealth, when Britain was introduced as a territory for the first time, sometimes explained as the 'Isle of Britane' or, in one 1655 case, 'the three nations of England, Scotland and Ireland'. This might be a local reflection of the national policy of dealing with Royalist soldiers by sending them to Barbados – in 1654, the Parliamentary commander General Monk was empowered to transport 'to any foreign English plantations such of the enemy now in arms in the Highlands . . . as often and in such numbers as you think fit'. The government also examined the possibility of transporting to the West Indies 'all masterless, idle vagabonds, and robbers, both men and women', but were advised that this would rouse the whole country against the regime.[22]

It would not be surprising if there was modification by Commonwealth-appointed sheriffs, as this interference was widespread in many areas of Scottish law. The decline in witchcraft prosecutions at this time, for example, has been interpreted as a consequence of the Cromwellian government's appointment of judges of a very different temperament from that of their royal predecessors (and the return of witch-hunting in 1660 to the reinstatement of the old 'Scottish' traditions under resurgent royalist rule). Use of the 'English' colonies as a destination for Scottish criminals seems to have grown by individual action and local order, rather than through any particular policy. Under royal government, Scotland was not usually involved in the English processes of convict transportation, but in the 1670s, there were signs of the beginning of an integrated system allowing shipment to what were still, technically, purely *English* colonies. It may be the Restoration government was picking up a policy suggestion from the Interregnum. In 1678, there was correspondence with Virginia:

The King to Thomas Lord Culpeper, Governor Herbert Jeffreys, Lieutenant-Governor and the Council of Virginia. To permit Ralph

Williamson or his assigns to land and dispose of fifty two convicted persons of Scotland, sentenced to be transported to our English plantations and such others as shall be convicted in Scotland and sentenced to be transported and delivered into Williamson's custody, without hindrance or molestation, any law, order, or custom of Virginia to the contrary notwithstanding.[23]

This refers, not to the rebel Covenanters seized after the battle of Bothwell Brig the following June, (one of three major Presbyterian revolts against the Stuarts after 1660), but to the group, including Alexander Peden, that was sent to London with the intention to pass them on to Virginia (but the venture failed – see Chapter 4). Covenanters were appearing both rebellious and stubborn, the latter a character shared by an equally obstinate government:

No less recalcitrant royalist regimes transported Scots to the colonies after Bothwell Brig and Argyll's rising, offering precedents for the wider transportation movement of the eighteenth century, like the two fathoms of rope bought by the burgh of Stirling in 1700 to restrain the unfortunate 'Laurence M'Lairen quhen sent to America'. In general Scottish felons were less likely to be transported than their English compeers, but only because Scots law reserved transportation as the punishment for its most fearsome criminals.[24]

Around 1700 or soon after, though, local jurisdictions seem to have adopted English custom even when there was no legal framework to support it. In one case, the Justiciary of Argyll and the Isles, whose judges were appointed by the Duke of Argyll as a private jurisdiction, were inventive in making use of multiple punishments. Ordinary thefts were, as elsewhere, punished by corporal punishment and banishment from the shire of Argyll or, in cases of cattle or horse theft, from 'this realm and never to return thereto', or from 'that part of Great Britain called Scotland'. The convicts were usually given a number of days by which time they should have removed themselves. In 1721, however, Donald Glass McNicholl, convicted of theft, was sentenced to be whipped through Inverary and have his ear nailed to the gibbet for an hour. Thereafter, his moveable property was to be seized, and he was to be 'banished this realm and transported to His Majesties plantations in America conform to the late Act of Parliament and not to be found in this realm again under pain of death'. Yet, the *English* legislation referred to, the 1718 Transportation Act, was very clear, as clause 8 stipulated that 'Provided always, that nothing in this Act contained shall extend or be construed to extend to such Persons as shall be convicted or attainted in that Part of Great Britain called Scotland'. Formal legislation authorizing the same processes in Scotland as the English law was not introduced until 1766, but the Argyll court continued to specify America as the destination of certain convicts.

It is a measure of how independent these private jurisdictions were before their abolition in 1747.[25]

These examples show that banishment from seventeenth- and eighteenth-century Scotland was a fundamental aspect of the criminal law. Indeed, Argyll's courts were developing one practice that had long been adopted by the Justiciary Court in Edinburgh, of banishing men from the kingdom to go into the armed forces, though after 1707, the judgement might include from 'the United Kingdom of Great Britain'. One man was forced to sit in the 'juggs' (a form of stocks or pillory) with a noose around his neck until delivered to a particular army company and so 'transported out of the jurisdiction'.[26] In Edinburgh, at the Justiciary Court the previous century, this had been common practice up to the civil wars. The judges there heard a wide range of cases from many parts of Scotland and, in addition, found themselves tangling with the Privy Council which, in some cases, ordered banishment without a formal trial. The majority of cases leading to banishment in the 1630s and 1640s involved theft and, if the accused were reasonably young men, they were destined for the armed forces, to serve the king 'in the wars' and never to return. In some instances, the victims had petitioned for the penalty, suggesting that the value of the goods stolen was such as to put the crime in the higher level, deserving the death penalty, as occurred in one crime committed in England, the victim acting to save the perpetrator, his servant, who had stolen many precious jewels and gold objects. There was a procedure for returning, apparently like that in England, for it was forbidden to do so 'without special licence'. Those who returned without it, as one man did in 1642 to defend a civil case in court (to settle his affairs, he claimed), could find themselves in difficulties. It was deemed that he had behaved 'contemptiously', and was liable to the death penalty.[27] The procedure for recruiting men into the armed forces abroad usually involved them doing so 'of their awin consent', and being allocated to a particular recruiting officer. Eight men in 1635 (one of them guilty of stealing 10 sheep), for example, agreed to join the company of Captain Thomas Moffet, who, other sources indicate, was recruiting soldiers for Sweden that year. A burglar and pickpocket in 1639 was sent to the 'partis of Germanie' with one Colonel Stewart, possibly the Robert Stuart who was also recruiting for Sweden. William Barr, convicted in 1639 of stealing five silver spoons from his master Sir James Hamilton, was allocated to Colonel Alexander Erskine, who was taking hundreds of men to France. The official commissioning of recruiters for overseas service, and the licence given them to gather up prisoners of all kinds, including 'vagabindis and sturdie beggars', provided a convenient opportunity to the courts to pardon and dispose of these men.[28]

Many other offences before the Justiciary earned banishment, some of them after a kind of careful reduction of the crime to a level below that of a capital offence. Adultery, as we have seen, was a capital crime, but if reduced to bigamy or fornication, the offenders could be banished. This happened to one fortunate man in 1631, and another in 1650, though the latter was also whipped. The logic of this seems to be that marrying a second time was a kind of perjury, and could therefore be treated slightly more leniently. As Brian Levack has observed, 'despite the severity of Scots law in this regard, executions for adultery were rare. Many notorious adulterers were banished rather than hanged'. Several cases of men guilty of sexual assault also resulted in banishment. One man, accused of an attempted rape of a 10-year-old girl, was banished by order of the Privy Council. Another, John Rylay 'agreed' to be banished for rape, with the acquiescence of the victim's father – she was described as a 'young virgane'.[29] In one unusual case of murder, the killer was a girl of only 10 years, and the victim, a boy of only six. She was required to do penance in front of the Kirk Session of her congregation, and banished to beyond a 12-mile limit from the parish.[30] Crimes for which banishment was also imposed included interpersonal violence of many kinds, defamation, such as alleging falsely that someone was a witch, and even witchcraft itself. One woman in Kirkcudbrightshire in 1700 was banished (for the second time), for being unable to repeat the Lord's Prayer, and causing the minister's house to come tumbling down, and also causing him nearly to drown a day later.[31] These cases indicate that there was a search for non-fatal penalties – secondary punishments in fact – in ways that parallel similar efforts at the same time in England. Foreign wars provided certain opportunities, and so did the willingness of both victims and perpetrators to countenance lifelong exile.

The formal processes of criminal transportation, on the English model, were created in Scotland by the 1766 Act. As Ekirch has commented, there was a kind of harmonization with English judicial practices, but perhaps with much less central direction than in England. It was already an established custom that condemned criminals could petition for transportation, and the 1766 law seems to have reinforced the use of the penalty for lesser offences. The rate of reprieve from execution, though, was much lower than in England, and the numbers sent to America less. There was public money for organized and large-scale shipment of convicts, for example, but the courts often continued to allow those sentenced to arrange things themselves, by making 'private bargains for passage to America'. For the poor, this meant sometimes a very long and potentially dangerous wait in an unhealthy jail before they could obtain a place on a ship across the Atlantic. The individual responsibility of the criminal for their own punishment could therefore be a terrible burden for the poorest, but a blessing for those with resources to compensate the ships' captains for both the costs of their passage and the likely profits from their indenture. The convicted criminals were pardoned, as Anne Davidson was in 1762 for 'child murder, on 'condition of transporting herself for life', while George Innes, from Bengal, convicted of stealing, was sentenced to seven years transportation, and was allowed to be indentured to Thomas Alves, a planter and merchant, who offered to take him to Jamaica. Flexibility seems to have been the key feature of the Scottish system of transportation, much as it was in the practice of banishment.

These were hardly standard English ways of doing things, and indicate that what happened in Scotland was, in fact, a kind of synthesis of old and new practices – one that left banishment *and* transportation side by side in an uncertain framework where the distinction was not obvious.[32]

One peculiarly Scottish feature was that the accused scheduled for trial could petition to be banished, and receive a sentence without having been found guilty. As a handbook for Scottish magistrates noted, 'rather than run the risk of a more severe punishment upon trial and conviction, the accused offers to be banished from the jurisdiction, under certification of imprisonment, or the like, in case of return', but such a person had at least to have been committed for trial first, and the offence specified. The sentence of banishment therefore would specify the punishment to be inflicted if the person returned, and all that would be required in that circumstance was the correct identification of the person by the public prosecutor rather than any formal trial. The punishment for return was often whipping and further banishment, rather than death, though there was great variety in this area. In 1789, for example, at Stirling, one James M'Nab was accused of theft and petitioned for banishment, 'which, being consented to by the Advocate-Depute, he was accordingly banished forth of Scotland for seven years'. By contrast, at the same court, Andrew Paton was convicted of theft, and sentenced to 'banishment for life, his service adjudged for seven years', meaning he was to be transported to the colonies for indentured servitude. In Dumfries, a sentence of banishment for 14 years inflicted on an accused forger came with 'certification of whipping and re-transportation' if he returned within the time. Reports and sentences mix up the old and new language, with 'banishment' and 'transportation' being used interchangeably.[33]

The distinction between the meaning of Scottish banishment and sentences to transportation, however, became a matter of legal and political debate in 1794 during the trials of members of the National Assembly, formed in deliberate imitation of the French revolutionary model, which met in Edinburgh. Several of those who were prosecuted were English delegates, and this provoked a discussion about the relationship of English to Scottish concepts of 'sedition' and also about other crimes of speaking against the state and government, as traditionally defined in Scottish law, such as 'leasing-making', a crime of attacking the reputation of the monarch or their government, which under a 1703 Act would only attract banishment. The sentences of 14 years transportation for sedition – a crime imported from English law – therefore provoked understandable debate about whether the activities of the accused were threatening to the government, and hence seditious, or merely insulting, and therefore 'leasing-making'. This was subject to careful analysis by David Hume in his *Commentaries on the Law of Scotland* published a few years later, and remained problematic. In the same trials, there arose a debate about whether transportation to a specific place was known in Scottish law for this and other offences. The prosecution was understandably keen to show that it was. In Parliament, in March and

April 1794, there was much debate. Scottish lawyer and MP William Adam, who had once fought a duel with Charles James Fox, in a long speech in the House of Commons concerning these trials, questioned the nature of the charges and the legality of the sentences. If the crime was properly leasing-making, then banishment, not transportation, was the appropriate sentence. Under banishment, he said, 'transportation is not included'. Because sedition was a crime unknown in Scottish law, 'it would be contrary to law to punish that offence by *transportation*, and not warranted by law to inflict pain of death for returning from such transportation'. His definitions are significant given the Scottish practices outlined here:

> By *banishment* I mean mere expulsion from the society, country or realm, to which the expelled person belongs; leaving every other country open to his approach, without restraint.
>
> By *transportation* I mean not only the expulsion of the person transported the realm or society to which he belongs, but his being sent to another place, which he cannot quit, and in which he must remain, in a situation of servitude, as in America formerly; or under a military despotism and servitude, as at Botany Bay now.

For him, banishment meant '*simple expatriation from Scotland*, and nothing more' – by contrast, transportation was 'an *arbitrary punishment* by the law of Scotland', which referred to the consequences of a pardon from capital convictions at the discretion of the king. A few weeks later, in a debate brought by the Earl of Lauderdale about the same trials, Lord Mansfield replied to the critics. Lauderdale had pointed out that 'transportation supposed that the court had authority over the place to which they transported. But as Scotland never had colonies till the beginning of the present century, they could not exercise transportation'. He, too, argued that the offences could not have been sedition. By way of reply, Mansfield ducked some of the objections, but went for a simple merger of the two words, 'What clearly shows the sense in which the courts of Scotland understood the word banishment is, that the sentences which they generally pronounce, the word "banish" is generally used in the sentence, where the punishment is transportation'. That was certainly true, but not all uses of the word 'banishment' involved sentences to transportation, though most sentences to transportation refer to banishment. The confusion continued in Scotland until both were abolished in the mid-nineteenth century.[34]

In the eighteenth century, the pattern of routine banishment by Scottish courts was reported in the English press as one of the interesting features of Scottish law. For example, in 1751, the London papers reported the case of a discharged soldier who, sent to buy herrings, defrauded a man by doubling the price he had actually paid for them from sixpence to one shilling, and was ordered to stand in the pillory for an hour with a dozen herrings around his neck, then to be banished from the 'city and liberties for ever'. In the same edition, three men involved in a riot in Lanark were reported as banished from Scotland for three years, on pain of being whipped and banished again for another three years. Banishment – or transportation – became the most common punishment for participation in public disturbances or riots in Scotland after the 1760s.[35] In the early nineteenth century, the penalty for returning had become less severe – in 1819, a local Dundee woman, Ann McKenzie of Hilltown, was imprisoned on Christmas Eve for 'not obeying the Sheriff's sentence of banishment'. The whipping of women had become unfashionable, as sentiments changed.[36] Banishment from Scotland itself, though, eventually provoked protests – from England. In the early nineteenth century, Northumberland MPs were raising the problems caused by the Scottish practice – Sir M. W. Ridley, it was reported in Parliamentary debate,

> hoped that the learned lord would take into consideration the disadvantage under which those English counties, which were near the Scotch borders laboured, in consequence of the system of banishment out of Scotland, which formed one of the punishments awarded by the Scottish law. Thus an unfortunate Scotchman, if banished from his native country for his misdeeds, immediately sheltered himself in Northumberland, and was by no means sorry to give up his peat fire for a comfortable chimney corner in a neighbouring town. For his own part, he could not conceive how this banishment could be considered as a penalty. On this point he could not but quote the opinion of the poet, by whom it had been wittily said, 'Had Cain been Scot, God had reversed his doom, Not forced to wander, but remained at home'.

Forced migration to England had become a reward, not a punishment, by this time, it seems. Eventually, the practice was abandoned, but Scotland was unusual in its forms of banishment, as well as in the complexity and longevity of their use.[37]

3

Religious persecutions and banishment

The experience of exile was not new for those communities persecuted for their religious beliefs in the seventeenth century. Indeed, many religious minorities in Europe in the previous hundred years since the Reformation had been scattered by political repression. Things were little better after 1600 – some, like the French Huguenots after the revocation of the Edict of Nantes in 1685, suffered wholesale expulsion from their country. Many others, without such forceful mistreatment, had nevertheless endured periods during which their leaders or most influential members had been in exile abroad, and the community had had to survive by maintaining international networks. This had, in fact, been a common factor in the creation of the first English Protestant communities, dependent on English Bibles printed overseas and smuggled into the country. Later, both Catholic and puritan groups in the sixteenth century were sustained through their contacts with continental centres of learning and printing, where personnel could be trained and returned to England. Catholics still looked to the English School in Rome or Douai, where many priests were trained, and Protestants to the Netherlands, Switzerland or Germany. Experience of exile, then, was common and an important factor in sustaining dissident faith communities – indeed, it was perhaps one factor in creating the identities and collective memories of these groups.[1]

Exile, however painful, was, its victims hoped, temporary. It is unclear whether seventeenth-century governments regarded it in that way, and banishment, particularly if it involved long-distance removal, could be both more permanent and more hurtful. A number of different jurisdictions in the British Empire in the mid-seventeenth century adopted a policy of formal judicial prosecution and expulsion of members of religious groups. In England and Scotland, this took place largely after 1660 under a restored monarchy whose government was widely suspected of Catholic loyalties. In New England, by contrast, the puritan authorities turned on the same targets from a very different religious viewpoint. The victims, mostly Quakers and Covenanters, suffered for several decades the intermittent repression of their meetings and the banishment abroad of members for attending those meetings. Significantly, the most forceful Protestant groups, those English Presbyterians and Independents who had played so prominent a part in the Civil Wars and Oliver Cromwell's government during the Interregnum, were largely ignored by the authorities in the 1660s and 1670s. Former radicals had been re-absorbed by the Church of England, at least on the surface, and even some extreme activists, like Digger Gerrard Winstanley, often hailed as a proto-communist, emerged in the 1660s as parish officers of the Anglican Church.[2] Ministers who had served under the Interregnum were another matter, and few kept their jobs under the restored bishops, despite the story in song of the 'Vicar of Bray' who adapted to every regime and kept his job. Most repressive measures were directed in the 1660s and 1670s at Protestant groups thought extreme or dangerous by their *fellow* Protestants. The legislation passed early in Charles II's reign, and repeated in a series of laws, formalized a situation that had been developing under the Cromwellian regime of the 1650s, when disturbances by Quakers and other groups had provoked savage reprisals in the form of public punishment. 'Although the worst possibilities were never realized, the Restoration did witness a persecution of Protestants by Protestants without parallel in seventeenth-century Europe'.[3]

Interregnum origins

Repression was the response of outraged local authorities to the Quakers' perceived threat on both sides of the Atlantic. Far from the 'quietness' for which they were later famous, the first generation of Quakers took to direct action, with both men and women preaching in public, disrupting services and insulting the respectable by refusing to show the customary respectful doffing of their hats. In addition, their refusal to swear oaths of any kind led them into all kinds of trouble, as these were fundamental both to expressing personal trustworthiness in everyday matters, such as legal arrangements and testimonies, and binding people to loyalty to state and church. Refusal to take an oath was usually a sign of a guilty conscience, as among those accused of crimes who refused to swear to their statements of innocence. Quakers were subject to attack in the 1650s from a number of directions in the local settings where they acted so disruptively, but there was no consistent legal framework providing the local authorities with powers to rid themselves of this kind of nuisance. For example, in a famous incident in Cambridge in 1653, Mary Fisher and Elizabeth Williams became involved in 'discoursing with some scholars from Sidney-Sussex College' and accused them of being 'Antichrists' because 'they had many whom they made gods of'. They refused to give their names to the magistrates on their arrest, and when asked their husbands' names, said they had no husbands but Jesus

Christ. They were whipped and 'put out of town'. More legalistically, a grand jury presentment in Cumberland in 1655 suggests that even those wishing to take action against the Quakers were uncertain if they had the authority to do so. This kind of jury, empannelled to review and endorse indictments (as they still do in many states of the United States) often served to articulate the anxieties of the respectable men of the county. They were concerned, they said, with 'our sadd and deplorable condicion, occasioned by the multiplicity and irregularity of the deluded sect called the Quakers', and began by specifying:

1 Their horride blasphemies and violations of the cleere and knowne fundamentall truthes of the Gospell.

2 Their notorious affronts to magistrates and ministers, whom they labour uncessantly by their scandalous speeches and pamphletts to expose to most infamous scorne and contempt, and consequently the whole nation to confusion.

3 Their apparent designe and common practise is to seduce and mislead the poore, ignorant, ungrounded, and unsetled people of these Northeren partes, and to involve them in most dangerous and detestable principles, worse then the Egiptian darknes. They are growne more numerous.

They requested of the judges 'that some speedie course be forwith taken, whereby piety may be preserved in purity, and the people of this county in safty', but it is clear that they were uncertain under what law action could be taken. There was less uncertainty in Parliament about James Nayler, who had entered Bristol on an ass, surrounded by admiring female followers, who alleged he was Christ. That was straightforward blasphemy, though the members were unclear what punishment could be authorized (see Chapter 1).[4]

New England

Similar official reactions developed in the colonies as the Quakers fanned out from England to the West Indies and North America to spread the word. The New England colonies reacted particularly severely, with the first legislation against the group. It was here that Calvinist traditional methods of discipline combined with English law – the origins of Quaker banishment lie, not in England, but in Massachusetts. The reputation of New England for, if not exactly inventing the persecution of Quakers, then taking it to a level of particularly excessive severity, was already entrenched by the mid-1660s. As a report to the authorities in London observed of the colony of Massachusetts Bay in 1665,

They have put to death and banished many Quakers on pain of death, and then executed them for returning, and have beaten some to a jelly, and been exceeding cruel to others, and say the King allows it in his letters to them, yet they pray constantly for their persecuted brethren in England. Many things in their laws derogatory to his Majesty's honour, the Commissioners desired might be altered, but nothing as yet done. Among others, who ever keeps Christmas Day is to pay £5.

How this developed over the previous 10 years had at first been out of sight of the London authorities.[5] In the mid-1650s, the same anxieties as were felt in England seem to have been shared in Massachusetts. On 14 May 1656, there was declared a 'publicke day of humiliation to seeke the face of God in behalf of our native countrie, in reference to the abounding of errors, especially those of the Raunters and Quakers'. Not content with praying for blessing, the authorities immediately followed with measures that were specific and severe. It was ordered:

that what Quaker soever shall arive in this countrie from forraigne part, or come into this jurisdiction from any parts adjacent, shall be forthwith committed to the house of correction, and at theire entrance to be severely whipt, and by the master thereof be kept constantly to worke, and none suffered to converse or speak with them during their imprisonment which shallbe no longer than necessitie requireth.

There were 5 pound fines for importing their books, as well as concealing them from the authorities. Any attempt to defend Quaker doctrines was to be punished by a 2 pound fine. Persistence in defending or maintaining these beliefs earned confinement in the house of correction 'till there be convenient passage for them to be sent out of the land, being sentenced by the Court of Assistants to banishment'.[6]

After a short while, these measures clearly were felt to have been a failure, and the next year, even more savage penalties were introduced, focusing on those who returned from banishment. Men, on a first return, would lose one ear, and on a second return, the other ear, while women would be severely whipped. On a third return, their tongues would be bored with a hot iron, and they would be sent away at their own expense. Moreover, these penalties, together with the previous ones, would apply not only to 'foreign' Quakers but also to 'all and every Quaker arising among ourselves'. Finally, in October 1658, the authorities decided to increase the threat to outsiders, and allowed that, after a jury trial and conviction, foreign Quakers could be sentenced to 'banishment upon paine of death'.[7] Although these laws made Massachusetts legendary in Quaker history, the actual tally of victims was small, as Pestana has pointed out – four were executed, Marmaduke Stephenson from Yorkshire, William Robinson from London, William Leddra from Barbados and, most famously, Mary Dyer from Rhode Island, the only

North American. All had returned from banishment, in Dyer's case, after she had watched the executions of Stephenson and Robinson, standing with a noose around her neck as they were hanged. She was reprieved through 'the petition of hir sonne, and the mercy and clemency of [the] Court', and 'had liberty to depart within two days, which shee hath accepted of', it was reported. By May 1660, she had returned, and, confirming her identity, was condemned to death according to her previous conviction. By contrast, at the same time, a couple who had also returned, Joseph and Jane Nicholson, were given 'further clemency, as yett to give them respit', and banished again. They were eventually allowed to go to England.[8] Although efforts were sometimes made to remove convicted Quakers to specific destinations, they were, in these cases, unsuccessful.

The process of banishment had been made less 'fire and forget' and potentially more organized in 1659, as local authorities were empowered to sell the Quakers to 'any of the English nation at Virginia or Barbados', perhaps in the hope that this would contain them in a structure of indentured servitude. However, there is little evidence that this device was adopted. On at least one occasion, a Quaker sent to England 'without punishment', Christopher Holder, returned 'presumptiously', to be banished again on pain of death – at the same time as Dyer and the others were being prosecuted for a capital offence. Those who 'entertained' Quakers, that is, gave them food and shelter, were also being rigorously pursued at this time, along with those who guided them in their travels.[9] Problems of religious differences between husbands and wives arose where the latter were Quakers. Towards the end of 1660, the authorities decided in the cases of Margaret Smith and Mary Traske, that 'there being some women Quakers in prison liable to sentence of bannishment, whose husbands are innocent persons in that respect, so farr as wee know, and are inhabitants of this jurisdiction', they should be kept at hard labour and 'meane diet' in the house of correction, until the court ordered their release, and 'that the sentence of banishment . . . be suspended, any lawe to the contrary notwithstanding, unlesse their husbands shall choose to carry them out of this jurisdiction, and not returne without leave first obteyned'.[10]

These policies were reported to England, and provoked something of a scandal. By 1660, a pamphlet war in England, started by Francis Howgill's *Popish Inquisition newly erected in New-England* (1659) and Humphrey Norton's *New England's Enseigne* (1659), had thrown the Massachusetts authorities on the defensive. In their petition to Parliament in December 1660, the General Court of the colony expressed their hope that their defence of the repressive policies 'will abundantly satisfy concerning our proceedings against the Quakers' and that no one would force them to permit Quakers 'their libertie here (which God forbid)', since this would be worse than 'destroying us and ours by the sword'.[11] Nevertheless, their actions were broadcast even more effectively by Edward Burroughs' *A Declaration of the Sad and Great Persecution and Martyrdom of the People of God, called*

Quakers, in New England (1661). This was the most serious denunciation of religious persecution in Massachusetts, and gave all the details, providing the full statistics on his front page:

> 22 have been banished upon pain of death, 3 have been martyred, 3 have had their right-ears cut, 1 have been burnt in the hand with the letter H, 31 persons have have received 650 stripes, 1 was beat while his body was like a jelly . . .

Burroughs was hoping to impress with these figures, aiming to convince the king to end the punishments. This was reinforced by George Bishop of Bristol, who in his pamphlets *New England Judged, Not by Man's, but by the Spirit of the Lord* (1661), and *New England Judged: The Second Part* (1667), talked of the martyrdom of the Quakers. Like other writers, Bishop was more dramatic and polemical, as Pestana has emphasized, varying their style according to the likely religious sympathies of their readership.[12] From the first, Quakers drew on what has been called the 'Protestant theory of persecution', which had developed since the start of the Reformation and which became part of the way that their sufferings were recorded and published in the eighteenth century, yet the New England experiences were exceptional. 'The killings of the Quakers suggest that in the 1650s, Massachusetts Puritans were markedly more hostile to pluralism and toleration than Cromwell and the other leading English Puritans'.[13] Burroughs had his way. Although Massachusetts reiterated its legislation in May 1661 with the full panoply of punishments including banishment 'on pain of death', and executed Mary Dyer a month later, Charles II wrote to Governor John Endicott in September ordering the release of all Quakers condemned to death or corporal punishment. In late November, the laws in force against the Quakers were suspended until further notice. All they were left with was an order against vagrancy, which, in traditional English style, relied on the deterrence of whipping, and this was confirmed in 1662 as the only law available.[14]

It is surprising, nevertheless, that one of Charles II's subsequent responses in 1665 to New England's repression of Quakers was to endorse the 'sharpe law' that had proved necessary on both sides of the Atlantic. He made it clear that he did not want to encourage any 'indulgence' towards the Quakers, 'whose being [is] inconsistent with any kind of government'. The mutual influences of old and New England were established here, as the Massachusetts proclamations in 1658 were the first to establish the association of Quaker meetings with 'sedition' and to specify the punishment of banishment on pain of death. Years later, the Massachusetts authorities were still trying to justify their policies because the Quakers had behaved so 'insolently and contemptuously' towards authority and their executions were justified, not because of their religion but, like those of Jesuits and Catholic priests in Elizabeth I's time, for 'their breach and contempt of his majesty's laws'. Eventually, after a review of those areas of colonial law that had been found to be 'repugnant to the laws of England', they repealed the law making death the penalty for Quakers returning to colony. This was almost 20 years after the last execution.[15]

The threat to good government was the core of allegations against Quakers, and it was here that England copied the colonies. In Maryland in the late 1650s, the refusal of Quakers to swear to take the 'Engagement' to promise to assist Lord Baltimore's regime led to accusations that their 'principles tended to the destruction of all government'.[16] This was echoed in England only in part because the Parliamentary authorities concentrated on suspicions of heresy and blasphemy, despite Oliver Cromwell's personal commitment to liberty of conscience. The theme of sedition, however, was taken up after the Restoration in 1660, and accusations of sedition and the punishment of banishment became the hallmark of English laws in the subsequent decade, though unlike in Massachusetts, the death penalty was avoided. When Virginia passed its own legislation against the Quakers in 1663, it was modelled largely on that of Charles II's England the year before, rather than on the proclamations of New England, and it made careful reference to legislation from Elizabeth I's reign designed to maintain the supremacy of the Anglican Church. This time, the colony copied from England. As in the English laws, banishment was established for a third offence of attending a seditious meeting. The legislation accused several groups of 'separatism' and holding 'sundry dangerous opinions and tenets'. A significant adaptation had to be made as monetary fines were translated into pounds of tobacco. This example points to the workings of 'regionalism' of law in the colonies, within a transatlantic world of circulating texts and legal ideas, the different religious establishments of the two colonies sharing a common idea of sedition, but contrasting versions of the established religion to be defended. As in other areas of law, local legal cultures varied between the colonies.[17]

Restoration England

In some ways, the laws of the Restoration were less severe in terms of penalties than the somewhat *ad hoc* practices that had gone on before – corporal punishments (under vagrancy laws) were generally discarded. There were developments in the criminal law at the same time under Charles II that paralleled the policies applied to religious groups, particularly the adoption by judges of the use of transportation for those more serious criminals reprieved from the gallows, which suggests that the changed colonial situation with the new colonies in the West Indies offered a chance for more merciful penal policies. The idea of transporting the Quakers and Baptists may have arisen from earlier laws directed at vagabonds and 'gypsies' and from these contemporary practices of the criminal courts (see Chapter 1).

With regard to religious groups, however, transportation was repeatedly embodied in English laws of the Restoration and provided one of the primary threats to Quakers and Baptists until the 1670s. A raft of laws was directed at dissenters of all kinds, though Quakers were often singled out for particular mention. Horle notes the 'myriad of law enforcement agencies' directed at Quakers, with ecclesiastical courts attacking non-payment of tithes and imposing excommunication, which debarred them from many legal rights, and the secular courts prosecuting for refusal to take the oath of loyalty and attending illegal meetings. This was experienced by Quakers as a multi-pronged attack on many fronts, with multiple forms of punishment from fines, distraints of property and imprisonment, often without a specific term. The new element in the 1660s was transportation to the West Indies.[18]

The legislation applied in criminal prosecutions of Quakers varied extensively, from late sixteenth-century Elizabethan statutes concerning illegal conventicles and taking the oath of supremacy to special laws passed in the 1660s against conventicles. Two Acts entered Quaker records of sufferings as the first and second 'banishment' laws, but in fact, it was that of 1664 that led to sentences of transportation from the courts. In addition to those, use of the Elizabethan laws placed the Quakers under an obligation either to conform or swear an oath to 'abjure the realm, with refusal resulting in a death sentence' because that resistance was, by definition, a felonious action. The key offence in both England and Scotland was holding or attending an illegal conventicle. There were doubts as to what a 'conventicle' actually was, and to have the by-then famously quiet meetings of the Quakers defined as both seditious and a 'riot', for which one group were prosecuted, often seemed extreme. Quakers themselves pointed to the contradiction of a peaceful 'riot', and the absurdity of prosecuting for sedition – which meant the verbal expression of words that might damage the government – people who were largely silent in their worship. 'If there are no seditious words spoken, no seditious gestures used, why should it be taken as a seditious meeting, and the persons punisht [sic] for for what they are not, nay for what they most abhor to be?', said one Quaker pamphleteer. Another argued that 'it is so far from being what it pretends itself to be, to wit, a law to punish the guilty' but instead punishes those who '(to use the Kings own words in the aforementioned Declaration), *do modestly and without scandal perform their devotion in their own way*'.[19] To Anglican clergymen, however, it seems that 'such meetings were worse than riots, posing a clear and persistent danger to the established order of church and state'.[20]

The legal framework established in the early years of Charles II's reign bore down on any kind of Quaker refusal to conform. They could be prosecuted not just for assembling (to the number of five or more), but for refusing to take oaths or encourage to refuse to do so – even in print – and were, in addition, banned from serving in corporations such as guilds or town councils. Under both the pieces of legislation that came into force in 1662 and 1664, it was only at the third offence that they might have to 'abjure the Realm; or otherwise it shall and be lawful to and for his Majesty, his Heirs and Successors, to give Order, and to cause him, her or them to be transported in any Ship or Ships, to any of his Majesty's Plantations beyond the Seas', as it was put in the first law. Under the second, which reiterated this, but added the condition that if, at the third offence 'such Offender shall refuse to plead the general Issue', then they could be transported for seven years 'to any of his Majesty's foreign Plantations, *Virginia* and *New England* only excepted'.[21]

Trials – 1664–5

Although there were many prosecutions in the early 1660s, the impulse to prosecute for transportation seems to have been the result of the 1664 Act. As arrests and trials took place in London in the autumn of 1664 and spring of 1665, the wave of repression was reinforced at the instigation of the Court. An order to the Lord Chief Justice in March 1665 expressed the King's wishes:

> Calling to mind the advices we of late receive from all parts of this kingdom of the more than ordinary insolence to which the Quakers and sectaryes are now of late grown, he hath thought fitt for ye example and to represse in this conjuncture of affaires especially the insolence of those people that such of the as have been upon the late Act been condemned before your Lordship or other the justices in London or Middlesex to be transported beyond the seas, he commands speedy order for their transportation.

Yet, only a few days earlier, he had ordered nine Quakers imprisoned in York on a *praemunire*, that is, for not taking the oath of allegiance, who had been in jail at least two-and-a-half years, to be released, 'being moved wth pitty and compassion towards them'.[22] There is little systematic contemporary evidence of these trials, though there are both pamphlets published by the Quakers themselves at the time, and orders from the Privy Council arranging their transportation. Both these were copied faithfully in the two great collections of Quaker 'sufferings' published in the eighteenth century, which relied heavily on the records of their national 'Meeting for Sufferings', which was established in the 1670s. These two collections (the more famous of which was edited and published by Joseph Besse in 1753) were devoted to lists of victims and their punishment, and were global in scope, covering all communities in Britain, Ireland, the West Indies, North America and parts of Europe such as Malta.[23]

In the light of what we know from these disparate sources, the striking feature of the distribution of sentences to banishment is their unevenness across the country, with none at all in many counties. 'Sporadic and capricious' is one judgement of the general character of prosecutions of the Quakers. In addition, the cases were nearly all in 1664 and 1665. Quaker authors attributed this to the personal malice of local authorities, such as the Mayor of Bristol in 1664–5, who was responsible for the incarceration of at least 145 Quakers, and the attempted banishment of several more. In terms of sentences to transportation, Hertfordshire's courts produced the largest number – nearly 30 – but much larger counties, such as Yorkshire, saw only seven. The worst situation was in London where hundreds were arrested over more than a year of repression, and jails and lockups of all kinds were filled with Quakers awaiting trial or shipment to the colonies. With arrests beginning soon after the 1664 Act came into force, by the spring of 1665, as many as 150 Quakers had been sentenced to transportation in London and Middlesex courts. With regard to some batches of those who had been convicted, the sentences were carefully targeted with, in one instance, the women sent to Jamaica and the men to Barbados (19 people – 9 women and 10 men).[24]

The total number sentenced to banishment differs slightly in the two major eighteenth-century publications of Quaker *sufferings*, but was certainly more than 200, and these sources provided names for about 140 from London. Exactly how many actually left remains rather more difficult to establish. Horle argues that 'some Friends, however, were successfully transported to Jamaica, Nevis and Barbados, while one was sentenced to Virginia as a slave. But of more than two hundred and fifty Quakers sentences to transportation, only about twenty were actually transported'.[25] Certainly, the Privy Council orders suggest an effort to rid the country of some Quakers in the spring and summer of 1665, with specific numbers being allocated to individual ships and their masters going to specified destinations. In March, the *Amity* with seven Quakers was ordered to Nevis, the *Jamaica* with three to Jamaica, and the *John and Thomas* with six to Barbados – it was specified that they were not to return for seven years. Much larger numbers were also order that month, with the ships masters of the *Black Eagle* being given 60 Quakers and the *John and Sarah* 50 Quakers, but they were to 'defray the cost of their own transportation', which indicates that, by paying for the voyage, they were able to buy themselves out of any indentured servitude on arrival. The Governor of Jamaica, the intended recipient of the largest batch, was told:

> That you be required and you are hereby required to receive the said Quakers into your Charge, and for such of them as shall defray costs of their owne transportation, that you permit them to remaine there and not to returne for England within the space of seaven years. But for such as shall be at the charge of transporting, you are to cause them to be employed and kept as servants in that Plantation for the term of seaven years. And this his Maj[esty's] Command you are to see punctually performed.

The group from Hertfordshire were sent much later, in July, on the *Nicholas*, but this was, in fact, the second attempt to transport them.[26]

The Hertfordshire Quakers sentenced to banishment were moved to the Thames in London for shipment, and at the end of 1664, a famous incident occurred when the captain of the contracted ship, the *Anne*, refused to take seven of them to the West Indies, and set them ashore at Deal in Kent. Although he had been contracted to take them at 5 pounds for Barbados, 6 pounds for Jamaica, the captain Thomas May swiftly developed misgivings, and refused to take them onboard. When they arrived on his ship in his absence, he set off down the Thames and abandoned them in Kent. Reports of this began to circulate almost immediately, with one alleging May had left them because they had brought him bad luck. In December, orders were issued to arrest the seven freed men. At the same time, an arrest warrant for May was sent to the Warden of the Fleet. The warrant was not served until 1666, and May could not have an opportunity to explain himself. At the same time, the sailors of the *Anne* petitioned for their unpaid wages going back twenty months.[27] Such opposition to shipments were recorded with satisfaction by the Quaker memorialists, and are known in at least two other episodes. One was in London, when the crew of the *Black Eagle* under Captain William Fudge created difficulties about loading 55 Quakers in 1665. Another was at Bristol, as was reported to the authorities, when eight men of the crew of the *Mary Fortune* of Bristol petitioned that:

> Three Quakers were brought to their ship for transportation, but they durst not carry away innocent persons, who walk in the fear of the Lord; are persuaded the King does not wish to make void the Act that Englishmen shall not be carried abroad without their consents; moreover, these men are bound by no indenture or agreement for their passage; and there is a law in Barbadoes that whosoever brings thither any persons against their wills, and not being bound by indenture, shall be liable to such penalties as the law may inflict, and also shall be forced to bring them back to their habitations; have therefore put these men on shore again.

There were three Quakers sentenced to transportation and the crew claimed that the King could not really intend to transport them, as he 'hath not made void the Late Acte of the Nation, which saith no Englishmen shall be Carryed out if his native Countrie against his Will, and hee or they that do so Carrie them shall forfeit great penalties'. In addition, they said, they were afraid of what might happen if they turned up in Barbados with these men:

> And further we know that there is a Law in Barbadoes that whosoever doth bring any person or persons into the aforesaid Ileland against their Wills and not being bound by Indentures shalbe under such penalties as the law may inflict upon them, and also forced to bring them back to their habitations again, and we also know that they are innocent

persons and they do desire to walk in the feare of the Lord and that they was put on our shipp against their Wills; Neither are they bound by any Indenture, Neither hath anyone agreed for their passage; and we find that our Maister hath no order, nor any ones hand save him and us from Comeing under such penalties that the law may inflict upon us for Carrying them in this nature: for these reasons and many more we have put them on shore, Not that they have made any escape, But that we have set the at Liberty to Go Whither they please.

Only the episode involving the captain and crew of the *Anne* resulted in legal reprisals, though there was no court proceeding. The Hertfordshire people were ordered for shipment in the plague-stricken summer of 1665–10 men for Barbados, and 11 for Jamaica, and they seem to have left without difficulty on that occasion.[28] The *Black Eagle*, however, was the unfortunate ship in the summer of 1665. With 120 people in their jails, and a plague outbreak on their hands as well, the authorities in London tried to load 55 people into Captain Fudge's ship (also called the *Black Spread-Eagle* in Quaker sources) in August 1665, six months after he had been given the contract. Perhaps because of the 'pestilence', the sailors on board refused to load all but four of their passengers and the rest were taken back to Newgate. A second, successful attempt was made, this time with troops from the Tower of London. Thirty seven men and 18 women were in the party, the men, it is said, kept below decks. Captain Fudge was soon arrested and imprisoned for debt, and it was early in 1666 that the ship eventually set sail, by way of Plymouth. By that time, 6 women and 21 men had died. Soon after setting out, the *Black Eagle* was captured by a Dutch privateer, who, realizing that they were of no use as a means of bargaining in a prisoner exchange, sent them home again with 'a passport and certificate'.[29]

Towards respectability

For the last half of the seventeenth century, the national and local pictures of relations between the Quakers and the community around them concur – there was a move from outrageous challenge to other Christians to an acceptable respectability and even a form of integration. Though still subject to repressive laws, the threat of banishment was removed when the 1664 Act was replaced in 1670. The repudiation of violence and rebellion helped, though Friends were still being arrested locally in the 1683 panic of the Rye House Plot. By the time of Monmouth's rebellion two years later, they were less likely to be suspected of disloyalty, as their business and colonial interests had made them well-known participants in the national project of America. Apart from the famous involvement of William Penn in Pennsylvania, Friends provided substantial finance and organization for the small but significant colony of East New Jersey. Ironically, it was to that colony that rebellious Scottish Covenanters were banished in 1685, another people who left collective memoirs of their oppression. Nationally, at least, Friends had been transformed from dangerous seditious sectaries to being 'sober and useful inhabitants'. They were still, in their own eyes, a suffering people – something that confirmed their faith in many ways – but were also increasingly acceptable on the national scene of business and politics. In the colonies of the West Indies, records suggest that Quaker merchants and planters were increasingly integrated and formed part of the vital supporting economic community for the colonial authorities. There were still difficulties, the pacifism of the peace testimony in particular offending colonial authorities who needed white settlers to have a capacity for violence (see Chapter 8), but the acknowledgement of their contribution seems grudging in tone, relationships between Friends and the colonial governments seem to become practical and collaborative by the 1680s.[30]

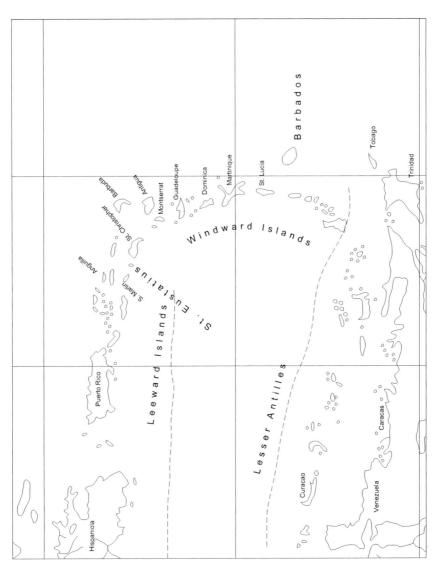

MAP 2 *Eastern Caribbean [detail from Emmanuel Bowen's* An Accurate Map of the West Indies *(1740 or 1752)].*

4

Rebellion in Ireland, England and Scotland 1649–88

Ireland

The transplantation of Irish by Cromwell within Ireland to the West – 'To Hell or Connaught' was accompanied by the shipping of thousands of people abroad – from hell to Barbados, as one author has put it.[1] Garrisons who surrendered, rebels who were captured and those who volunteered for military service in the pay of friendly countries (that is, those not hostile to the Cromwellian government) were all sent away. The combination of internal and external movement, in a period of war and famine that led to a falling native population, had few parallels in European history. The English were moving Irish people in large quantities in the 1650s, some to the colonies as prisoners, others as 'voluntary' exiles to the service of European powers. Garrisons were wise to surrender, as both Donagan and Ó Siochrú have established – the rules of war encouraged the granting of quarter to those who surrendered in advance of an attack but, if quarter was refused, no mercy could be shown if the subsequent assault proved successful. Cromwell actively pursued this policy, as he reported himself. At the 'storm of Tredah', that is, Drogheda, in September 1649, he attacked a large number of Royalist troops – after burning one of three crucial defensive towers, he recorded, that:

> The next day, the other two Towers were summoned; in one of which was about six or seven score; but they refused to yield themselves: and we knowing that hunger must compel them, set only good guards to secure them from running away until their stomachs were come down. From one of the said Towers, notwithstanding their condition, they killed and wounded some of our men. When they submitted, their officers were knocked on the head; and every tenth man of the soldiers killed; and the rest shipped for the Barbadoes. The soldiers in the other Tower were all spared, as to their lives only; and shipped likewise for the Barbadoes.

He reported this to the Council of State in blunt terms of its policy effective-ness as well as its semi-legal justification in terms of the rules of war:

> The Enemy had made three retrenchments, both to the right and left [of] where we entered; all which they were forced to quit. Being thus entered, we refused them quarter; having, the day before, summoned the Town. I believe we put to the sword the whole number of the defendants. I do not think thirty of the whole number escaped with their lives. Those that did, are in safe custody for the Barbadoes. Since that time, the Enemy quitted to us Trim and Dundalk. In Trim they were in such haste that they left their guns behind them. . . . This hath been a marvellous great mercy. The Enemy, being not willing to put an issue upon a field-battle . . .

He may have realized the effect of this, and repeated the justification in the second letter in phrase, which suggests that if the policy did not work in subsequent actions, then there were grounds for 'remorse and regret':

> I am persuaded that this is a righteous judgment of God upon these barbarous wretches, who have imbrued their hands in so much innocent blood; and that it will tend to prevent the effusion of blood for the future. Which are the satisfactory grounds to such actions, which otherwise cannot but work remorse and regret.

The massacre of garrisons and inhabitants of towns that had refused to sur-render reached its peak in these actions at Drogheda, an act that undermined Cromwell's personal reputation throughout Europe. His army, he thought, had lost only 100 men, and one figure of 3,552 deaths of Royalist soldiers and local civilians seemed, even to contemporaries, dubiously precise.[2]

By the middle of the 1650s, Royalists were assessing the contradictions in the character and actions of Cromwell, 'He dislikes shedding blood; but is very apt "to barbadoes" an unruly man, has sent and sends us by hundreds to Barbadoes, so that we have made an active verb of it: "barbadoes you"', went one judgement on his character in an intercepted letter. The use of transportation of surrendered enemy soldiers was also a feature of the intimidatory tactics adopted by General Monk in Scotland and seems almost to have been the standard policy of the Cromwellian regime for those unfit for service on the Continent.[3] To be 'barbadosed', therefore, was a continual threatening presence for many on the fringes of the British state, and while it was also threatened in England, it was so to a far lesser extent. Only in Ireland, however, was this policy widened to sweep up a large number of the poor and destitute, including a great many women and children, whose value as indentured servants was keenly felt in the newly acquired colony of Jamaica (seized from the Spanish in 1655). Within the West Indies, there were large movements of military forces and civilians to take advantage of this new acquisition, too.

Rounding them up

The policies by which so many Irish were transported to the West Indies is badly recorded, though the results are fairly clear in the reports from the Caribbean. The distinction between voluntary, forced and judicial processes is almost impossible to discern. The policy began after Drogheda and became part of the techniques for dealing with rebel soldiers. Very soon, the net widened to include a large number of the poor and those rendered helpless in the face of the forcible resettlement of Catholics in the West of Ireland. The 'transplantation', in effect, was accompanied by a very real threat of transportation. The traditional view is that 'Ireland must have exhibited scenes in every part like the slave hunts of Africa', with 'agents actively employed through Ireland, seizing women, orphans and the destitute to be transported to Barbados and the English Plantations in America'. The English government eventually became alarmed at the methods used, of which there were many complaints. It reported that up to 6,400 men, women and children had been sent by 4 March 1655 when 'all orders were revoked'. The 'men-catchers', the government admitted, had employed men 'to delude poor people by false pretences into by-places and thence, they forced them on board their ships'. They had even treated the English as badly as the Irish.[4] Despite these official misgivings, the servant trade went on, as it did in England, unchecked. 'The authorities in Dublin, concerned by the "great multitudes of poor swarming in all parts of this nation" welcomed this trade in human cargo as a means of clearing the country of vagrants', and of emptying the jails. This has to be understood as an additional suffering inflicted at the end of more than 10 years of warfare in the 1640s that had already cost Ireland between 15 and 20 per cent of its population. Transported to the West Indies, it was said, the Irish had to labour 'under [a] yoke harsher even than that of the Turks'.[5]

The development of forcible removal from Ireland was probably viewed by the English authorities as a form of mercy. The arrogance and prejudices (both racial and religious) of the English government are clear from the patronizing tone of Henry Cromwell's correspondence with London – he was appointed by his father in 1655 to deal largely with the internal divisions in the army in Ireland caused by the rising influence of the Baptists. Suggesting that the government settle disbanded soldiers in Jamaica, he added that there would also need to be a female population as well, and, in the face of their reluctance, he admitted that, 'Concerninge the younge women, although we must use force in takeing them up, yet it beinge so much for their own good, and likely to be of soe great advantage to the publique'. In another letter discussing a plan to send 1,500–2,000 'younge boys' of 12–14 years to Jamaica, he expressed the hope that 'who knows, but that it may be a meanes to make them English-men, I mean rather, Christians'. In this, he may have been following a precedent in 1653–4 when young Irish people were shipped to New England and Virginia.[6]

Selection of the transported

The policies of banishment pursued in Ireland in the 1650s were a mixture. With regard to surrendered soldiers, as had already happened after the fighting in England and Scotland, they were either allowed to go into foreign service or sent to the west Indies. As the re-settlement or 'transplantation' of Catholics to the west got under way, recalcitrants were threatened either with death or Barbados. This, described, with only a little exaggeration, as 'ethnic cleansing', caught up some of the former Catholic landowners as well as their tenants and workers.[7] Then there were other sources of trouble, such as Catholic priests. Finally, there were the poor, particularly women and young men, who were required to supplement the developing economies of islands like Jamaica.

One set of documents from November 1655 gives very detailed data on one shipload out of Waterford, which contained 39 people – 19 of them were women, three were priests, and there was one married couple with their daughter. The authorities in Dublin ordered the removal of this group, apparently because some were alleged to have been 'privy' to a murder in Kildare (though the two condemned for the killing were excepted) – it included the inhabitants of Lackagh Castle. It is likely that they were not untypical. Priests were commonly transported, along with large numbers of the landless 'proprietors' who had been the objects of transplantation, pushed westwards to Connacht, sentenced to death for non-cooperation and then pardoned for the West Indies. Henry Cromwell in 1655 was responsible for a less savage view with regard to Catholic priests, executions being largely replaced by transportation. This could be a kind of voluntary exile on the Continent, like those who went into foreign service, but transportation to the West Indies was threatened in response to any signs of recalcitrance.[8]

In the West Indies

The numbers of Irish people sent to the West Indies is uncertain, Population estimates from reports from the islands suggest that 'by the 1660s as many as 12,000 Irish resided in the Caribbean, compared with 50,000 African slaves'. A description of Barbados by the authorities in 1667 surveyed the available resources of available white men, that is, available as a military resource, as:

> Not above 760 considerable proprietors and 8,000 effective men, of which two-thirds are of no reputation and little courage, and a very great part Irish, derided by the negroes as white slaves; and indeed except the proprietors, merchants, tradesmen, officers, and their dependants, the rest are such as have not reason to discern their abuses, or not courage to leave the island, or are in debt and cannot go.[9]

Some Irish were regarded as a threat from the outset. Transported Catholic priests were not always welcomed in the West Indies, and in Barbados in 1655 and 1656, the Council inquired into at least seven of them, deciding with regard to a group of four to give them 15 days to leave the island and go to 'any place outside the Commonwealth of England'.[10] Irish servants were also not regarded very highly, the fear being that they might link up with angry Africans in a general revolt. In fact, as a number of contemporary observers commented, the slaves were remarkably passive, compared with whites. The 'great combination' that Richard Ligon noted had occurred shortly before his visit in 1647 had attracted 'the greatest number of servants', but not slaves. His view was that they could not overcome their ethnic and linguistic differences, being selected from a wide range of African origins.[11] Yet, there were occasional reports of alliances between blacks and whites, particularly the Irish whites. In it was reported to the Barbados Council that 'that there are several Irish Servants and Negroes out in Rebellion in ye Thicketts and thereabouts' and troops had to be ordered to find and detain them. In 1657, with some reports of personal misbehaviour towards their masters, there was a general crisis of confidence about the Irish servants:

> Whereas it hath been taken notice that several of the Irish Nation, free men and women, who have no certain place of residence, and others of them do wander up and down from Plantation to Plantation, as vagabonds, refusing to labour, or to put themselves into any service, but continuing in a dissolute, lewd, and slothful kind of life, put themselves on evil practices, as pilfering, thefts, robberies, and other felonious acts, for their subsistency, and endeavouring by their examples and persuasion to draw servants unto them of said Nation to the same kind of idle, wicked courses, as complaints to that purpose hath daily made to appear; and, informations having been given, and oath made before myself and Council, that divers of, as well Freemen as Servants, have of late uttered threatening words, and menacing Language, to several ye inhabitants of this Place, and demeaned themselves in a very Peremptory and Insolent way of carriage and behaviour; and, that some of them have endeavoured to secure them selves with Arms; and others now forth in Rebellion, and refuse to come in; by all which it appears, that could they be in a condition of power, or had opportunity, they would soon put some wicked and malicious design in execution.

Respectable householders meeting such wandering Irish were ordered to check their credentials, particularly to see if they had forged tickets from their masters, permitting them to be away from their place of service, or fake testimonials of their freedom provided at the end of their time. Nor was anyone to sell arms and ammunition to the Irish, or any Catholic, especially as the war with Spain was continuing and becoming very difficult for the Commonwealth in the Caribbean.[12] Yet some who had been troublesome to the authorities in the 1650s became reasonably well established and even owned a little land and property after 20 years in Barbados. The need for solidarity among the whites probably overrode any remaining sense of difference between the Irish and non-Irish. This was not exactly a form of integration since their identity as Irish servants was still clear, as the 1667 report above indicates, but racial membership came increasingly to dominate social relationships in slave societies in the West Indies and elsewhere.[13]

Survivors

It is hard to reconstruct the careers of these banished Irish, though one or two of the wealthier classes can be traced back to the Commonwealth period.[14] A rare accidental narrative of the voyage into the Atlantic is the petition found in the British government's intelligence files from an Irish woman stranded in Portugal:

> The bearer hereof Finella Cullava is a poor Irish widdow, and a catholick, which, in mere hatred to our holy faith, the Inglish heretycks sente her, in company of many other catholicks, slaves for the islands of the Barbados; and it pleased the Lord, that the ship, in which they were imbarked, was by foul weather forced into the port of Lisbon, and could not proceed in her intended voyage; for which reason this poor woman, and the rest of the Catholicks, remaine in this Christian citty, where they undergoe many necessities. Therefore it will be a charitable worke for every faithfull Christian to helpe them with their almes. In testymony of the truth, I have paste this certificate, written in the colledge of our lady of Oration, in the street called the Faugus das Farinias in the citty of Lisbon, the 21st of October, 1657.

No record survives of any response.[15]

Others turned up with various difficulties in Massachusetts. In 1661, two Irish servants in Essex County refused to serve their master (whose fields of maize, more than 10 acres, were standing unharvested) because, they claimed, they had already served more than the four years they would have done in Barbados. He brought a case against them for not working, saying that they were all the workforce he had, and that 'consequently all his cattle, fence and family were left destitute'. They said, by way of reply, that:

> We were brought out of our owne Country, contrary to our owne wills and minds, & sold here unto Mr Symonds, by ye master of the Ship, Mr Dill, but what Agreement was made betweene Mr Symonds and ye Said master, was never Acted by our Consent or knowledge. Yet notwithstanding we have indeavored to do him ye best service wee Could these seven Compleat yeeres, which is 3 yeeres more then ye use to sell ym[them] for at Barbadoes, wc[which] they are stollen in England. And for our seruice,

we have noe Callings nor wages, but meat and Cloths. Now 7 yeares service being so much as ye practise of old England, and thought meet in this place, and wee being both above 21 years of age, We hope this honoured Court and Jury will seriously Consider our Conditions.

The court's verdict was to check the legality of the contract, which in any case should not have extended to beyond 1663, and in the meantime, the two men (both over 21, suggesting that they had been indentured at a young age) agreed to go back to their service until the inquiry had been completed. There, the records end, though it is worth noting that adult servants, such as the Scottish soldiers sent to New England after the battle of Dunbar, could be indentured for six, seven or eight years.[16] Apart from these few voices, the Irish in the West Indies can be heard only in the accusations of their enemies.

Cromwellian banishment of rebels

The policies of repression in Ireland were never fully duplicated in England or Scotland by the Cromwellian regime, though they were threatened at times, and the use of banishment to the colonies as a means dealing with political rebellion became established almost by default. The Penruddock or Salisbury Rising of 1655, a Royalist rising possibly incorporating some disappointed Levellers, produced trials and narratives of banishment in both personal memoirs and petitions from the women left behind. The reality of the threat in this rebellion was at one time doubted by historians, particularly in the nineteenth century, but all agree that whether the rebellion was genuine or not, the judicial consequences were real enough, with executions and many banished to the West Indies. The details of the background and the suspicions about Cromwell's foreknowledge – and, perhaps, manipulation of the plotters to his advantage – are not relevant to this chapter. The events seem to indicate that a half-cock rising took place, involving a mixture of Royalists and others hostile to Cromwell's rule. The conspiracy had probably been much more widespread, but action elsewhere was forestalled by the disaster in the West Country. 'However feeble and abortive the actual attempts at insurrection in March 1655 were, the conspiracy from which they sprang was real, general and dangerous', according to Firth. The links with Levellers in the conspiracy are not proved, though three colonels were arrested in the autumn of 1654, suggesting that an alliance of Anabaptists and Levellers in the Scottish army was posing a threat. The evidence against the prisoners in the Thurloe papers, plus intercepted letters, indicate that the Salisbury or Penruddock rising was real enough.[17]

John Penruddock of Compton Chamberlayne, Wiltshire, led an abortive Royalist insurrection in the west, but was easily defeated by Parliamentarian troops under the command of Captain Unton Croke from the

garrison at Exeter . . . Penruddock and his associates, known as the Salisbury rebels, were tried by a commission of oyer and terminer at assizes
held at Exeter, Salisbury and Chard. John Penruddock was sentenced
to death, but the majority of the rebels, although receiving sentences of
death, were transported and sold into indentured servitude in Barbados.
However, seven of the rebels besides Penruddock and his next in command, Colonel Hugh Grove, were executed.

Probably some 39 men were sentenced to death, of whom about eight were
reportedly executed. A few years earlier, following their defeat at Worcester
and Dunbar in 1651, hundreds of soldiers, primarily but not exclusively
Scots, had been deported to the West Indies, and this was the policy adopted
with regard to Penruddock's men. This may have been the first time that
English rebels were treated in this way. The number may have been about 70,
though records are not precise. The most important feature of this episode,
however, is that the captives were put on trial before deportation, a process
that featured in all subsequent domestic rebellions.[18]

Secretary Thurloe kept careful records, not only of the trial and the
verdicts, but also of protests of the accused about the procedures adopted.
This included a petition from Marcellus Rivers on behalf of both himself and
other prisoners 'being with some scores more freeborne Englishmen sould
into slavery' to merchants who, he said, 'hope to continue and encrease
England's slavery by an unheard-of wile'. Some of the transported had
been acquitted and he himself had faced charges of high treason, but the
grand jury did not find the indictment valid – it was not a 'true bill' – but
nevertheless, he was transported too. Other defendants played a legal game
with the assize judges, challenging the selections of the jury by peremptory
challenges, and protesting against the procedures. Penruddock issued a
challenge (as was his right, to reject a juror without giving any reason) to
28 of those selected. The defendants also petitioned in protest, demanding
their rights to see the indictments laid against them, to know the names of
the potential jurors, and to have representation by counsel, citing Coke and
other legal authorities in support of their demands. Above all, they argued,
how could they have committed treason, defined as making war against
the king, when all royalty had been abolished? Their document ran to 35
clauses, with many similar arguments, often referring to recent cases such
as that of John Lilburne. Despite this, the majority were transported to the
West Indies, guilty or not.[19]

Barbados narratives

It is from these rebellions against Cromwell's rule that we have the first
printed accounts of experiences of transportation to the West Indies, and
the kind of life the transportees endured there. A German soldier, Heinrich

von Uchteritz, captured after the battle of Worcester and transported to Barbados, has left one the best-known accounts of being a servant, which he was for about five months on the island. The prisoners from Worcester, more than 1,300, were held for some months before being shipped in 1652 to the West Indies, where each was sold, he said, for 800 pounds of sugar. Von Uchteritz was bought by a man called Whittaker, 'who had one hundred Christians, one hundred Negroes, and one hundred Indians as slaves' (this referred to Amerindians, *wilde* or savages in the original German). His main complaints about his time there were that 'I had to sweep the plantation yard the first day; on another day I fed the pigs and thereafter I had to do the kind of work usually performed by slaves'. In addition, 'our food was very bad and consisted only of roots', mostly cassava and potatoes (which 'tastes almost like chestnuts'). After several months, Whittaker sold him to some German merchants for the same price he had originally paid, and von Uchteritz was to pay the merchants the amount of money 800 pounds of sugar would raise in Germany, after his return.[20] There are few signs here of the brutality of the servant system, though the sense of indignation is strong.

Marcellus Rivers and Oxenbridge Foyle, after their return, left a graphic account of their 1655 shipment to Barbados. During the five-week voyage from Plymouth, they and their companions were 'kept lockt under decks (and guards) with the horses, that their souls through heat and steam, (under the Tropick) fainted in them, and never till they came to the Island, knew whether [*whither*] they were going'. On arrival, they were all sold, and without any consideration of status or age, gentry or 'divines', were 'rendered all alike in this most insupportable Captivity, they now generally grinding at the Mills[,] attending the Furnaces, or digging in this scorching Island, having nothing to feed on (notwithstanding their hard labour) but Potatoe Roots, nor to drink but water with such roots mashed in it'. They were whipped as rogues 'for their masters pleasure', and made to sleep in 'styes worse then [than] hogs in England'. They had, he says, never seen the faces of the men who pretended to own them, the 'merchants that deal in slaves and souls of men', who had unlimited power to enslave the innocent, and bring them to 'this place of torment'. Rivers and Foyle claimed to be petitioning Parliament on behalf of both themselves and 70 others 'sold (uncondemned) into slavery', and the 1659 pamphlet also includes four supplementary letters, probably by Rivers. He apologized for the 'rude approach of a slave' who had recently escaped from the 'Protestants' purgatory', and repeated his innocence of involvement in the 1655 rising, though he had been in the king's army up to 1644. Again and again, he accuses the authorities of allowing the illegal removal of men by 'men-stealers', and their abuse in the colonies, 'a thing not known amongst the cruell Turk' (comparisons with the Turks – 'Turkish treatment' being an ordinary phrase for acting badly towards someone – had become almost standard by this time). Ironically, for a Royalist, his pamphlet was published, it records on the front cover, 'in the eleventh year of England's Liberty', that is, since Charles I's execution.[21]

These accounts accord with others from the same decades of the 1640s and 1650s. As Larry Gragg has observed, 'servants faced a rigorous work regimen': 'the planters had developed a system which invited the most violent abuses, a harsher system than that in England'. This was admitted as such by the 1661 Act, which conceded that some masters 'have exercised violence and great oppression to, and upon their Servants, through which some of them have been murdered and destroyed'. Slaves, though, had a much worse life, all observers agreed.[22] Even so, indentured servants were, in turn, worse off than those driven into European exile, in foreign service or hanging around the courts of the Continent. Of these gentry scattered around the Continent by the British and Irish wars of the 1640s and 1650s, it was said by one exile, 'banished men find very little business besides books'. But it was with dread that such exiles heard of news from home. As one reported in 1655, 'the prisoners of the Tower shall, 'tis sayd, be Barbadozz'd. God make us ready for the worst of times, if yet we can have worse then these'. Published accounts of the island, such as that by Richard Ligon in 1657, reinforced its reputation for cruelty and slavery in all but name.[23]

Covenanters and Rebellion 1660–85

If the Quakers in England were subject to some levels of persecution, including banishment in the 1660s, the policies in Scotland towards religious dissidents were both more severe and more likely to be a response to armed conflict. The history of religion in seventeenth-century Scotland is replete with conflicts, both between dissenting churches and the state, and between apparently closely related groups of believers. Presbyterianism formed the most vehement communities of belief, and, after the disappointment of the Restoration, the most consistent opposition both to the episcopal organization of the state church and to the royal power that imposed it. Presbyterians had proclaimed the Covenant in 1638 in opposition to both Charles I and his bishops and they had not changed their views by 1660. The result was a pattern of recurrent revolt and defeat between 1660 and 1685, from the Pentland Rising in 1666 to the failures of the joint rebellions by the Duke of Monmouth and the Earl of Argyll in 1685. However, this matching of the 'Bible and the sword' was an incoherent series of risings, with little to show for them – Presbyterians were rarely united in their attitudes to the state, or able to draw upon their considerable popular support. Repeatedly, it seemed in retrospect, they were plunged into a 'killing time' reminiscent of the first conflicts under Charles I, one in which execution went hand in hand with strategies of banishment, as the authorities resorted to transportation of the most intransigent or uncooperative Convenanters to the colonies. When they wrote their history in the early eighteenth century, Presbyterians were able to view it as one of suffering, vindicated by the eventual liberation of the Glorious Revolution of 1688 and the formation of a Presbyterian Church of Scotland. In this way, they laid down their claim to be the foundation of Scottish freedom and identity. Protestantism had entered the very definition of what it was to be Scottish much earlier than this, and it remained – and remains to this day – a subject of disputed national stories, as between Presbyterian, episcopal and Catholic Scotlands. Covenanter history was as much a constructed narrative as Jacobite or Gaelic histories of Scotland, of course, and therefore stands as one of the most continuous interpretations of Scotland since the 1600s. In the nineteenth century, any historical scepticism about, for example, the two women recorded in later accounts as condemned to death and drowned for their Covenanter beliefs in Wigtown in 1685, was met with a mixture of distress and passionate defence. The sceptics based themselves on early eighteenth-century criticism of the Whig and Covenanter views of James II's alleged cruelty, such as that by Sir George Mackenzie, who argued that 'as to sending People to the Plantations. It is answered, that none were sent away, but such as were taken at Bothuell [Bothwell] Bridge or in Argyle's Rebellion; and the turning Capital Punishment into Exile, was an Act of Clemency, not Cruelty'. With regard to the use of torture in the cases of religion and rebellion, he noted that 'it is allowed not only by the Law of our Nation, but of all Nations except England'. By contrast, pro-Covenanter histories of the 28 years of repression from 1660 to 1688 spoke of repeated experiences of martyrdom, and maintained this version of history through continual repetition of the stories of personal courage and sacrifice. Scotland's history thus remained a source of contention rather than agreement.[24]

From the first year of the Restoration, Covenanters knew that they could not win control of the church in Scotland, but they were scarcely united as to what they should do to rectify the situation. As Walter Scott wryly put it, 'it has been often remarked, that the Scottish, notwithstanding their national courage, were always unsuccessful, when fighting for their religion. The cause lay, not in the principle, but in the mode of its application'. Primarily, the problem lay in the factious nature of Presbyterianism in Scotland, divided between those who wanted no compromise with the secular structures of authority, and those who felt that there was something to be gained from a relationship with the state, if it could be established on their terms.[25] The Restoration government, however, was uninterested in a dialogue, and resorted to increasingly severe measures that paralleled those directed against the Quakers in England in the 1660s. Covenanter meetings were deemed illegal 'conventicles' in 1662, and by a subsequent Act of 1670, refusal to give evidence before the Privy Council of Scotland about them could be punished by heavy fines or banishment to the 'plantations in the Indies'. Holding a 'house' conventicle also incurred heavy penalties of having to find sureties for good behaviour, and imprisonment until they were found, 'or else enact themselves to remove out of the Kingdom, and never return without His Majesties Licence'. Between the Pentland Rising in 1666 to the 1680s, 'transportation to Barbados, Virginia or Tangier was the usual fate of those who proved too obdurate' and refused to make peace and compromise with the government. On occasions, this led to even more severe proposals – in 1685, attempts were made to increase the punishment for preaching at a house or field conventicle from banishment to death.[26]

A martyr's story: Alexander Peden

Biographies of individual Covenanters, such as that of covenanting preacher Alexander Peden, were scarcely sober and factual stories – the narratives repeatedly involve the themes of a Godly people acting on His commands, and by contrast, the dire fate of any who opposed them. Thus, the stories show the severe judgement of God against any who oppressed Peden, recording their messy deaths, and showing the providential character of his life by demonstrating his ability to predict these judgements. His personal exile was in the 1670s on the Bass Rock in the Firth of Forth for several years, and in 1678, he was nearly banished again, this time to Virginia. He, with about 60 others was sentenced to be transported to the colonies, on pain of death if any returned. Naturally, he prophesized correctly that 'the ship was not yet built that should take him and these Prisoners to Virginia or any other English Plantations in America'. They were successfully shipped to London, however, where the captain hired to take them across the Atlantic refused to do so. They had been represented to him as 'Thieves, Robbers and Evil-doers, but when he found they were all grave Christian Men, banished for *Presbyterian* Principles, he said, he would sail the Sea with none such'. They were set at liberty without any oaths or bonds, and returned to Scotland. This, at least, was the triumphant story told by Peden's hagiographer, but Robert Wodrow's account is more prosaic – Ralph Williamson, who was to collect them in London, was not there, and the captain who had brought them from Leith was so reluctant to pay for their upkeep that he just let them go. Peden wisely fled to Ulster for a few years, but returned from his preaching there with 26 armed Scots to take part in the 1685 Argyll rising (dying the year after).[27] Covenanting texts of this kind in the early eighteenth century were not histories recalled in tranquillity, but campaigning documents designed to reinforce the Presbyterian hegemony established after the Glorious Revolution of 1688. Patrick Walker's account of Peden – 'The Prophet' – established the connection between banishment and injustice.[28]

The official responses to recurrent armed rebellions were not completely brutal, but each outburst of trouble resulted in some executions and, for the majority, transportation. In 1679, the revolt of Covenanters, including a large number of those who refused any compromise with the civil authorities, the followers of Richard Cameron known as the Cameronians, led to defeat at Bothwell Bridge. They had had initial success, and had invaded Glasgow, where they took down the severed heads of those executed for treason in 1666, and gave them careful burial. Defeated at Bothwell Bridge (or Brigg), many were transported to the West Indies.[29] According to Wodrow's history, the government was in some doubt as to the extent of the conspiracy, and were particularly interested to find out if there had been any correspondence with anyone in England:

> For discovering of all which, we do ordain you to offer them our royal pardon, if they discover and make out their information, and that you put them to the torture if they refuse to inform in what you have pregnant presumptions to believe they know. When this is done, we do in the next place approve the motion made by you, of sending three or four hundred of these prisoners to the plantations, for which we authorize you to grant a warrant in order to their transportation, and we will thereafter send another warrant from hence for receiving them in that plantation for which they are to go, you giving information to our secretary of the place to which they are to be sent.

The use of torture became part of the legend of Covenanter suffering ('fiery matches betwixt their fingers'), and the implied contempt in one remark in the official records – 'The rabble may be transported to the plantations, never to return' – indicates that disposal of the ordinary participants was a matter of political convenience. After some delays, 257 prisoners were taken to a ship owned by Edinburgh merchant William Paterson on 15 November 1679, lying at Leith, to start the dangerous journey to America round the north of Scotland and the Orkney Islands. A winter journey by that northern route was always a risk, and the ship was wrecked. Only about 50 ('about forty, some say fifty') of the prisoners were taken off, the rest 'lost, or rather murdered', says Wodrow.[30]

Less dramatic accounts of the consequences of the 1679 rebellion emerge from the interrogation of William Kelso in Lisburn, Northern Ireland, by a local magistrate, George Rawdon. He had been in the rebel army, and decided to leave with his family, he claimed, and, after the defeat at Bothwell Bridge, fled to Ireland, hoping to find a ship going to Dublin and then London. He was a surgeon, and had been persuaded to join the rebel army by his neighbours. At the same time, a ship's captain reported seeing boats come from Scotland, on one of which were some heavily armed men, one of them a gentlemen, who said they, too, had fled after the rebel defeat.

These cases demonstrate, as does Peden's mobility between Scotland and Ireland, that exile and banishment were closely associated in the mutually supportive Presbyterian diaspora. The authorities were right to suggest that Ireland formed a bolthole for rebellious Scottish Presbyterians.[31]

The process of clearing up after 1679 went on for years, and there were continual efforts to force the Covenanters to conform. In 1684, more were banished and transported. Six men were ordered to the Low Countries, described as 'West Flanders', one of them for refusing to say 'God save the King', because the words imputed 'an owning of his person and government', of which he thought no Christian would approve. In other cases, the king agreed to send 'penitent' rebels to the plantations even though they had not taken the 'test' or oath – 'great multitudes were at this time sent away to the plantations, by virtue of this power. I cannot so much as do justice to a great many of these good people, by recording their names: as far as the council-records go, I have noticed them, but there were many sent away from Glasgow and other places of the country, that I have no distinct account of', recorded Robert Wodrow. On 17 May, the council banished to the plantations a list of men from different places, 'William Laing in Hawick, James White in Douglas, John Harper in Fenwick, Gavin Muirhead in Cambusnethan, John Gardner in Monkland, David Jamison "a sweet-singer", James Balfour in Fife'. Their alleged crimes were rebellion and reset that is, harbouring, of rebels.[32] They were conveyed to the custody of Walter Gibson of Glasgow, who was required to obtain a certificate confirming their delivery. 22 were shipped – the testimony of these, Wodrow claims, is 'before me', and were sent to (South) Carolina – the charge was supposedly refusing to call Bothwell-Bridge a 'rebellion'. At least another 15 were sentenced. The ship produced an accidental transportee, Elizabeth Linning, who was on board visiting one of the prisoners when the ship sailed. On arrival in America, the ship's captain tried to sell her into indentured servitude, but she challenged him successfully by making a legal appeal to the colony's governor. After a hearing, she was released. The others were mostly forced into servitude, and stayed there. As Wodrow sums up their experiences, 'in short, most part of the prisoners died in Carolina, and scarce half a dozen of them ever returned to their native land'. These transportees and their experiences have entered the history of the Presbyterian Church in South Carolina, part of the history of a community formed from voluntary migrants and those 'banished for religion's sake to a savage wilderness'.[33]

The next year, 1685, Argyll's rebellion produced more people to be shipped to the colonies – on this occasion, the destination was East New Jersey, Scotland's first true colony, ironically, partly funded by London's increasingly integrated Quaker business community. It was also a time when gratuitous cruelty seemed to accompany the use of banishment of Covenanters, and groups were rounded up and sent to New Jersey. Two processes combined in this year, the disposal of Covenanters arrested since the preceding autumn who had expressed support for a radical Cameronian manifesto, and the punishment of the rebels who supported Argyll. The most famous of those banished in 1685 were already in custody when Argyll's rebellion broke out. In addition to those seized in Scotland, Scottish Presbyterians attending a conventicle in London were also gathered together in Edinburgh for appropriate punishment. Among the men from London were two 'students of divinity', Alexander Sheils, who was exiled to the Bass Rock, and John Fraser, who was transported. As Argyll's rebellion started, about 270 prisoners, both men and women, were moved to the castle at Dunnottar on the North-East coast near Aberdeen, to be held in what became known afterwards as the 'Whigs' Vault'. That summer they were sentenced in batches to be banished, and handed over to George Scot of Pitlochrie to be taken across the Atlantic.[34]

The judicial processes were scarcely formal and proper. The sentences were usually for refusing to take the oaths of obedience to royal authority provided under the religious legislation. While women could be drowned for refusing to take the oath, and men were shot out of hand, the penalties inflicted by the Scottish Privy Council were relatively merciful. Repeatedly, groups of the accused were ordered to be marked for life, the men by having an ear cut off, the women by being branded, usually on the cheek. Both the authorities and the subsequent Covenanter historians called this being 'stigmatized', recalling Christ's stigmata, and it had been an occasional practice since the 1660s. The clerks to the Council recorded the summary of their actions – 'banished in all, 177, of which there is to be cut in the eare, 49; delayed in prison, 15; remitted to justice, 11; dismist and liberat. [freed], 40. [total] 292'. At least 20 of the banished Covenanters were women.[35] At the same time, the authorities were processing the prisoners taken from Argyll's forces. They threatened them with torture of the 'boot', though were legalistically uncertain whether evidence obtained in that way could be used against other accused. It was also reported that the Duke of Hamilton 'opposed this torturing much; and alledged that, at this rate, they might, without accusers and witnesses, take any person off the street, and torture him'. Some of the 'common' prisoners were ordered to be given to George Scott for transportation, and, like the others, 'to have a piece of their lug cut off, by the Hangman, and the women disowning the King to be burnt in the shoulder, that if any of them return they might be known by that mark and hanged'. The group that left that September for East New Jersey was therefore a composite one, consisting of obdurate Presbyterians, rebels and some individual criminals, including four women accused of murdering their own children. Sir John Lauder left an account of the voyage of George Scot of Pitlochie:

and a great many other peeple, some of them criminall prisoners given him by the Privy Counsell; others, who ware distressed by poverty, debt and captions, or ware whoores or prodigal wasters. A 3rd sort ware of phanaticall principles, and dissatisffyed with the Government. They sailed from Leith to the new plantation in America, of East New Jersey . . . Ther fell a tumult and mutiny betuen him and John Johnston drogist, another undertaker, who should have the dispiseall and use of the ship cabin. By crosse winds, they ware put in to the West of England; but after 4 moneths sailling, arrived ther, and Pitlochie and above 60 more dyed by the way.

The results were long remembered, as individuals made their way back to provide the crucial accounts of their sufferings.[36] Not all died, and some made their way in the new colony or in New England, where they were welcomed as refugees from religious persecution. This was the story of minister John Fraser, one of those hauled up from London and transported. After a number of years in New England, where he married a fellow passenger on the terrible journey from Leith, he and his wife returned to Scotland in the safer times of William and Mary and settled in the Gaelic area of Ross. Others stayed and gave support to the Presbyterian community in New Jersey, later taking part in a distinctively Scottish part of the general 'Great Awakening' of early eighteenth-century North America. A similar return was effected by Gilbert Milroy from Jamaica, though he had, at first, suffered some difficulties, with his master ordering him to work on Sundays. However, he seems to have become overseer of the African slaves, who made several attempts on his life. Like Fraser, he waited until after the Glorious Revolution before returning. The Scots seems to have been valued servants, whatever the cause of their transportation, and clearly came to see their own place in the racial and economic hierarchy of a slave colony. As one Scot, John Menzies wrote in verse about his situation,

> Ile owe no blush then as a debt to shame
> Because that I noe slavish servant am.[37]

The Presbyterians of Scotland in the seventeenth century were, therefore, the other group whose members suffered banishment from Britain because of a fundamental official mistrust of their beliefs and political loyalties. The Presbyterians, like the Quakers, could be described as a 'suffering people', if only because their troubles were carefully recorded in the works of providential character by men such as Robert Wodrow in the eighteenth century. But with a large Catholic and Protestant Episcopal population, Scotland was not yet safe for the Covenanting tradition, and Wodrow's work, in particular, was produced after the 1715 rebellion in order to reinforce the awareness of continued dangers of rebellion and a return to the 'killing time' of the 1680s. This is history emphatically written from the point of view of the winners, trying to establish their own experiences as the primary victims of oppression and sole claimants to a legitimate dominance of Scotland. It underplays other state violence between the 1660s and 1680s, particularly against Highlanders, but only in the long struggle against the Covenanters was banishment so consistently used.[38]

The Western martyrs of 1685

The rebellions of 1685 in England and Scotland mark a crucial step in the development of banishment – they were the first outside Ireland to end in large numbers of captives being sent to the colonies. Those transported could also portray themselves as martyrs of James II's tyranny and return in triumph to write their own experiences into the history of the country. In effect, they were only temporarily losers, and one of the few groups of losers to become winners a few years later. The accounts of the English events of that year, written by those who were participants or witnesses, are, like Covenanter history, full of the language of martyrdom and vindication. This makes their accounts uniquely difficult to treat as historical sources. Most of the personal accounts are also shaped by a sense of victimhood or divine providence, and many collected and published long after the events were produced with polemical aims in mind. Traditional histories have not helped to form a balanced view of the 1685 risings – Macaulay, for example, has been blamed for enshrining myth into history rather than subjecting it to severe criticism. Yet, he was not entirely devoid of perspective – in particular, he looked at the numbers killed afterwards. 'All the executions of 1715 and 1745 added together will appear to have been few indeed when compared with those which disgraced the Bloody Assizes', he wrote of the consequences of Monmouth's rebellion, but was more sceptical about some of the more fanciful local legends passionately repeated in the West Country. In England, as in the case of contemporary incidents in Scotland, these events became the stuff of legends, and that, in fact, has been the problem for more sober historical analysis. The 'western martyrology', published within a few years created the image of the repression following the risings, and set the tone for post-1688 histories until the end of the nineteenth century.[39]

The events of 1685 were a key phase in the 'crisis of monarchy' that Tim Harris has analysed so thoroughly, but also figured in the development of the 'Protestant empire' that Pestana has asserted was fundamental to the colonial enterprise of the British state.[40] The events of 1685 entered subsequent history of the Glorious Revolution because this was the moment when James II began to lose the support of the middle ground of English and Scottish politics. In 1683, the failure of the Rye House Plot and the executions of Algernon Sydney and Lord Russell had provoked a more serious and desperate contemplation of violent revolt against James, which Argyll and Monmouth attempted to carry out in a coordinated pair of risings in Scotland and England in 1685.[41] Yet, the two rebellions of that year were not successful in mobilizing widespread support and were quickly suppressed by a loyal, largely professional, military force. The failure was partly because the two men could not coordinate their actions, for the Earl of Argyll had to pay his men to keep them with him and was short of funds to mount an extensive campaign. The lack of any mass rising in support, particularly from the county leaders and their followers, even in South-West England, left Monmouth short of fighting men and equipment. Fear of civil war, because of memories of the 1640s and 1650s, in part lay behind the reluctance of many to start the vicious process again. It was the poorer people who joined, making the rising 'a local and predominantly plebeian affair'. But this did involve thousands, rather than the few hundred who supported Argyll, and the official reprisals were brutal. Monmouth's overhasty attempt at a night attack at Sedgemoor left his army defeated, and those fleeing the battlefield were easily captured and some were slaughtered on the spot in the villages of Somerset. Twenty two were hanged summarily at Westonzoyland, one of them a Dutch gunner and a deserter from the royal army, and someone recorded later seeing a 'range of Gibbets so decorated to good length' along the moor from Westonzoyland to Bridgwater.[42]

The subsequent trials in the West Country produced many death penalties for treason and 'making war on the king', one or two scandalous executions such as that of Alice Lisle, and many men sent to the colonies. It seems likely that of the 1,300 or so captives, 250 or so were executed and about 850 confessed, were pardoned and transported. Many may have died in jail. The term of transportation was for 10 years. Peter Earle calculates that about 7 per cent of the whole rebel army was executed, and these were about a fifth of those captured and put on trial.[43] The legal tactics adopted set the precedents for future government practice in the aftermath of the 1715 and 1745 Jacobite rebellions. As in the 1655 rising, the government policy was to subject all captives to judicial process. With about 1,300 people to process, and many more swept up in the panic of arrests following the rising, the authorities faced a problem of bringing successful prosecutions for treason (which required two witnesses). Though they ordered the arrest of many suspicious people, including nonconformist ministers and others, the core business of the summer was the processing of the rebel prisoners. With regard to minor offenders, such as those who had expressed 'seditious' words of sympathy for Monmouth, the penalties were confined to whipping, sometimes with repetitive brutality, for both men and women. William Wiseman of Dorset, for example, for publishing a seditious libel, was sentenced to be 'whipped at Dorchester and every market town in the county'. Others, such as the suspected preachers, seem to have been released after a few months.[44] With the overriding need for a judicially convincing outcome, and reluctant to have too many time-consuming trials, the authorities resorted to bluff and blackmail against the rebel prisoners. The aim was to ensure either a guilty verdict through a trial or a confession of guilt from all of them. The process had to be both swift and successful in delivering suitable outcomes, ones that allowed the government opportunities for both severity and mercy. One problem was the unpredictability of the subsequently infamous Judge Sir George Jeffreys, the Lord Chief Justice, while another was the various tactics adopted by the local authorities to persuade people to confess. As Macdonald Wigfield has observed, in his study of the rebels, without evidence from two witnesses, most of the accused could have been safe from conviction. One report from the Ilchester, though, reported how the county clerk

> wheedled them to confess how far they were concerned; pretending, if they would confess they would do them all the kindness they could at the assizes; and so drew out of them all they could, in the hopes of favour, and then went in and writ down their examinations; which I was eye-witness of . . . It was such a piece of treachery to betray them out of their lives . . . . Some were terrified into confessing in hopes of pardon, and then hanged, whom otherwise they could have had little against.

However, when selections were being made for transportation, it was possible to work a counter-deception against the jail authorities. Somerset man John Coad, who had deserted from the county militia to join Monmouth, recorded how he was advised by the officer selecting 200 people for Jamaica to stand forward if someone failed to respond to their name being called, and he observed a number of men saving themselves in this way. He did not follow their example, but

> there stood a poor woman of Charde, a stranger to me, who observed one of the company unwilling to be transported, came after me and pulling me to the man, [who] hastily shifted himself out of the string and put me in his place, and told me if I was called, his name was Jo Haker.

Coad also came from Chard, and this may have been one reason for the offer, but since he was well known in the county, he was somewhat apprehensive. Nevertheless, he managed to avoid the certain death that one army officer had warned him was his lot as a deserter and rebel.[45]

Although executions were carried in large numbers throughout the West Country, transportation saved most of them. As Clifton has observed, however, 'the scale of James II's sentences was new to England, for 850 men received the ten-year sentences to obligatory labour in the West Indies'. The extension of the time of service to 10 years, double the normal period, was one of James II's particularly mean orders, and resulted in many complaints of financial losses after the Glorious Revolution of 1688 from planters who had bought these servants. Judicially, though, James continued a consistent policy throughout 1685 of refusing to pardon and free many people. Death or banishment constituted the only options for all but a few. Nearly all of the transported were men, often from an artisan or agricultural background as ploughmen or farmworkers, as Clifton has shown from some of the occupational details provided on particular shiploads or prisoners. Whether all those sentenced to transportation were, in fact, shipped is not clear, so the case of the one woman, Jane Price, listed as being in Somerset's jail at Wells with the rebels to be transported, cannot be followed in detail. Of the more than 800 sentenced to transportation, at least 612 are known to have been taken in eight shiploads from Bristol and Weymouth, to Jamaica and Barbados. Those responsible for shipping were a strange mixture of James II's favourites, including his Queen. The basic figures published by Whig accounts in the decades after 1685 are generally thought to be fairly accurate by modern historians.[46]

The rebellion and its aftermath in the trials and executions were in some ways well documented in contemporary accounts, but evidence of the consequences for the great majority who were ordered for the colonies is scarce.[47] There are two personal accounts, the most famous being that of Henry Pitman, tried at Wells, whose story published a few years later has provided some twentieth-century myths. It was this story that formed the basis for Rafael Sabatini's novel *Captain Blood* (1922), the tale of an Irish physician who was transported and turned pirate (filmed most famously by Michael Curtiz with Errol Flynn and Olivia de Haviland in 1935). Only some of the key facts were changed. Pitman was with Monmouth's men, and he was captured by pirates after escaping from Barbados in a small boat. As Peter Earle puts it, 'Henry Pitman's relatives . . . paid £60 to George Penne (the shipper he described as a 'needy papist') but had to serve in the plantations until he made a "dramatic escape" in an open boat'. His account of his own sufferings displays great detail (for example of the royal order to the Governor of Barbados setting down the conditions of their 10-year servitude, which he prints in full), and, also perhaps, knowledge of the accounts being published after the Glorious Revolution. Nevertheless, he has a gripping narrative of the deception and blackmail that induced many of the prisoners to confess in jail – 'confess and be hanged' for some. Another broken promise was made by shipper George Penne, who said that 'if they would not pay him now, he would give orders to his brother-in-law in Barbadoes that our freedom should not be sold us once after we came there', and they would be treated with 'more rigour and severity than others'. Supposedly able to 'make choice of some person to own as a titular master' on their arrival, he found himself in service to Robert Bishop (who also occurs as the wicked master in *Captain Blood*) and, though not officially indentured, unable to leave. Pitman tried to assert his status as a physician, and refused to work for Bishop in that capacity, and was beaten and put in the stocks. He had the advantages of class, since his relatives sent goods to Barbados, which he used to raise money to persuade a man to buy a small boat (promising that he could keep it later), and escaped with six other men. This then led to the most famous episodes – their capture by Spanish privateers (after a meeting with Indians in canoes), their abandonment on a shore where they had to eat turtles, and Pitman's eventual rescue by other privateers who took him to Puerto Rico. From there, he made his way home via New York. To be fair to him, he also published five pages of a full account of the fate (and successful return) of his companions.[48]

The second account, by John Coad, was preserved by his family, rediscovered and printed in the nineteenth century. It is more religious and providential than Pitman's account, and, in some ways, more innocent and less knowing. He had fought as a pikeman in Monmouth's army at two of the early skirmishes of the campaign, Keynsham and Philips-Norton, in the second of which he had been badly wounded. While recovering from his injuries, the rebellion was defeated and he was rounded up by the authorities and imprisoned in Ilchester jail. Threatened with certain execution, as described above, in October, he managed to insert himself into a batch of men being sent from Weymouth to Jamaica:

> The master of the ship shut 99 of us under deck in a very small room where we could not lay ourselves down without lying one upon another. The hatchway being guarded with a continual watch with blunderblusses and hangers, we were not suffered to go above deck for air or easement, but a vessel was set in the midst to receive the excrement, by which means the ship was soon infested with grievous and contagious diseases, as, the small pox, fever, calenture, and the plague, with frightful botches. Of each of these diseases several died, for we lost of our company 22 men, and of the sailers and free passengers I know not how many, besides the matter's mate and Esquire Linch.
>
> In the night fearful cries and groning of sick and distracted persons, which could not rest, but lay tumbling over the rest, and distracting the whole company, which added much to our trouble.

There was a shortage of water, and despite the supply of small beer on board, much thirst. The master 'that wicked wretch Edward Brookes', nevertheless, was forced to ask the prisoners to help him handle the ship in times of emergency. After six weeks and three days, they arrived at Jamaica. Coad then had complex dealings that resulted in him being 'sold' into service, but found friends among the 'Godly', and he seems to have fallen on his feet in this setting. He was allowed to visit friends (both carrying army titles) for private worship, and they seemed to have helped when the 1690 Proclamation of pardon arrived. He tells a convincing account of a collective petition to the Governor demanding freedom and return to England. He had certainly returned by 1692 when one of the friends wrote to him with an account of the great earthquake that destroyed Port Royal. It is not perhaps surprising that Macaulay called this the 'best account of the sufferings of those rebels who were sentenced to transportation'.[49]

In both these cases, the survivors were able to tell their stories, though in very different ways. As Clifton has observed, the leaders that failed Pitman and Coad became posthumous martyrs, and the whole episode was re-written in heroic mode. 'The Glorious Revolution transformed Monmouth's army from a collection of traitors, into a gathering of Protestant martyrs who had struck bravely but too soon. Heroes by posthumous accolade, they were seized upon by Nonconformists who after 1689 wished to justify full religious toleration for themselves'. Their main fault, it seemed afterwards, was bad timing.[50]

5

The Eighteenth-century Jacobite risings

The policies of British governments towards the eighteenth-century Jacobite rebellions differed in significant ways from the practices of the previous century. For one thing, there were no safe havens, except perhaps in service to the Russian government, for rebels to be sent to where they could continue as soldiers. France and Spain were a continual threat to British interests, and it was unthinkable to have an official policy that augmented their armed forces. The results of this changed context can be seen in the consequences of both the 1715 and 1745 Jacobite rebellions – there were no mass deportations to foreign service, and the transatlantic destination of most of those who were sent abroad suggests that this was seen as the safest, indeed the only, option. In other ways, there was continuity with the practices of the 1685 rebellions, particularly with regard to the use of trials and confessions to validate the government's intended fate of both the leaders and the mass of poorer rebels, which suggested that the British state was keen to establish a lawful framework for the penalties inflicted.

To contemporary commentators who supported the Hanoverian regime, including one who was probably Daniel Defoe, the repression of Jacobite rebels in the eighteenth century was nothing compared with the illegal actions of James II's government against the Monmouth and Argyll rebellions. 'Let the World compare the Legal Proceedings of the present Government with those inhumane Barbaritys . . . and then they will be able to Judge whither the Traiterous Faction has any Reason to Charge King George's Administration with Cruelty'.[1] He had a point, for the approach to processing the prisoners of the 1715 and 1745 risings was more careful and legalistic than in the seventeenth-century rebellions. Yet, the policies of the eighteenth century drew upon precedents established in the seventeenth century.[2] The fact that such punishments were still controversial, however, is suggested by this short factual pamphlet enumerating the executions, transportations and arbitrary legal procedures of James II's government – Hanoverian supporters felt the need to justify the punishment, and tried to show that this was more than the winners' justice of James II, but, on the contrary, it constituted just and merciful treatment – a clean break with previous bad practices. As Daniel Szechi observes, this was part of the Whig self-image of legitimacy established by the 1688 Glorious Revolution. Indeed, he rightly observes that 'one of the Whig party's most central beliefs about itself was that the Whigs had rebelled in 1688 to overthrow the kind of tyranny exemplified by James II and VII's treatment of the men who had followed James Scot, the Duke of Monmouth, into rebellion in 1685. They accordingly shied away from any notion that a Whig ministry might preside over the equivalent of Judge Sir George Jeffrey's "Bloody Assize"'.[3]

A key feature of both rebellions, therefore, was the contest over the legitimacy of the judicial processes. Government propagandists had to counter many of the critics of the Hanoverian regime who asserted that the policy was essentially spiteful and unjust – people who, to quote Defoe in another pamphlet, called justice 'revenge'. The war over the judgement of history was waged in deliberate speeches from the scaffold, in which the condemned attempted to undermine the legitimacy of the regime. Northumberland cleric William Paul, for example, apologized for pleading for his own life and begging to be transported, acknowledging that this seemed to accept the authority of the government, and asked pardon from his fellow Jacobites who were offended by his actions. In also providing a criticism of the Church of England since 1688 (despite his petitioning the Archbishop of Canterbury), he was also trying to undermine the Georgian establishment of a confessional state. As the government propagandist who replied to these speeches rightly observed, they were 'framed on purpose to spirit up the Faction to a New Rebellion', and reflected a resolve to 'delude the unthinking Populace, and make those Men Pass for Valiant and Glorious Martyrs'. The public sympathy for some of the executed, particularly the young Earl of Derwentwater in 1716, tended to make martyrdom, rather than just punishment, a very likely popular image.[4]

The processing of the Jacobite prisoners was certainly more legalistic, but the policies of 1715–17 and 1746–7 appeared at the time very much like ethnic and religious victimization. There were two major obsessions among the Hanoverian politicians – the Highlanders and the Episcopal Church, which seemed to support them in their ways. Both Highland culture and the Episcopal Church's traditions indicated that there were wellsprings of potential rebellion across a large part of Scottish society. The church's repression of Presbyterianism before the Glorious Revolution of 1688 was still a potent source of fear of Jacobitism, as Robert Wodrow's writings of the 1720s, carefully documenting the oppression and sufferings of the covenanting Presbyterians, suggest.[5] For him, despite the defeat of the 1715 rising, Jacobitism and the return of Episcopal oppression were ever-present dangers. The fact that the Presbyterians had acquired legitimate hegemony in Scotland under William and Mary meant they had a lot to lose. These twin features of Highland culture and Episcopal religion were intertwined into a cultural image of the rebel as subordinated by a feudal society and an oppressive church. The result was that Highlanders were mistakenly held to be solely responsible for both the 1715 and 1745 rebellions, and provided the primary image of Jacobitism in English publications of the period. Yet, the rebellions had much wider support among landed classes and poorer people in the lowlands and parts of the Borders than many contemporaries were willing to acknowledge.[6] Nevertheless, Highlanders and their society were clearly identified as a social and, above all, political, problem as long as they were able to maintain their traditions. As a result, the Highlands became the focus of repeated attempts at enforced social change and economic transformation, with the aim of making them safe for a Hanoverian government.

There was a paradoxical result of this over-emphasis, in that the 'common' rebels captured after both risings might be regarded as being of lesser culpability than their leaders. Highland society meant most were vassals or oppressed under-tenants of a feudal society – rebels had been 'forced out' to serve their lords under conditions of feudal land tenure that imposed military service. This hardly led to a policy of generous sympathy for the oppressed, as most ordinary captives were transported across the Atlantic in the aftermath both the 1715 and 1745 risings. It could therefore be argued, as Bruce Lenman has, that:

> If the treatment of the lower orders amongst the prisoners was casually brutal in its use of transportation, it was also basically contemptuous. What the government was determined to underline was that pleas that men had only been 'forced out' to serve in the rebel army by their social superiors would only be accepted if resistance to forced enlistment could be shown to be violent, well-attested and sustained . . . It was a formidable requirement, which only a few could meet.[7]

Feudalism was not a sufficient excuse, for the English courts, but politically, at least, it was a significant factor in granting mercy. When the authorities in Glasgow found themselves having to maintain, at great expense, more than 350 Highlanders who had been intercepted on their way home from Kelso, where they had deserted in 1715, they endorsed the many 'attestations' of their prisoners that they 'were forced out' and observed by way of additional evidence that nearly all were of the 'common sort'.[8] It was, in fact, well understood that 'forcing out' was not confined to the Highland clans, but was widespread elsewhere – even in Lancashire, it was customary for the Catholic tenantry to follow their landlord's cause, as they did in joining the 1715 rebellion on the way to defeat at Preston. It is possible that many of the ordinary rebels can therefore be regarded as 'victims of a dying feudalism', though whether they were *all* seen so at the time is more debatable.[9] It was because of these social structures that nearly all commentaries on the Highland problem focused on the levels of unfreedom and military service that combined to make the clans and their like prone to sheepish obedience when their lords rebelled. The pattern of what more than one writer called 'slavish dependencies' was one fundamental aspect of the way rebel armies were recruited, but was also present in some of their Scottish opponents' recruitment practices.[10]

Typical of the characterization of Highlanders was one report to the London government that recommended trying to change both the social structure and the culture of the society. It suggested abolishing feudal land tenure and making sure that rebel clan chiefs lost their estates, which they would not be able to leave to their children.

> 'Tis very obvious that it must be indispensably necessary in the first Place, to take away this Vassalage, and destroy the present slavish Dependance, by abolishing, in both instances, the Power of the Cheifs, so inconsistent with free, legal Government.

His picture was of an alien society:

> The Highlanders, by a different Habit, Language, manners of Living and Government, continue in their several Clans a distinct and separate People, and having little Intercourse are unconnected with the Nation in General, to the manifest detriment of the Public in many Respects. For while the Interest of the Rest of the Community consists in Justice and Tranquillity; Interest as well as Education leads these People to Confusion and Violence. The Principles of hereditary Rights and Slavery in which they are brought up, and their own abject Subjection to the Superiors or Chiefs of their several Clans confirmed by long traditional usage, easily lead them into Rebellion against a Government founded upon the Maxims of Liberty.

The separate (in fact, private) jurisdictions of the clan chiefs who could run their own legal system had to be abolished. Standard Scottish law and the English language had to be imposed, the latter by the establishment of Schools for the Instruction of the Highlands. The basic elements of a social revolution were to be imposed from above, with the same rhetoric of justification that had had been proclaimed in seventeenth-century Ireland – the poor would be set free from feudal oppressions and capricious masters. Some of this was attempted in the years after the 1715 rising, with laws forbidding the carrying of weapons (with heavy fines and transportation for non-payment), and sweeping plans for establishing schools, particularly in the Catholic areas. Major changes had to await the response to the 1745 rising, when private courts and jails, even those of the loyal Dukes of Argyll, were abolished.[11]

The myth of the Highlands and its alien society as the heartland of Jacobite rebelliousness nevertheless pervaded early eighteenth-century representations of the dangers. Yet, the evidence suggests that there was a substantial level of popular support for the two rebellions outside the Highland line, however vaguely it was defined and porous it was in practice. There were both popular and the 'high' cultures of Jacobitism, always interacting and overlapping, and often mediated through songs and music. In the 1715 rising, there was staunch support from some merchants, students and professionals in Aberdeen, and in the 1745 rising, the lists of prisoners compiled by the winning side suggest that many urban workers in small towns like Inverness, in un-warlike occupations such as tailoring, joined the Highlanders in the revolt[12] As Murray Pittock puts it, 'one of the chief errors . . . is to lay undue emphasis on the Highland nature of Jacobitism': Jacobitism was a 'complex culture of protest against the overthrow of a sacred monarchy' and 'the rapid development of the British state which followed the exile of the Stuarts'. Nevertheless, feeding the fears of his opponents, Bonnie Prince Charlie took pains to dress his *Lowland* troops in Highland dress.[13]

The two risings

The legal and political strategies of the '45 were derived from those pioneered 30 years earlier, and it is significant that legal officers were sent into the archives in 1746 to clarify the proper procedures for prosecuting and banishing rebels based on the practices of 1716. These precedents were central to the way the prisoners of the second rising were treated in 1746.[14] Geoffrey Plank argues that the legal problems produced by the policies of the 1715 rising led to much tighter procedures and stricter documentary evidence designed to pre-empt any legal challenges or delays.[15]

There were four essential principles established in 1716–17 that shaped the policies of 1746–7. First, the most obvious rebel leaders, those most responsible for starting the rising and recruiting the troops, were to be selected for trial on charges of treason (which, in one of its key formulations, meant 'levying war against the king'). These were mostly titled and landed Jacobites. Second, these trials could be held anywhere but, most importantly, they had to be held in England, even if most of the treasonable actions were carried out in Scotland. Third, the mass of the captives were to be subjected to minimal judicial processes, but 1 in 20 would be chosen randomly by lot to stand trial with their leaders. If any of these ordinary prisoners appeared particularly culpable of rebellious activities, they would be pre-selected for trial like their leaders while the rest went through the ritual of the lottery. Fourth, mercy was to be extended to the remainder as long as they agreed to beg for it (a way of forcing them to acknowledge the legitimate authority of the Hanoverian regime), and sign an agreement for indentured servitude in the colonies. They would then be transported. Though simple in theory, these principles were in practice muddied by other considerations, such as allowing some to go into voluntary exile, or even voluntary transportation to the colonies. In addition, resistance was quite sophisticated legally. Some rebels petitioned for pardon but refused to sign indentures. Others followed the practice of affluent convicts and managed to buy their own indentures from the ships' captains and escape servitude. From 1716 to the aftermath of the 1745 rising, there were sufficient gaps in the documentation, and uncertainty as to the law, to allow many to slip through and escape the full consequences of transportation. It is worth noting that the Jacobite banishments of 1716–17 preceded the passing of the Transportation Act which, from 1718, set up a more systematic framework for the treatment and containment of English convicts sent to North America. Transportation was a business still under development, and Margaret Sankey is right to point out that little attention has been paid to contribution that the government's experience with Jacobite rebels had in the development of criminal transportation.[16]

Executions were few, despite thousands being involved in the two rebellions, but even the sparing use of the death penalty, as we have seen, seemed to require Hanoverian supporters to win the argument against the scaffold speeches and statements by Jacobite 'martyrs'.[17] One crucial precedent after the 1715 was the use of a lottery to decide who should be tried, and who offered pardon on condition of transportation (which they had to sign for and agree to) – 1 in 20 was chosen for trial. The role of the judges in choosing who would be tried and who 'lotted' was made explicit in government instructions, and the purpose was to identify the most culpable:

> The most considerable of Note and condition as well as the most criminall of the Inferior Rank, that all such should be distinguished and sett apart and that the lotts should afterwards be drawn among the Bulk of the Inferior people but notwithstanding this drawing Lotts Evidence was to be continued to be got against every individual person of any rank or degree and that as well from among officers and soldiers of the Kings Troops as from any of the prisoners themselves.

In this way, the 'inferior' were subject to random selection for trial and probable execution, while their superiors, those of 'note', had already been taken out of the pool and scheduled for court proceedings.[18] The 'gentlemen or persons of substance' were not to be transported, partly because this involved servitude and, therefore, would contradict the traditional social order, but also, suggested one official, 'to prevent the public from being deprived of the Forfeitures of such Estates, [and] not to delay delivering to the Merchants the Prisoners on account of this being an uncertainty in this Matter'. The commission forfeiting the estates did not get going until the end of 1716.[19] The 1745 prisoners were subject to even more careful classification – indeed, a whole class structure seems to have been worked out by the administrators, with the same policy of class differentiation in mind. In these respects, the treatment of the prisoners of the 1715 rising set the model for the subsequent processes of those of the 1745 rising, with class selection and the lottery of the poor shaping the destinies of different groups.

This policy ran into difficulties in 1716, as prisoners agreed to be transported, but refused to sign indentures for their servitude in the colonies – in other words, they refused the customary fate of English convicts reprieved from the gallows for transportation (which would only become statute law in the 1718 Transportation Act). It is unclear how many of those prisoners who conformed to the convention and signed a petition begging the King for mercy (and transportation) also refused to sign the indentures. Alexander Stewart's account of his transportation in 1746 gives an account of the experience and indicates that the prisoners were attempting at all times to retain the initiative as well as constructing strategies of resistance to, or at least frustration of, the process. His memoir reports the jail officers coming in:

> with a verie large paper like a charter, and read so much of it to us as they thout proper, and told us that it was to petition their king for mercy to us, and that it was to go of that night for London, and as soon as it came back we probably might get hom, or els transportation, which would be the worst of it; and that we behove to put down our names at the foot of it, and them that could not, and some that would not. Miller did it for them, and told me that I might be verie glade to doe it; for such mercy that was but to hang only one of twentie and let nineteen go for transportation, pointing to me in particular with his fingar, and told me if that Popish spairk had cairried the day he would have hanged nineteen of them and only let the twentieth go free.

He was sent to Maryland and escaped almost immediately with local help.[20]

In some of the retrospective histories of these rebellions, commentators argued that these legal procedures were not, in fact, required by customary notions of law and war. Francis Douglas, for example, in his history of the 1745 rising, noted the protest of one gentleman towards the end of 1746 against the cavalry grazing their cattle in his parkland, taking the officer responsible to court. But, in court:

> After stating the facts, it was observed that a mistake in the law runs thro' the whole complaint; inasmuch as the complainer supposes, that as in time of peace, or in the time of open rebellion, rebels must be tried and convicted by the civil courts before either their persons or goods can be

touched; but that the law stands directly otherwise: for that in an open rebellion, rebels are to be treated as enemies, and to be proceeded against by the military law, with which, in such cases the King is intrusted; and that the King and his legal officers have a legal power to destroy or seize the persons and effects of rebels without trial or conviction, in the same manner as if they were foreign enemies; with this remarkable difference, that rebels have no privileges allowed to enemies in a lawful war; as they are to be held as enemies, and not subjects, during the subsistence of the war, and after it are subjected to the pains and forfeitures inflicted by the laws of their country.[21]

The rights of the defeated rebels, this implied, were a privilege to be granted, not to be legally asserted. Yet, the Hanoverian government became increasingly, not decreasingly, anxious to be seen to act lawfully. Strictly speaking, the laws of war allowed the disposal of enemies and rebels without rights, even through death or slavery, but there were sufficient sceptics and critics among the government's own supporters to guarantee that legal forms were followed, particularly in the 1745 rising. Officers and men of the French military service, for example, whatever their national origin, were carefully separated from rebels for considerate treatment as prisoners of war. It was admittedly a fine distinction, since Irish and Scots were found in both categories, but one that may have mattered in Britain's relationship to its traditional enemies in the military struggles in Europe.

There were fiercer debates after the 1745 rising about the wisdom of the policies of execution and banishment. As one discussion in the press – significantly headed 'on civilizing the Highlanders' – remarked,

> I was as much against the rebellion as anybody; but I am neither for killing wretches in cold blood, nor transporting them into the plantations, where, the spirit of resentment remaining, they may possibly be more serviceable to the *French*, and dangerous to us, than in the *Highlands* . . . The great difficulty will be to make them industrious, and convince them, that a life of labour is vastly preferable to what they now lead.[22]

For the 'common sort' of rebel, this problem was safely transferred to the colonies.

The 1715 rising

The fighting in 1715 was over by mid-November, after the indecisive battle of Sherrifmuir near Stirling, and the surrender of the Anglo-Scottish rebels at Preston in Lancashire. It was the latter who formed the overwhelming majority of the prisoners.[23] Margaret Sankey's remains the almost definitive study of their fate, and of the twists and turns of government policy that led to so much exile and banishment. Like Geoffrey Plank, Sankey notes that, partly because George I's government was committed to going through as formal a legal process as possible, they were faced with continual challenges under both Scottish and English law. Things were made more difficult by the incorporation of the English protections given by the 1696 Treason Act into Scottish law after the 1707 Union. There was also the Scottish law against unlawful imprisonment and (in England) *Habeas Corpus*, both of which had been suspended for a year in the emergency. Despite the fraught context, the trials would still have to conform to the treason law.[24] These laws gave defendants much more information about the charges they faced and came close to guaranteeing 'due process' for the first time in a formal statute. The trials in 1716 were not the first trials of Jacobites under this framework, but they were the first *mass* trials for high treason after the union of the two kingdoms, and the imposition of uniform treason legislation.[25] Oddly, it was, in fact, the oldest rule of all, concerning the number of witnesses required, that caused the most difficulty in 1716. Two witnesses were needed for a treason prosecution, and their names had to be given to the accused ahead of the trial, and lawyers had to be appointed for the defence. Insuperable problems immediately arose with the processing of the 1,259 prisoners following the surrender at Preston, and even more difficulties were faced with attempts to prosecute those few taken in Scotland. The result was that trials were held in two concentrated periods, most of the Lancashire prisoners being tried in January and February 1716, and the most important and titled traitors coming before courts in London and Carlisle in the summer and autumn. To move the Scots to England and put them on trial required a repudiation of Scottish jurisdiction, and the process of marching prisoners through the streets of Edinburgh on the way to Carlisle produced a strongly hostile reaction from the local people, as well as from the (loyal) Scottish establishment, as being an insult to Scottish law. The first batches were sent to London in early 1716, with 16 arriving in January to await trial. After some delays, in September, several remaining parties were marched under guard and across the lowlands to Carlisle. An Edinburgh newsletter gave an account of the prisoners being publicly marched out of town, passing by the local precursor of the guillotine, the 'Maiden'. It looked 'ominous' for the gentlemen prisoners to be marched through the Grassmarket past the traditional place of execution, it observed.[26]

In Lancashire, meanwhile, the Preston captives had been classified, sorted and prosecuted. It proved a very difficult task for the authorities, led by lawyer Henry Masterman, who received continual instructions from Lord Townsend in London, many of which were hard to carry out. He was appointed by 30 November, just over two weeks after the surrender at Preston on the 13th, and in December, was authorized to dispose of the 'common prisoners by lot', by which 1 in 20 would be selected for trial for high treason and the rest transported as long as they petitioned the king for mercy (thereby acknowledging their guilt). This was a barely legal procedure that had been initiated by the Privy Council. With regard to prosecutions, he was exhorted to pay particular attention to the Lancashire gentry and collect evidence against them to ensure successful prosecution. The files left by Masterman and his colleagues reflect an enormous effort on their part both to follow their instructions and bring viable prosecutions to court.[27] There was no point in selecting people for trial if the evidence was not already available. In the many lists and notes left by the government agents, there is one which summarizes the feeble results of their efforts. After discounting the possibility of prosecuting more than half of the prisoners because of lack of evidence, and putting aside the 'gentlemen' against whom two witnesses could be found, the officials selected 1 in 20 of the 'inferior' sort for trial. Counting these with the prisoners who were under arrest and indictment as a result of county magistrates' activities during the rebellion, a grand total of 114 of the 1259 prisoners were deemed eligible for trial, less than a tenth of the whole. Table 1 shows a bureaucracy's love of legalistic precision, while simultaneously demonstrating the difficulties the administrators had in devising a working system. As in the methods used in the jails of the South West in the summer of 1685, a successful outcome, that is, many petitions and signed confessions for transportation, depended largely on bluff. However, the authorities were very attentive to the letters of the law in this deception.

It was hoped that all those who were not prosecutable, together with those not selected for trial by the lottery, would petition for transportation. On a number of occasions, it was reported to the legal officers that the King had expressed his 'hope' that no proceedings would be undertaken against those not selected:

> H[is] M[ajesty] hoped there would be no occasion to proceed to the Trial of any of those who had Escaped the Lotts neither was it HM's Intentions to go any farther than to strike a Terror in Case you should find a Combination among them to stand out agt the terms of Transportation which I expect to hear they have pretty generally submitted to by the return of the Messengers sent to Lancaster and Chester for that purpose but till that is done it will be necessary to keep them under such sort of Tie that thay may not appear as it were in defiance of the Government or think themselves secure as if they had done nothing to deserve Punishment.

If they went to colonies quietly, in other words, there would be no need for any further trials and executions.[28] In fact, there was little chance of a legal conviction against most of these men, and the pressure to make them petition was a kind of sleight of hand, involving bullying and threatening, whereby those who were never going to be tried were persuaded to plead guilty and petition for pardon. At least 206 are mentioned in one source in 1716 as refusing to sign a petition for mercy, and it was hoped by officials that the preparation of others for trial and potential execution

Table 1 *'Particulars and against who are or are not evidence'*

Gentlemen agt[against] whom noe particular evidence –	131
Inferior ditto	520
Gentlemen agt [against] whom are 2 particular witnesses	40
Gentlemen agt [against] whom are but 1 particular witness	40
Inferior agt [against] whom are 2 or more particular witnesses	383
[then repeats Gent with one witness but puts 40 in the column]	40
Inferiors agt [against] whom ditto [1 witness]	185
Inferiors agt [against] whom are 2 or more particular witnesses	383
	605
Total	1259
Lott men to be tried out of the 383	19
Inferiors appointed for tryall by reason of their degree of guilt	25
Gentlemen agt [against] who are one or more particular witnesses	40
Prisoners in custody by virtue of warrts of Justices of the peace to be tried because not entitled to draw lotts	30
In all to be tried	114

Source: TNA PRO KB 33/1/5/54.

would 'probably go far in breaking that Combination which seemed to be amongst them'. In any case, they were to be transported, and, in instructions to the governors of the colonies receiving them, were to be held 'in custody' until they had signed indentures. Then, they could be released into colonial bondage.[29] Many of the Jacobites with greater legal knowledge realized the legal weaknesses in this process, particularly where indentures had not been signed, and organized resistance was directed at challenging the legality of the procedures. The result was, as Sankey notes, that, just as those on the gallows produced the same forms of self-justifications which challenged the legitimacy of the Hanoverian state and church, so too from Lancashire to the Americas, Jacobite petitioners framed their resistance to the transportation orders with remarkable consistency.[30]

Nevertheless, even with little danger of a formal prosecution, a large number of prisoners did petition, even 113 'gentlemen' in custody at Chester. Only one of these – John Rutherford – was also on the lists of those from Chester to be sent to trial at Liverpool, though for one other, it was noted that there were two potential witnesses against him. Petitions were also difficult to obtain from prisoners of lesser rank. As noted earlier, 206 were recorded as refusing to sign in the various jails in the north-west, and a further 73 were judged too sick to do so.[31] Those sentenced to transportation after their petitions from Preston were not all taken out of the country – there were still appeals to be heard, and several were successful. Two men were able to bring 'particular circumstances' in their favour to the government's notice in May, but it was only in August, as the transports were preparing to sail, that they were taken off the ship and set free. For the rest, they were to be sent off willing to work as indentured servants (and like convicts), their indentures signed before departure in the presence of the 'chief magistrate' or mayor, if they were fit and healthy enough to do so.[32]

With the executions set, the transported selected, and a few left to be subject to trials in London, the judges left Liverpool with their job done. Some of the condemned had already been executed. In all, 33 were executed in various parts of Lancashire, the spread of terror to Preston, Wigan, Manchester, Lancaster, Garstang and Liverpool itself, carefully calculated to have an effect on the entire region. The executions began a few days after the start of the trials, and continued during them, in a deliberate effort to 'strike a terror' in case there was organized resistance to the conditions of transportation.[33] However, there was one legal difficulty to be overcome. Some of the prominent leaders at Preston, particularly those from Scotland and Northumberland, were sent to London for trial, which was far from the counties where their alleged crimes had been committed. In English law, the accused were to be tried where their crimes occurred, or else they had to be removed (by a writ of *a certiorari* and *habeas corpus*) to that county. Just as moving Edinburgh prisoners to Carlisle was legally dubious, so sending some of the Preston prisoners to London was equally questionable. Individuals such as 'General' Thomas Forster M. P. from Northumberland were formally attainted by Parliament to be tried for high treason. The others, in order to overcome the transference to London, required special legislation after the Liverpool trials had been completed. One London paper noted, 'the King came to the House of Lords with the usual Solemnity, and gave the Royal Assent to the Bill for the more easy and speedy Tryal of Rebels'. The Act 'for the more speedy Trials of such Persons who have levied War against his Majesty' observed that 'as the Law now stands', indictments were to be heard in the countries where the treasonable acts were committed, 'it will be very inconvenient to the public Justice of the Nation that the Judges should remain so long in the said Counties'. Therefore, the law allowed that 'all persons in custody before 23 January 1716 may be tried in such Shire as his Majesty shall direct. And no challenge for the Shire shall be allowed'. Thus, the decision to try some notable Northern English rebels in London acquired legal validity, but for these prisoners, even though they begged to be transported in some instances, transportation was not what the government intended.[34]

Szechi describes the whole process of the Hanoverian government's 'grim pageant of justice'. About 1700 prisoners had been seized in Scotland and England, from whom 34 'particular enemies' were selected and tried, and 17 executed; of the 47 chosen by lot, another 18 were executed, but most of the rest in both batches were convicted, with only seven acquitted. In other words, of the 81 were tried, 74 were convicted and condemned, and 35 executed – 47.3 per cent of the condemned, on these figures. Of the 1,500 or more left, 'a few dozen … escaped and then went into hiding and exile. What to do with the rest was a serious problem'. The first ships sailed in August 1716 with at least 638 prisoners, while it seems likely that those remaining in the English gaols were eventually released. More than 450 were sent to the North American colonies, and about 170 to the Caribbean. The king and his ministers originally expected that they would all be sold in the West Indies, where a seven-year indenture was always likely to prove a death sentence for transportees from the British Isles. In fact, most were sold in their first port of call in the North American colonies, which were desperate for skilled, fit labour that did not come with a 'proven aptitude for common felony'. Lenman may be right that the London government was not 'particularly interested in rounding up humble men who had probably acted throughout under the orders of their social superiors', but this group formed the major problem that they had to deal with. Above all, following this experience, there was no intention of trying anyone in Scotland after the 1745 rebellion.[35]

On the arrival of the 185 men sent to South Carolina, the Governor bought 'as many of them as he could in order to arm them and send them to the frontier to fight the Yammasee Indians, with whom the colony was at war'.[36] In Maryland, the Council logged the arrival of two ships with 135 rebels, and were forced to debate the legality of the whole process because of a petition from John Chalmers, one of the 55 from the *Good Speed*, who argued that there was no law authorizing their transportation. He went back to medieval law to make his case. This was brushed aside, but the Maryland authorities speedily resolved that, while they could not stop anyone buying rebel servants and setting them free, they would have to give surety for their ex-servants' good behaviour for seven years. In Virginia, the Governor and his Council faced both legal difficulties and resistance. Most of the difficulty arose from the people on the *Elizabeth and Anne*, from Liverpool. Only about a quarter of the passengers, 29 of the 112 on board, had signed indentures before the voyage, though they must have signed a petition for mercy. This refusal caused the authorities some irritation, and a procedure was developed whereby purchasers of rebel servants received a certificate from the Council confirming that it was the King's pleasure that they serve seven years. A second difficulty arose with another petition that cited the same legislation as John Chalmers', and similarly claimed that no British subject could be forced to serve without their consent or the suspension of the laws. There was clearly a consistent argumentative line in challenging their transportation. In addition, they complained of 'divers hardships imposed on them' by the master and owner of the ship. The Captain Edward Trafford was sent a copy of the protest and summoned to reply. Despite these delays, they were all sold successfully in the end.[37] Little is known about the subsequent lives of the rebel servants landed in the Chesapeake, but at least one of the 1715 rebels brought in that year, on the *Friendship*, did well. William Cumming served in various public offices, including as a member and clerk to the Lower House of the Assembly, and in 1751, executed a deed of trust to his son William, transferring all his real and personal property for the benefit of his creditors, including 117 law books, 40 slaves, 1 black and 3 white servants and silver plate.[38]

The 1745 rising

The 1745 rising marked a decisive point in the history both of Scotland and the British state. This was not just the last rebellion, but one that was decisively defeated in a way that prevented any renewal of opposition. Unlike the struggles of the 1715 rising, the Battle of Culloden was a crushing victory for the Hanoverian regime, and provided the opportunity to 'solve' the Highland problem once and for all. The consequences of the 1745 rising were therefore irreversible – there would no chance of rebels going safely home and waiting for the next rebellion, as happened in 1716, when the Earl of Mar's army just slipped away and was available to be called out less than four years later in a failed uprising. After 1746, the society that had seemed so prone to treason was changed utterly.

The consequences were, in part, because the 1745 rebellion was far more threatening than that of 1715. The scale of military defeats inflicted by Prince Charles Edward's army, followed by a march deep into the English Midlands, the extent of local support, particularly in Manchester, and the prolonged wait before final victory by the government forces, all added up to a more alarming picture. Despite the atmosphere of near-panic at the start, and the lust for vengeance in the aftermath, the strategies adopted towards Jacobite captives resembled those of 1716. There were more than three times as many executions, but the transportation policy continued to be the core of the government's method of dealing with the prisoners. The basic techniques were the same – persuading the majority to petition for mercy and transportation, randomly selecting 1 in 20 for trial, and making sure none of the leaders escaped prosecution and execution. The numbers were far greater than in 1716, but even allowing for that the proportion executed was higher. One issue that came up repeatedly was the right of the British state to try men in England for alleged offences committed in Scotland. This point was made continually in petitions, and also in court, when the trials eventually took place in London. It caused the law officers to pause and prove the legitimacy of the proceedings, but they pressed on thereafter.[39]

The study by Sir Bruce and Jean Gordon Arnot represents the best attempt to extract the statistical truth from the detailed administrative records kept by government officials on the 'remnants of the broken Jacobite army' captured at Culloden and in the aftermath of the battle. These figures cannot include the hundreds, perhaps thousands, who suffered starvation, destruction of property or random killing in the aftermath of the battle, as areas were brought under Government control by terror tactics such as those adopted by Lord Loudon, sent by Cumberland to Badenoch in May 1746 'for two or three days to burn and destroy that country which has not yet laid down its arms' – 'I believe they immediately will', he went on, observing the example of the McPhersons who had submitted to these techniques the same month.[40] Of 3,463 listed prisoners, '88 died of wounds or illness in prison; 120 were executed (including 40 deserters from the Hanoverian army), 936 transported, 348 banished (including 126 who were allowed to go to America), 1,287 set free (including 387 French and Spanish), and 684 whose fate is unknown, although a large percentage of these must also have died of neglect in the prison hulks to which the prisoners were taken'. Despite Cumberland's idea of transporting whole clans, 'not as slaves, but to form Colonies in the West Indies', transportation was confined to these prisoners, and those arrested as rebels subsequently. They were subject to careful filtering and processing, with trials and executions aimed at some, and a gradual procedure of pardon and transportation for the majority. Other captives were treated more summarily – when at least 32 deserters from the Hanoverian army were found among the Jacobite prisoners in and around Inverness, they were tried by court-martial and 'hanged on the spot'. 866 of the prisoners applied for the King's mercy, but only after many of the Scottish had been moved to the Thames and held in forts and ships. Here, a selection by lot was instituted, as in 1716, while others were pre-selected for trial. Of 430 prisoners listed by one Captain Eyre, for example, the lot chose 17 for trial randomly (slightly less than 5%), while another 75 had been 'set apart for Tryal or further Examination, and for Evidence, who have not been lotted'. The English who had joined the Prince's army in Manchester were particularly likely to be subject to trial and not granted the chance of release by lot. These were mostly local Catholics, and, unlike the gentry who had been the main focus of prosecutions in the previous rising, of more ordinary social standing. The English recruits to both rebellions, though, seem to have provoked great alarm and a more repressive response from the government. In the documents, the language of class and hierarchy was faithfully produced when summing up the social statuses of the captives. Prisoners were 'common men', 'really gentlemen', 'not properly gentlemen but above the rank of the common men' or of 'a lower degree than the preceding'.[41]

Although it has been suggested that 'the government did not worry about "plebeian Jacobitism"', the data collected on the prisoners of the 1745 rising suggests not only Lowlander participation, but recruitment of a fairly ordinary kind of men. Among the Jacobite prisoners held on the *Liberty and Property* on the River Medway after Culloden, for example, were five tailors (one a 'taylor and staymaker' from Inverness and another who had been 'in the King's army and taken at Falkirk'), a miller, a weaver, a wine cooper or barrelmaker, a tutor, a writer described as 'servant to Mr Mitchell', a house carpenter, a shoemaker, and, more useful for military purposes, two blacksmiths and a 63-year-old 'out pensioner of Chelsea [Hospital]', or army veteran. They were not all wild Highlanders. As Neil Davidson has suggested, the proletarians and bourgeoisie alike took part and probably volunteered freely.[42]

Once they had petitioned for mercy, all that needed to be done was commission ships to take them to the colonies. While they waited, conditions on the ships on the Thames grew worse. A Mr Minshaw was sent down to the Thames in August 1746, where he was to inspect the conditions on the *Pamela* and take down the names of the prisoners:

> and on my looking down into the hold, where the prisoners then were, was saluted with such an Intollerable [over: smell] that it was like to Overcome Me, tho' I was provided wth proper herbs and my nostrilles stopped therewith. After seating ourselves on the Quarter Deck the prisoners were called up one by one; such as were able came and on being asked, told their names, in what Regiment or corps they served, of what age they were, and where born; The Number of those who came on deck were 54, many of whom were very ill, as appeared by their countenance and their snail creep-pace in assending the ladder, being only just able too crawl up; 18 who were left below were said to be utterly incapable of coming on the Deck unless by help of a sling, which was not thought necessary as two of the most hardy of the Guard went down into the hold, and took account of their Names etc., a fair copy of which, as well as the List taken above Deck I would have transcribed, but the commanding officer who wrote the list taken above chose to do it himself and send as mentioned in his letter.
>
> To hear the Description given by the Guard, who went into the Hold, of the Uncleanness of that place, is surpassing Imagination, and too nautious to describe, so that that, together with the malignant fever raging among them, and another odious distemper peculiar to Scotchmen, is such a Complication of Disorders, that if not timely remedied by a speedy removal from the ship (which is very small) is such feared will terminate in a more dreadful disorder than any herein before mentioned.[43]

It had become a matter of urgency to arrange transportation. After a period of bad-tempered negotiation, Liverpool merchants were hired to take people from the prisons in Cheshire and Lancashire. Samuel Smith was the main contractor, and he tried to negotiate 6 pounds for each man transported, rather than the usual 5 pounds given for convict transportees.

And that to Virginia and Maryland, which is a shorter passage than to the West Indies but in time of war consideration ought to be had to the great difference of Expence [sic] in the Freight, Provisions, Men's Wages, Insurance, the which swells to amount above one half – therefore I hope their lordships will not think Six pounds per Man too much, for that Sum I will adventure to engage to disperse the in the different parts of the Continent of America and the West Indies in such manner as to answer fully the end proposed.

He never obtained the higher fee, though a rival shipper, Alderman Gildart of Liverpool, offered to take the rebels for 5 pounds and 10 shillings. Smith was also demanding in other ways. He supposed that his agents would receive assistance from the port officials in arrival until they 'can make a proper Disposition of them among my friends, who I fancy will make them usefull Members of Society and in time they may possibly become good subjects'. This was in September 1746, but the project was delayed by a number of escapes from the jails, and even from the ships in harbour. He wrote in November:

I am now convinced that it is absolutely necessary that an act of Parliament sh'd be pass'd to make it Death in case any of the Rebells return to great Britain or Ireland, and in place of my having their service during their Lives, I believe it will be right to have a clause in that act to oblige the Transported Rebells to serve a certain Limited number of years not to exceed fifteen.

In fact, this was in train, and was implemented in legislation as the shipments began, in 1746. For the first time, transported rebels were put on the same legal footing as ordinary criminals, and the authorities could rely on that legislation rather than the customary rules that had been so loosely defined in the previous rebellions.[44]

Gradually, shiploads of Jacobites left London and Liverpool in 1747, with different destinations in mind and very different outcomes. Samuel Smith's final account claims he had shipped 453 prisoners by the end of 1747, 270 from London and 183 from Liverpool, but he lost some on the way. He was paid half the 5 pound fee on leaving, and half on landing them in America (or on proof of their deaths on the way). One group sent to the West Indies were intercepted by a French privateer, but Smith was able to gain the necessary affidavit proving that the loss was not his responsibility, reporting:

That 150 were taken near Antigua in the Ship *Veteran*, John Ricky master the 28 June last [1747], by the *Diamond*, a French Privateer, Paul Marsat

Commander, and carried into Martinique, as appears by the affidavit
annexed, sworn at St. Christophers by Mr Francis Hamilton.

The French authorities in Martinique seem to have recruited some of these
men for their regiments in the Caribbean. More seriously, 12 men of the 140
on the *Frere* from London to Barbados died on the way, which is probably
not an extreme loss, given their terrible conditions of confinement before
they left. Their arrival and sale into indentured servitude were carefully
logged by the local authorities. As Geoffrey Plank has pointed out, these
men had not signed any indentures before leaving, unlike the voluntary
servants, nor had been indentured to the ship's captain, as happened with the
convicts. Despite this potentially damaging legal difficulty, things seemed to
have gone smoothly. In Jamaica, a kind of explicit blackmail was practised,
in that 'though the men were bound over for lifelong service when they left
Britain, those who signed the indenture in Jamaica had their term reduced to
seven years'.[45] The 33 men on the *Johnson* (or *Johnston*) to Maryland from
Liverpool were the only ones to be sent to the North American colonies.
They were logged into the colony by both Samuel Smith and the local
records, which took down the masters to whom they were sold.[46]

Stories of Jacobite resistance and survival

The military value of the Scottish prisoners was often a matter of discussion
in accounts of their forced or voluntary migration. According to Alexander
Stewart's narrative, all the men on his ship were sold into servitude to
gentlemen, except three or four who 'went with two of the common
buckskins'. His own contract was with Benedict Calvert, who accepted an
offer by Stewart's friends to pay him the price he had paid for it, and so he
was set free. His story provides one of the few accounts of banishment to the
colonies, and more importantly, of return to Scotland. In the same period,
criminals sent to the colonies gave accounts of their return only when on
the way to the gallows.[47] That some local families in Maryland and Virginia
had Jacobite sympathies, and Jacobite origins, seems undoubted, though
they were not numerous.

Some Jacobite sympathies nevertheless appear in public after the
transportations of the 1745 rebels, but they are few. The actions of two
Jacobites in Maryland who, it was reported, had only just arrived in the
colonies – possibly transported as prisoners of the 1745 rising – aroused the
wrath of local authorities:

Annapolis Maryland, 8 September [1747]: the Grand-Jury of the Assize
for this County (which ended this Day) found Bills of Indictment against
Two of the rebels lately imported, for Drinking the Pretender's Health,
and some other treasonable expressions; for which the Court adjudged,

(as they were Servants, incapable of paying Fines) that they should be well whipped at the Whipping Post, and stand in the Pillory, which Sentence was immediately put into Execution.

Some servants may have been either Jacobite transportees or have Jacobite sympathies. Among the Virginia runaway notices in the newspapers in early 1751 was a group of three men and one woman who had escaped from Charles County.[48] One man was Irish, the second an African slave, and the third was:

> *Thomas Long*, about 5 Feet 9 Inches high, has a Scar on one of his Hands, black Hair, sandy Beard; had on when he went away a Cotton Jacket and Breeches, and a Felt Hat, but it is thought he has other Cloaths with him: He was a Scotch Rebel.

A few years later, in 1755, seditious words were reported spoken by a James Castello, of Chester County Pennsylvania – 'King George has no more right to the crown of Great Britain than I, and if he had his just deserts, he would have his Neck cut off', he was accused of saying, and he was also said to have drunk the health of the French King and the Pretender. He pleaded guilty at quarter sessions, and was sentenced to one hour in the pillory.[49] These were unusual, though local legends of transported Jacobites remain strong in the modern United States. Most historians of, for example North Carolina, doubt that the Highland community there was recruited from Jacobites, but there were Jacobite mutterings early in the eighteenth century appearing before the courts as sedition. Although ardent Jacobites cannot have been many in the colonies, it may have been fear of them that led Maryland to propose an Act 'to disable Persons transported into this Province for being concerned in Rebellion against the King, from voting for Delegates to serve in the Assembly'. But by that time, at least one of the 1715 rebels had not just voted, but been elected (William Cumming, above).[50] Jacobite exiles rarely included North America and the Caribbean in their networks, perhaps because the most ordinary men were there, while the gentry scattered to the European Continent.[51]

PART TWO

Continuity and Change: British North America and the Caribbean

6

Banishment and criminal transportation in the British Atlantic World

In the seventeenth century, as we have seen in Chapter 1, gypsies and vagrants, rebels and criminals, Quakers, Catholics and Covenanters were transported from England and Wales, Scotland and Ireland to the growing empire of the English across the Atlantic. This was especially true of the middle decades of the century, when the Caribbean was the preferred destination adopted by the authorities, though it was superseded by the Chesapeake before the century's end. While English settlers were guaranteed the rights of Englishmen in their charters, allowance was made for local circumstances. The legal systems on both sides of the Atlantic were similar and the practice of expelling those who were deemed troublesome, threatening or rebellious was replicated in the colonies in the seventeenth century. Nevertheless, after the Glorious Revolution of 1688 and the post-Revolutionary settlement in the three kingdoms, this pattern that had already begun to diverge in relation to Native Americans, diverged further. Although the threat posed by religious minorities, or at least the Protestant sects, receded on both sides of the Atlantic, in the colonies of the Caribbean and North America, legislators came to define and redefine those who threatened the social order. Yet, one of the main planks of the English criminal law in the eighteenth century – the punishment of criminal transportation for misdemeanours in addition to felonies – was not consciously adopted in the colonies, at least not for the same purpose or on the same scale as in the mother country.

Wealth and power were key motivators in the quest for overseas expansion. Spain and Portugal led the way, but claims to far off places could only become a reality when they acquired permanent populations subject to the authority of the European claimant. Colonies were costly to establish and maintain, especially in the early decades, as England found in the case of the Roanoke failures in 1585 and 1587 and the early years of Jamestown after 1607, and the Scots were to discover somewhat later in the Darien disaster of 1698–1700. Colonies had to have strategic importance, mineral or other resources and a ready supply of manpower.[1] Richard Hakluyt, the greatest advocate of expansion in Elizabethan England, emphasized the positive features that such expansion could bring whereas Sir Francis Bacon, writing a generation later, warned of the dangers of making settlements overseas for the wrong reason and in the wrong way. What gave colonies one of their long-term justifications was their utility as places of banishment for political opponents, defeated rebels and religious dissidents and another was separating out unwanted elements from the parent society, such as condemned criminals, vagrants and other undesirables sentenced to criminal transportation who would also serve as a reservoir of labour and swell the colonial populations. Hakluyt and Bacon anticipated most of the positive and negative issues facing aspiring imperial powers in early modern Europe when they sought to extend their influence at the expense of their neighbours. In advancing a number of arguments in favour of colonization in late sixteenth-century England, Richard Hakluyt included the transplantation of vagrants and masterless men whose wanderings around the countryside and infestation of cities and towns threatened the social stability of Elizabethan England. Also, suitable candidates for exclusion were 'Condemned men and women, in whom there may be founde hope of amendment'. Neither wanted nor required at home, such people might contribute to the 'well peopling of America' and to the production of those goods and services for which England was dependent on its continental neighbours. Sir Francis Bacon took a different view, cautioning against planting new colonies with unworthy people:

> It is a shameful and unblessed thing to take the scum of people and wicked condemned men to be the people with whom you plant; and not only so, but it spoileth the plantation; for they will ever live like rogues, and not fall to work, but be lazy, and do mischief, and spend victuals, and be quickly weary, and then certify over to their country to the discredit of the plantation.[2]

By transporting condemned criminals to overseas colonies, judicial authorities in England and Wales were in effect banishing them but the sentence was not one of banishment. Unless sentenced to life, criminals were not barred from returning home but they were liable to execution if they returned prematurely, though there is little evidence that many did return. While all those sentenced by the courts to criminal transportation were dispatched overseas and could be said to have been banished temporarily, those banished without due process such as rebels, religious dissidents and political opponents fell into a different category. Technically, they were not subject to criminal transportation; they were not required to work and their status was, in theory at least, temporary. Banishment and criminal transportation were not the same thing but with the growth of overseas settlements, they came more closely to resemble each other and it was not always easy to distinguish between them. That the practices of colonial powers influenced those of their colonies is axiomatic, though metropolitan authorities also learnt some of the prejudices and practices of their colonies, particularly with regard to 'race'. There was no standard pattern across the British colonies in North America and the West Indies, but in the seventeenth century at least, there were still marked similarities with the mother country.

Religious expulsions in the colonies

As the Quakers became objects of persecution in Restoration England, the same was true of England's American colonies. As we saw in Chapter 3, Massachusetts gained notoriety in England when it executed four Quakers from Rhode Island and Barbados after having expelled them on a number of previous occasions. Yasuhide Kawashima described banishment as 'a typically Puritan way of keeping the society intact by weeding out the undesirable'. It was considered 'as serious a punishment as the death penalty, [and] was applied from the very beginning of colonization to all kinds of criminals'. Nan Goodman notes that during the first year of settlement, when the population of Massachusetts was less than 1,000, 14 people were banished from the colony, that is 1.4 per cent of the population. Nor did this percentage decline as more settlers arrived. From these figures, she argues, 'we can infer an obsessive if futile effort on the part of the Puritans to use banishment to keep their community free of undesirables'. Massachusetts's most famous exile, Roger Williams, spent 17 years contesting with John Cotton, who was responsible for his expulsion, the legitimacy of his banishment.[3]

Colonies such as Massachusetts and Virginia barred the Quakers from entering, settling, holding meetings and preaching in public and sought to expel those who were already there, but such restrictions were not sufficient to deter the Quakers. One such Quaker was George Wilson, imprisoned in Carlisle in England in 1659, who travelled to Massachusetts, only to be expelled in 1661, after which he went to Virginia. Arrested and confined in chains in Jamestown where he subsequently died, Wilson wrote to the governor and Assembly, protesting against anti-Quaker legislation and advocating religious toleration.[4] Sir William Berkeley, the newly restored royal governor of Virginia prosecuted the Quakers rigorously. In the summer of 1660, he wrote to county sheriff Richard Conquest, complaining of his failure to put a stop to 'the frequent meetings of this most pestelent sect', ordering him not to allow any further meetings or conventicles. In March 1660, the Assembly alerted Virginians to the threat posed by the Quakers, denouncing them as 'an unreasonable and turbulent sort of people . . . teaching and publishing lies, miracles, false visions, prophesies and doctrines, which have influence upon the communities of men both ecclesiasticall and civil endeavouring and attempting thereby to destroy religion, laws, communities and all bonds of civil societie'. An Act of March 1662 sought to reinforce the position of the Anglican church, enforcing attendance at parish churches through a system of fines that increased according to the length of the absences. If a person was absent for a year, he or she was required to provide security for their good behaviour. Quakers attending 'unlawfull assemblyes and conventicles' would face a fine of 200 pounds of tobacco for each offence. Meeting in December 1662, Berkeley's next assembly made the Quakers the first order of business. In an Act 'prohibiting the unlawfull assembling of Quakers', they were portrayed as an even greater danger to society than previously thought. They were denounced as people who had taken up 'sundry *dangerous* opinions and tenets' and who, 'under pretence of religious worship', were assembling 'in greate numbers in several parts of this colony to the greate endangering its publique peace and safety and to the terror of the people by maintaining a secret and strict correspondence among themselves . . . '. They had separated themselves from the rest of his majesty's loyal subjects. An escalating system of fines was now imposed on the Quakers in breach of the law and a system of rewards was introduced to solicit information from the public at large and put pressure on magistrates and other officials to enforce the law. If, from the time of the Act, five or more met together for religious worship, if found guilty, they were to pay a fine of 200 pounds of tobacco; for a second offence, 500 pounds of tobacco and for a third offence, they were to be banished from Virginia to a place appointed by the governor and the council. To restrict the entry of Quakers into Virginia and punish those who were already there, the Assembly adopted a system of rewards and punishments. They imposed a stiff penalty of 5,000 pounds of tobacco on masters of ships bringing Quakers into Virginia, half of which was to be paid to the informer. Officials and magistrates were subject to similar penalties, half of which was to go to the parish in question. In September 1663, John Hill, the high sheriff of Lower Norfolk County, represented to the house that Mr John Porter, one of the burgesses for the county 'was loving to the Quakers and stood well affected towards them, and had been at their meetings, and was so far an Anabaptist as to be against the baptizing of children'; Porter admitted the charge but argued that his presence at Quaker meetings could not be proved. When the oaths of allegiance and supremacy were tendered to him, he refused to take them and was dismissed from the house.[5] James Horn argues that 'the upheavals caused by the revolution in England and the demise of royal government in 1652 followed eight years later by the Restoration, served to complicate religious differences in the colony and sharpened political antagonism between Anglicans, Nonconformists and religious radicals'.[6]

In March 1658, political power in Maryland, which had seen a successful Quaker penetration of the colony under the puritan commission that had ruled Maryland for some months, surrendered its powers to Lord Baltimore's officials. The assault on the Maryland Quakers that followed was harsh and brutal. Josiah Coale and Thomas Thurston, who entered Maryland from Virginia, became principal targets of attack. On 2 August, Thurston was brought before the governor and council, who ordered his banishment within the next 10 days. All Marylanders were forbidden to 'receive, harbour, or conceal' him after 10 August. Should he return, he was to be sent to the nearest justice of the peace and then whipped with thirty lashes.[7] In these legislative measures, Virginia and Maryland shared in the general persecution of Quakers in the British Atlantic, and in some degree, Massachusetts and Maryland invented some of the most severe penalties, far more severe than those inflicted in England after 1660. Characteristically, the colonies entered the general historical memories of the Quaker community's books of 'sufferings' as among the worst examples of the repression they had experienced.

Expulsion of the Jews from Barbados

How the expulsion of some Jews from Barbados and Jamaica can be categorized is more problematic. When trading and residence rights were granted to Jews in 1661, their petition had been supported by local planters, and they were described as men who had 'behaved themselves well'. Within a short space of time, however, complaints by Sir William Davidson who alleged he was 'much damaged' by them and the failure of certain Jews on Barbados to find the promised gold mines alienated the King, Charles II. A mixture of religious, economic and political factors as well as personal grievances appeared to have been in play and on 1 March, 1664, orders were sent to Lord Francis Willoughby, 'cheife Governour of our Islands' or 'the Commander in chief' of Barbados 'for the time being':

> Whereas certaine Jews hereafter named have under pretence of a Gold Mine within some of our Plantations in the West Indies and their Ability to discover and improve the same, fraudulently induced us to make them free Denizens of our Kingdom of England with power to trade every where, as our Native Subjects do. And whereas besides abusing us thereby, they have also very much wrong'd and damnified Our Trusty and well beloved servant Sir William Davidson Knt and Baronet Gentleman of our Privy Chamber in Ordinary, drawing him to great expenses and falsifying their Oaths and promises made unto him, as We are informed. We have therefore thought fit to declare our pleasure concerning the said Jews, that their Patent of Denization so obtained from us is and shall be so esteemed and held as void and frustrate to all intent and purpose, and that they shall not have or receive any benefit thereby . . . .

Having compensated Sir William Davidson for his losses and recovered trade goods from others, the Jews were 'to be banished off Our said Island never to reside or trade there again without our Express and particular Order'. It was also ordered that a gold chain given to Isaac Israel de Piso by the king to encourage the project should be recovered 'such false and faithless persons being altogether unworthy to beare or retaine any such mark of our Royal favour'.[8]

Political expulsions

Following Bacon's unsuccessful rebellion in Virginia in 1676, Governor Berkeley meted out summary justice to rebel leaders. Some he hanged, others were ordered for transportation. Bacon's Rebellion was the culmination of three decades of misrule, corruption and abuse of power but its immediate cause was hostilities with Native Americans – raids by the Doeg and Susquehanna Indians from the Maryland side of the Potomac River. Nathaniel Bacon, a relative newcomer to Virginia and well connected, sought a commission from Governor Berkeley to lead a campaign against the Indians but it was refused. Berkeley had no desire to destabilize relations that he had worked so hard to establish, but Indian relations were only one of the grievances of Virginia's settlers. Bacon proceeded anyway and, as in King Philip's War, Virginians fell upon local Indians who were not allied to those who were raiding the colony's frontiers. Life was difficult for Virginia planters. The overproduction of tobacco had led to low prices and restrictions on the colonial trade, initially imposed by the Commonwealth and then by the restored monarchy, eliminated alternative outlets for trade. Freemen, released from indentured servitude in ever increasing numbers, lacked opportunity to make their way in Virginia society. Between 1664 and 1667 and 1672 and 1674, England was at war with the Dutch, during which periods, tobacco ships 'were captured on the high seas, converted to military use in England, or burned at anchor in Virginia by Dutch raiders'. Tobacco rotted at the quayside for lack of vessels. Defence measures were costly and ineffective. Freemen, bereft of opportunities, followed Bacon in sizeable numbers. When Bacon died in mysterious circumstances, Berkeley prevailed. The rebellion was suppressed with 'unremitting fury' that was viewed with astonishment by 'even the most hardhearted' of the governor's supporters.[9]

Among those banished from Virginia was John Jennings, clerk of the County Court of Isle of Wight County, one of the centres of the rebellion. Jennings petitioned Herbert Jeffreys, Berkeley's successor as Governor of Virginia and former member of the commission sent out to investigate the uprising, and the Council of State. Having received sentence of 'banishment and transportation out of Virginia', Jennings sought to delay his departure from the colony 'since by reason of the late Rebellion his estate has been so wasted that he has not the money to leave, and because it would peril his life to undergo the said sentence in his aged, sick and weak condition'. He was also responsible for the care of 'a poor wife and children'. With the advice of two councillors, Jeffreys delayed Jennings' departure for three months. On September 5, Jennings' wife Mary received power of attorney to collect his debts, to let his plantation for a period of three years and to sell some of the animals, but Jennings died before his sentence could be carried out.[10] The assembly meeting in February 1677 confirmed the order of banishment on John Taylor and John Richins who 'having been notoriously active in the late horrid rebellion, be, and hereby stand banished out of this country'.[11] Jeremiah Hooke, Jonathan Wisedom and Thomas Warr were brought to court on 22 March, 1677,

> for their being notorious actors, aydors and assistors in the late rebellion, and petitioning rather than to come to a trial for the same that they might be banished, the court doth therefore order that they may be banished for the term of seven years, either to New England, Barbadoes, Jamaica, or any other of the islands, and not to returne within that time under the forfeiture of being prosecuted according to law, and that they depart the country within two months, and give good security for their good behaviour during their stay in the country.[12]

Also sentenced to banishment was Henry West. Unlike the previous instances of banishment, West's case gives us some idea of the personal cost of banishment to the individual. Henry West had been tried for treason and rebellion along with his brother William and five others at Green Spring by court martial on 24 January 1676–7. All except Henry were found guilty and sentenced to be 'hanged by the neck until dead'. Henry was found guilty of the same crime but being 'not so notorious as the rest', he was sentenced to seven years 'banishment to England, Barbadoes, Jamaica or any of the islands'. He was allowed to retain 5 pounds from his estate to cover the cost of his departure. Henry went to England, where he presented a petition to the King seeking mercy and forgiveness for himself and his brother. In the petition, he described how he and his brother William had been 'seduced' into accepting a commission under the rebel Nathaniel Bacon to go against the Indians who, 30 years previously, had 'inhumanly murthered' their parents. Colonel Bridger, one of Berkeley's principal adherents, had persuaded his brother to surrender with the promise of a 'free and full pardon'. 'But as soone as they were come in & had surrendered themselves to Coll. Bridger the contrary to his promise immediately bound them both & sent them to the Governor at green Spring'. Sir William Berkeley brought them for trial before a Council of War and though his brother was 'only in arms' and had never done injury to any person or estate, he was sentenced to death by martial law. The petitioner 'who was wholly innocent of any crime and had been always peaceable and loyal' and against whom nothing was or could be proved' was, after a long imprisonment, sentenced to be transported 'into England'. He was forced to give a bond to leave Virginia by a certain day, which led 'to his utter ruine'. His 'wife & several small children are thereby reduced to extreme poverty & left in a most forlorne condition'. He petitioned to be discharged from the penalty that he would face if he returned to Virginia, which he described as 'his native country' and 'where his wife and Children are'. He was anxious to leave before the last ships of the year sailed for Virginia. He also petitioned on behalf of his brother who, having been sentenced to death, 'made his escape out of prison & hath ever since absconded himself'. He was willing to take the oath of obedience and give security for 'his future good behavior' as many guilty of worse offences had already done. The petition was read in Council on 21 November 1677 but no decision was recorded.[13]

Native Americans

It was in their relations with indigenous people that a gulf opened up between what settlers might do to their own and what they might do to others. Native Americans were not Christians and therefore lacked the attributes associated with the true faith. There were suspicions from the start, but following the Indian rising of 1622 in Virginia, the English writer Edward Waterhouse expressed the view that by their actions, the settlers in Virginia were released from their obligation to behave towards them in accordance with the rules of war and law of nations:

> Our hands which before were tied with gentleness and faire usage, are now set at liberty by the treacherous violence of the Sauvages. . . . So that we, who hitherto have had possession of no more ground than their waste and our purchase at a valuable consideration to theire owne contentment gained; may now by right of Warre, and law of Nations, invade the Country, and destroy them who sought to destroy us; whereby wee shall enjoy their cultivated places, turning the laborious Mattacke into the victorious Sword. . . . and possessing the fruits of others labours. Now their cleared grounds in all their villages (which are situate in the fruitfullest places of the land) shall be inhabited by us, whereas heretofore the grubbing of woods was the greatest labour.[14]

As in Ireland, where the population was composed of the wrong sort of Christians, much was to be gained from attitudes such as these among land hungry people.[15]

King Philip's War 1675–6

With this kind of attitude becoming stronger in the seventeenth century, Indians who surrendered to the settlers could expect little mercy. During most of the century, captives were sold to their enemies or sold into slavery in the Caribbean. In this respect, there was little distinction between the treatment meted out to indigenous people in the southern colonies and those in the region of New England. Attitudes, however, may have differed from the earlier decades, when colonists tended to invoke the law of nations, while in later decades, the Indians were regarded as subjects rather than independent peoples. The bloodiest Indian war in New England was triggered by the hanging of three Wampanoag Indians for the murder of an Indian from one of the praying towns in Massachusetts in the spring of 1675, but grievances were longstanding relating to economic, cultural and religious issues. The frontier fell back as Indians attacked 52 of the region's 90 towns, destroying 12 of them. According to Jill Lepore, the sale of Indians 'into foreign slavery' started early in the war in the summer of 1675, but 'widespread systematic enslavement came only a year later, when large numbers of Indians surrendered or were captured'. 'In effect, captured Algonquians were the rewards of war, to be punished to the public's satisfaction or distributed in the same manner as relief funds.'[16]

Indians taken prisoner in Bacon's Rebellion and King Philip's War, if not executed, were condemned to slavery in the Caribbean or sold to enemy Indians. While this process might involve court proceedings in Massachusetts and Plymouth, it was also carried out by individuals for personal profit. As relations between settlers and tributary Indians deteriorated in Virginia in the years before Bacon's Rebellion, Governor Berkeley conceded the need to employ terror against them. His appeal for a search and destroy mission against those intruding into the back parts of the colony was welcomed in Rappahannock County, especially by justices residing on the south bank of the river. Agreeing with the governor on the need to intimidate local Indians and make an example of 'foreign' Indians, Justices Thomas Goodrich, John Catlett, John Weir and Humphrey Booth assured Berkeley that no further incentive would be needed to promote the expedition than the prospect of selling captured Indian women and children as slaves. In New England, both formal and informal processes were used to 'secure' the colonies and profit for individuals. These Native Americans were denied the status of prisoners of war. By refusing to recognize Indian warriors as fighting by the laws of war and within the laws of nations, the actions of the courts and of individuals, though both ethically and morally questionable, were legally acceptable.[17]

The case of the Nanziattico People, Virginia 1704–5

In the late seventeenth century and throughout the following century, frontier wars were usually part of wider conflicts between European powers, especially Britain and France. Such wars had implications for both settlers and Native Americans as new tactics were adopted and the

fate of captives became more complex. War having been declared between
England and France in 1702, the Reverend Solomon Stoddard advocated
the use of specially trained dogs against the Indians on the Massachusetts
frontier in 1703. He believed that the Virginians had successfully used
them in the late seventeenth century. When the daughter of the Reverend
Williams failed to return from Canada with other hostages, her fate was
the subject to diplomatic exchanges in Paris.[18] Bacon's Rebellion in 1676,
however, had spells the end of that period of Virginia history when the
Indians posed a real threat to the security of the colony. Yet, anti-Indian
sentiment in Virginia remained strong. Distrust of local Indians, desire for
their surviving lands, and an even greater fear of those who dwelled beyond
the settled parts of the colony had by no means diminished at the beginning
of the eighteenth century. When planter John Rowley and his family were
murdered in the upper parts of Richmond County, Virginia in 1704, the
atrocity galvanized into action the entire military and judicial apparatus
of the county, neighbouring counties and a large part of the colony, but it
did not lead to all-out war as initially feared and as had occurred in King
Philip's War and Bacon's Rebellion a generation earlier. Virginia Indians
were too weak to mount a coordinated campaign against the settlers and
when the Nanziattico people, having fled to the frontier, were taken into
custody by local militia forces, the case against them was handled in the
courts not by a sustained military campaign. The case, which was heard
in October 1704, resulted in the hanging of the adult men, a sentence
carried out at once. The fate of the surviving members of the Nanziatticos
hung in the balance when it was recommended that they should be tried
under the dormant law of 1680 under which, when an Englishman was
murdered, the Indians of the nearest town were answerable for it 'with
their lives and liberties'. This act, first introduced in 1663 and applicable
only to 'foreign' Indians – those living outside Virginia – had been extended
in 1665 to all Indians, but repealed one year later on the grounds that it
was too arbitrary.[19] If the Nanziatticos were found guilty, they should be
transported out of the colony. This course of action, recommended by
the Richmond County court, would promote 'the future peace, quiet, and
security' of Virginia and 'meet the particular satisfaction of the inhabitants
of these parts'.[20] Although the members of the Virginia Council found no
evidence to suggest that the remaining members of the Nanziatticos were
implicated in the murder of the Rowley family, they agreed to their removal
to the capital Williamsburg where they spent the winter in the public jail.
In May 1705, the House of Burgesses considered their case. The House
took a hard line. Determining that the Nanziatticos were most likely
guilty, it adopted the commission's recommendation of transportation out
of the colony. It was a measure, according to the House, dictated by fatal
experiences in the past. The Indians, the House claimed, were a people 'of
revengeful temper, never forgetting what they apprehend to be Injurys'. All
those over the age of 12 who were regarded as the most dangerous were

to be transported to England or the West Indies. Members of the Council disagreed proposing that an old Indian man called Madox Will and his wife Betty be set free and women and girls, with two exceptions, be sent not to the West Indies, but to the Eastern shore of Virginia. The House refused to budge and the Nanziatticos were sent to Antigua to be sold as indentured servants for a period of seven years. They were banished from Virginia for life and never to live again in any Indian town.[21] Most things were done according to the laws of Virginia and England, but what was distinctive was the fate of the children under 12 years of age. These were to be divided between the members of the Council who cast lots for them. The Governor was allocated four and each member of the Council one. The children were to serve until they were 24 years of age. They were forbidden from living in another Indian town on pain of being transported to England or the islands and sold into indentured servitude for a further seven years.[22]

The Yamasee War 1715–16

While the survivors among the Nanziatticos were being sentenced to indentured servitude, the South Carolina merchants were still involved in a profitable slave trade with the Caribbean but not, as in the case of Bacon's Rebellion or King Philip's War a generation earlier, in prisoners of war. The government in Charleston was weak and could exercise little control over events in the interior. The trade in slaves was notorious and highly profitable to the traders, but the consequences for the indigenous population were dire. The coastal Indians with whom early settlers had engaged on reasonable terms were virtually exterminated. As traders penetrated further into the interior, they manipulated the Indian peoples, turning allies into victims. Victims of slave raiding, the Tuscarora of North Carolina sought to secure their survival by transporting themselves from the traders' reach by negotiating a refuge in Pennsylvania. Negotiations, however, broke down. They were more successful with the Iroquois confederacy located further north below the Great Lakes, becoming the sixth member of the confederacy. When South Carolina traders began seizing women and children for sale as slaves for debts incurred by the Yamasee, the Yamasee revolted, leading to a war that brought the colony close to destruction.[23]

New subjects for transportation: Slaves

By the second decade of the eighteenth century, South Carolina had a slave population comparable in size to its white population. When Indian slaves were added to the total of slaves, they exceeded the white population. Some of South Carolina's earliest settlers had come from the Caribbean, in particular from the island of Barbados, where the production of sugar, requiring large capital investment, squeezed out small planters. When South Carolina was founded, the islands of the Caribbean were already slave societies.[24] Though Barbados had not yet experienced a slave uprising, conspiracies and rumours of conspiracies were frequent. As Jerome Handler has written, reprisals were swift and brutal though 'perhaps not uncharacteristic of the age'. 'Slaves were burned alive, gibbetted, beheaded, and castrated'. There were few Amerindian slaves in seventeenth-century Barbados, but some were from New England. Barbadians knew of 'King Philip's War' in New England and of Indian attacks on white settlements in Maryland and Virginia. In response to these events and in the wake of the alleged 1675 plot on Barbados, the legislature passed a measure prohibiting the importation of 'Indian slaves and as well to send away . . . those already brought to this island from New England and the adjacent colonies, being thought a people of too subtle, bloody and dangerous nature and inclination to be and remain here'.[25]

Other colonies, also developing new legal frameworks incorporating slaves and free blacks, adopted the penalty of banishment. In 1691, the Virginia Assembly forbade masters from freeing their slaves unless they paid for their transportation out of the colony within six months of the date of manumission in an attempt to curb the growth of a class of free blacks and mulattoes, a measure originating in the Council. In the same year, whites who married 'a negro, mulatto or Indian' were to be banished from Virginia forever. Subsequently, the grounds on which slaves could be manumitted were narrowed, being limited to approval by the governor and council for some singular service such as the disclosure of a conspiracy. A Pennsylvania law provided for the transportation out of the province of any negro, slave or free who was convicted on the charge of attempted rape, or 'robbing, stealing, or fraudulently taking and carrying away any goods, living or dead, above the value of five pounds'. The cost was to be borne by the owner of a slave or the person himself, if free.[26] In 1714, the South Carolina Assembly passed an Additional Act for the Better Ordering and Governing of Negroes and All other Slaves, which appeared to pull back from its current legal practice, though hardly for reasons of altruism. Sentencing slaves to death for felonies 'of a smaller nature' had been found to be:

> of great charge and expense to the public, and will continue (if some remedy be not found) to be very chargeable and burdensome to this Province, Be it *therefore enacted* . . . That all negroes or other slaves who shall be convicted and found guilty of any capital crime (murder excepted), for which they used to receive sentence of death, as the law directs shall be transported from this Province, by the public receiver for the time being, to any other of his Majesty's plantations, or other foreign part, where he shall think fitting to send them for the use of the public.

The value of the slave was to be appraised and paid to the master out of the public treasury. Three years later, in 1717, the legislature rescinded the relevant clause in the act. It was claimed that it had encouraged slaves 'to commit great numbers of robberies, burglaries and other felonies, well knowing they were to suffer no other punishment for their crimes, but transportation, which to them was rather an encouragement to pursue their villanies'. In 1722, the legislature passed a very lengthy act 'for the Better Ordering and Government of Negroes and Other Slaves' which, specifying the use of branding and whipping in great detail, may have been intended to achieve the same purpose as the earlier Transportation Act.[27]

The Virginia Colony turned again to transportation in response to an alleged slave conspiracy based on Middlesex County in 1723. The colony, it was reported, has been lately threatened by 'frequent disorderly Meetings of great Numbers of Slaves in a riotous and tumultuous manner, who by reason of their Secret Plotting and confederating among themselves could not be convicted by such Evidence as the Laws now in force require'. Some of the ringleaders were now in custody, information having been given against them by other slaves who accused them of 'conspiring and contriving to rise up in Arms and kill and destroy several persons' in Middlesex County and elsewhere in the colony. They also threatened the lives of those concerned in exposing 'their wicked designs'. In order to prevent this, slaves involved in the conspiracy should be transported to Barbados, Jamaica or some other islands in the West Indies, there to be sold as slaves. Should they return to Virginia, they faced the death penalty. The slaves were identified as 'Dick, a Negro Slave of Matthew Kemp, Gentleman, Tom, otherwise called Bambeo Tom, Slave of Thomas Smith Gentleman, Sanco, Isaac, and Jeffrey, Slaves of Armistead Churchill, Gentleman, Robin, Slave of John Rhodes, planter, Sam, a Negro Slave of Elizabeth Burwell, Widdow of Nathaniel Burwell, Gentleman, deceased, And Sam, a Negro Slave of Elizabeth Richardson, Widdow'. Should a slave be brought back into Virginia against his will, he might be pardoned by the governor or commander in chief on condition of being transported again. Archibald Blair and William Robertson, two gentlemen of Williamsburg, were appointed to convey the slaves out of Virginia and account for the proceeds of their sale. The slaves were valued at between 20 and 50 pounds.[28] The link between 'race' and transportation developed most fully in Virginia after the Revolution. While white officials hanged at least 635 enslaved men and women between 1785 and 1865, 983 were transported, bought 'from under the gallows'. They would be sold to 'persons who guaranteed to transport them out of the United States to places from which they could not return to Virginia'. Schwarz identified Spanish Florida, Cuba and the Dry Tortugas 'or some other deadly location' as likely destinations.[29] Linebaugh and Rediker observed that 'in the red wake of many a plot or insurrection in plantation America came a mini-diaspora in which the leaders of the events were sold off, frequently away from their families and communities, to buyers in other parts of the Atlantic'.[30]

Slave conspiracies

Transportation was used in the case of lesser conspirators in the Antiguan conspiracy of 1736. It was used not only for some allegedly involved in the conspiracy, but also for witnesses and freedmen who may or may not have been caught up in it. On 11 April 1737, the legislature passed an Act for banishing 47 slaves. These were later transported to North America. Other transportees who were initially intended to go to Lisbon or 'such other place' were later reported bound for nearby Hispaniola, the Spanish American mainland or other territory belonging to Spain. David B. Gaspar, the authority on the Antigua conspiracy was unclear why these destinations were chosen 'but [it] would be interesting to know'. The legal documents in the case are vast and complicated. Decisions appear to have been taken, then changed, new evidence was found, witnesses changed their stories and some 'were fled from Justice'. The Act was no different from others of its kind in similar circumstances. Owners were guaranteed compensation for their losses. Those transported were to be banished from all the Leeward islands, not just Antigua. Those still on the islands after 1 July 1737 were to be executed as felons. Those importing them would forfeit 200 pounds American money, the slaves were to be seized, made to work for the government, then banished again. It would seem that even before this Act had been passed, the legislature had made an agreement with Arthur Wilkinson to transport the 'Criminals' to Hispaniola or the Spanish American mainland or to sell them to the French or Spaniards at some of those places 'provided he may have a reward of half their Gross Proceeds'. The legislature, however, had difficulty in recovering the proceeds of the sale from Wilkinson, who had taken the slaves away on an armed sloop. News of the conspiracy appeared in the press on both sides of the Atlantic.[31]

Historians differ in their views on how extensive the Great New York slave conspiracy of 1741 was. Linebaugh and Rediker incorporate it into a vast proletarian Atlantic enterprise while Lepore takes serious issue with the validity of Horsmanden's record of the trial and the presentation of slave evidence. T. C. Davis sees not one vast enterprise, but a number of smaller ones, Peter Hoffer, despite reservations, argues the plot was real. It resembled similar conspiracies in the Caribbean and the Denmark Vesey conspiracy in South Carolina in 1822.[32]

Daniel Horsmanden, a member of the Supreme Court, published his *Journal of the Proceedings in the Detection of the Conspiracy found by some white People in Conjunction with Negroes and other Slaves for the burning of the City of New York in America* in 1744 in defence of the decision of the court and the punishments inflicted on the alleged conspirators. The proceedings of the court and the punishments meted out were roundly condemned by critics at the time and by subsequent historians. The punishments were similar to those imposed in the Caribbean and on a similar scale, On 4 July, however, 42 men were recommended for pardon and transportation The owners of the slaves were to receive compensation for their sale and within five days, the first transportees were taken on board the ship *Mayflower*, which was bound for Madeira. Lepore identified 50 slave transportees gleaned from Naval Office Records in the National Archives. Consigned to six vessels, they were distributed around the Atlantic rim among Dutch, British and Portuguese colonies. Islands were preferred. On 9 July 1741, the *Mayflower*, Robert Beatty master, sailed for Madeira with 8 transport Negros'. On 15 July, the *Catherine*, John Stout master, left for Madeira and Lisbon with 13 transport negros on board. Three days later, on 18 July, the *Sarah* of which Abraham Brasher was the master, carried '2 Transport Negros' for Newfoundland. It was almost two weeks before the next vessels departed on 31 July – the *Stephen & Elisa*, with Richard Langdon, master with '2 Transport Negros' for Curaçao and the *Stephen*, with Elias Rice, master with '20 Transport Negros' for St Eustatia. It was another two weeks before the final transports left on the *William and Mary*, with Jacob Kiersted, master, a vessel owned by Jacob and William Walton, with '5 Transport Negros' destined for Madeira.[33]

The second Maroon War and the case of the Maroons of Trelawny Town 1795–6

The case of the Maroons of Trelawny Town, Jamaica, principals in the second Maroon War of 1795–6, throws up similarities and differences with aspects of the foregoing cases. While the governor and assembly wanted these Maroons removed from the island as quickly as possible, there was no question of them being sold into slavery in Jamaica or elsewhere, or of trying them for treason or as rebels. By the 1790s, it could be presumed, their status as freemen inhibited such actions but it did not preclude their removal.

Communities of runaway slaves were relatively rare in North America compared with the Caribbean and South America due to the inverse ratio of slaves to freemen and the nature of the terrain. Following the failure of British forces to suppress the Maroons in a campaign lasting from 1725 to 1739, treaties established a 'quasi autonomous state' in the interior but committed the Maroons to track down and return runaways. The agreement collapsed after several decades as relations between the Maroons and the settlers deteriorated. The Maroons, according to the pro-slavery historian of Jamaica Bryan Edwards, declared war on the British and embarked on a 'bloody rampage of killing, plundering, and burning' that resulted in the widespread destruction of livestock, people and plantations.[34] After a bloody campaign, they surrendered to Colonel George Walpole who made an agreement with them that they would not be deported from the island. That they were, in fact, banished from Jamaica in accordance with the wishes of the governor and the majority of the assembly without any discernable legal proceedings and carried to Nova Scotia without the approval of its governor and unknown to British authorities had parallels with other cases of banishment in the eighteenth century, most notably that of the Acadians, though the numbers in question were much smaller, being around 538. While the Maroons were powerless to resist once they had surrendered and especially after they had been put on board vessels at Port Royal, they were not powerless to protest nor were they without friends in high places. They petitioned the Jamaica Assembly and the British Parliament, wrote to the press and details of their case appeared in publications in London and Halifax. Not only did what Miles Ogburn calls the 'transatlantic geography of imperial communication' give them a voice, the context in which these events occurred had also changed from earlier decades. Rebellion had broken out on St Domingue, Wilberforce's campaign against the slave trade had gathered momentum, black loyalists had sailed for Sierra Leone and the opposition in Parliament could use the episode as a stick with which to beat the government.[35]

Nova Scotia was not to the liking of the Maroons though, at first, things seemed to go relatively well. They arrived in midsummer 1796 when the weather was fine, but then they encountered two lengthy winters, the worst since the founding of Halifax in 1749. Governor John Wentworth sought to promote Christianity and agriculture among them. Strangers to both, Wentworth judged their acquisition was essential to the long-term success of the Maroons in Nova Scotia. Whether they could adjust to the climate was unclear. Wentworth's plans fell apart due to the slow progress of the Maroon settlements, the failure to convince the Maroons that this was their best route forward and the steady undermining of Wentworth's strategy by subordinates as well as the hostility of local whites. The prospect of changing their location to somewhere where the climate was preferable and where they could exercise their military prowess grew stronger and after three and a half years of petitioning and pleading, the Maroons left for Sierra Leone.[36]

Colonel George Walpole negotiated a surrender agreement with the Trelawny Maroons – one of several Maroon communities – which both sides regarded as binding. The campaign against them involved the purchase of blood hounds from Cuba and their Spanish handlers (chasseurs). It was this issue rather than the breach of faith that was first raised in Parliament. Reading in the *Morning Post* an account of this transaction which he described as 'an extraordinary circumstance of horror and barbarity', General Macleod brought the subject before Parliament as a matter of the utmost concern since it sullied the 'honour of the House, and the credit of the nation'.[37] It was in the following year that Walpole, now elected to Parliament, raised the matter of the violation of the treaty which he had made with the Trelawny Maroons.[38]

Despite the promise that they would not be deported, Jamaica's Governor Alexander Lindsay, Earl of Balcarres, made the decision to remove them from the island. They were put on board two transport ships at Port Royal though where they should be sent was undecided. New Brunswick, Sierra Leone and the Bahamas were considered. As in the case of the Acadians, when the governors of the mainland North American colonies and authorities in the English seaports had no knowledge of their coming, the governor of New Brunswick, Sir John Wentworth, learnt of their imminent arrival after they had set sail. Like Governor Lawrence in Nova Scotia, Lindsay wished to act against the Maroons without engaging in extended legal proceedings. He took pre-emptive action and tried to cover his tracks later. Lindsay got an act through the Jamaica Assembly for the deportation of the Maroons on 1 May 1796. After two months at sea, they arrived on 21 and 23 July. There were 528 in number. Bryan Edwards credited Governor Lindsay with defeating 'all the projects, and rendered abortive all the hopes of these pestilent reformers'. He defended the use of dogs, citing William Paley that if the needs of war were justifiable, all means necessary to end it were also justifiable. He denigrated the character of the Maroons. Reconciliation was impossible and ridding the country of the Maroons was the only solution. The question was raised in Great Britain of whether the colonial governments had the legal right to banish a set of miscreants who had been 'guilty of felony, murder and treason'. Perhaps not in other times, but it could be justified in the present 'when the bonds of society were loosening and atrocious and abominable crimes were being committed'. While claims were made that the Maroons were protected from banishment by treaty, it was also believed that the general was released from his obligation to them.[39]

Criminal transportation

Transportation to English colonies in the West Indies and North America was a punishment imposed by English courts in the seventeenth century on felons – those guilty of serious crimes – but the experience of banishment, as we have seen in earlier chapters, was also shared by religious dissidents and political enemies. Colonies such as Virginia, however, had some success in resisting the importation of the former but not the latter two categories. New England colonies and those of the Chesapeake (Virginia and Maryland) also employed the practice with regard to religious dissidents and political enemies, but also in relation to slaves and Native Americans.[40] Dutch settlements in North America also witnessed the expulsion of serious offenders and political rivals and Dutch influence was probably responsible for the practice of whipping offenders out of New York in the eighteenth century. Linda Biemer identifies banishment as the only serious punishment imposed on women in New Amsterdam (for 'indecent exposure or "whorish behavior"') and cites one case of a woman banished to Holland. The Court Minutes of Rensselaerswyck identifies one man sentenced to the pillory followed by banishment 'in accordance with the wisdom of the fatherland'; another, having already been banished twice, to be banished from the colony 'forever' while yet another found guilty of murder, was banished from the colony 'again'.[41]

British convicts began arriving in the American mainland colonies in substantial numbers following the passage of the Transportation Act of 1718. The origins of the Transportation Act are not altogether clear, but John Beattie has argued persuasively that the search for a punishment less than death had become acute, and the use of imprisonment under 1706 legislation had resulted in the jails becoming full, particularly with women. London authorities were desperate, not for the first time, to dispose of some of their prisoners. More than 50,000 men, women and children were transported from Britain and Ireland to the British colonies of the Caribbean and mainland North America between the Transportation Act of 1718 and the outbreak of the American Revolution.[42] Transportees were those either sentenced to death by the assize courts and subsequently reprieved on condition of transportation or those sentenced directly to transportation by the same courts. What swelled the total number of convicts were convictions in the lower courts – quarter sessions courts – where justices of the peace could now hand down sentences of transportation for lesser offences (misdemeanours) for the first time. Though permitted under the Act of Settlement, only a few people were transported from England for vagrancy (see Chapter 1). These were generally from the Scottish borders and the south-west. The case of Ireland was different. The proportion of vagrants to criminals, permitted under a 1707 Act of the Irish Parliament, was much narrower.[43] Of the mainland colonies in North America, Pennsylvania, argue Marietta and Rowe, appears to have been influenced by the Transportation Act of 1718 in ordering some culprits to 'depart the colony', but it did not and could not be compared with the role of transportation in the British system of punishment.[44]

According to Duncan Campbell, about half of the transportees were shipped from the Home Counties where the trade was subsidized by the government. Though the cost of transporting prisoners from London and the Home Counties was subsidized by the government, elsewhere in the country, the trade was supported by local rates. Prisoners awaiting transportation might wait for months, even years, to be put on board ships. One woman gave birth not to just one child but two while still in Durham gaol while awaiting transportation. Some died before being transported. Shippers tended to select those who would sell quickly. If shipped from the north, convicts endured longer voyages than most, especially if the vessels carrying them first sailed north around the Orkneys and Shetlands. However, if shipped alongside 'free' servants or other passengers, conditions might be better but crossing the Atlantic was hazardous at best. Some in the north were taken overland to London to join the larger vessels leaving the Thames whereas in the south-west, they might be carried to ports on the Bristol or English Channels. Some vessels were wrecked before they left the Bristol Channel. Others might run low on rations if the journey time was extended by bad weather or unforeseen circumstances. London vessels carried the largest numbers of convicts, sometimes as many as 300 or more.

Most convicts were destined for the tobacco growing plantations of Virginia or Maryland, Shippers sought to improve the appearance of their convict cargos before they were put up for sale in the hope of higher prices. Cargoes were advertised in newspapers together with the location of sales. Sales might be held at one or more places along the riverbanks of Virginia's mighty rivers or near the mouths of creeks in Maryland. If some remained unsold, they were taken inland, moving along well defined circuits from one county courthouse to another. Despite efforts in the 1720s to bar their sale in Virginia and Maryland, there was always a market for them and not only among the poorer sort of planters. The attraction was the regularity of supply and the longer terms of service. Convicts might have been sentenced to terms of seven years, 14 years or life, but they seldom served longer than seven years. Labour in these colonies was not a requirement laid down in the legislation sanctioning transportation but a consequence of the inability of almost all prisoners to pay their passage across the Atlantic.

What convict workers actually did in the colonies is not easy to recover. In the seventeenth century, convicts laboured alongside indentured servants, but with the growth of slavery in eighteenth-century Virginia, their tasks were more varied. Planters wanted skilled workers if they could get them and some were employed in early industrial ventures such as the Ridgely iron works. Some claimed to be artisans and runaway advertisements reveal a range of skills which they themselves claimed. Towards the end of the century slaves, Indians, Irish, convicts and women could be found on some large plantations. There is little evidence that those transported were drawn from some criminal class. Most likely they were a cross-section of the working population, as were those who later sent to Australia. Towards the end of the colonial period, convicts were sent increasingly into frontier counties where agriculture was more diversified and their skills could be profitably employed. They left little impact on Chesapeake society most likely because of their inability to rise from their lowly status. Some convicts failed to adjust to life and labour in the colonies. Coming from mostly urban locations, confined to isolated farms and back breaking work, they could not cope, as in the case of Jeremiah Swift who murdered his masters' children and John Hesbrook who murdered his master and attacked his mistress. It was not that these men were inherently vicious but that their new environment made them so.[45]

'Felons of distinction', 'Felons of inferior note' or 'the common sort'

Most transportees fell into the category of the 'common sort' but though exceptional, 'felons of distinction' were not unknown. Such cases as that of the lawyer Henry Justice, however, illustrate the importance of status and class within the punishment system. In May 1736, the *Gentleman's Magazine* reported the case of Henry Justice of the Middle Temper Esq. who was tried at the Old Bailey, for stealing books from Trinity College Library in Cambridge. He pleaded, that in the year 1734, he was admitted Fellow Commoner of the College,

> whereby he became a Member of that Corporation, and had a Property in the Books, and therefore could not be guilty of the Felony, and read several Clauses of their Charter and Statutes to prove it. But after several Hours of Debate, it appear'd he was only a Boarder or Lodger, by the words of the Charter granted by Hen. 8, and Q. Eliz. So the Jury brought him in guilty of the Indictment, (which is Felony within Benefit of Clergy, so Transportation,)

On 10 May,

> Mr Justice was brought to the Bar to receive Sentence, and mov'd that as the Court had a discretionary Power, he might be burnt in the Hand and not sent abroad. First, for the sake of his Family, as it would be an Injury to his Children, and his Clients, with several of whom he had great Concerns, which could not be settled in that Time; second, for the Sake of the University, for he had Numbers of Books, belonging to them, some in Friend's Hands, and some sent to Holland, and if he was transported he cou'd not make Restitution. As to himself, considering his Circumstances, he had rather go abroad, having liv'd in Credit till this unhappy Mistake, as he call'd it, and He hoped the University would intercede for him. The Deputy Recorder commiserated his Case, told him how greatly his Crime was aggravated by his Education and Profession, and then pronounced. That he must be transported to some of his Majesty's Plantations in America for seven years.

As a 'felon of distinction', Henry Justice was not alone. On Monday the 17th, early in the morning, the felons ordered for Transportation set out from Newgate:

> Those of the common Sort were conducted on Foot, by a proper Guard, from Newgate to Black Fryare Stairs, where they were put on Board a close Lighter and carried down to Blackwall, and there put on Board a Ship belonging to Jonathan Forward, Esq; bound to his Majesty's Plantations in America; but the Felons of Distinction had a little more Respect shewn them; *Mr Wreathcock* the Attorney, and *Mr Ruffhead* the butcher, condemned for robbing Dr Lancaster, went in a Hackney Coach to Blackwall; and *Mr Bird* the Bailliff, condemned with Two more for the same Robbery, and *Mr Vaughan*, commonly called Lord *Vaughan*, because of his being nearly related to a noble Family, went to Blackwall

in another Hackney carriage, with Keepers in each Coach to guard them; and the above-mentioned *Henry Justice*, Esq., went to *Blackwell* in a third Hackney Coach, with Jonathan Forward, Esq; to attend him . . .

On Board the Ship likewise these Five Gentlemen were treated with Marks of Respect and Distinction; for the Felon of 'inferior' Sort were all put immediately under the Hatches, and confined in the Hold of the Ship, as usual, but these Five were conveyed into the Cabbin; which by Agreement, they were to have the Use of during their Voyage; and as they pay for their Passage, it is supposed that as soon as they land, they will be set at Liberty, instead of being sold as Felons usually are: Thus, by the wholesome Laws of this Country, a Criminal who has Money (which Circumstance, in all other Countries would aggravate his Guilt, and enhance the Severity of his Punishment) may blunt the Edge of Justice, and make That his Happiness which the Law designs as his Punishment.[46]

In these vivid descriptions, which are some of the few concerning the cases of apparently untouchable gentleman thieves, we can see the class distinctions of the convict trade. The importance of the press in providing these images cannot be overstressed. For most ordinary convicts, however, the most that can be found are brief references in the English press recording their arrival. More dramatically, their personal descriptions are in the runaway advertisements in the colonial press, where details of clothing, appearance, bodily markings and personal styles are given. Ironically, they received more attention in America than in England. Yet, few successfully returned, despite the stories of Henry Justice and his like. They vanish into the general history of the poor of North America, like most of their fellow servants.[47] The Treaty of Paris in 1783 at the end of the Revolution put a formal end to the convict trade from Britain to her former American colonies though the last known arrival of a convict ship was the *Jenny* from Newcastle, which landed its cargo in April 1776. Some cargoes arrived from Ireland and it was anticipated that they would work digging the Chesapeake–Ohio canal but the project failed.[48] The American colonies were never penal colonies, but when the British tried again in a new place, they exchanged the Atlantic for the Pacific and a model of colonies with convicts for a colony of convicts.

The Atlantic colonies

When the English colonies in North America sought to replicate the political and legal systems of the mother country, – after all, that was what their charters enjoined them to do – the sentence of transportation intended to fill the gap in England between the finality of the death sentence and the brevity of whipping, was not really an option because there was nowhere for colonial authorities to send their criminals. They could hardly send them back to England and Wales, Scotland or Ireland and they were unlikely to be welcome in the colonies of other European powers in the Americas. Therefore, this feature of English law was largely missing in North America, but not entirely as growing European and American experiences combined and culminated in the formal expulsion of Native Americans in the seventeenth and eighteenth centuries. The use of banishment in Britain's American colonies suggests continuity with the past but in North America and the Caribbean, banishment for political purposes rather than criminal offences was the norm. Seventeenth-century colonists, however, made good use of banishment to rid themselves of hostile natives, rebellious settlers, religious zealots and fractious individuals. Barbados was more expansive. Records for the 1650s 'mention traitors, pirates vagabonds, felons and rebels among those serving time in the West Indies'.[49] But as order and stability came to characterize most colonies in the following century, banishment as well as transportation as a criminal punishment became increasingly associated with 'race' and slavery, that is, until the American Revolution. There was, however, one major exception – that of the Acadians or 'French Neutrals' as they were also known – who are the subject of the next chapter.

MAP 3 *Nova Scotia [detail from John Mitchell's* A map of the British and French dominions in North America *(1757)]*

7

The Acadians:
A people without a voice?

The expulsion of some 7,000 Acadians from Nova Scotia followed by further expulsions during the Seven Years War, many of whom died as a consequence of their removal due to the conditions on board the transport vessels, the disease-ravaged environment of the seaports where they landed and the impoverished and harsh conditions of their lives in exile, has been described by John Mack Faragher as 'one of the most horrific episodes in North American history'.[1] In an odyssey that for some lasted decades, the Acadians found themselves dispersed and relocated among the seaports and inland towns of Britain's North American mainland colonies, the coastal towns of England and France, the French and English islands of the Caribbean, French Guyana, the South Atlantic and Spanish Louisiana.[2]

The process of removal began with 'those about the Isthmus', the Chignecto district, 'all of whom were in Arms and therefore entitled to no favour from the Government', wrote Lieutenant Governor Charles Lawrence to Colonel Robert Monckton. These people had 'always been the most rebellious', it was alleged. 'A sufficient number of transports were to be sent up the bay with all possible dispatch for taking them on board'. The measure was to be kept as secret as possible to prevent any attempts at escape and to prevent them from carrying off their cattle and other goods.

And the better to effect this you will endeavour to fall upon some Stratagem to get the men both Young and old, but especially the heads of families, into your power, & detain them till the transports shall arrive, so as that they may be shipped off - for when this is done it is not much to be feared that the women and Children will attempt to go away and carry off the Cattle. But lest they should, it will not only be very proper to secure all their Shallops, boats, Canoes, & every other vessel you can lay your hands upon, but also to send out parties to all suspected roads and places, from time to time, that they may be thereby intercepted.

Those of Grand Pré, Annapolis Royal and Minas were targeted next and finally those from the southern tip of the peninsula Cap Sable. The decision to disperse those banished from Nova Scotia among Britain's North American colonies was intended, according to Naomi Griffiths, to eradicate 'the idea of an Acadian community.'[3]

Much has been written about these events. From the start, the question on one side was who to blame and, on the other, how could the removals be defended. The French government accused the British of maltreating those Acadians who spent the war years in England and violating the law of nations and the Abbé Raynal, the first person of address the issue, was biting in his criticism of the British. At the end of the eighteenth century, Andrew Brown sought to recover crucial documentation from state records relating to the whole affair. Thomas Haliburton published a well-balanced account in 1829 but most nineteenth-century accounts were highly partisan. The most recent work by Plank, Griffiths and Faragher revisits the old issues in greater depth and detail, but also seeks to achieve an objectivity that was beyond the reach of earlier historians, while Christopher Hodson traces the extraordinary story of the Acadian diaspora in the context of British efforts to consolidate their empire in light of their defeat of the French in the Seven Years War, while the French sought to reinvent a new one beyond the reach of the British and built on more enlightened principles.[4] The role of Charles Lawrence, Lieutenant-Governor of Nova Scotia, is no less central to the latest body of work as it was to studies in previous centuries. Though Griffiths argues that Lawrence 'may have known what he was about and why', she nonetheless raises a number of questions which still perplex historians. Who influenced the decision to remove the Acadians not just those around Chignecto but all of those residing in Nova Scotia? How influential was Governor Shirley of Massachusetts? What were Lawrence's instructions from London? Did the naval commanders attending the Council meetings in July 1755 play a significant role in decision making? Besides, proposals for moving the French population from the peninsula were not entirely new; they were included in the Treaty of Utrecht. By 1755, however, the Acadians were well entrenched and the majority had little inclination to move.[5]

The military context

In order to assess the fate of the Acadians in the colonies of mainland North America, it is important to take into account the military context. While war between Britain and France was declared in 1756, fighting was already taking place on the frontiers of the colonies as early as 1754 when George Washington led an expedition against French incursions in the backcountry. The Albany Plan of Union, a pioneering attempt to bring the colonies together for military purposes had failed, but it is important to note that

Nova Scotia did not take part in the conference. Only Nova Scotia and Georgia were excluded, being 'infant colonies'. Though no agreement was reached, cooperation between smaller numbers of colonies was usually the norm and was also true of Massachusetts and Nova Scotia. The importance of the Indian frontier cannot be underestimated. Matthew Ward argues that Indian warfare on the frontier was not random but systematic. 'Between 1754 and 1758, war parties of only a few hundred Indians, supported by the French in Canada, paralyzed Virginia and Pennsylvania, two of the most important British North American colonies, whose populations numbered in the hundreds of thousands'. Hodson has also explored the importance of the Indian frontier, but unlike earlier historians, he has focused on the south-eastern frontier in relation to his discussion of the Acadians' experiences in South Carolina and Georgia.[6]

The Acadians: A people without a voice?

Although Faragher argues that, 'At precisely those points when their testimony is most wanted', the Acadians 'are voiceless', they were not among those who laid out their thoughts or told their stories. They did not keep diaries, print newspapers, engage in extensive correspondence or write their histories. Even so, their voices can be heard in collective and individual responses in petitions to assemblies, councils and governors, to agents in England and authorities in France but these were integral parts of the diaspora, they did not preceed it.[7] The government of Nova Scotia was in the hands of the governor and council. The removal was executed swiftly and brutally. Griffiths singles out the fall of Beausejour on 16 June 1755 as the tipping point. When the British took this French Fort, they found 300 armed Acadians among those who surrendered, though they claimed, not without some justification, that they were under duress. Charles Lawrence, *de facto* Governor of Nova Scotia, received no official sanction for his actions nor did he write to the Board of Trade, informing them of the Acadians' removal until October 1755, months after the decision to remove had been taken. Neither did he inform colonial governors ahead of time that they were shortly to receive boatloads of 'French Neutrals'. Jonathan Belcher, Jr, a New Englander, recently appointed chief justice of Nova Scotia, provided Lawrence with a smokescreen for the removals. Belcher designated the Acadians 'rebels' on the grounds that they had given aid and comfort to the enemies of England. Though the claim was not without foundation, it was scarcely true of the majority. In addition, he denied that the Acadians were British subjects because they had refused to take an unqualified oath of allegiance for fear it would commit them to taking up arms against the French. When Nova Scotia changed hands for the umpteenth time in 1713, a change confirmed by the Treaty of Utrecht, the former French subjects became British, as was usually the case when international boundaries were redrawn.[8] The question of the oath remained problematic but it was more of an irritant than a portent of betrayal. Belcher's third rationale was one of expediency. A declaration of war was anticipated, the military situation was deteriorating and Acadian removal would be timely and advantageous.[9]

The decision to remove such a large population and its execution were unprecedented in British North American history. Charles Lawrence received no official sanction for the decision or the manner of its execution, but neither was he reprimanded, and the policy of ridding Nova Scotia of its Acadian population was continued by his successor Jonathan Belcher, Jr. The final decision seems to have been taken at a Council meeting attended by two admirals – Boscowen and Mostyn.

Removal

The Acadians were the envy of land-hungry New Englanders and long regarded as a threat to British designs for the development of Nova Scotia on account of their religion, language, relations with neighbouring Micmac Indians and failure to take the oath of allegiance. Their expulsion – as 'French Neutrals' rather than 'Acadians' as they became known – involved the seizure of thousands of men, women and children, the destruction of their communities and the seizure of their property. The process of removal was swift and ruthless. John Winslow, Colonel of one of the two Massachusetts regiments sent to Nova Scotia, wrote vividly of the events at Grand Pré in which he played a pivotal role. At three in the afternoon of 5 September, the French inhabitants gathered at the church at Grand Pré as ordered. There were 418 men. A table was set up in the centre of the church from where Winslow, attended by some officers and using translators, delivered the following orders. The French inhabitants of Nova Scotia, it was declared, had for more than half a century, though indulged, failed to respond.

> The Part of Duty I am now upon is what tho[ugh] Necessary is very Disagreable to my natural make & Temper as I Know it Must be Grievous to you who are of the Same Specia . . . . [y]our Lands & Tennements, Cattle of all Kinds and Live Stock of all Sortes are Forfitted to the Crown with all other your Effects Saving your money and Household Goods and you your Selves to be removed from this his Province.
>
> Thus it is Preremtorily his Majesty's orders That the whole French Inhabitants of these Districts be removed, and I am Thro[ugh] his Majesty's Goodness Directed to allow you Liberty to Carry of[f] your money and Household Goods as Many as you Can without Discomemoading the Vessels you go in. I shall do Every thing in my Power that all Those Goods be Secured to you and that you are Not Molested in Carrying of them of [f] and also that whole Familys Shall go in the Same Vessel and make this remove which I am Sensable must give you a great Deal of

Trouble as Easey as his Majesty's Service will admit and hope that what Ever part of the world you may Fall you may be Faithfull Subjects, a[nd] Peasable & happy People.

Winslow then declared them the King's prisoners. Similar scenes were played out across Acadian settlements in Nova Scotia but there was some resistance. Jedediah Preble wrote from Fort Cumberland to Winslow on 5 September that Major Frye, having been ordered:

to Burn the Buildings and bring of[f] the Women & Children the number of which was Only Twenty Three which he had Sent on Board and Burnd 253 Buildings and had Sent 50 Men on Shore to Burn ye Mass House and Some other Buildings which was the Last they had to do. 'when about 300 French & Indians Came Suddenly on them Kild Doctr March, Shot Lieut Billings thro[ugh] the Body & thro[ugh] ye Arm & Kild or Took 22 and wounded Six more they retreated yo ye Dikes and Majr Fry Landed with what men he Could Get on Shore and Made a Stand but their numbers being Superior to ours were Forst to retreat.[10]

The governors of Britain's mainland colonies had no advance warning that boatloads of French Neutrals were about to arrive on their doorstep. Lawrence's circular letter to the Governors 'in relation to the French inhabitants of Nova Scotia' was dated Halifax, 11 August 1755. It was sent with the vessels carrying the exiles away from Nova Scotia not ahead of them.

The success that has attended His Majesty's Arms in driving the French from the Encroachments they had made in this Province furnished me with a favourable Opportunity of reducing the French Inhabitants of this Colony in a proper obedience to his Majesty's Government or forcing them to quit the Country. These Inhabitants were permitted to remain in quiet possession of their Lands, upon condition they should take the Oath of Allegiance to the King within one year after the Treaty of Utrecht by which this Province was ceded to Great Britain: with this Condition they have ever refused to comply without having at the same time from the Governor an assurance in writing that they shou'd not be Called upon to bear Arms in the defence of the Province, and with this General Phillips did comply of which step his Majesty has disapproved and the inhabitants pretending therefrom to be in a state of Neutrality between his Majesty and his enemies have continually furnished the French and Indians with Intelligence, Quarters, Provisions and Assistance. In annoying the Government and while one part have abetted the French Incroachments by their Treachery, the other have countenanced them by Open Rebellion, and three Hundred of them were actually found in Arms in the French Fort at Beausejour when it surrendered.

Notwithstanding all their former bad behaviour, as his Majesty was pleased to allow me to extend still further his Royal Grace to such as would return to their Duty, I offered such of them as had not been Openly in Arms against us, a continuance of the possession of their Lands, if they wou'd take the Oath of Allegiance unqualified with any Reservations whatsoever, but this they have most audaciously as well as unanimously refused, and if they wou'd presume to do this when there is a large fleet of Ships of War in the Harbour and a considerable land force in the Province what might not we expect from them when the approaching Winter deprives us of the former and when the Troops which are only hired from New England occasionally and for a small time have returned home.

As by this behaviour the Inhabitants have forfeited the title to their lands and any further favour from the Government; I called together his Majesty's Council at which the Honble Vice Admiral Boscowen & Rear Admiral Mostyn assisted to consider by what means we could with the greatest Security & effect rid ourselves of a set of People who would forever have been an obstruction . . . and as they consistently collect themselves together again, it will be out of their power to do any mischief and they may become profitable, and it is possible in time faithfull Subjects.

As this step was indispensably necessary to the Security of this Colony I have not the least reason to doubt of your Excellencys concurrence and that you will receive the Inhabitants i now send and dispose of them in such manner as may best answer our design in preventing their Reunion.

Lawrence sent a copy of this letter to the Board of Trade with his letter of 18 October in which he informed the Board of the removal of the Acadians. It was received on 20 November and read five days later.[11]

New England colonies

When William Shirley, Governor and Commander in Chief, suggested to the House of Representatives of Massachusetts that they consider sending commissioners to a meeting in New York, to consult on what might be done 'for the Security of his Majesty's Territories against the Invasion of the French' and to recover the territory lost, they politely declined. Only the King was equal to the execution of such a project. They pointed out 'That this Province have from their first Settlement been engaged in Wars with the Native Indians and the French Canadians . . . '. They were exhausted. The result was that the first anyone knew that some of *the* Acadians' were destined for Massachusetts was when they arrived in Boston harbour though reports of their detention were appearing in the colonial press in early September. On 5 November 1755, the House was informed that several vessels were lying in Boston Harbour carrying 'a considerable Number of French People from Nova Scotia who are in a suffering Condition on many Accounts'. A committee of five, appointed to inquire into their circumstances, reported back to the House. The same day that they found 'the Vessels too much crowded, their Allowance of Provisions per Week short, and too small according to that Allowance, to carry them to the Ports they are bound to, at this Season of the Year, and their Water very bad', the House interviewed merchants Apthorp and Hancock 'whether they were impowered to do any thing for their Relief and more comfortable subsistence'. Governor Lawrence, it appears, had given them no directions, 'but that they were ready to afford the Masters of the several Vessels, any Help, or to supply them with any Stores and Provisions they stand in Need of on their own Accounts'. On the next day, having interviewed the masters of the vessels, the House concluded that it was not safe to allow the transport vessels with the French people on board 'to proceed on their respective Voyages, under the present Circumstances' and confined the vessels to the port.[12] Quarantined for a number of days by the port authorities who feared they would spread disease among the resident population, they were temporarily housed on Boston Common. Many had only the clothes on their backs. Hutchinson and a few others took in some of the aged and infirm. By the spring of 1756, it was assumed they would be able to support themselves. Those who were unable or unwilling to work would by bound out.[13]

The House recessed on 7 November but appointed another committee to determine what should be done with the inhabitants of Nova Scotia 'as are or may be sent hither'. It was more than a month later that a bill was brought in, making provision for the inhabitants of Nova Scotia deported by their own government. The Council voted on 16 December that the Lieutenant Governor write to Governor Lawrence to acquaint him, that although they had admitted the French Inhabitants of Nova Scotia, they expected to be reimbursed for all present and future charges. Should any more of the inhabitants of Nova Scotia be sent to Massachusetts, they would not be admitted unless the government of Nova Scotia indemnified the province for all charges. The bill was given a first and second reading on 22 December. On 27 December, the House learnt that another vessel with a considerable number of French Neutrals on board had arrived the previous night. Directed to attend the House, Captain Livingstone, the master of the transport vessel and Messrs Apthorp and Hancock, Boston merchants and owners of the vessel, informed the House that their orders were to deliver the Neutrals to Boston and, on receiving a certificate from the governor 'of their being landed', to apply for payment. They had no further instructions. The House appointed a committee to consider the best course of action when the Deputy Secretary presented a letter from Governor Lawrence to the Commander in Chief of the province. This was Lawrence's circular letter to governors dated 13 August.[14]

Since the latest arrivals from Nova Scotia had reached Boston in mid-winter, they were 'in great Danger of sufering during this rigorous Season' unless some provision was made for them. In the absence of instructions from Governor Lawrence or Governor Shirley, it was ordered that the committee dispose of them:

> in such Towns within this Province, as they shall judge least inconvenient to the Public: And the Select-Men or Overseers of the Poor of the several Towns to which they may be sent as aforesaid, are hereby authorized and required to receive them; and employ or support them in such Manner as shall incur the least Charge. And the said Inhabitants of Nova-Scotia being so received and entertained in any Town shall not be construed or understood to be an Admission of them as Town Inhabitants; the Court relying upon it that some other Provision will be made them, without any Expense to this Government'.[15]

Eight months later, the House was informed on 14 August 1756, that more French Neutrals had arrived 'and in a suffering Condition'. They had arrived not from Nova Scotia but from the Southern Colonies in a flotilla of canoes and were detained while entering Barnstable Bay. There were 99 of them. They had been originally sent to Georgia and were making their way back to Nova Scotia. They had obtained passports from the governors of Georgia, South Carolina and New York, which the Deputy Secretary was ordered to lay before the House. A strict search was to be made for any papers they might be carrying. A quick decision was taken on where to send these latest arrivals – 5 to the town of Rochester in the County of Plymouth and the remainder to 11 towns in the County of Bristol, each town receiving between 5 and 20 French Neutrals. Since the financial burden on the Colony was considerable, some relief was sought from the government of Nova Scotia. There were rumours that more were coming along the sea coast 'in the same manner'.[16]

However desperate the condition of the Neutral French was, they were still seen as a threat. Shortly after the arrival of those from the southern colonies, a committee of the House embarked on a review of the legislation relating to them, only to find there was no provision restricting their mobility. A bill to prevent them from 'travelling from Town to Town' without permission was ordered to cover this oversight. In September, it was found that they had not been removed from Boston, as anticipated. In October, a petition from the select-men of the town of Marblehead in the county of Essex, read on 7 October, registered further concerns:

> that by Reason of the Situation of the French Inhabitants of Nova-Scotia, now in [the] said Town (most of the Men being Mariners) they are in Danger of their taking some Vessel out of Marblehead or Salem Harbour, and making their Escape in the Night; and praying the said Men may be remov'd from [the] said Town'.

On the same day, a memorial from the select-men of the town of Charlestown, 'praying that the French Inhabitants of Nova-Scotia now in [the] said Town, may be removed into some other Town in the Country'. The House was receptive and the French inhabitants, who numbered 49, were reallocated to other towns. In late October, the overseers of the poor of the town of Salem in the county of Essex requested that the inhabitants of Nova Scotia lately ordered there, be removed to some inland towns 'where less danger may be suspected from them'.[17]

Most of the Acadians remained in Massachusetts for the duration of the war, seven long years. They found outlets for their grievances in petitioning the governor and council. Their complaints related to payment in kind rather than wages, the quality of their accommodation and, most especially, the treatment of their children. James Morris, late an inhabitant of Nova Scotia, petitioned the House:

> that in the Place where he, with his Family are situated, by the late Order of the Court, they can procure nothing but Victuals for their Labour; and praying that customary Wages may be allowed them for their Work, so that they may be enabled to provide Cloathing, to prevent their suffering, during the Winter Season.

The petition was dismissed.[18] Dispersed across many small towns, they were meanly provided for and their children taken away from them and placed in the households of strangers, a practice unfamiliar to the Acadians but common enough in Old and New England. According to Faragher, François Mius petitioned the Massachusetts governor 'about the conditions in which he, his wife and ten children were obliged to live in "if drawing breath in the depth of want and misery may be called living"'. His family had been sent to Tewksbury where they were allocated a property 'with rotten timbers, broken glass, and a hearth that amounted to nothing more than a few stones piled up, with a hole in the roof substituting for a chimney. His family was being "smoked to death [and] that at every blast of wind they expect the House to be down upon their Heads, and think it a miracle that it has stood for so long"'.[19]

Jean-Baptiste Guédry lodged a similar protest. "[W]ithout any regard or pity", the authorities of Wilmington had assigned his family a house that lacked a roof. When it rained, they had to move the bed, but when it snowed, there was nothing they could do. His situation was desperate. As Faragher summarized it, 'He had no firewood or food, and his wife and children were barely surviving on acorns gathered in the nearby woods'.[20]

Joseph Michael from Annapolis Royal who lived with his wife Marie Boudrot in Marshfield complained about two selectmen who had come to his house and taken away his two sons. The older boy was sent to work as a labourer on a farm owned by Anthony Winslow, a cousin of Colonel

Winslow, while the younger boy was sent on board a vessel owned by
Winslow's son in law. In another case, Claude Bourgeois and his wife Marie
Leblanc, also from Annapolis Royal, complained that:

> Ten or twelve men came and took away from him two of his daughters . . .
> At that time employed in spinning for the family the poor remains of the
> flax and wool which they had saved from Annapolis.

When Bourgeois reclaimed his daughters, public support for the family was
withdrawn and they could no longer pay their rent. Nine men from six
towns made a collective protest. The men protested that they were 'afflicted'
on account of their children. It was bad enough to lose their farms by 'being
brought here and being separated from each other', but that was

> Nothing in comparison to that which we are now bearing in having our
> children torn from us before our eyes. It is an outrage on nature itself.
> Had we the power to choose, we would prefer to give up our bodies and
> souls rather than be separated from our children.[21]

While the Massachusetts Council was not unresponsive to the plight of
the Acadians, they offered no practical help but merely advised the town
authorities to refrain from binding the children out but the practice
continued. The Acadians were seriously disadvantaged. As Pierre Boudrot
complained, he did not understand the English language or customs; many
did not know where or how to apply for redress 'and the country people do
just what they please with them'.[22]

The governors' responses

Lawrence does not seem to have given much thought to what impact
the arrival of hundreds of alien people – French in origin and Roman
Catholic in religion – would have on the inhabitants of the British colonies
of mainland North America, most of whose frontiers were endangered if
not already enflamed, nor to their problematic status. Were they British
subjects – Lawrence's statement implied that they were, or were they
prisoners of war, as some of them believed?[23] Colonies with a significant
mix of peoples were fearful that the French Neutrals would make common
cause with their minorities. Governor Morris of Pennsylvania wrote to
fellow Governor Jonathan Belcher of Connecticut in November 1755,
having just failed to get his Assembly to pass a satisfactory militia bill,
that Governor Lawrence had sent him 800 Neutral French, 'whom I am
at a loss how to dispose of . . . if they were dangerous in Nova Scotia,
will they not be more so here'? He complained that the Neutrals might go
with intelligence to the Indians and French, 'who were invading us in all

parts' or with the aid of the German and Irish Roman Catholics, 'forment some comotions to favour the French designs' in this and neighbouring colonies.[24] Belcher was sympathetic:

> Your Assembly seem still as deaf as Adders, to the Defence of the King's Honour . . . if things go on much longer . . . it must bring fatal Ruin and Destruction, upon the fine Province of Pennsylvania . . . . I am, Sir, truly surprised how it could ever enter into the Thoughts of those, who had the ordering of the French Neutrals, or rather Traitors & Rebels to the Crown of Great Britain, to direct any of [them to these colonies.]

Belcher was resolved to prevent their landing should any be sent to Connecticut. 'They should have been sent directly to old France'. The colonies already had 'too great a number of foreigners' for their 'own good and safety' and the Acadians would be too ready to join with Irish Papists and others 'to the ruin and destruction' of the King's colonies. But regardless of Belcher's views, it was not in his power to prevent the arrival of approximately 620 Neutral French in New London.[25] Connecticut passed an act similar to that of Massachusetts in which families were dispersed among all the towns, with local officials responsible for aiding 'the sick and indigent and maintaining strict discipline over the able-bodied', preventing them from moving from one place to another or gathering 'in potentially dangerous groups'.[26]

Maryland

When 913 exiles arrived at Annapolis from Minas in Nova Scotia, the government of Maryland adopted a different strategy though the result in the end was not dissimilar to the outcome in New England. The initial response to them was not unsympathetic. 'They appear very needy and quite exhausted in provisions', reported the *Maryland Gazette*.

> As the Poor People have been deprived of the Settlements in Nova Scotia and sent here (for some very Political Reason) bare and destitute, Christian Charity, nay common Humanity, calls on every one, according to their ability, to lend their assistance and help to these objects of compassion.

Private charity, rather than state aid, was expected to provide for the exiles' wellbeing. Convened in emergency session and after considerable debate, the Council voted to apportion the exiles among the several counties 'where they would be expected to rely on charity for their relief'. The results, according to Faragher, 'were disastrous'.[27] One group of exiles was forced to live for days without shelter in the snow-covered countryside, huddling together for warmth until a local minister secured housing for them. Many were reduced to begging from door to door. When local officials complained about vagabondage, the Maryland Assembly passed an act in the spring of 1756 authorizing them to jail indigent Acadians and bind out their children 'to some person upon the best terms they can make'. The Maryland Council engaged in a serious debate over the status of the French Neutrals. Edward Lloyd was convinced that the only proper designation for them was 'prisoners of war' but the Council preferred to describe them as 'wayward subjects'. Lloyd preferred 'prisoners of war' because 'we cannot devise any other honourable way of depriving those people, who were all Free born, of their Liberty'. It was true that no declaration of war had been made at the time, but Lloyd did not think this was a problem. Lloyd was particularly concerned over how the colony's actions, as well as those of the Council in Nova Scotia, would be viewed in London. He invoked the law of nations as the yardstick by which the transactions of both would be measured. Lloyd wished James Hollday, the recipient of the letter, to present his views 'in the proper places in England'. The letter also reveals fears about the impact the Roman Catholics might have on the colony's slaves.[28]

Virginia -even less welcome 'Faragher'

Acadians, according to Faragher, 'were even less welcome in the southern colonies where the government took steps quickly to get rid of them'. When Robert Dinwiddie, Lieutenant-Governor of Virginia, wrote to General William Shirley at the end of October 1755, he informed him that he had recently received a letter from Admiral Boscawen in which the admiral announced he was about to sail for England but would be leaving behind a force sufficient to defend Nova Scotia. He did not, however, Dinwiddie told Shirley, make any mention of what was to be done with the 'neutrals' residing there. Two weeks later, Dinwiddie received an express from Hampton Roads at the entrance to Chesapeake Bay. It came by night and reported that two sloops had arrived and four more were 'daily expected' carrying 'French Neutrals' from Nova Scotia. Dinwiddie's reaction to the arrival of over 1,000 exiled Acadians was shock, dismay and resentment. As he wrote to Governor Lawrence, he had had no notice of their coming and was, therefore, unable to make appropriate preparations to receive them.[29] Of all the mainland colonies, Virginia was the only one that expelled the Acadian exiles from North America for a second time. The reasons for this must be understood not only in the context of continental factors, but also, and more importantly, factors particular to the colony of Virginia.

As Adam Stephen wrote to George Washington in early October 1755, Virginia's frontiers were in a parlous state. Border settlements were in danger. 'The Smouk of the Burning Plantations darken the day, and hide the neighbouring mountains from our Sight. . . . Unless Relief is Sent to the Back inhabitants immediately None will Stay'. Two weeks later, Washington was writing to Dinwiddie of his concern that the French would seek to recruit the 'southern Indians – the Cherokees the Catawbas and others to their cause' and urged Dinwiddie to send 'a Person of Distinction' to counter their influence.[30] Dinwiddie was already a worried man before the 'French Neutrals' arrived on his doorstep. He was weighed down by 'concern and fatigue' over military affairs in British America. He wrote freely to James Abercromby, the Virginia agent in London, that should the government at home choose to replace him, he would welcome the prospect. War between Britain and France had not been officially declared but the two powers had been in conflict with each other on the margins of empire in North America for many years and a declaration of war was anticipated. Dinwiddie was dispirited by the response of colonial assemblies to appeals for funds for a campaign against the French:

> [T]he bad Conduct of all the Colonies, particularly the Proprietary Governments, is very unaccountable, [and] has occasioned such a Backwardness in giving proper Aid and Assistance that I am really wore out with Concern. I never heard [of] or saw a People so very defective of their Duties to His.Majesty's Commands, so absurdly neglectful of their Liberties, Lives and Estates.[31]

Virginia was vulnerable not only because of its extensive frontier, but in the event of war, it was also vulnerable from the sea. It was 'monstrous' Dinwiddie wrote to the Earl of Halifax, that so large a colony as Virginia had no forts, 'or one Great Gun fit to be Mounted for your defence; that a small Privateer may come into the Capes, robb and plunder every Plantation on the different Rivers, if the Station Ship should happen to be absent'. He had written to the Board about the guns needed to put the colony in a defensive state, but there was another problem – the colony had no engineers Though there were 36,000 men in the militia, they were mostly freeholders who would not serve except in 'imminent danger' and they would not serve outside Virginia.[32] Dinwiddie saw the problems on the Virginia frontier as a consequence of General Braddock's defeat earlier in the year and the march of the remnants of his army to Philadelphia. General Braddock's defeat was beyond Dinwiddie's comprehension. 'The Defeat of General Braddock appears to me as a dream', he wrote to Halifax, 'when I consider the Forces and the train of Artillery he had with him', while 'the precipitant march of the remaining Part of the Army for Philadelphia has occasioned much Clamour here, and really great Destruction among our back Settlers'. Dinwiddie urged the home government to pay the 'poor People' in the backcountry whose horses and wagons Braddock had impressed.[33] He wrote to Sir Thomas Robinson. Virginia had experienced 'a violent Drought which was likely to occasion a short Crop and the great scarcity of all Grain', as a consequence of which, the governor had found himself obliged reluctantly to forbid the export of wheat, bread, and flour. In response to pressure, Dinwiddie rescinded the prohibition and a proclamation to this effect appeared in the *Virginia Gazette* published on 12 December 1755.

Dinwiddie anticipated that the inhabitants of Virginia would be hostile to the arrival of such large numbers of refugees because of the mayhem on the frontier, where the perfidious French and their Indian allies were 'now murdering and scalping our frontier Settlers'.[34] Dinwiddie's preference was to disperse the exiles among the counties and seek an Act of Assembly to restrain them within certain limits. Contrary to Lawrence's assurances, he did not expect the French Neutrals to become 'either good Subjects or useful People'.[35]

On receiving news of the arrival of the first Acadians, Dinwiddie hurriedly summoned a meeting of the Council but since few of the councillors appeared and the affair was 'of such great consequence to this Country', he prorogued the meeting for a few days in the hope of attracting larger numbers. Dinwiddie's relations with the Assembly were poor. Only half the members of the assembly had turned up for the session called for 29 October and they proved awkward and fractious. Dinwiddie dissolved the Assembly, preferring to take his chances with a new election. Yet, he cancelled the meeting of the Assembly called for January 1756 despite the outstanding problem of what to do with the thousand or so exiles who had been deposited in Virginia. Dinwiddie had failed to persuade the earlier Assembly to contribute men and money for the projected expedition against the French at Crown Point. The earlier pistole fee controversy in which the governor had imposed an additional fee on land grants had also alienated members of the House of Burgesses.[36] It is from Dinwiddie's correspondence that we get some insight into what the exiles expected from their new environment. In his most detailed letter concerning the French Neutrals dated 24 November, Dinwiddie assured Secretary Robinson of his efforts to put the colony in as defensive a position as possible, 'considering we have no Fortifications to defend us from any Invasion by Sea, but must depend on the Ships of War that may be ordered us for our protection'. It is here that Dinwiddie raises the question of land for the 'Neutrals'. It is clear from this letter that Dinwiddie expected to provide land for the Acadians though he recognized that it would cause problems.

> Our Lands in the lower part of y's C'try [are] chiefly taken up and [are] private property, so y't I cannot assign these People any, and it is not the least reasonable to give them Lands on our Frontiers where the Fr. And their Ind's are robbig and murder'g our People.[37]

In a short letter to the Earl of Halifax and an even shorter one to the Board of Trade of the same date, Dinwiddie wrote of maintaining the French Neutrals until the next spring 'when they shall have Lands assigned them to settle on'. From the longer letter to Halifax, we get some idea of how Dinwiddie managed to persuade the Council to admit the 'Neutrals' though by a slim margin. Members of the Council had questioned the right of another governor and council to tell them what to do. Dinwiddie argued that since Admirals Boscowen and Mostyn had assisted the Council in Nova Scotia, he concluded that the decision to deport the Neutrals was consistent 'with the Safety of the whole Colonies, as the Fr. had pushed their whole Strength to N. Scotia'.[38]

The Council advised the Governor 'to postpone the determination of this affair, till some proper persons were sent down to Enquire particularly into the number of families these people consist of, and into their circumstances, also to learn whether they were willing to take the oath of allegiance to his Majesty without any reservation, would conform themselves to the laws of this Country and not transgress the limits assigned to them without the governor's permission'. Two members of the Council, Philip Ludwell and the Commissary met the French Neutrals at Hampton 'where they were arrived with the following Proposition: First, that they were admitted as Fellow Subjects, if they would take the Oath of Allegiance without any Reservations. Second, that they would be peaceable Subjects, conform and submit themselves to the Laws of this Colony. Third, that they would not depart from the Governor or Commander-in-Chief'. Dinwiddie continued,

> The Gent'n returned, say: As to the first, they have already sworn Allegiance to His Majesty: that they never forfeited it, but are punished for the faults of others. As to the other two Articles, they will cheerfully submit, but they wanted a free Exercise of their Religion, and to have their Priests, which I ordered the Gentlemen to let them know was by no means to be allowed, or must be admitted consistent with our Constitution, and they think they will in Time, take the Oath of Allegiance again. The next point was their maintenance till next April, before they can possibly be settled. It's so contrary to the sense of the People in general of admitting them among us, that I am persuaded the Assembly will give them no Assistance. It was therefore agreed by the Council that they are to be supported from the 2s per hogshead Revenue. The Balance thereof is so very small that I fear it will exhaust the whole.[39]

Less is known about what the French Neutrals thought about their circumstances in Virginia than in any of the other mainland colonies. There were no petitions to the Assembly, no private correspondence and few reports in the press. Few editions of the *Virginia Gazette* for 1755 and 1756 survive. Where and how the French Neutrals spent the winter is unclear. It may have been on board the vessels that brought them to Virginia or as one report in the *Pennsylvania Gazette* stated, 'Part of them remain at York, Part are near this City, and Part are sent to the Eastern Shore'. Yet, this is the only report that claims they were distributed in this way. They were probably kept on board the transports for the winter, though some were 'placed in quarters on land where they aroused further suspicion by fraternizing with Negro slaves'. Dinwiddie reported that one group plotted to run away with a sloop from Hampton, which obliged him to place a guard over them for two months. It was alleged some young men got back to Quebec. In the spring of 1756, Dinwiddie suggested that the French Neutrals might be dispersed among the eastern communities on the model of Maryland, but the burgesses would have none of it.

> The Danger we apprehend from such a number of Neutral French Roman Catholics being suffered to continue among us [makes it] Imperative they Be immediately shipped to Great Britain to be disposed of as H M shall think proper.

The Council agreed, as did Dinwiddie. He wrote to his superiors 'nervously' that he hoped 'that this step will meet with your approbation as I could not shun consenting thereto from the general clamour of the whole Country'. The first ship left with 299 French Neutrals for the English port of Bristol in May 1756. All the rest were sent off in the next two weeks – 250 for Falmouth, 340 for Southampton and 336 for Liverpool. They arrived 'unannounced in England at the beginning of the summer'.[40]

South Carolina

The *South Carolina Gazette*, published on 20 November 1755, announced that on Saturday there arrived under convoy of His Majesty's ship *Syren* Charles Proby, Esq., Commander, from the Bay of Fundy in Nova Scotia, a ship, a brigantine and a sloop carrying 471 Neutral French. The ship carried 210, the brigantine 137 and the sloop 124. 'and we hear, that several Children have been born in the Passage, on board each Vessel'. The following week, the paper reported that 'The General Assembly of this Province have been sitting since Thursday last; but, we don't hear, that they have yet determined, how the 600 *Neutral French* lately arrived hear shall be disposed of'. Two weeks later, the same paper reported that 'On Thursday the Four Transports with *Neutral French*, came up to Town; and on Monday those People were landed here: But in what Manner, or whether, they are to be distributed among us, we cannot yet inform our Readers'. The omens were not propitious. It was not until six months later and, after several abortive but disturbing escape attempts, that the Assembly devised a scheme to 'dispose of' the Acadians throughout the colony. One fifth would remain in St Philip's parish, Charleston, while the rest were divided among the remaining parishes, where they would find work or be contracted out by the churchwardens. They would only earn food and clothing. The scheme did not work as intended, as many daily resorted to Charleston and appeared to South Carolinians to be gathering as 'one body', a burden to St. Philip's parish. At the peace of 1763, many opted to sail for Haiti.[41]

In February, there were reports in the press of two parties of French Neutrals trying to make their way north and of thefts perpetrated by them. On 12 February, it was reported in the *Pennsylvania Gazette* that there were still 30 persons missing. On 1 April 1756, came some startling news from neighbouring Georgia. The Acadians who had been sent to Georgia had received the Governor's permission to leave the province and,

> have built Boats to transport themselves hither; and on Monday about 200 of them, in 10 of those Boats, arrived in *Wappoo* Creek, within a few Miles of this Town, convoyed from *Port Royal* by one of our Scout Boats. [L]est they should attempt to do any Mischief by the Way. What is proposed to be done with them, we have not yet learnt; but surely, it was not considered in *Georgia*, that we had already enough of them to maintain. We hear, these People are infatuated with a Notion, that they shall obtain Leave to pass, in like Manner, thro' all the Governments on this Side of Nova Scotia, 'till they reach it; but such have not considered, to what End they have been removed from thence'.

Five weeks later, it was reported in the *South Carolina Gazette* that on the previous Sunday 'upwards of 80 *Acadians* went from hence in Canows, for the *Northward*: The Country *Scout-Boats* accompany them as far as *Winyah* and that 'Yesterday upwards of 50 more of those People went for *Virginia*, in the Sloop Jacob Capt. *Noel*. At the end of May, the *Pennsylvania Gazette* published a report from Charles Town:

> that an Offer has been made to the *Acadians* here, to supply them with Vessels, &c, at the Public Charge, for transporting themselves elsewhere, as they have frequently solicited (or rather demanded;) but that having refused to accept the Offer, because not exactly corresponding with their own Humor, a Method has been fallen upon that will render it less troublesome and expensive.
>
> Those that went from hence some Weeks since, stopt at several of the Inlets (if not all) on our Sea Coast (Northward) and at Winyah raised their Boats to proceed, with the more Safety, farther.

It also included the report of 80 and 50 moving north, which was included in the *South Carolina Gazette* of 7 May.[42] The Council, it seems, had an alternative scheme to use the Acadians to work on the fortifications of Charleston. The Governor urged the General Assembly 'to consider with all possible Dispatch, in what Manner a proper Distribution may be made of the *French Acadians*, by which His Majesty's Intentions concerning them may be complied with (Whose Royal Will and Pleasure it is, that they shall remain here), and which may, at the same Time, prevent their being burthensome or dangerous to the good People of this Province'. That they had been distributed according to an Act of assembly was reported in the 29 July issue of the paper. News of the movement of the little boats had reached New York by the end of June, when the *Pennsylvania Gazette* of 1 July reported, 'We hear a great Number of the French *Neutrals*, some say seven Boat Loads, who were permitted to leave Georgia and South Carolina, are arrived and stopt in Monmouth county, somewhere near Shrewsbury, in the Jerseys; and a Council is called at Elizabeth Town about them'.[43]

Georgia

On 14 December 1755, the Neutral French passengers were allowed to land and given 10 days worth of rice for each person. Boats were to be provided for them. Some were to go to Frederica and the rest to Midway Great and Little Ogachee and Joseph's Town. The Clerk of the Council was to write to the magistrates about the new arrivals to be placed in their care. When the Council 'received a petition from the French People lately sent here from Nova Scotia setting forth that many were in 'a Sick and Languishing Condition and incapable of supporting themselves', a week's Provisions was allowed to those who were 'sick and in need'.

Commissary Russell was to inquire into their numbers and report to the Governor. Over two years later, Governor Henry Ellis, Georgia's new governor, told the Board that he had visited the French Neutrals the previous day 'and was much affected to see such a Number of Distressed People surrounded with large Families of helpless Infants, and proposed to the Board their having a Portion of Land allotted to them for the making a Garden, which might enable them to obtain a more comfortable support by which Necessaries such Garden would afford them for their own Consumption, and by the money to be made of the Residue at a Market. If the Means was approved his Honor intended to supply them with all Manner of Garden Seeds'. The Board approved.[44]

When Lawrence wrote to the Board of Trade in a letter dated 5 August 1756, he had already caught wind of the audacious attempt by some Acadians to return to Nova Scotia 'by coasting' along the shoreline of Britain's mainland colonies. He was informed by some of HM's captains 'that the French Inhabitants which were transported from hence last year to Georgia and South Carolina, had obtained permission and even procured small vessels at the publick Expence and embarked on board them in order to return to this province by coasting from Colony to Colony; and that several of them were actually on their way. I lost no time in writing to the different Governors upon the Continent to the eastwards of those two provinces, representing to them in the Strongest Manner the danger we should be exposed to should these people succeed in their undertaking, and entreating them severally to use their utmost endeavours to prevent it by both land and sea'.[45]

The French Neutrals in England

Acadian exiles began arriving in England from Virginia in June 1756. London newspapers noted their arrival. On 22 June 1756, the *Gazetteer and London Daily Advertiser* reported 204 Neutral French arriving at Falmouth aboard the *Fanny*. *The British Spy* carried the same report a few days later. News of the arrival of *The Virginia Packet* at Bristol with 300 of the Neutral French on board, 'a great part of whom are women and children', appeared in the *Public Advertiser* on 29 June. Several hundred more were expected. Eleven days later, the *British Spy* noted the arrival of the *Bobby* at Southampton 'with 293 neutral French on board', though five days later, the *Public Advertiser* put the number at only 200.[46] Just as colonial governors had had no notice of their coming, so too did English authorities find themselves in a similar situation. The government protested vehemently that colonial governors had no right to expel the Acadians from their lands and certainly had no right to send them to England, but it did not send them back. Responsibility for 'the French Neutrals' was passed to the Admiralty and by the Admiralty to the Medical Department's Sick and Hurt Board whose secretary John Cleveland would serve as the intermediary between the Board and the Admiralty. Though the government and local authorities were careful to distinguish between French prisoners of war and the 'Neutral French' in terms of their legal status and treatment, it gave responsibility for both groups to the same bodies of men. The treatment of French prisoners of war was covered by the rules of war and they could be and were exchanged for British prisoners of war, especially officers, if the warring parties found it convenient to do so. The rules of war also made provisions covering neutrals, but the French Neutrals were actually British citizens and so their situation was not really analogous. Cost and security were the guiding principles adopted by the Admiralty.[47]

   On arrival, the Acadians aroused curiosity among local people and fervid activity among officials. At Bristol, 'vast Numbers of the Citizens' were reported to be 'flocking daily to see them'. But there was also uneasiness for they had been sent by the Governor of Virginia 'who was apprehensive that they would go and join their countrymen and the Indians in their interest'.[48] The immediate problem presented by the Acadians was the provision of basic needs – for food, shelter and clothing, the most difficult of which was shelter. Men, women and children over the age of seven were to receive a daily allowance of sixpence for their subsistence and children under seven, three pence. The committee's agent in Bristol and Falmouth, Mr Guiguer, first thought about lodging the neutrals at Knowle, a large county house that he had already considered and rejected as a prison for French prisoners of war in the current conflict, though it had served that purpose in the last war. Guiguer dismissed the idea on the grounds that it was too far away from Bristol. He was also doubtful whether its present owners would be willing to let it to house the exiles. Quartering them in private houses was also dismissed as impractical. The solution he adopted was to rent a number of large warehouses 'at an extreme end of town', though even here, he faced local opposition. The mayor thought the French Neutrals might prove a nuisance while the Governor of the Mint, the Manager of 'all that relates to the poor' of Bristol, opposed the landing of the Neutral French within the Liberties of the city 'lest they should acquire a right of settlement, being deemed His Majesty's subjects'. The proprietor's demands were at first extravagant, but it was finally agreed that the warehouses would be rented in the first instance for three months with a power of retaining them at the same rate, 'as long as the public service should require'. Having lodged the exiles in the warehouses, the agent informed them of the King's provision of sixpence per diem for every man, woman and child over seven years of age and three pence for those under this age and issued instructions for the 'preservation of regularity and order among them'. Guiguer reported back to the committee that the exiles had arrived with no money, that they appeared well disposed towards these measures and that they regarded themselves as subjects of the King. Not one of them 'expresses any desire to return to France'.[49]

Efforts to have the 'French Neutrals' with private families in Southampton and Liverpool failed. Mr Eddowes, agent for prisoners of war, obtained possession of the Great Tower, which had served as a magazine for Hessian troops in the town. Like Knowle, the Great Tower had been fitted for the reception of prisoners in the last war. He had acquired straw for bedding, which he thought preferable to that used by the Neutrals on board the ship, which needed airing on account of 'the great stench' of the ship. Eddowes also found another place about a quarter of a mile from the town fitted out for mariners and divided into apartments, though 'it wants some small repairs'. The agent asked whether these people should be continued in the tower 'as at present' or be removed to the other building. He recommended the latter, which he believed offered 'the cheapest and most eligible Lodging'.[50] The medical department wrote to Cleveland on 30 June 1756 that they had heard from their surgeon and agent at Liverpool informing them of the arrival of the Snow *Industry* from Virginia with 243 French Neutrals on board. They had sent the necessary directions for their subsistence and lodging in accordance with their Lordships' orders.[51] Reports from Falmouth suggest some Acadians found lodging in private houses but there was not enough room for everyone. It was being suggested that alternatives could be found at Killgalli and if the people agreed, they wished to commission the premises. They would also continue to seek private housing 'in any Neighbouring Towns or Villages'.[52] The Admiralty apparently did not find this arrangement satisfactory – it was too costly. The medical department ordered their agent to seek a reduction in the cost of private lodgings or seek out alternative accommodation in barns and warehouses. Overtures had apparently been made to one individual who owned a large storehouse but it was not in a condition to receive them. On learning of the official disquiet with existing arrangements, the French Neutrals 'were much affected and absolutely refused to go'. The agent responded by telling them, in accordance with his instructions, that they might remain where they were if they could get the cost reduced; if not, they must move as soon as possible. 'Our Agent was also told that the Neutral French at other places were very well content with like Accommodation'.[53]

Mr Bromfield, the agent in Liverpool, wrote to the committee to acquaint them with the Neutrals' complaint about the 3d allowance and 'desired to have the same quantity of Provisions as before'. One person was already infected with the smallpox and two others 'have the Appearance of that Distemper breaking out on them which he feared would prove to be general'. The agent noted that the burials of children could not be conducted for under 10s and 'as it would be difficult to keep accts of the prices of medicines', he suggested that 6s 8d should be allotted for each Cure. Medicines were to be charged 'in the manner pointed out by the Board'. He would seek out 'a House without the Town' and let the Board know 'the Terms on which it may be had'.[54] Despite their daily subsistence, there were times when the exiles went without. 1757 was a famine year in England. Little wonder then that the Committee received applications from the Neutral French, complaining of the insufficiency of their present 'Allowance for that purpose, occasioned by the dearness of Provisions, by their own little stock of Money which they had on their arrival being expended, and the few Cloths they brought with them worn out, and as their Situation does not admit of their Working and they receive no other Subsistence than the sixpence per Diem from this Office; We Humbly recommend them to their Lordships as real Objects of Compassion, & if their Lordships should be pleased, to Augment their Allowance'. They proposed an extra 3d *per diem*.[55] In July 1757, the Committee again wrote to John Cleveland that they had received another application from the Neutral French 'complaining of the insufficiency of their present Allowance to support them and buy them a few Necessaries'. They urged Cleveland to inform the Admiralty in addition to their letter of 13 July.[56] In 1759, it was the French prisoners of war who aroused public sympathy. A report from Liverpool dated 9 October 1759 declared that the prisoners there 'were in great want of Cloathes' and a subscription had been opened on their behalf. Fifty pounds had been raised, by which means 'those people had been furnished with all things necessary to keep them in the winter'. John Wesley opened a subscription at the Methodist chapel in Bristol 'for cloathing for some of the French prisoners who are almost naked'. 20 pounds was then spent on shirts and waistcoats for 'the most necessitous among them'.[57]

Sickness

The first indication of sickness among the exiles was a brief reference in Eddowes's report on the difficulties he had had to overcome in making arrangements for the accommodation of the French Neutrals in Southampton. He noted that several were sick 'with dangerous Symptoms'. He had found a place 'a little distance from the Town' for them. That sickness was affecting all the exile communities was apparent to the committee by early August, when they reported that accounts had been received 'from all the places where such people are that there are many Sick among them'. Upwards of 200 were now ill of various disorders, particularly the small pox. The surgeons who were employed to attend them were of the opinion that the disease would affect 'the greater part, if not all of them'. The committee had directed 'all proper Care to be taken of the people, and that they should be furnished with the necessary Medecines and Nurses'. The committee warned the Admiralty of the increase in costs. The committee repeated their assurances in their letter of 17 September 1756 that they had given their agents 'the most clear and positive Instructions' to assist the sick 'with Medecines, Nurses and every other Conveniences proper for their Condition, and that all possible precaution should be made Use of to prevent the spreading of Distemper, by keeping the Sick as Remote as they could be from the Well'. There was no neglect of their Lordship's instructions or want of fidelity 'to the Public Trust' on their part. The committee did not think the mortality among the French Neutrals, 'great as it has been', was exceptional especially when their circumstances were taken into account – 'their Long Voyage, their Change of Climate, their Habits of Body, their other disorders, and their irregularity and Obstinacy, often complained of by the Surgeons'. There was no foundation 'for Supposing that the distemper has been even peculiarly fatal to them'.[58]

Work

The Neutral French were not supposed to work, lest their employment antagonize the local work force, but in 1756–7, those living in Southampton were given permission to work on repairing the turnpike between the town of Southampton and the city of Winchester but it took an act of Parliament to approve the repairs and permit the employment of the Neutrals. Even so when approached by the Committee for 'Managing the Affairs relating to the Turnpike', the medical department wrote to the Admiralty, informing them that they had always turned down such requests from the Neutrals in the past despite frequent solicitations but this time the shortage of local labour led to the committee's acquiescence but it was an exception.[59] In April 1760, the medical department received a complaint about the employment of French Neutrals. The Committee confirmed that the French Neutrals were not allowed to work in order 'to prevent the Clamour of Labouring People in the Towns where they resided'. The Committee declared that they had never deviated from this policy, except once, in the case of the turnpike being built between Southampton and Winchester and that was for 'want of hands' and only 'for a short time'. It would seem that the Admiralty was willing to allow the Neutrals at Bristol to work, for the Committee sought confirmation of this apparent decision. The Committee asked whether the same privilege should be awarded to those of Penryn, Southampton and Liverpool. If so, they suggested that the 6d per day allowance might be reduced 'to ease the Government of part of the great Expence which that Lodging, Care of the Sick and Allowance of sixpence per day . . . occasions'.[60]

Laws of nations

The deaths of so many in the exile communities shortly after their arrival in England led the French government to launch a formal protest. It queried whether their 'sickly and unhappy condition' was the result of a 'Want of the assistance and Care proper towards People in their Circumstances'. Secretary of State Henry Fox transmitted the French protest to the Lords of the Admiralty, who passed it to the medical department, who in turn passed it on to their agents. The reports they received from their Southampton and Bristol agents reassured them that everything that could be done was done. The French had charged the English with violating the laws of nations, a serious accusation which suggested that English behaviour towards the Neutrals had failed to meet the standards expected from civilized nations. For a nation that prided itself on liberty and law, the charge was indeed serious. The committee's letter of 17 September 1756 to John Cleveland was mostly concerned with defending itself against charges of neglect and the abuse of prisoners. The letter from the French government to Secretary of State Henry Fox raised questions about the adequacy of provisions made for prisoners in Bristol and Sissinghurst. Those in the former were in Bristol pending the completion of their prison in Exeter. The Lords of the Admiralty sought reassurances that the complaint was groundless, for such representations were 'very Dishonourable to the Nation, and if causelessly made, matters ought to be set in a just light to Foreign States, to turn over as much as possible the prejudices conceived upon the Spreading such Complaints'. The committee reassured the Lords of the Admiralty that there were no grounds for these Representations.[61]

Housing French prisoners of war and French Neutrals in the same town, as was the case in Falmouth and Penryn, was likely to have unfortunate consequences. In 1759, French Neutrals were accused of assisting the 800 French prisoners at Kegillick in their bid to escape, which allegedly came close to success. When the prisoners built an extensive tunnel, the French Neutrals were accused of disposing of large quantities of earth that the prisoners had dug up in order to facilitate their escape. The Neutrals allegedly had 'constant intercourse with the prisoners' and were supposed to have supplied them 'with every instrument suitable to their purpose'.[62] Not only could the Neutrals supply intelligence to the prisoners, they could also procure firearms for them 'at the intended hour of escape'. Twenty had actually got away on two boats. A letter from Falmouth dated 6 August 1759 protesting against these activities proposed moving the Neutrals 'into some inland town' but they stayed where they were. When the war ended, the French sent vessels to collect them, though they indicated they would prefer to return to North America.[63] Of those sent to the North American colonies by Governor Lawrence, those in Massachusetts had aspirations to go to France but there was no funding available. Some returned to Nova Scotia, though their lands now belonged to others; more went to French Canada. Those in other colonies scattered across the Atlantic world.[64]

The French grab

In May 1763, *Lloyd's Evening Post* reported that a flat-bottomed boat from Bologne had arrived at Southampton to take prisoners from Winton on board and sailing for France at the same time were the *Dorothy* and the *Ambition* with French Neutrals from Southampton and Bristol. Three weeks later, the *London Evening Post* reported that 220 of the French Neutrals brought to Liverpool from America in 1756 embarked on board the *Sturgeon*, a French cartel, but 'were forced back by contrary winds. The French Commander proceeded from hence towards Carlisle and Scotland'. A cartel was daily expected from France for the French prisoners of war. The *London Evening Chronicle* carried the same story on the same date. Though they were apparently being rescued, this was not what they wanted. In response to a British government inquiry as to their wishes, they said 'we hope we shall be sent into our countries, and that our effects etc. which we have been dispossessed of (notwithstanding the faithful neutrality which we have always observed) will be restored to us'. They also asked to be compensated for their huge losses.[65] Though these were the first vessels to leave England carrying the Acadians to the next stage of their lives, this process was being duplicated around the Atlantic world. Relocated to seaport towns in North-East France, they did not integrate into French society.[66] Some became unknowing victims of French aspirations to re-establish themselves as an imperial power in the Caribbean and South Atlantic in ill-judged settlements at Kourou (Guyana), at Môle Saint Nicholas (St Domingue) and the East Falklands. Only the latter offered some hope of success but the French government withdrew the settlers in the face of diplomatic pressure from Britain. Twenty years later, some of them were gathered together in the place for which they are now famous, Spanish Louisiana. Others returned, not to Nova Scotia, but to French Canada.[67]

MAP 4 *Maryland and Virginia [detail from Lewis Evans,* A General Map of the British Colonies in America *(London: Carrington Bowles, 1771)].*

8

'Arbitrary, unjust and illegal': Philadelphia Quakers on the Virginia frontier, 1777–8

While the responses of the Acadians to their expulsion from Nova Scotia and subsequent diaspora leave much to the imagination owing to the shortage of personal documents, the Philadelphia Quakers exiled to Virginia in September 1777, though few in number, kept diaries and journals, individual and collective, and corresponded with their families – not only with their wives but also with their children. More significant still are the public protests they issued, which challenged the grounds on which they had been taken into custody and the banishment they endured. While detained in the Free Mason's Lodge in Norris Alley, they kept up a steady stream of public protests – remonstrances, memorials, protests and addresses – to the Supreme Executive Council of Pennsylvania, the Congress of the United States and to the inhabitants of Pennsylvania. When they reached the Pennsylvania boundary, they challenged the right of the state authorities to send them into another jurisdiction where they had no authority. In Winchester, Virginia, they continued their protests, adding Patrick Henry, the governor and the Council of Virginia to the list of their recipients. They also challenged the legal authority of the county lieutenant of Frederick County, John Smith, to hold them in confinement. Their arguments were based on solid legal grounds; they were skillfully crafted and models of their kind. What was at stake, they argued, was not merely the rights of those held prisoner in Free-Mason's Lodge and banished to Virginia, but those of every citizen of Pennsylvania. Collectively, these Quaker records, together with personal correspondence, provide a valuable insight into the experience of banishment suffered by a blameless, though perhaps somewhat insufferable, group of people – at least, that is how members of Congress and the Supreme Executive Council of Pennsylvania regarded them – but who in challenging the new revolutionary organs of government and its agents, especially over the use of warrants and oaths, contested not merely the justice of their treatment in the light of the revolutionary principles they purported to espouse but their very legality. It also illustrates the limits of appeals for justice, however well founded, in the face of power. For their persistence, they deserve more than a footnote in the history of the Revolution.[1]

But why should such a small group of well-to-do Philadelphians become the object of such fear and resentment? In the seventeenth century, Quakers were unwelcome in most colonies, and laws excluding them and banishing them only came to an end in the first quarter of the eighteenth century. By then, Pennsylvania had been founded as a Quaker colony (1680), a refuge for persecuted Quakers in England and the colonies. Though the power of the Quakers remained formidable long after their proportion of the population had diminished, the pacifist policies of their government survived as long as relations on its borders could be contained. Immigrants were attracted to the colony by the availability of land. Irish and German migrants flooded in, many of them settling on the volatile frontier. Thayer identifies 1755 as the year in which Quaker power crumbled before the threat of French expansion in the Ohio Valley. The attempt of the Quakers to maintain a pacifist position once fighting had broken out damaged them irreparably. 'Moreover, the Quakers had over a number of years, accumulated a considerable number of political enemies who were now in the ascendancy'.[2]

'Tolerance often is an early victim of revolution', writes Richard Bauman. Initially, the Quakers had supported the opponents of British policy. They had also given generously to the beleaguered population of Boston after the British had blockaded the port following the Boston Tea Party. As the situation deteriorated and the prospect of war loomed, their commitment wavered, especially when the assembly voted large emissions of paper money in June (£35,000) and November (£80,000) in 1775. Led by the 'resolute' Israel Pemberton – whose taxes during the French and Indian War had been collected by forced sales of his property – the Quakers denounced the Assembly measures as both 'illegal and arbitrary'. The Quakers 'were reminded both in and out of their meetings that the paper money was issued for waging war' and that they should not use it.[3]

Philadelphia was not only the capital of Pennsylvania, it was also the largest and richest city in the 13 mainland colonies. It was a thriving port and the point of entry for large numbers of European immigrants who headed for the frontier and the Valley Road of Virginia that afforded them access to the back parts of the Carolinas and Georgia. It was the seat of government of the colony and the successor state of Pennsylvania.[4] The Superior Executive Council met there, the assembly met there and so did the Congress of the United States. The Executive Council and the Congress were deeply implicated in the plight of those who became known as 'the Virginia exiles'. Having publicly named and, with considerable fanfare, expelled a number of leading Quakers together with a smaller number of non-Quakers, neither institution was willing to accept responsibility for the consequences. While anti-Quaker sentiment continued to build steadily – Friends were fined or imprisoned for not bearing arms or not paying taxes, for not illuminating their windows or shutting up their shops when popular sentiment demanded otherwise – it was the landing of General Howe and the imminent threat to the city of Philadelphia that brought the question of Quaker loyalty to a head.[5] Material purporting to come from the 'Spanktown Yearly Meeting', forwarded to Congress by General Sullivan, caused outrage. In his letter to Congress from Hanover, New Jersey, dated 25 August 1777, Sullivan claimed that among the baggage taken on Staten Island on the 22 August, a number of incriminating documents had been found implicating the Quakers in providing intelligence to the enemy. He enclosed copies of three of them, one of which solicited information about American troop movements and two of which provided intelligence about them. Sullivan accepted these papers as proof that 'Quakers at the Meetings Collected Intelligence & forwarded [it] to the enemy'. The Quakers were 'the most dangerous Enemies Ameri[ica] knows & Such as have it in their power to Destress the Country more than all the Collected Force of Britain'. As Sarah Logan Fisher wrote in her journal, 'no yearly meeting ever existed there' and the papers were 'a notorious forgery'.[6]

On 28 August 1777, a committee of Congress consisting of Richard Henry Lee, John Adams and William Duer reported that they had examined the 'testimonies' and concluded that certain persons of wealth and substance were 'with much rancour and bitterness, disaffected to the American cause' and likely 'to communicate intelligence to the enemy, and in various other ways to injure the councils and arms of America'.[7] Adams was no friend of Israel Pemberton. Writing over 30 years later of his arrival in Philadelphia in 1774 to attend the First Continental Congress as one of the representatives of Massachusetts, he was invited to meet some Gentlemen who wished to discuss 'a little Business' with the Massachusetts delegates at Carpenters Hall.

> We all went at the hour, and to my great Surprize found the Hall almost full of People, and a great Number of Quakers seated at the long Table with their broad brimmed Beavers on their Heads. We were invited to Seats among them: and informed that they had received Complaints from some Anabaptists and some Friends in Massachusetts against certain Laws of that Province, restrictive of the Liberty of Conscience: and some Instance were mentioned in the General Court and in the Courts of Justice, in which Friends and Baptists had been grievously oppressed.

Adams was greatly surprised and offended 'at seeing our State and her Delegates thus summoned before a self-created Trybunal, which was neither legal nor Constitutional'.[8] Richard Henry Lee, another member of the three-man committee, wrote to fellow Virginian Patrick Henry, governor of the state, enclosing copies of the incriminating evidence, so he could see for himself 'a uniform, fixed enmity to American measures' which, with the 'universal ill fame of some capital persons', had led to 'the arrest of old Pemberton and several others, to prevent their mischievous interposition in favour of the enemy at this critical moment when the enemies army is on its way here, with professed design to give this City up to the pillage of the soldiery'. That day, Congress had ordered that the 'Quaker Tories' be sent to Staunton in Augusta County, Virginia. Lee hoped that Henry would ensure their security 'for they are mischievous people'.[9]

The committee of Congress not only examined the evidence provided by General Sullivan, but also took into consideration a year-old pamphlet signed by John Pemberton. It was addressed, 'To our friends and brethren in religious profession in these, and the adjacent provinces' on behalf of the Meeting of Sufferings held at Philadelphia and New Jersey dated 20 December 1776 and included the following paragraph:

> Thus we may with Christian fortitude and firmness withstand and refuse to submit to the arbitrary injunctions and ordinances of men, who assume to themselves the power of compelling others, either in person or by other assistance, to join in carrying on war, and in prescribing modes of determining concerning our religious principles, by imposing tests not warranted by the precepts of Christ, or the laws of the happy constitution, under which we and others long enjoyed tranquillity and peace.[10]

It was denounced as seditious. The committee earnestly recommended that since certain persons 'have uniformly manifested, by their general conduct and conversation, a disposition highly inimical to the cause of America', they recommended to the Supreme Executive Council of the state that they 'apprehend and secure the persons of Joshua Fisher, Abel James, James Pemberton, Henry Drinker, Israel Pemberton, John Pemberton, John James, Samuel Pleasants, Thomas Wharton, sen, Thomas Fisher, son of Joshua, and Samuel Fisher, son of Joshua, together with all such papers in their possession, as may be of a political nature'. There was 'strong reason' to believe that those named maintained 'a correspondence and connection highly prejudicial to the public safety, not only in this state, but in the respective states of America'.[11]

What made the arrests a matter of urgency was the approach of the British army. It was necessary:

> for the Public safety of this time, when a British Army is landed in Maryland, with a professed design of enslaving this free Country, & is now advancing towards this City as a principal object of hostility, that such dangerous persons be accordingly secured.

The arrests were to be carried out by a 'suitable number of friends to the Public cause' – in other words, those who could be trusted – and the number to be detained was increased to 41 – Joshua Fisher, Abel James, James Pemberton, Henry Drinker, Israel Pemberton, John James, Samuel Pleasant, Thomas Wharton, senior, Thomas Fisher, Samuel Fisher (sons of Joshua), Myers Fisher, Elijah Brown, Hugh Roberts, George Roberts, Joseph Fox, John Hunt, Samuel Emlen, junior, Adam Kuhn, D. M. Phineas Bond, William Smith, D. D. Reverend Thomas Combe, Samuel Shoemaker, Charles Jervis, William Drewitt Smith, Charles Eddy, Thomas Pike (Dancing Master), Owen Jones, junior, Jeremiah Warder, William Lennott, Edward Pennington, Caleb Emlen, William Smith, Samuel Murdock, Alexander Stedman, Charles Stedman, junior, Thomas Ashelton Merchant, William Imlay, Thomas Gilpin, Samuel Jackson, Thomas Afflick and John Pemberton.[12]

The books and papers of John Hunt, who lived on the Germantown Road 'about five Miles off the City' and John Pemberton, Samuel Emlen and others, 'leaders in the Society of Quakers', merited special attention. As for the rest, discretion was called for. Those whose names were marked with an X could be offered the opportunity to remain in their own homes, provided they gave a written promise that they would not do anything '*injurious to the United Free States* of North America, by Speaking, Writing or otherwise, & from giving intelligence to the Commander in Chief of the British Forces, or any other Person whatever, concerning public Affairs'. If such a commitment was not forthcoming, from those refusing as well as those against whose names there was no mark, a suitable place should be found for their confinement consistent with their status. The Free Masons Lodge was suggested as it was not the wish of the Council to commit 'many of the persons to the Common Gaol, nor even to the State Prisons'. On 2 September 1777, 19 of those named were rounded up and committed to the Free Mason's Lodge. They were joined by a further seven the next day and on the fourth, by John Hunt, Israel Pemberton and Samuel Pleasants.[13]

Arrests

On 3 September, the Supreme Executive Council received a detailed report from those authorized to make the arrests. The account was divided into sections. Those who, for one reason or another, had not been arrested were dealt with first. Joshua Fisher was reported to be so ill that he could not be moved, but gave verbal assurances to those who came to arrest him. Abel James was allowed to remain on his plantation on promising to appear before the president of the Council when summoned and not to speak, write or give any intelligence to the enemies of the United Free States of America. Hugh Roberts, who was '70 years or upwards', declared that he had never spoken or in any way shown himself to be hostile to the liberties and independence of America since the conflict with Britain had begun. He had given his word and he would be seen again at 2 o'clock that afternoon. George Roberts' wife was pregnant and ill. He would be visited again with his father. Samuel Emlen Jr was confined to his bed. Samuel Shoemaker promised not to leave his house and claimed he had nothing to do with the meetings of sufferings and disapproved of Pemberton's paper. Jeremiah Warder was old and infirm. He gave his verbal parole. No papers could be found at the homes of most of these men, except Warder, but even in his case, their value as evidence was doubtful. Samuel Emlen's desk was broken open, but nothing was found.[14]

Others like James Pemberton had been arrested, but no incriminating papers had been found at his home and the same was true of Thomas Wharton, Sr., Thomas Fisher (son of Joshua), Samuel Fisher (son of Joshua), Myers Fisher, Jos. Fox, Reverend Thomas Combe, Charles Jervis, William Drewitt Smith, Owen Jones, Jr., Charles Eddy, William Imlay, Thomas Gilpin and Thomas Afflick. However, papers of a public nature belonging to the monthly meeting were found at the home of Henry Drinker when he was arrested. '[A] number of Papers in a brown Bag led to John Pemberton's arrest while William Lenox, Junr, was found with "a Pocket Book & some papers" and "Edward Pennington, and John Hunt with some papers"'. Others took the oath and were discharged. Adam Kuhn, D. M, produced a certificate proving he had taken an oath to the United States. Caleb Emlen, originally listed as 'not to be found', when arrested, took the oath as required by law, and 'was discharged'. William Smith, described as a broker, had been arrested, but 'his Chamber was locked up' and the key was in somebody else's possession. Samuel Jackson was 'out of Town' and 'no search has been made for his Papers as yet'. Israel Pemberton, John Hunt and Samuel Pleasants proved more obdurate. When Colonel Bradford, Colonel Will, Major Keer and Mr Loughhead tried to arrest them at Pemberton's house, they refused to leave unless they were arrested by a civil officer. It was also reported that Phineas Bond had changed his mind and wished 'to renounce his parole'. Colonel Nicola, the town major, was ordered to take him into custody. The next day, the dissidents were ordered to Staunton 'agreeable to the resolve of Congress'.[15]

Sarah Logan Fisher has left an account of how three men came for her husband Thomas Fisher. They offered him parole if he would agree to remain a prisoner in his own home, but he refused, upon which, the men told him 'he must go with them & be confined to the Lodge'. Her husband demanded to see their warrant. What they produced was a piece of paper, allegedly an order from the Congress recommending to the Executive Committee that they take measures against all those who 'by their conduct or otherwise [had] shown themselves enemies to the united states'. On the morning of her husband's arrest, she related, the Council had sent out deputies 'to many of the inhabitants whom they suspected of Toryism &

without any regular warrant or any written paper mentioning their crime, or telling them of it in any way, committed them to the confinement'. In the end, her husband went quietly, 'without waiting to have a guard sent for him'.[16]

The first visitors who came to see the prisoners were turned away though 'towards evening, most who applied were admitted' but on the next day, '[s]ome of us conversing through the windows, were ordered by the guards to desist, and one of them presented his gun, cocked, and threatened to fire'. The incident led to a meeting with the town major, but it transpired he was not in command of the guards, but had only been ordered by the President and Council to furnish Colonel William Bradford with the men. The inmates then complained to Bradford about the misbehaviour of some of the guards, but Bradford declared he had nothing to do with the guards or any charge over the prisoners. He did, however, produce a paper signed by George Bryan, vice president of the Council when challenged to disclose on whose authority they were confined. It set out the recommendation of Congress that the Council should take up and confine a number of persons by name, and all others who by their general conduct had shown themselves to be inimical to the United States, etc. 'which he read to us', after which they desired to be heard in their own defence, and demanded a copy of the warrant.[17] While the prisoners insisted on their right to be heard, the Council was adamant in its refusal to hear them.

Council refuses to hear the prisoners in person

On 6 September 1777, the Supreme Executive Council informed John Hancock, President of Congress, that they were too taken up with important business to give the prisoners a hearing that 'could answer no good purpose'. They defended their actions, claiming 'the restraint of suspicious persons, in like exigencies as the present, may be abundantly justified by the example of the freest nations, & most judicious [writers]'. They urged Congress to assume the responsibility for hearing and disposing of the prisoners in Masons' Lodge and those on parole, advising Hancock that few Quakers were willing to make 'any promise of any kind'. George Bryan, vice president of the Council, had earlier sought the advice of Congress over where they should send them. Having approved the detention of the prisoners, Congress recommended Staunton in Virginia.[18]

Two days earlier, Israel Pemberton, John Hunt, and Samuel Pleasants, attended by their attorneys, had sought a hearing before the Council but without success. The Council declined to admit them on the grounds that it was the Congress that had originally ordered their arrest, to which Pemberton, speaking on behalf of all three men, observed that they had not been arrested and that as freemen, they claimed the right of being heard in their own defence. They argued that theirs was 'a case in which every freeman in the State is interested' and they demanded this right. The secretary replied on behalf of the Council that the Council has ordered this arrest in consequence of a recommendation of Congress, 'and they do not, at present, think proper to hear Mr. Pemberton, Mr. Hunt, and Mr. Pleasants'.[19] In response to the Council's order for their immediate arrest, Pemberton, Hunt and Pleasants drafted a remonstrance, which was published in Robert Bell's pamphlet *An Address to the Inhabitants of Pennsylvania* in Philadelphia in 1777, included in Robert Jackson's Dublin edition of the same pamphlet (1778) and in the *Gentleman's Magazine*. From their own knowledge and the advice of others on their rights and privileges as freemen, they denounced the order for their arrest as 'arbitrary, unjust and illegal'. It was their duty to remonstrate against it. Short and lucid, the principal tenents of the remonstrance were incorporated into the protests of others.

The remonstrance of Pemberton, Hunt and Pleasants

In the remonstrance, Pemberton, Hunt and Pleasants sought to justify their claims:

> The order appears to be arbitrary, as you have assum'd an authority, not founded on Law or Reason, to deprive us, who are peaceable men, and have never born arms, of our Liberty, by a military force, when you might have directed a legal course of proceeding; – unjust, as we have not attempted, nor are charged with any act, inconsistent with the character we have steadily maintained of good citizens, solicitous to promote the real interest, and prosperity of our country, and that it is illegal, is evident, from the perusal and consideration of the constitution of the government, from which you derive all your authority and power.
>
> We, therefore, claim our undoubted right, as Freemen, having a just sense of the inestimable value of Religious and Civil Liberty, to be heard before we are confin'd, in the manner directed by the said order; and we have the more urgent cause, for insisting on this our right, as several of our fellow citizens have been some days, and now are confin'd by your order, and no opportunity is given them to be heard; and, we have been inform'd, that it is your purpose to send them, and us, into a distant part of the country, even beyond the limits of the jurisdiction you claim, and where the recourse, we are justly and lawfully intitled to, of being heard, and of clearing ourselves from any charge, or suspicions, you may entertain, respecting us will be impracticable.[20]

To the President and Council of Pennsylvania: remonstrance of the subscribers . . . now confined in the Free Mason's Lodge

The prisoners detained in the Free Mason's Lodge had drafted their remonstrance to the President and Council of Pennsylvania a day earlier. They began by describing the manner in which they had been taken from their homes and conducted to the Free Mason's Lodge, where they had been 'kept in close confinement' and 'under a strong military guard for two or more days'. Failing to obtain copies of the warrants from the messengers who had arrested them, they remained in detention 'unaccused and unheard'. Subsequently, having obtained a copy of the warrant, they took 'the earliest opportunity' to lay their grievances before the council, whom they held responsible for their detention:

> and of claiming to ourselves the Liberties and Privileges to which We are entitled by the fundamental Rules of Justice, by our Birth-right and Inheritance, the Laws of the Land; and by the express Provision of the present Constitution, under which your Board derive their Power.

They continued,

> We apprehend, that no man can lawfully be deprived of his Liberty, without a Warrant from some Persons having competent Authority, specifying an Offence against the Laws of the Land, supported by Oath or Affirmation of the Accuser, and limiting the time of his imprisonment until he is heard., or legally discharged, unless the Party be found in the actual Perpetration of a Crime. Natural Justice, equally with Law, declares that the Party accused should know what he is to answer to, and have an opportunity of shewing his innocence.[21]

The prisoners then cited the ninth and tenth clauses of the state Constitution, the former guaranteeing the rights of the accused to a fair trial and the latter the protection of persons and property. A man should know the charge against him, be heard in his own right, be able to call witnesses in his favour, be tried in a public trial and if found guilty, it must be by a unanimous verdict. The tenth clause guaranteed the protection of persons, 'their houses, papers, and possessions against arbitrary search or seizure without Oaths or Affirmations first made'. The prisoners challenged the legitimacy of the warrant used to detain them, which did not match the requirements of the constitutions 'in this or any free country, both in its substance, and the latitude given to the messengers who were to execute it, and wholly subversive of the very constitution you profess to support'. The warrant did not identify their alleged offences, but allowed the messengers to search 'all papers belonging to us, upon a bare possibility that something political may be found'. It also required papers, 'relative to the sufferings of the people called Quakers, to be seized'. No limit was placed on the duration of their imprisonment or time appointed for a hearing. Since the warrant lacked these elements that were 'an absolute requirement' in making a warrant legal, they concluded that the 'warrant, and the proceedings thereupon' were 'far more dangerous in its tendency, and a more flagrant violation of every right which is dear to Freemen, than any that can be found in the records of the English constitution'. This was a damning and damaging indictment of the Council's behaviour. The prisoners demanded an audience to prove their innocence.[22]

An Address to the Inhabitants of Pennsylvania

The first item in the pamphlet published by Robert Bell was *An Address to the Inhabitants of Pennsylvania*. It was also the title of the pamphlet. It began by challenging the image that the Council had sought to present of the detainees 'as men dangerous to the community'. The authors owed it to:

> our country, to our families, to those who have heretofore held us in esteem, and to the general welfare of society, to address you, and lay before you, a particular state of the most dangerous attack, which has been made upon the cause of civil and religious freedom, by confining, and attempting to banish, from their tenderest connections, a number of men, who can, without boasting, claim to themselves, the characters of upright and good citizens.

They described how a few days earlier they had been called upon 'by persons, not known as public officers of justice' to subscribe their names to a paper promising not to leave their homes, and to be ready to appear, on the demand of the President and Council. They should refrain from doing anything injurious to the 'United Free States of *North America*' 'by speaking, writing, or otherwise, and from giving intelligence to the Commander of the *British* forces, or any other person whatever, concerning public affairs'. Aware of their innocence, they rejected the proposal. They demanded to know on whose authority the orders were made and of what crimes they were accused. Some were informed that they were detained by the authority of Congress, while others were read 'part of a warrant, from the President and Council'. None were allowed 'the indisputable right, of either reading or copying it'. On refusing to subscribe, they were conducted to Mason's Lodge, 'where they remained in close confinement, under a military guard, for twenty-four hours'. They expected to be informed of the cause of their arrest and to have an opportunity of defending themselves. They demanded a copy of the warrant to find out what 'heinous crimes' they were charged with 'to justify such rigorous treatment'. They were astonished to discover that a *General Warrant* had been issued against them, which did not specify their offence or appoint a judge or other authority to hear their case. No limit was set to their confinement nor did this 'extraordinary warrant' give any power to the messengers 'to break and search not only our own, but all the houses their heated imaginations might lead them to suspect'. They described the warrant as 'this agent of modern despotism' and included it in the publication to give the public 'a better idea of the arbitrary spirit it breathes'.

The protestors demanded 'as a matter of right', to be heard both before the Council and the Congress. The demand 'was reasonable in itself, founded on the immutable principles of equity, and warranted by the constitution under which the Council derive every power they claim'. This focus on the nature of the warrant and the dangers implicit in it was an essential feature of their appeal to the public.

The powers granted by this warrant are such, as in any free country, where the laws, and not the will of the governors, are the standard of justice, wuld be reprobated, as overturning every security that men can rely on – Yur houses, which by the law of the land, arc your castles against invaders, your chambers, your closets, your desks, the repositories of your deeds, your securities, your letters of business, or friendship, and other domestic concerns, which every man naturally wishes to keep within the circle of his own family, are permitted to be broken, searched, exposed to the prying eye of malignant curiosity, and all this, without any well-founded cause of suspicion . . . Nor can any man think himself safe, from the like, or perhaps more mischievous effects, if a precedent of so extraordinary a nature, be established by the tame acquiescence with the present wrong.

On learning that they were to be sent to Staunton, which they understood had been determined by the Congress, the prisoners in the Free Masons' Lodge sent a remonstrance to the Congress dated 5 September 1777, in which they demanded a hearing in the full confidence that they could demonstrate 'the falsehood and injustice' of the damaging charge made against them and to allay the suspicions being entertained of them.[23]

Third remonstrance to the President and Council of Pennsylvania

In a third remonstrance addressed to the President and Council of Pennsylvania dated 8 September – the prisoners had received no reply to their previous remonstrance – they found it necessary to protest again

'against your extraordinary mode of treating us'. They protested they were
to be banished to Staunton, a place where the Council had no jurisdiction,
'and to which we are utter strangers'. They asserted that this decision was
not only 'the violent infringement of the laws and constitution which you
have engaged to govern by, the hardship is heightened by the particular
situation of that county at this time'. The Indians had already commenced
hostilities on the frontiers of Virginia, 'not very far distant from the place
of our intended banishment, as though you could find no place of security
without endangering our lives'.[24]

On this occasion, the detainees took up the issue of the oath. The Council
were willing to discharge them, so they stated on 5 September, provided they
would take the 'Test required by law or the new Test framed by yourselves'.
Even if they had the right to do this, 'we think it very improper to be made
to men in our situation'.

> You have first deprived us of our liberty, on one pretence, which finding
> you are not able to justify, you wave, and require as a condition of
> our enlargement, that we should confess ourselves men of suspicious
> characters by doing what ought not to be expected from innocent men.

They noted that:

> This kind of procedure is not new in history; for tho' the great Patriots of
> the Revolution found better expedients for the security of their government
> than what arises from Oaths of abjuration, yet the annals, both of Old
> and New England are stained with accounts of men, in circumstances
> similar to our own; dragged before Magistrates, on the bare suspicion of
> crimes; of whom Tests, which they conscientiously scrupled to take, have
> been afterwards demanded, as the condition of their enlargement.[25]

How could the *Supreme Executive Powers* ask more of them than the law
required?

> By the Test Act every inhabitant may take the Test, and enjoy all the rights
> of Freemen, or decline it, and submit to a deprivation of some of them, of
> which are expressed in that act; but no power is given to any officer
> of justice whatsoever, to tender it to any person except in particular
> circumstances, and as the charge against us is not founded on a breach of
> that law, it is evident you exceeded your authority in putting it to us.

The detainees charged the Council with usurping the legislative power that
belonged to the Assembly 'while the Assembly was sitting under the same
roof'. They accused the Council of creating an *ex post facto* Law. If, in
fact, they were as dangerous as the Council suggested, taking either test
would not protect them. 'That men of bad principles will submit to any Tests
to cover their dangerous and wicked purposes is evident to all who have

been conversant in public affairs'. They invoked the example of 'the great Lord Hallifax' who, during the Glorious Revolution of 1688, had presented the crown to King William and Queen Mary 'in the name of the People of England'. Halifax placed no faith in oaths. 'As there is no real security to any state by oaths', he declared, 'so no private person, much less statesman, would ever order his affairs as relying on it'. The detainees repeated their demand to know the reason for their commitment and 'to have a Hearing in the face of our country'.[26]

On the following day, 9 September, the Council sought to strip the men confined in the Free Masons' Lodge of their citizenship. They resolved that the 22 named individuals who had refused to confine themselves to their homes, refused to refrain from corresponding with the enemy and declined to give any assurance of allegiance to this state 'do thereby renounce all the privileges of citizenship; and that it appears they consider themselves as subjects of the King of *Great Britain*, [and] the enemy of this and the other United States of *America*'. The Council defended its actions on the grounds that 'persons of like characters, and in emergencies equal to the present, when the enemy is at our doors, have in the other States, been arrested and secured' when suspicions arose about their behaviour and refusal to acknowledge their allegiance to the states. The prisoners were to be removed to Staunton without further delay. They should be treated according to their characters and stations, as far as may be consistent with the securing of their persons'.[27]

Preparations for the journey

At ten o'clock that night, the prisoners received notice that they were to leave the next morning, to which they responded with a further 'Remonstrance and Protest addressed to the President and Council of Pennsylvania'. On this occasion, they did not invoke the law or the Constitution, but rather, the rights of mankind. They protested that 'contrary to the inherent rights of mankind', they were being condemned to banishment *unheard*. They particularly objected to the charge against them of refusing 'to promise to *refrain* from corresponding with the "enemy"', since it insinuated that they had 'already held such correspondence', which they 'utterly and solemnly deny'. The tests being proposed were not binding in law and 'not withstanding our refusing them, we are still justly and lawfully entitled to all the rights of citizenship, of which you are attempting to deprive us'. They had never been given the opportunity to prove their innocence 'and remove suspicions which you have laboured to instil into the minds of others', which 'you knew to be groundless'.[28] The failure to grant them a hearing was a constant refrain found in all their protests and one that would continue when they went into exile.

Town major, Lewis Nicola, presented his instructions concerning their removal to the prisoners in Masons' Lodge, to which they responded with a list of queries. How were they to be sent into banishment? If in carriages, of what sort and how many? Would they be furnished with baggage wagons and, if so, how many? What provisions and stores would be provided for so long a journey? What number of beds and bedding? Who was to pay their travelling expenses and how would they be supported during their absence from their families and businesses? Could those whose families and businesses needed to be attended to before their departure 'have liberty to repair there' and would they be allowed to correspond with their Friends during their absence? They also insisted on obtaining a copy 'of their Commitment to that Country, & of the Orders accompanying it' so they would know how they were being represented and 'in what manner' they would be treated. Could they apply 'to the Officers of any Government in which we may be, for Redress of any Grievances we may be under'? The place of banishment became Winchester rather than Staunton and use of the prisoners' own carriages was preferred.[29]

Leaving Philadelphia

Thomas Wharton wrote hurriedly to his wife Rachel on 2 September, informing her that he was well and that they had learnt they were to be 'sent off that day' though he thought it would probably be the following day. Though earlier instructions were issued, because the military situation kept changing, soldiers initially assigned to escort them were needed for military duties elsewhere. When they finally left on 10 September, they found the streets around their houses crowded with men, women and children. The countenances of the people was sombre as they witnessed the cruel and undeserved measures inflicted upon the Quakers. Thayer describes how they

> were drove through third street to the upper part of the city and from thence to the falls of the Schuykill, a spectacle to the people, who by their countenances sufficiently tho' silently expressed the grief they felt on this extraordinary occasion, nor were any marks of approbation of our hard sentence & suffering given except by a very few of the lower class, until we had crossed Vine Street, where a rabble, consisting for the most part of boys . . . threw some stones at one or two of the hindermost carriages.[30]

Four days later, Wharton wrote from Carlisle how the party had crossed the Susquehanna River in carriages, on horseback and in canoes. After a disagreeable journey of 17 or 18 miles, they had arrived the previous evening in Carlisle 'and got into pretty good quarters'.[31] The people behaved 'very civily' towards them. Taking a walk around the town, which was about the same size as Trenton, a person called down to him from a window. It was Dr Keasley, who reported he was in 'good health' but closely confined in the gaol. Dr Keasley was a well-known Tory. When the lawyer Isaac Hunt was being 'carted through the streets' of Philadelphia for defending a profiteer, Keasley, thinking that the following throng were targeting him, aimed a pistol

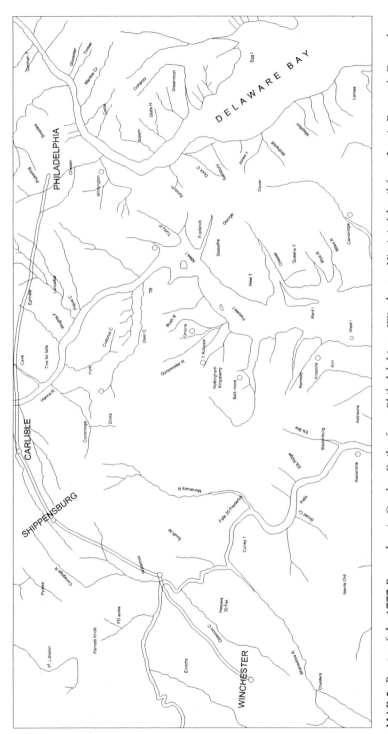

MAP 5 *Route of the 1777 Pennsylvania Quaker Exiles from Philadelphia to Winchester, Virginia [detail from Lewis Evans, A General Map of the British Colonies in America (London: Carrington Bowles, 1771)].*

through an open window at the crowd, 'was grabbed and pulled through the window and hustled off to Committee headquarters at Bradford's Coffee House'. According to Thayer, he refused 'to admit any wrong doing or ask for pardon, whereupon the Committee ordered him paraded through the streets but would not let the mob tar and feather him'. The evening after he was released, 'the mob threw stones and bricks through his windows, but did not attempt to enter the house'. Soon after, one of the doctor's letters to England was intercepted and found to contain information inimical to the patriotic cause. Keasley was jailed. Sometime later, while languishing in prison in Carlisle, he died.[32]

The journey

James Pemberton also recorded some episodes of hostility encountered along the way. When passing through Reading, where they arrived at about two o'clock, 'there appeared to be much enmity among the people, and some stones were thrown at us'. A mob had gathered in front of their lodgings to receive them and John Pemberton and James Starr were pulled from their carriage and attacked. Repulsed by their escort, the mob did not disperse until assured by Colonel Morgan that the men were harmless. But, there were also Friends who visited them en route with offers of accommodation and gifts of food. Their baggage followed them and, when it fell behind, they negotiated with their escort for a delay so that it might catch up with them, one of their party having only one shirt to his name. It was when the party reached Pottsgrove on 14 September, that Levi Hollingsworth and Benjamin Pratt caught up with them and the legal issues surrounding their banishment entered a new phase. Hollingsworth and Pratt were carrying writs of *habeas corpus* for nine of their number. The purpose of this historic writ, writes Paul Halliday, 'was and is to bring a prisoner before a judge in order 'to signify the crimes laid against him', and thereby ensure that law is honored in holding or releasing him'. These were served on their escorts Samuel Caldwell and Alexander Nesbit, who refused to accept them. Even so, those who had not applied for the writ, now agreed to do so. Benjamin Bryant, joined by Nathaniel Walker, undertook to pursue the matter.[33]

When application was made to Thomas McKean, chief justice of Pennsylvania, it was granted. McKean wrote a spirited defence of his action to John Adams when he learnt of the dissatisfaction in Congress regarding his granting of the writ to 20 persons 'confined in the Free-masons Lodge in Philadelphia'. 'Next to the approbation of a good conscience' wrote McKean, he esteemed, 'the good opinion of good men, and of my friends in particular'. The writs were applied for in conformity with the directions laid out in the statute of 31 Car 2, ch. 2, 'and the only authority for the confinement that I saw was the copy of a letter from the Vice-President to Colonel Lewis Nicola'. He had not 'received a letter or seen a newspaper from Philadelphia for a fortnight nor could he learn of any particulars respecting this affair from anyone whom I met', with the exception of the two people who presented the writs to him. They offered him a pamphlet stating their case, which he refused to read, stating that he would make his decision on the basis of the returns to the writs. McKean then outlined the history of the writ in Pennsylvania. The Habeas Corpus Act, he argued, was part of the legal code of Pennsylvania and:

has always justly been esteemed the palladium of liberty. Before that Statute the habeas corpus was considered to be a prerogative writ and also a writ of right for the Subject and if the King and his whole Council committed any Subject yet by the opinion of all the Judges in times when the rights of the people were not well asserted nor sufficiently regarded a ha[beas] cor[pus] ought to be allowed & obeyed, and the distinction taken was that in such a case upon the return the prisoner was to be remanded, but if the commitment was by part of the Lords of the Council he was to be bailed. By the [sta] tute I need not mention to you the many cases on this head in our books had I now to rec [blurred] all discretionary power in the judges is taken away, and a penalty of £500 sterling imposed for a refusal in the vacation to allow the writ. So that if I had forgot the oath I had taken but a few days before, common prudence would have prevailed upon me not to have incurred the forfeiture of ten thousand pounds sterling, and also as a judge to have subjected myself to the just censure of the judicious dispassionate and the more especially when no injury could arise by returning the writs and bringing the parties before me, save a little delay, the expence being borne wholly agreable to the statute by the prisoners. If upon the return of the Process I had shewed any partiality to the prisoners or sought occasion to favor men inimical to a cause, I have espoused with as much sincerity and supported and will support with as much zeal, as any man in the Thirteen United States, then I might have been deservedly blamed & stigmatized, but censure previous to this was, to say no more, premature and injudiciously bestowed. No Gentleman thought it amiss in the Judge who allowed the *habeas corpus* for Ethan Allen & his fellow prisoners upon the application of Mr Wilks. Even the Ministry despotic as they were did not complain of it, but evaded them by sending the prisoners out of reach, Fiat Justitia, ruat caelum is a sentiment which pleases me; And faithful Judges ought not to be subjected to unnecessary difficulties. I told him that in almost every war since the making the statute, the like had been done in England. . . . You know however the struggles in parliament from time to time whenever this has been moved by the ministry. I could do more. . . .

The Assembly then suspended the writ, as was the common practice during wartime.[34] During the second week of their journey, the party arrived at Winchester, where they were destined to remain agreeable to the authorities in Pennsylvania. Arrangements were made ahead of time for them to lodge at the premises of Phineas Bush. They had met John Smith, county lieutenant who would have charge of them in Frederick County, the previous evening when Daniel Levan, sheriff of Berks County who commanded their escort from Reading, delivered to him the several papers relating to them from the President and the Council. Smith found them weighty and unintelligible and would not agree to receive them into his custody without further time to consider them. 'We then supped and at a reasonable time retired to rest, and our baggage wagons not being come up in which were the beds several brought from home and there not being sufficient accommodation for all our company'. Wharton went to lodge at the house of two Friends near the town.

Arriving at Winchester

When the exiles arrived at Winchester, they met with a hostile reception. Men 'under arms' gathered noisily around the house where they were to lodge. They were militiamen from the town and neighbourhood who had earlier in the day escorted Hessian prisoners from the town 'further into the country'. They did not want the Quakers in Winchester. Lieutenant Smith and Isaac Zane failed to allay their fears or persuade them to disperse. The crowd demanded the immediate departure of the exiles, preferably to Staunton 'as first ordered'. When they did not disperse, Smith and Zane again interceded with them. It was finally agreed that the Quakers could remain so long as they were under strict guard, that no Friends were allowed to 'converse' with them and they were confined to their lodgings until the Lieutenant received further directions from the Congress and the Governor of Virginia. The tumult subsided. Pemberton attributed their escape from injury to 'Divine Providence'. That evening, the exiles agreed that they should represent their situation to the Governor and Council of Virginia, explaining how they came to be sent into the province 'by the arbitrary power of unrelenting men' and as was their practice, 'appointed a Committee for that purpose'.[35] Pemberton was convinced that 'the industrious malevolence of our persecutors at home in dispersing their falsehoods and forgeries among the people, where we were to pass' was responsible for the hostility they met en route. An instance of this was apparent when, on opening a packet directed to the Lieutenant of Augusta County in their presence, it was found to contain 'the wicked forgery relating to intelligence from Spank town yearly meeting' which he conceded they had 'done too little to refute in our several publication . . . only to find it captivates the minds of the ignorant & deluded multitude'. Their remonstrance to Congress was prepared that afternoon, 'considered, transcribed & signed'. The county lieutenant also wrote to Congress to seek clarification of his orders in relation to the prisoners. He and they exchanged letters and they were sent off together. The exiles requested some small changes in the letter of the county lieutenant, believing they were harmful to the society. The county lieutenant described his predicament:

> The peculiar situation of these prisoners has left me at a loss what part to take. On examining the papers addressed to the sheriff, I found the orders so exceedingly confused that I could not discover upon what terms the prisoners should be received, nor in what manner they were to be supported during their continuance here.

He had been informed by the sheriff that they had been sent to Winchester at public expense and that the prisoners expected to be maintained in this way while confined here. But he had received no orders to make such provision and it was not 'the usual mode of treating men of their order in this State'. Quite simply, he did not want responsibility for the prisoners.

> The inhabitants in this part of the country, are, in general, much exasperated against the whole Society of Quakers. The people were taught to suppose these people were Tories, and the leaders of the Quakers, – and two more offensive stigmas, in their estimation, could not be fixed upon men; in short, they determined not to permit them to remain in Winchester, for fear of their holding a correspondence with the Friends in adjoining counties. It was with the utmost exertion of my influence with an enraged multitude, that I prevented the greatest violence being offered to these men, and that only upon a promise that they should be continued here no longer than Congress should give orders for their removal.

Though their behaviour since their arrival had been inoffensive, the lives of the prisoners were in danger should they remain in Winchester.[36]

The exiles prefaced their queries by outlining the circumstances of their removal and how 'they remonstrated repeatedly' to the President and Supreme Council of the State of Pennsylvania,

> the injustice of the proceeding, against them, and asserting their innocence, demanded a hearing as the inherent right of every freeman, but could obtain none. They were ordered to be *sent to Virginia unheard*. In order to avail themselves hereafter, they protested regularly against all the proceedings, respecting them as *arbitrary, unjust, and unwarranted by any law*. They were removed from their families by force (after having again protested against all the actors under the President and Council,) to Reading, where writs of habeas corpus, *allowed by the Chief Justice of Pennsylvania, were served on their keepers, who refused to obey them.* They were removed from thence to S. Pauling near the line of Maryland, where they again protested against the power of their keepers to carry them beyond that line. They were then brought to the state of Virginia, where they protested in the same manner. All these protests were regularly made in the presence of witnesses.

The exiles prepared a list of legal questions for their captors. Addressed to the County Lieutenant John Smith, who was already in a state of confusion over his orders, they queried whether he believed them to be prisoners of Congress or the Council of Pennsylvania or prisoners of war. If they were prisoners of Congress, did he have any authority to take charge of them? If he deemed them prisoners of the Council, did the papers he had received give him authority to take charge of them and if he considered himself authorized to take charge of them, would he provide for their comfortable accommodation at Winchester, 'according to their character and stations, should the papers referred to direct'?

Remonstrance to Congress

The exiles described how they were now under strict guard in Winchester, where they had been sent on Congress's recommendation 'on suspicion of being dangerous men, inimical to our country, and holding correspondence with the British army'. As before, they utterly denied the truth of this accusation. It was on Congress's information that the President and Council of Pennsylvania 'have banished us to a part of this Continent of which we have heard very disagreeable accounts, but which, from our short experience, far exceeds the description'. The lieutenant had not received instructions to take charge of us or provide for our support. 'He has only undertaken to provide for our personal safety until he receives further instructions from you'.

> In this difficult situation we now find ourselves among strangers, whose passions and prejudices have been excited against us; who, from the manner of our being sent here, are impressed with a notion that we have been convicted of some heinous offences, and cannot be persuaded that any public body in America, would so severely punish men on bare suspicion, and who disclaim the right of the Council of Pennsylvania to send persons so circumstanced out of their own government.

False information regarding them had been circulated, one packet being opened in their presence 'was found to contain nothing but a newspaper fraught with anonymous falsehoods and forgeries, tending to render us odious in the eyes of the people'. They protested that since the President and Council claimed that they wished 'only to secure our persons, and prevent our correspondence . . . places might have been found for that purpose without endangering our lives'. If the President and Council 'were ignorant of the state of this country' that might be an excuse for sending them there. They protested as before that had they received a hearing, they would be able to remove 'every suspicion entertained against us'. It was pointless 'to go through the many arguments we have already used to the Council and yourselves. It is sufficient to remind you that we are reduced to our present dangerous situation by your means; and as the Council have no pretence of jurisdiction in this place, on the principles of justice and humanity, you ought to extricate us from it'. If the members of Congress really believe in the principles of liberty so often found in their publications, they should not be offended by 'the firmness 'with which we have thought proper to assert it'. The Governor and Council of Virginia, however, received a fuller account of their circumstances.[37]

Life in Winchester

Loneliness, boredom, isolation, a sedentary existence and living among strangers are all part of the hallmarks of banishment. The cases examined in this book are of groups, mostly small, with the exception of the Acadians, but all except the Acadians, were separated from their families and former employments. They were also transported to an alien climate and an unfamiliar terrain to which they found it difficult to adjust. What banishment meant to the exiles in personal terms is less easy to discern since their letters could be censored and their wives complained that they could not write freely. Some indication of the personal loss they anticipated was perhaps best expressed in one public statement they made before leaving the city. They complained they had been banished 'unheard, into an obscure corner of a country, near three hundred miles distant from our parents, our wives, our children, our dear and tender connections, friends and acquaintance' from whom, they derived 'protection, assistance, comfort, and every endearing office' and to whom they owed the reciprocal duties of care. Their lives had been lived in close-knit communities, yet were linked to much wider networks of family and Friends that transcended boundaries and extended across oceans. Kinship networks clearly supported the wives and families they left behind.[38] Despite the incidence of violence they encountered as they passed through Pennsylvania and Maryland and on arrival at Winchester, it was also a notable feature of their journey that everywhere they went, in the different towns and inns where they stopped and lodged along the way, they knew people, they had Friends. Deposited in Winchester, the exiles expressed 'their earnest longing for news of their families and the public prints'. The health of their children and wives, two of whom were pregnant when they left Philadelphia, was a constant worry. Correspondence was irregular, dependent on who was passing through Winchester or going to or coming from Philadelphia.[39] The exiles were discrete in their private correspondence in commenting on politics lest they be misunderstood and it compound their problems. Co-religionists were a source of comfort and information. Some came specifically to visit them, often bringing gifts of food and drink. Others were travelling in the light, carrying the gospel to dark corners of the land or going to or from quarterly meetings in neighbouring states or monthly meetings such as in nearby Hopewell. In their journals and correspondence, they wrote about the frequency of their Quaker meetings, about the texts they adopted, which Friends were moved by the spirit to speak, and when meetings were silent. Their meetings were attended by local Friends and others who were interested in or merely curious about their forms of worship. The size of their meetings grew, sometime attracting as many as 60, 70 and even 80 people so that when they were offered access to local premises used by Lutherans and Calvinists, they accepted. The exiles were also visited by local and state dignitaries, among whom was John Augustine Washington, brother of the general, and one of the Fairfaxes with whom they discussed agriculture. In terms of news, they appear to have been relatively well informed. From a variety of sources, they learnt about recent events – about Burgoyne's defeat at Saratoga, the heavy casualties on both sides at the battle of Germantown and General Howe's bloodless entry into Philadelphia.[40]

Easing of restrictions

During their first week in Winchester, no person was allowed to converse with the prisoners at Mr Bush's, exception having been taken to Friends who had visited them on their first night. Thereafter, people wanting to converse with the exiles had to obtain permission from their landlord. The prisoners learnt that the riot which had greeted them on their first evening had been deliberately orchestrated to discredit them lest their influence was such as to persuade young men in the vicinity not to sign up for the patriot cause. On 6 October, they were able to take their first walk, having obtained written permission to go as far as the spring attended by a sentinel. They could talk only among themselves. A while later they were given permission to walk anywhere in the town but only during the daytime. One of their number but not a Quaker, Drewitt Smith, obtained permission to practise as a doctor and with an assistant to go anywhere in the town and countryside to see patients.[41]

Accommodation

Accommodation remained something of a problem. Bush's lodging house was too small to accommodate all the Philadelphians and some found lodgings at Friends' houses in the locality. When the Board of War informed the county lieutenant that the exiles were expected to pay for their own accommodation and expenses, Bush sought to raise his rents. His offer of a daily rate of 12s 6d for which the exiles had to provide their own bedding, drink (water excepted) and washing was too high and alternatives were sought. At this point in their exile, the Philadelphia Quakers reviewed their journal and established a committee to revise it.[42]

Sickness and death

The almost constant cold and dampness affected the health of all and Thomas Wharton suffered a continual battle with gout. The affliction struck him within a week of his arrival and remained with him until his return to Philadelphia. At times, a doctor bled him, but that did little to relieve the pain in his head. John Hunt died on 31 March 1778 from complications following the amputation of his left leg. Wharton placed the blame for his death on the authorities who condoned their 'unjustly suffering'. James Pemberton recorded in his *Memoirs* that on 28 February, Thomas Gilpin 'appeared in a very unfavourable way, being reduced to great weakness, though not afflicted with much pain'. A few days later, he recorded that 'our fellow sufferer, Thomas Gilpin, was taken from this transitory life, having borne his sickness with great patience. He was favoured with his understanding to the last'. He was only 48 years of age. The day after his death on 3 March, he was buried in the Friends' graveyard at Hopewell.[43]

Escapes

On 9 December, William Drewitt Smith (a druggist or doctor) went for a routine ride but did not return though the exiles had agreed to keep each other informed of their movements. Two months later, on 16 February, Thomas Pike, the fencing master, also disappeared. Neither man was a Quaker. Both escapes brought repercussions for those they left behind and Drewitt Smith returned to a mixed reception in Philadelphia[44] The measures adopted after Pike's escape had more serious consequences, especially as it coincided with accusations against Owen Jones, Jr (who had acted as substitute for his elderly father), of speculating 'in the conversion of gold to Continental currency to the debasement of the bills'. On the basis of letters that had been intercepted, the Board of War ordered that Jones be closely confined and that all the exiles be removed to the more distant town of Staunton, their original destination. Access to writing materials was withdrawn except if used in the presence of the county lieutenant until such time as 'they affirmed that they would not act "against the Independency of the United States of America"'. These demands prompted further appeals to Congress and the Supreme Executive Council and the employment of a local attorney, Alexander White, to plead their case before the Congress, then meeting at York and the Council at Lancaster.[45]

The exiles challenged the justice of these orders arguing that they were no more valid than those which had carried them into exile in the first place. They declared that their correspondence had related solely to family matters and that the county lieutenant declined to censor their letters. In dealing with local tradesmen, they had always used local continental currency. Gold had been used in only one transaction. As for moving to Staunton, it was virtually impossible, given the weather and the condition of the roads, besides which, the age and health of some of their number 'made such a venture hazardous, especially as it was not known what facilities would be available to them there'. Congress postponed any decision until 5 January, while the Supreme Executive Council declined to consider the case since the exiles were 'Prisoners of the United States'. Congress could therefore either release the exiles or restrain them.[46]

Thomas Wharton wrote to his cousin, Thomas Wharton Jr, president of the Supreme Executive Council, for the first time, describing their hardships and requesting that they not be sent to Staunton but he was hardly diplomatic. 'Thou gave thy consent to this Unheard of Cruelty, without so much of a single Proof being taken to justify the same.' He urged his cousin to consider 'that, it is by virtue of your Warrant We were seized and made Prisoners, and therefore all the Hardships and Distresses which we may Suffer lays at your door,' he continued. A similar letter from fellow exile Edward Penington was enclosed with his own.[47] When President Thomas Wharton Jr, did write to Thomas Wharton the exile, it was to inform him of the measures to be taken against traitors, especially those who had assisted the British during the occupation of the city. He also sent an extract from this letter to Rachel, Wharton's wife, with the proposed penalties that included the confiscation of estates and caused consternation among the exiles' wives. Good news arrived on 25 January when it was learnt that the move to Staunton was suspended.[48]

The women left behind

Like other women who found themselves in revolutionary situations, the wives of the Virginia exiles could draw not only on the support of the wider Quaker community and their network of kinfolk, but also drew strength from their growing experience of managing their households and providing for their families. In late January, Sarah Logan Fisher wrote in her diary that she intended to visit her husband in the spring. Several other wives were contemplating the same thing should there be no prospect of their release in the spring. She did not relish the prospect of the journey, believing it would be attended 'with great difficulty if not danger', adding, 'A voyage to England would appear a triffle to it'.[49] There was widespread support for the exiles, especially from Quaker Meetings in the state. There was talk of a prisoner exchange. In February and March, a veritable stream of

Quakers and prisoners' wives visited Lancaster and York on their behalf. On 15 March, the exiles received word from Lancaster 'that four of our near relatives and wives . . . had come up there a few days before to use their endeavours to obtain justice from our persecutors, and a release from our unmerited banishment'. They were Phoebe Pemberton, wife of Israel, Mary Pleasants, wife of Samuel, Susanna Jones, wife of Owen and Eliza Drinker, Henry's wife.[50] Mary Pleasants wrote to George Washington on behalf of herself and 'the rest of the suffering and afflicted parents, wives, and near connections'. They had received news of the death of one of the 'Virginia exiles' and that divers others were 'much indisposed'. The women sought Washington's support to allow one or more wagons and their drivers to carry medical supplies to the men. Washington sent the letter to President Wharton for his concurrence.[51] In Winchester, Thomas Wharton fretted over the Council's dalliance. 'I see but little prospect of a return to My Dear Connections while this Civil War continues'.[52]

However, in March 1778, the Council informed Congress that the improvement in existing conditions would allow the exiles to return 'without danger to the commonwealth or the common cause of America'. Anderson argues that both the Council and Congress had come to believe that holding the exiles was damaging the American cause. On 16 March, Congress ordered the Board of War to provide for the prisoners' release but it was 8 April before the decision was sent to the exiles. On the same day, Francis Bailey and Captain James Long received instructions to go to Winchester to escort the prisoners back to Pennsylvania. Initially they were to be released at Shippenburg, but at the exiles' request, this was changed to Lancaster. They would not, however, be reimbursed for any expenses. Thomas Wharton, Jr., instructed Bailey and Lang to treat the former prisoners 'with that polite attention and care which is due from men who act upon the highest motives to Gentlemen whose station in life entitles them to respect, however they may differ in political sentiments from those in whose power they are'. These orders were very different from those of the previous year.[53] News of their impending release reached the exiles when James Pemberton received a letter from Timothy Matlock, the Council secretary. It cautioned against returning precipitously in violation of existing laws. They needed permission from the Council or Congress or Washington to cross American lines in order to reach Philadelphia, which was still held by the British. Though Lang and Bailey arrived in Winchester on 17 April, their horses needed resting and the Quakers were advised to go on ahead and the escort would catch up with them at Frederick, Maryland. Furnished with passes from Bailey and Lang, '[t]he exiles began their journey in small groups from their scattered lodgings. Wharton and Charles Eddy moved out on the eighteenth; others followed their example the next day. On the morning of the twenty-first, Wharton, together with Eddy, Penington and the three Fishers, linked up with the main body at John Hough's house in Loudoun County east of South Mountain . . . . From there they travelled at a leisurely pace to Lancaster, arriving at the state's temporary seat-of-power on the twenty-fourth'.[54]

Henry Drinker and James Pemberton called on Thomas Wharton, Jr. the next day seeking to arrange an appearance before the full Council. At Wharton's suggestion they submitted a written statement, which demanded that they be restored to 'the full enjoyment of liberty [of which] we have been so long deprived'. Once again, the Council refused to admit them but issued an order to each prisoner 'which shall be deemed a discharge'. There was some disagreement over what this meant. The exiles would have preferred 'pardon' or 'parole', but the Council considered it an exoneration.[55] Two days later and after an absence of eight months, the exiles entered Philadelphia, still occupied by the British. James Pemberton recorded in his *Memoirs* how 'as we approached the city of Philadelphia, we observed the devastation committed by parties of the English army in their excursions – the fences being generally laid waste, and the fields of grain and corn left exposed – together with houses destroyed, and left desolate; which sorrowful prospect prevails generally within a few miles round the city'.[56]

Hostility to the Quakers

Though the Quakers were only one of a number of dissident religious groups, they were pre-eminent among them. They had once dominated the colony of Pennsylvania, but their numbers and influence were significantly reduced by the time of the Revolution. Even so, they were known for their wealth and conspicuous for their attempt to keep a low profile in the contest between Britain and the colonies. With the British in occupation of Philadelphia, Eliphalet Dyer wrote to Joseph Trumbull from Lancaster about how the hopes expressed in his last letter had been dashed:

> we then entertained that the Enemy could never penetrate the Country & possess themselves of the (*great*) Capital of this State yet all this they have done & without any loss or may say almost without a gun being fired at them since instead of the Country rising for their defence & surrounding & harassing the Enemy in every Movement the Militia which were Collected have principally run of [f] & left the genll with his Continental forces to shurk for himself. This State is torn to pieces by factions in Government, Quaker, Dunker, Milese & Moravians in religion whose principles not only prevent them from fighting but Induces them to disaffect others & to give all possible Aid to the Enemy. (Moravians excepted).[57]

Opinions did not change following the return of the exiles. 'Nothing can equal the barefaced Falsehood of the Quakers & Tories in this City', wrote Samuel Adams. 'These Quakers are in general a sly artful People, not altogether destitute, as I conceive, of worldly Views in their religious Profession'.[58] Writing after the British army had quit Philadelphia, Josiah Bartlett wrote home 'how [t]he faces in Philadelphia were much altered but the Whigs are returning fast, so that it begins to look more natural'. As for the Quakers, 'The majority of the Quakers remain the same dark, hidden, designing hypocrites as formerly – however as the laws of this State are very strict against all persons who do not take the Oath of allegiance to the State and abjuration of the King of England, not allowing of their buying or selling, receiving debts and in short nearly outlawing them, the Quakers many and I believe most of them are coming in with a sanctified phiz and taking the oath of affirmation, for if you touch their worldly interest you touch their conscience and their best beloved deity'.[59]

According to Marietta and Rowe, the 'Quakers suffered most from the new state government. Their homes were entered violently and all sorts of personal effects were confiscated. More than three dozen Quakers were arrested and seventeen exiled to Virginia without trial or conviction'. Robert Oaks argues that the coming of the Revolution did not require the Quakers to find new policies in response to it for they could simply continue to obey 'the rulers God had set over them'. Royal officials made few demands of them, requiring neither oaths nor much by way of goods and services. The problem for the Quakers came when the patriots 'demanded proof of their support for the new regime'. What happened next was an episode 'conducted throughout in a most arbitrary and unjust manner, and was prompted largely by hysteria and vindictiveness . . . the conduct of the affair was unnecessarily severe in the light of the actual behaviour, advanced age, and peaceful demeanor of the accused'.[60] 'Nothing that the British had done' observed Leonard Levy 'equaled the violation of privacy rights inflicted by Pennsylvania on its "Virginia Exiles" in defiance of the state constitution'.[61]

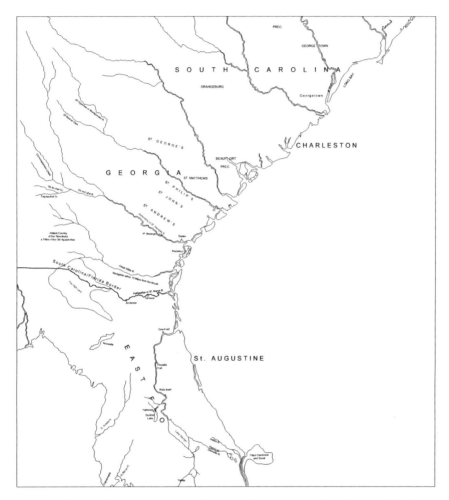

MAP 6 *The southern colonies, Charleston to St. Augustine [detail from de Brahm et al.,* A General Map of the Southern British Colonies in America *(1776)].*

9

'Strangers and prisoners in a strange land', St. Augustine 1780–1

After a siege of six weeks, Charleston, South Carolina, the only city in the southern states worthy of the name, situated at the tip of the peninsula between the Ashley and Cooper rivers, and major Atlantic seaport, surrendered to the British on 12 May 1780. They occupied it for the next two years. Three months later, on 16 August, the British at Camden inflicted the heaviest defeat suffered by the rebels during the course of the war. Of General Horatio Gates's forces, which numbered more than 3,000 Continentals and militia, over 1,000 men were killed or wounded and 800 taken prisoner. It was also in the southern states, especially the Carolinas and Georgia, where pre-war social and political tensions were most acute, that partisan militias with scores to settle could not be contained within the conventions of the rules of war and the law of nations. Though the years from 1776 to 1779 were relatively quiet, when the British launched their southern campaign in the belief that pro British sentiment was strong in the region, civil war raged thereafter. It was mistakenly anticipated that those supporting the British as well as those defeated by them would accept protections and swear oaths of allegiance to the king, so returning them to their former status as British subjects under the crown.[1]

Sir Henry Clinton, Commander in Chief of the British forces, described the articles of capitulation of the city of Charleston as 'formed in the mildest spirit of moderation throughout, with a view of convincing those misguided people that Great Britain was more inclined to reconciliation than to punishment'. Most important was the stipulation that the town and its fortifications be surrendered; all Continental troops become prisoners of war until exchanged; militiamen be returned to their homes as prisoners on parole; and everyone in the city became a prisoner on parole. Also, the sick and wounded were to be cared for, private property protected, officers were allowed to keep their horses, swords, pistols and baggage.[2] The use of paroles was central to the agreement. A parole was essentially a voluntary agreement dependent for its enforcement on concepts of honour and shame, but the violation of parole could have serious consequences. Major General William Moultrie in a letter to Colonel Balfour defined it as follows – 'A parole is a sacred act between parties, which if violated on either side, is void in itself'. The British general Cornwallis, Clinton's subordinate, and the senior American officer in Charleston, Major General William Moultrie met to discuss one such problem in June 1780, which resulted, somewhat surprisingly, in the referral of the issue to Congress. That this was agreed by both sides reflects the delicacy of the issue. Congress resolved that if it was 'properly' informed that a US citizen who was a prisoner of war had breached his parole, it would investigate the incident 'in accordance with the law of nations and the rules of war' and 'that in the meantime there is no cause to apprehend, from any such instance said to have happened, that prisoners who have duly observed their paroles can, upon any just principles, incur the danger of suffering by means of the misconduct of any other'.[3]

What led to the above resolution was the case of South Carolina Judge Henry Pendleton. When William Moultrie responded to the request of General Cornwallis that he meet with him at General Patterson's quarters, Moultrie found himself:

> Very politely received in the drawing room, upstairs; after some little conversation respecting his rout[e] through our backcountry, and telling me what a fine country we had, and that he had taken all our stores, laid in different places; he then informed me that Mr. Pendleton had broke his parole, and was gone off; he therefore hoped I would order him back, or the officers who were held prisoners at Haddrell's-point should suffer for it: upon which I told him, I was not accountable for any man's parole but my own: he said he had a right to discriminate, and take some one in confinement, for Mr Pendleton. I told him he might do as he pleased, but that his lordship was too much of a soldier, not to know that every one was accountable but for his own parole, and for no other; besides, that Mr Pendleton was a civil officer, I therefore could have nothing to do with him: I told his lordship that I would write to Congress, for them to decide upon the matter: upon which he was satisfied, and said he would forward the letter to Sir Henry Clinton; which letter I wrote, dated the thirtieth of June, and sent it to Lord Cornwallis, who forwarded it to Sir Henry Clinton; and by him sent to the President, who laid my letter before Congress; and upon investigating the matter, they passed a resolve, justifying Mr. Pendleton's conduct; and sent a copy, of the resolve, to Sir Henry Clinton.[4]

Pendleton's justification for his alleged breach of parole was that on the day he made his escape, he was informed by a friend, who had it from a

British officer (Captain Constable) that if he did not get away that day, it was determined, by a party of Tories headed by William Holliday, who kept the corner tavern, to take him from his quarters that night, and hang him at the town gate. Pendleton counterfeited Major Benson's hand, and made out a pass, by which means he got away.

In his letter to Congress dated 30 June, Moultrie informed the President of Congress Samuel Huntington that it was:

> the earnest desire and expectation of his Excellency Lord Cornwallis and the Hon. Brig. Gen. Patterson, that the Hon. The Continental Congress do interpose in this affair, and give the speedy remedy which is due in such cases by laws of nations and of war; and which they have formally demanded through me; intimating, at the same time, that unless Mr. Justice Pendleton is by authority ordered immediately to return to his parole, the prisoners now on parole will suffer for this offence.

He pointed out though it was probably unnecessary for him to do so, that:

> [s]uch a violation of honor, as well as those rules and principles which all civilized nations have established and ever held sacred in the conduct of war, I am sure by the respectable body over which you preside will be deemed highly criminal, and as meriting the severest punishment; as in its consequences the misery of thousands may be involved; and such an offence is an injury to mankind in general.

Moultrie also took advantage of the occasion to inform Congress that the 'situation of the continental hospital, and the officers and privates, prisoners of war, is truly distressing, and such as calls for the immediate attention of Congress'.[5]

Banishment

Early on the morning of Sunday, 27 August, 1780, 29 people, all prisoners on parole in Charleston:

> were suddenly taken from their habitations, by armed Soldiers of the British Troops under the direction of Major Benson, and Captain MacMahon, by order as they said of General Cornwallis, and Felon like, conducted to the upper part of the Exchange, and there detained under an Officers Guard till about Ten of the Clock, when Boats being provided for their reception . . . conveyed [them] from thence down to the Armed Ship, *Sandwich*, under command of Capt. William Bett, moored near to Fort Johnson's ruins. The Captain received them on board politely, but knew nothing of their coming until half an hour

before their arrival. . . He apologized for not being able to entertain them properly with Dinner . . . [Furthermore] being unprovided with Bedding, and every other necessary suitable to our circumstances, the Captain undertook for our relief, by going up to Town to wait on the Commandant there, Col. Nesbit Balfour, and obtained leave for our friends, not only to supply us with necessarys, but also for their coming on board to visit us. We also had civil usage from all the under Officers and Men on board, and by the Evening were furnished from our homes with Bedding &c.

This was how Josiah Smith Junior, one of those detained by the soldiers, described his experience. A merchant of Charleston, he kept a detailed journal of events, from the seizure of the 29 men to their release and arrival in Philadelphia almost a year later.[6]

The prisoners

These were no ordinary prisoners, as the deference extended towards them suggests. The most senior of those taken up was Christopher Gadsden, the Lieutenant Governor of South Carolina, along with three members of the Privy Council – Thomas Ferguson, David Ramsay and Richard Hutson. Early in the siege of Charleston, General Lincoln had urged the governor, John Rutledge, and the Council to leave town, 'their being in the country would keep up the civil authority, and be more useful than they could possibly be, by staying in town'. The Governor had strongly objected to this because it would reflect badly on him. Eventually, it was agreed by the prisoners on 12 April that the Governor and three of the Council left the town and the Lieutenant Governor Christopher Gadsden and five others of the Council 'remained within the lines'. A significant number of the other detainees were members of the House of Representatives but also held additional civil and military offices, such as Peter Timothy, Clerk of the House of Representatives; John Edwards, member of the House of Representatives and Commissioner of the Navy Boat; Edward Blae, First Commissioner of the Navy Boat and member of the House of Representatives; Edward Rutledge, member of the House of Representatives; Hugh Rutledge, Judge of the Admiralty Court and member of the House of Representatives; Anthony Toomer, Isaac Holmes and William Hazell Gibbes, all members of the House of Representatives; Thomas Heyward, Assistant Judge and member of the House of Representatives; Alexander Moultrie, Attorney General and member of the House of Representatives; Josiah Smith Jun', Commissioner of the Navy Boat and member of the House of Representatives; John Loveday, Messenger to the Privy Council; John Sansum, Deputy Marshall to the Admiralty Court; Richard Lushington and Jacob Read, Captains in the Charles Town Militia;

Thomas Savage Gentleman; John Ernest Poyas; Doctor John Budd; Doctor Peter McCrady as well as George Flagg who was described as a painter and John Todd, an Innholder. David Ramsay was convinced that the reason for their removal was that Balfour believed that the 'silent example' of such influential men was deterring some Charlestonians from returning to their former allegiance and accepting British 'protection'.[7]

From the first, the prisoners challenged the legitimacy of their detention; they tried to hold the British army to account, and sought to fix responsibility where it lay. They insisted that any instructions regarding them should be put in writing; otherwise, they would have no authority. They would not forget the rough manner in which they had been seized – 'felon-like' was how Josiah Smith described it. As in the case of the Philadelphia exiles, concerted efforts were made to discredit them with local residents. David Ramsay, who was also one of their number, wrote in his *History of the Revolution in South Carolina* how 'reports were immediately circulated to their disadvantage, and every circumstance managed so as to induce a general belief, that they were all apprehended for violating their paroles, and for concerting a scheme for burning the town, and massacreing (sic) the loyal subjects'. Guards were placed at their houses and private papers were examined.[8] Aware that they had not, 'at least wilfully' broken their paroles, the prisoners 'were not a little anxious to know' why they had merited 'such Cruel Treatment'. By noon the next day, they had drafted a memorial to Colonel Nesbit Balfour, the Commandant of Charleston, described by William Moultrie as a 'proud, haughty Scot' who 'carried his authority with a very high hand', which they delivered to Captain Bett. The detainees protested that they were 'Citizens of Charles Town' and that:

> by the articles of Capitulation agreed to by Sir Henry Clinton, Citizens were to be considered as Prisoners of Warr on Parole, and to be secured in their Persons, & Property, while they observed their Paroles: that after the surrender, they severally gave their Paroles acknowledging themselves to be Prisoners of Warr, upon Parole to his Excellency Sir Henry Clinton, and thereby engaged until exchanged or otherwise released . . . , to remain in Charles Town, until permitted to go out by the Commandant, and that they should not in the mean time do or cause to be done anything prejudicial to the Success of his Majesty's Arms, or have Intercourse, or hold correspondence with his Enemies, and to surrender themselves when required, which Parole your Memorialists have endeavour'd strictly to observe, nor are they conscious of the least violation of it. . . . . Your Memorialists cannot conjecture the Reasons of such extraordinary severity, nor by what means they have forfeited those privileges expressly secured to them by the Articles of Capitulation – they request that full and speedy inquiry may be made and wish to know what is the nature of their offence and who are their accusers.

Before noon, Major Benson boarded the *Sandwich*, and presented Gadsden with a paper stating that, on the orders of the Commandant, he was to inform him:

> that my Lord Cornwallis being highly incensed at the late perfidious Revolt of many of the Inhabitants of this province and being well informed by papers that have fallen into his hands since the defeat of the Rebel Army, of the means that have been taken by several People on parole in Charles Town to promote and forment this Spirit of Rebellion. His Lordship in order to secure the quiet of the province, finds himself under the necessity to direct the Commandant to order several Persons to change their place of Residence on Parole from Charles Town to St. Augustine . . .

The document was unsatisfactory being neither signed nor dated. That evening, Captain McMahon came on board the *Sandwich*, and delivered a verbal message to the company:

> That Lord Cornwallis considered the Persons sent on board this Ship to be then Prisoners on Parole, but for reasons of policy, thinks it necessary the place of their residence should be changed from Charlestown to St. Augustine. Those who think this proceeding an infringement of the Capitulation are considered as Prisoners on Board, and as such to be delivered at St. Augustine, those who dissent therefrom are to sett down their names.

Before the company had concluded its discussions of the implications of this statement, Captain McMahon left the boat and returned to Charleston without waiting for an answer. On the morning of 4 September, the Company was asked to renew their paroles for the duration of their voyage and residence at St Augustine. Lest there was any doubt over the meaning of the word 'parole', it was spelled out:

> I consider the word Parole to mean that the Gentlemen while on board, and at St. Augustine are not to do anything whatever prejudicial to his Majesty's Service. If the Gentlemen are retaken, it is not expected that they are to return to any part of America under the British Government, but are to consider themselves on Parole.

When all but Lieutenant Governor Gadsden had complied, the discussion turned to practicalities. The detainees enquired about rations and were assured that three weeks allowance for all of them was then on board. They had already asked Captain Bett whether, when at St Augustine, they could send for goods from Charleston and have them conveyed at government expense. They also asked for the commandant's permission to carry with them 'Fifty barrils of Rice and other provisions'. These terms were agreed.[9]

Moultrie's Intercession

As the senior commanding officer of the American prisoners, William Moultrie sought to avert the departure of those sent on board the *Sandwich*. He had not known about this affair until he read about in a paper on 29 August, where he found the names of the men listed. They included:

> the names of a number of the most respectable gentlemen, inhabitants of this state; most of whose characters I am so well acquainted with that I cannot believe they would have been guilty of any breach of their paroles, or any article of the capitulation, or done any thing to justify so rigorous a proceeding against them: I therefore think it my duty, as the senior continental officer, prisoner under the capitulation, to demand a release of those gentlemen, particularly such as are entitled to the benefit of that act. This harsh proceeding demands my particular attention; and I do, therefore, in behalf of the United States of America require that they be admitted immediately to return to their paroles; as their being hurried on board a prison-ship, and, I fear, without being heard, is a violation of the 9th article of the capitulation. If this demand cannot be complied with, I am to request that I may have leave to send an officer to Congress to represent this grievance, that they may interpose in behalf of these gentlemen in the manner they shall think proper.

Moultrie received a reply not from Balfour, who refused to answer the letter 'wrote in such exceptionable and unwarrantable terms', but from Benson, his subordinate, who informed Moultrie that Balfour would not 'receive any further application from him upon the subject of it'.[10]

Departure

Until their removal from the *Sandwich*, the detainees 'were daily receiving necessaries' from their friends in Charleston, and 'favour'd with the Company of many of them on board'. All were well treated by Captain Bett and his officers, receiving breakfast, dinner and coffee and in the evening 'at his own Table in turn, as there was room for it'. On Sunday, learning of their imminent departure, the vessel was crowded with friends and relatives who 'came down to take a melancholy leave of us',

> and a grievous sight it was indeed to Husbands parting with their distressed Wives, Fathers bidding Farewell to their beloved Children, and Friends separating from Friend, perhaps many never to meet together again.

'This Tearful season' ended when they were transferred to the transport ship, *Fidelity*. A much smaller ship than the *Sandwich*, already on board were 11 of their fellow citizens. Two of those originally taken into custody, Thomas Savage and Peter Faysseroux, were released, the former because he was 'in a very bad State of health' and the latter, a doctor at the Continental Hospital, where conditions were very poor, was presumably needed in Charleston, while another, Alexander Moultrie, was permitted to travel separately with his family. Smith named the additional deportees – mostly political and military figures, but also including the Reverend John Lewis, rector of St Paul's parish. The others were John Neufville, late of the Privy Council; William Massey, Colonel and Deputy Muster Master General; William Johnston and Thomas Grimball, who were members of the House of Representatives; Robert Cochran was a Powder Receiver; Thomas Hall, a late Captain in the 2nd Regiment; William Hall, Commander of St Briggt Notre Dame; William Livingston, late Captain in the Militia; John Mouat, Lieutenant in Cannonier Company and James Hampden Thomson, teacher at the Academy in Charleston.[11]

The journey

The voyage to St Augustine was unremarkable but it was uncomfortable not because of the weather but because of the crowded conditions on board. Those banished to St Augustine were accompanied by 26 of their 'servants' (that is, slaves). Also making the journey to St Augustine were 15 invalid soldiers. Ten seamen had also been put on board to defend the ship in the event of an attack by the enemy, in addition to the regular crew which, according to Josiah Smith's calculation, made a total of 106 souls. 'We were,' he wrote, 'not only much crowded under Deck, but also found it very disagreeable above from the Crowd of Sheep, Hoggs, and Poultry, laid in for our use on board and at St. Augustine'.

They weighed anchor at 7 o'clock on Tuesday morning, 5 September and, helped by favourable winds, reached the bar at St Augustine early Friday morning. Their voyage had taken 72 hours, during which time they did not see another vessel. It would take twice as long to disembark. Bad weather delayed their landing and it was not until 13 September that a large schooner was able to get alongside their vessel. It took off military equipment for the government, 32 pounds of rice and 15 hogsheads of rum, while the next morning, another schooner 'took on board all our Baggage, live-Stock Poultry and other provisions'. After dinner, 'the whole of our Company and Servants, went on board' – they were '37 Whites & 26 Blacks' – but the schooner ran aground on a large sandbank and they were 'obliged to spend a very disagreeable night there with very little Sleep, among Sheep, Hoggs and Poultry, most of us being put to the necessity of laying on Deck, in the Sails, and in a large Boat alongside'. They went ashore the next morning at about half past eight, to be met by William Brown, Commissary for Prisoners, who conducted them without a guard of any sort to the State House, an imposing but unfinished building. Upon learning that they had not yet breakfasted, Mr. Brown furnished them with a good one from his own house, 'of Coffee, Tea, and hott bread, well butter'd'.[12] Although proprieties such as this were observed, which reflected the class and status of the Americans, it was not an indicator of their subsequent treatment.

The parole

No sooner had the Americans finished their meal than the commissary presented them with a copy of yet another parole to which they were required to agree. Shortly after, Patrick Tonyn, Governor of East Florida, his Secretary and Lieutenant Colonel Glazier, Commandant of the Army, accompanied by several of his officers, appeared at the State House. Christopher Gadsden, acting as spokesman for the group, asked for a minor alteration in the parole and took the opportunity to complain about the harsh treatment meted out to them when first arrested. Interrupted by the Governor and Commandant, who declared they were not there to argue with him but wanted to know whether he would or would not sign the parole, Gadsden replied that his honour would not permit him to do so. When he refused, wrote Smith, 'he was taken from us by an Officer and immediately conducted to the Castle', where he was kept in close confinement. For his obduracy, Gadsden was to pay a harsh price. As he described his experience after his release, he was imprisoned in the castle for 42 weeks, during which time none of his friends were permitted to see him because of his refusal to subscribe to another parole. 'I told them I had kept the first as a Gentleman, defy'd (and do still defy) them to prove the Contrary and was determined never to take a second which wou'd imply a Breach of the first'. Again, he protested at the treatment he received when first detained, which was more severe in his case than that of his friends owing, he believed, to his superior station as Lieutenant Governor and the fact that he was not mentioned in the Capitulation. The latter, Gadsden believed, gave his captors an opportunity of treating him 'with Rigor and Contempt'. He thought it was his duty to the general cause 'to Refuse to the last giving a Second Parole', that he might be seen as a 'Standing protest against such outrageous Tyranical Conduct'. His sense of isolation deepened when orders were given to officers in the Castle not to convene (sic) with him:

> however many of them often did, and all of them behaved with Decency. I never had the least Insult offer'd me there. Once indeed there was an Order against lighting a Candle In Consequence of which [I] went without for two or three Nights, but the Pitifullness of this they were soon asham'd of themselves.

Eventually, he was allowed some exercise in being permitted to walk 40 yards from the door where he was confined.[13] Gadsden's detention was presumably intended to serve as a warning to the others. If that was the case, it served its purpose. The exiles subscribed their names to the parole despite the fact that it restricted them to much narrower bounds than they had enjoyed in Charleston. They hoped that 'in a little time our prudent conduct might induce the Commandant to enlarge our limits'. The parole dated 15 September enjoined the subscribers, designated prisoners of war, 'upon the Honour & Faith of a Gentleman, hereby severally given to Lieut. Col. Glazier Commandant of the Garrison', that while they remained in East Florida, they would 'not do anything prejudicial to the Service of his Majesty George the Third, King of Great Britain' and that they would confine themselves to the designated limits within the town of St Augustine. Having bound themselves to observe the parole, they found themselves subjected to a further humiliating ritual:

> we were desir'd to walk below Stairs to the Parade, where, near to the North Door way of the State house, was standing the Governor, Commandant and others before mentioned, who . . . directed that we should walk out, one by one, as our names were called, the which having so much the appearance of passing under the Yoke, could not but be very grating to us.[14]

Humiliation and insult were to prove daily features in the lives of the exiles. William Brown who served as an intermediary between the exiles and the Commandant informed them on their second day that general orders had been issued requiring them to attend for roll call at the State House twice a day. The demand came as a surprise 'as we had so recently pledged our Honour in our Parole to the Commandant'.

> This we could not but look upon as a kind of fresh Insult to our Persons, as it not only carried a suspicion of our Honour, but also put many of us to the inconvenience of dancing attendance in the warm part of the day, when we would rather be retired to our apartments, there to improve ourselves by Reading &c.

Recognizing that their fate was in the hands of the Commandant 'and that our Noncompliance might Induce him to plague us more in some other way', the exiles agreed that, 'however humiliating such a measure must be to us', they would comply, 'provided we were Served with the Order in Writing'. It was delivered the next day. According to the General Orders, the rebel prisoners were to appear 'at Gun Fire in the Evening, and at Guard Mounting in the Morning at the Town House where the Commissary will attend and Call the Roll of their names, and Report to the Captain of the day if any are absent'. The exiles were also required 'to put some Badge of Distinction on their Negroes and other Domesticks so as they may be known' but 'No Rebel Uniform, or any Coats in Imitation of British or French Regimentals' could be worn and if any soldier was seen or known to associate 'with any of the Rebels', he or they would be tried by court martial for disobeying orders. The exiles complied by having their 'servants' wear 'a Red colour'd Badge' made in the shape of a heart around their necks, 'the form & colour, we are told, is not pleasing to the Officers'.[15]

More detainees

A further 25 prisoners joined the Charleston exiles on 25 November. Colonel Balfour took the initiative in removing these men, explaining to General Cornwallis that he had 'been obliged to take up some more of the violent and principal men that were upon parole, and have shipped them board the *Sandwich,* just going as a convoy to St. Augustine'. He defended his action on the grounds that it was necessary. The need for this measure 'was as evident to every person, whom I consulted upon it and much pressed by Moncreiff and Simpson'. He praised the men's 'assiduity'.[16] The 25 prisoners who joined the Charleston exiles were a more diverse group than the earlier parolees. They included General Griffith Rutherford and Colonel Elijah Isaacs of the North Carolina Militia, who headed the list. Arthur Middleton was a member of the Continental Congress; Daniel DeSaussure, John Berwick and Henry Crouch were members of the Assembly; there were also Edward Weyman, Marshall of the Admiralty Court, George Abbott Hall, Collector, State Custom House, Edward Darrell, Commissioner of the Naval Board, Daniel Bourdeaux and John Spall Cripps who were merchants of Charles Town; John Wakefield, Quarter Master of Militia; Doctor Noble W. Jones, former Speaker of the Georgia House of Assembly; William Logan was a merchant, Richard Beresford was the late A. D. C. to General Moultrie; William Lee, Captain in the Militia; while Thomas Savage (from Georgia), Samuel Prioleau Junior, Philip Smith, Benjamin Cudworth, Morton Wilkinson, Benjamin Waller, Christopher Peter were all planters; and Joseph Bee and Benjamin Postell were 'vendue masters'. It was most likely the banishment of these men that prompted Thomas Bee's speech in Congress on 26 December, as a result of which George Washington was instructed to seek an exchange in his subsequent correspondence with Clinton. Like those already banished to St Augustine, the new batch of prisoners were to be removed 'without the Shadow of a charge against them'. Thomas Bee, one of the state's representatives in Congress, surmised that the reason for their removal 'was the Influence they may have on the other Inhabitants', few of whom had been induced to take up protections offered by the British. David Ramsay had drawn the same conclusion.[17]

Accommodation

The exiles in St Augustine did not suffer from want of housing, food, clothing, company or contact with their families. In these respects, they fared rather well and it was reported in Congress that they were in good spirits.[18] Vessels of various sizes sailed regularly between St Augustine and Charleston and the exiles employed agents in Charleston to purchase and despatch goods on their behalf as well as assist in business affairs. In his journal, Josiah Smith describes how the exiles set about organizing their lives in their new environment. After the first nights, when they slept on mattresses on the floor of the state house, they divided themselves into three messes. The first mess consisted of eight gentlemen who rented a stone built house with a large orange garden on the north-west corner of the Parade, which they rented for 70 pounds per annum from the rector of the town. This presumably was the Grove. The second mess was made up of 17 people who rented a large wooden house belonging to Spencer Man, which was 'very pleasantly situated near the River, on the north-east corner of our Parole Limits'. The rent was high at 120 pounds per annum. The house was two stories high and 75 feet long. It contained four large rooms on each floor 'near twenty foot square, with a Piazza the whole length on the South Side so that the four Chambers above, by having the Stairway from one Piazza to the other, are all private, and contains four Lodgers in each'. The house had extensive grounds suitable for a large garden. John Loveday, one of the exiles who was 'a professed Gardenest', was to put the garden 'into prime order' and appointed to the office of steward of the mess. Through the friendship of a number of people, it would 'soon be well stocked with Plants, herbs &c'. The third mess consisted of 12 people who took quarters in the State House 'until they could make out better accommodations'.[19]

Food

The exiles placed substantial orders for food and drink with their agents in Charleston. One order cost 85 pounds and included an order for '12 Packs playing Cards' though there was some dispute over freight charges, although previously agreed by Balfour. Food was also available locally but there were some problems. Fish was abundant, but local residents complained that since the arrival of the exiles, the price of fish was much increased. The exiles obtained leave for their servants to go out and catch fish and oysters 'for our use, and for which purpose, our Mess have this day purchased a handy & handsome Cypress built Canoe from Mr Alexander McQueen at a moderate price of Five Pounds Sterling'. When the Americans found it difficult to buy milk in St Augustine, it being expensive and shortweight, Smith's mess resolved to buy a Milch

Cow 'in order to afford us a constant supply of Milk for Breakfast & Coffee in the evening' and 'through the kind assistance of Mr. William Binnie', they purchased that day a cow and calf, 'about 8 Months old, for Five Guineas'. The price might seem high, but it was not really 'when tis consider'd that fresh Beef in Market, sells readily at Six pence the pound, and doubt not the Calf when sold there, will bring at least half that Sum'. They celebrated Christmas Day in some style. They enjoyed 'a very good dinner of Roasted Turkeys & Pig, Corn'd Beef, Ham, Plumb pudding, and pumpkin Tarts &c was provided by our Mess'. They invited the members of the mess at Parole Corner to join them and 'we dined together Thirty in number very heartily, and many of the Company as merrily Spent the Evening by a variety of Songs'.[20]

Family and friends

Boredom characterized exile regardless of location and letter writing appears to have been one of the principal ways in which exiles coped. Like the Philadelphia Quakers, what concerned the exiles most was the separation from their families. Fear of sickness, reports of sickness, especially small pox, references to death among family, wider kinship networks and business associates who often overlapped were a constant worry. The well being of their wives and children in the absence of the head of household or close relative who could support the family worried them most of all. Verbal reassurances that their immediate families were well brought comfort and relief to the exiles. Some family letters were concealed in parcels of clothing or food stuffs not because they contained incriminating information, but because they were regarded as personal and therefore private. When, following the death of his wife, George Abbot Hall, one of the company, was permitted to return to Charleston 'to see after his numerous & helpless Children there', he carried letters from Smith to his wife, to each of his four children, to his relative and attorney George Smith, to Dr W. S. Stevens and 'to Mr Wm Binnie relative to some money due our Mess for two Sheep sold by him'. Given the traffic by land and sea between Charleston and St Augustine, the exiles could often find 'a sure hand', people they knew, to carry letters for them. Smith also used a free black woman and a female slave who were sailing to Charleston as carriers on at least two occasions.[21] The exiles enjoyed a regular correspondence with their families though it was sometimes interrupted by bad weather or unforeseen incidents. Like the Quaker exiles banished to the Virginia frontier, their correspondence was monitored and suspicion was easily aroused. Smith offers little indication of how wives fared in the absence of their husbands, but David Ramsay in his *History of the American Revolution* wrote how women bolstered their husbands' resolution when they were tempted to throw in their lot with the British.

Smith identifies only one woman, the wife of Benjamin Cudworth, who travelled to St Augustine to visit her husband.[22] Families and friends learnt of their safe arrival at St Augustine relatively quickly, receiving their first news from the exiles on 22 September. Despite a gale, Smith recorded how letters from the prisoners reached Charleston in four days. It was 'a very boisterous and dangerous Season' but 'we were all safely landed . . . at this unhoped for, and disageeable Town of St. Augustine' where they were 'to remain as Prisoners of War on Parole in a very circumscribed, and we fear, Insulted situation, until released by Congress in a way of. . . .Exchange for British Prisoners in their hands'. Nothing further was heard from them for more than a month as high winds prevented ships sailing for Charleston in October. The weather got worse. It began to 'Rain and blow excessive hard', high tides flooded part of the town, the sea running 'through some of the Lanes up into the Second Street, above 150 feet from the Bay':

> The Water surrounded the whole front part of our dwelling, damaged the front fence not a little, washed away a good deal of Ground for about 20 feet within our Yard, and from the Second Street water broke into our Garden, where it lay about 48 hours, and there by destroyed all the Vegetables that we had but a little before planted out, and which had given us a fair prospect of supplying our Table very soon with lettuce, Carrots, Raddish, Mustard, Scallions, Shelots, Cabbage and other Greens, so that, as 'twere in a moment our expectations were cut off – much damage has been done to others, and 'tis thought that the Crop of Oranges will be much hurt, as the Trees appear to be blasted, both fruit and leaves changing their colour and continually dropping to the Ground.[23]

Mockery

The exiles had to endure mockery from soldiers as well as local residents. The former were more officious. The raising of the siege and suspension of operations against Savannah on 9 October was celebrated in St Augustine:

> by the shew of Colours at Sun Rising, and Triumphant situation, on the Vessells in the harbour, also by the firing of Cannon at noon, with a Royal Salute of 21 Guns from the Castle, a Dining together of Officers and Inhabitants, also a Ball at night for the Ladies. – But to Crown all, a truly ridiculous company, consisting mostly of Officers, headed by their Veteran Commandant, all of them seemingly much heated by liquor and attended by their Regimental Musick &c Paraded the Street on the following morning between 7 & 8 O'Clock, who in passing by our habitation, Insulted us with the tune of Yankey Doodle &c the which tune has also been often Struck up by the relief Guards in their Marching

to & from the Castle, doubtless by way of Insult, and in derision to our Company of suffering Americans.[24]

Two weeks later, at sunrise on 21 October, when merchants Moss and McCleod, Mr Lewis, the governor's nephew, and a young British officer called Hewlett who,

> having Spent the preceeding night at a Ball with the Ladies, . . . well warmed with Liquor in the morning when being attended with Fife & Drum and other Musick, they ambled through the principal Streets of the Town as a company of Serenadors, but when they came in Sight of our dwelling, changed their merriment into Insult by having struck up the Tune of Yankey Doodle, some of their attendants holding out Pumkins & throwing an Orange or two at the front of the House, and in this deriding manner they meanly passed our Habitation and ended their Drunken Frolick.

At roll call that evening, the company complained to the commissary in the expectation of receiving a 'proper Apology from them to us for such rude behaviour' but got only a verbal expression 'of having unintendedly disobliged' them.[25]

Private insults were not always easy to interpretate. When they first arrived, John Imsie, a shipwright formerly of Charleston, sent them 15 pumpkins but they were at a loss to explain its significance. Were they a gift or an insult? They suspected the latter because, on the night before they landed, Imsie had erected a large pair of gallows 'no doubt as a Spectacle desig'd for us'. They had not seen it as it was taken down the following morning. When they received a second 'gift' from John Imsie, of 10 large pumpkins, though sent 'in a deriding way', they would 'make a good Garnish to our table'.[26]

News

David Ramsay claimed that the exiles had only limited access to information about the struggle between Britain and her former colonies and that it was coloured in favour of the British. There is little of a political nature in Smith's journal, but he does refer to newspapers such as the *Royal South Carolina Gazette, the Jamaica Gazette* and *Rivington's Gazette,* which seems to bear out Ramsay's conclusion. Smith also learnt of Rodney's and Vaughan's capture of St Eustatius and its impact on American shipping but there is little else. Smith, however, took particular interest in the movement of ships in and out of St Augustine. He recorded the names of the vessels, what type of ships they were, the cargoes they carried, where they had come from and where they were headed.[27]

Presbyterian versus Anglican

Unlike the Philadephia Quakers, religion brought no solace to the Charleston exiles, who became embroiled in a conflict with the governor over holding their own services. Smith was the son of a Presbyterian minister and there were others among the exiles who were Presbyterians. When a rumour circulated that the Governor had taken offence at their holding religious services in their dwelling house and that the practice should be discontinued, they had already held four services. Since it was a verbal message, they told Commissary Brown that they did not think themselves bound by it and 'therefore would continue our devotions' as they had been doing 'until they received a written order sent by the governor to Mr Brown'. This summary dismissal of his instruction clearly irritated the Governor, who nonetheless put his concerns in writing to Commissary Brown and made his displeasure known. 'You are also to mention to these Gentleman, that I consider Messages deliver'd by you as sufficient weight and authenticity, and that it is in compliance of your request, that I descend to this manner of Satisfaction, which Lieut. Col. Glazier also desires may be understood to be expressive of his Sentiments'. On the substance of the issue, Governor Tonyn wrote:

> Having been informed That the Rebel Prisoners forgetful of their Parole, have very Improperly held private Meetings for the purpose of performing Divine Service agreeable to their Rebellious Principles, and as such proceedings are tho't highly Injurious to his Majesty's Government, and of a seditious Tendency, and an Infringement of their pledge of Honour. I desire you will acquaint them that such Meetings will not be allowed, and that Seats will be provided for their reception in the Parish Church, where it is expected they will observe the utmost decency.[28]

Smith maintained in his diary that their intention was only to observe the Sabbath appropriately, but they were charged with conducting 'proceedings of a seditious Tendency, and violation of our Parole and pledge of honour, this we absolutely deny', but with one exception on the part of their reader and that was not repeated. Nor did they 'so much as once court, or enjoy the company of any one Inhabitant, in our Sabbath Assemblies'. Inviting them to the parish church where seats would be provided for them and where they should observe 'the utmost decency' was 'an Insult upon our understanding'.

> for cou'd it be expected that we cou'd with the least sincerity Join in prayer for the daily destruction or disappointment of our Brethren & friends or implore Success to a Man that has countinanced every kind of Oppression & Cruelty towards our connections, and all with the view of enslaving us & our Posterity, to whom we have sworn, that we will never be Subject, while we can have the power of remaining Free Citizens of

the United States of America . . . . rather than Join in such hypocritical petitions, and perhaps be insulted with Sermons calculated to affront us, we have resolved to refuse our attendance on divine Service at the Parish Church and patiently put up with the loss of such, at our own dwelling, there silently to spend our returning Sabbaths, in the Best manner we can, by reading and meditation . . .[29]

It came as a surprise then to the exiles when, after several months, at the roll call on the evening of 19 January, Mr. Brown read to the Company 'a most extraordinary Paper or Letter' in which they were accused of ingratitude in light of the indulgences shown them. Their parole, it asserted, was simply written; it did not contain difficult legal phrasing. It was intended to make their confinement 'as easy as possible', but the prisoners had failed to make an adequate response. 'I pass over your haughty & arrogant behaviour, and shall only remark on the Improper use made of the Indulgence granted to correspond with your friends, letters have been sent from you, answers have been receiv'd from your friends in Carolina of a most dangerous Tendency, and inconsistent with the paroles you have given – I consider these as grateful returns for the Indulgencies I have granted, and the Civilities you have received. These letters will be laid before proper Judges, and due notice shall be taken of them'. He cautioned them against continuing such practices and if not they would bring down 'severe Vengeance' upon themselves.[30] The prisoners responded indignantly. Was it an indulgence, recorded Josiah Smith,

to be confined to the inner Square of the Town of St. Augustine when before our removal from Charles Town we were not prevented from walking all the Streets, around the outskirts there, even up to the lines of Fortification, and this thro' any and every part of the day.

Was it an indulgence, to be obliged to attend Roll Call Twice a day at the State House. When at Charles Town we never were requested to give our attendance, or answer to our Names until the day for reasons of policy we were order'd to change our residence from Charles Town to St. Augustine, which was the 27th August 1780.

Was it an indulgence Towards us, that we shou'd be permitted to send letters to, and receive the like from, our friends in Carolina (after being first examined by the Commissary, the Commandant, or others of the Military, and thereby the Secrets, and necessitys, of our Selves & families &c to them be made known) when no such restraint was laid upon us in Charles Town, we there having free liberty to correspond with our friends abroad, so that we were careful to write nothing contrary to the Paroles we had given after the Capitulation.

Was it an Indulgence to us, when himself or Officers did 'tis said all in their power to irritate the Inhabitants here, against our Persons, by advising them not to have any communication with us, so that through fear of Offending the Military they (with three or four excepted) were continually Shy of our Company, and of holding Conversation with us.

And as to his Civilities towards us, We know of none (unless this may be deemed one). The granting of liberty to our Servants, to go out about the harbour, and down to the Barr for the Catching of Fish and Oysters for our use, and this not done till we had through Mr Brown the Commissary, requested such leave . . .

'And as to the charge of haughty and arrogant behaviour', they were ignorant of such,

unless the declining to pull off our Hatts, or bowing our Bodies to the Gov'r Commandant, or his Officers, at passing them, can be interpreted as such, and which we do not, as Strangers and Prisoners in a Strange land, think it our duty to do, unless drawn thereto; by compliments of that sort first offered on their part. And as from their former behaviour towards us, we have no reason to expect from them Civilities of this sort, we shall be content to do without.[31]

As time passed, the circumstances of some exiles became more difficult. In March, Smith reported that two of the members of the mess – William Hazel Gibbs and Isaac Holmes whose 'supplies from Home being but small' had left the mess to take a single room at a dollar a week 'in hopes of living at much less expence' and 'confined their diet chiefly to their Rations from the Kings Store'.[32]

Washington, Clinton and The Law of Nations

While the detainees focused on the legitimacy of their detention in light of the articles of capitulation of the city of Charleston and the practical implications of their banishment, Congress framed its discussions and correspondence in broader conceptual terms, invoking the law of nations and the rules of war. When delegates from South Carolina informed Congress in late September that there were good grounds to believe that 'a number of respectable citizens of South Carolina, prisoners of war by the capitulation of Charleston', had been seized and confined 'on board a ship of war', Washington as Commander in Chief was directed to inquire of Sir Henry Clinton, the British Commander in Chief, whether such arrests had been made and for what reason. Under a flag of truce, Washington sought confirmation of this information, requesting a quick response. Clinton replied three days later, acknowledging the report, but noted that the persons detained 'had entered into a plot for the destruction of the place where they were protected, and that the officer commanding there had found it necessary to interfere'. No formal report had been made to him and he knew of it 'only from common fame'. Clinton assured Washington that Lord Cornwallis, with whom he was well acquainted, was 'incapable of straining the laws to take away the lives and liberties of the innocent'. In his response dated 16 October 1780, Washington begged to differ. The nature of the 'supposed plot' to destroy Charleston appeared 'ill-founded' and 'in the present situation of things improbable'. He wished that he could agree with Clinton 'as to the spirit which actuates your officers', but letters recently intercepted (copies of which he enclosed) 'breathe a very different temper'.

> They not only profess a flagrant breach of the capitulation of Charleston, and a violation of the laws of nations, but, under whatever forced description the unhappy objects of the severity are placed, it is in a form and carried to an extreme, at which humanity revolts.

Washington urged Clinton to use his authority and influence to prevent measures being implemented that would aggravate the 'rigors of war' and result in 'the most disagreeable consequences'.[33] Yet Cornwallis had reported to Clinton in a letter dated 3 September that:

> ever since the Reduction of Charlestown a number of the Principal & most violent inhabitants have held constant meetings in Town & carried on Correspondence with the Country to keep up the flame of Rebellion & impose on the ignorant by spreading false reports throughout the whole Province to encourage the disaffected & intimidate the others.

Cornwallis had thought about seizing the men before leaving Charleston but preferred to wait until some decisive action had occurred between the two armies. After the British success at Camden, he had directed Lieutenant Colonel Balfour, the Commandant at Charleston, to apprehend those whom the loyalist head of the Charleston Board of Police – Mr James Simpson, former attorney general – 'thought the most dangerous among them'. Cornwallis enclosed a list of the men sent on board the *Sandwich* on 27 August who were destined for St Augustine. He also appears to have deferred to Simpson on the issue of the terms of the capitulation. 'Mr Simpson', he wrote 'is clearly of opinion that the changing their place of residence on Parole from Charleston to St Augustine is no breach of the Capitulation'. In any event, he had 'intelligence of their corresponding with the enemy, of their 'propagating false reports & receiving General Gates's Proclamation'. Cornwallis did not doubt that the measure would appear 'as just as it was expedient'. Whether this letter reached Clinton before his correspondence with Washington is unclear. If it did, then he deliberately misled Washington and Congress.[34]

Exchange/non-exchange

In November 1780, Congress resolved that the Commander in Chief 'insist upon an exchange of those persons, prisoners of war under the capitulation of Charleston alluded to in the order of the 23 day of September last'. Washington did not act upon this instruction as he explained in a letter to John Matthews because he was 'so totally unacquainted with the state of the southern prisoners' that he decided against entering into negotiations with Sir Henry Clinton, on the idea of a 'general exchange'. Consequently, nothing particular had been done about the gentlemen who were confined in St Augustine, Washington did not believe that the enemy 'would consent to a partial exchange of persons of the most considerable influence in the southern States, and who, besides, are pretended to have made themselves obnoxious'.[35] Yet, William Moultrie wrote to General Greene on 30 January 1781 that he had been informed in a letter from John Matthews that a general exchange had been agreed between General Washington and Sir Henry Clinton. The following February, John Matthews wrote to George Washington seeking news about the exchange of prisoners, for 'almost every near connexion I have, are now in the power of the enemy'. Washington, however, had not pursued the matter because the Americans lacked suitable candidates to exchange with the British.[36] Balfour, in a letter to Moultrie, which he received on 30 March 1781, informed him that Lord Cornwallis had 'in vain applied to General Greene for an equitable and general exchange of prisoners, finds it necessary, in justice to the king's service, and those of his army, who are in this disagreeable predicament, to pursue such measures, as may eventually coerce it'. Balfour had orders 'to send all the prisoners of war here, forthwith to some one of the West-India Islands'. This was to take place by the middle of the next month and transports had been arranged. This presumably was a measure intended to force the Americans to cooperate.[37]

The return

On Sunday, 8 July 1781, two schooners with provisions for the garrison also carried news that 'all persons made Prisoners (both Regulars & Militia) in the Southern department, from the beginning of the American War, to 15 June 1781 were generally exchanged', but, wrote Smith,

> to embitter our Joy on this happy occasion we discovered in the Charlestown Gazette of 27th of June a Garrison Order of the 25th directing that all the Wives and Children of the partys thus exchanged, must depart the province by the 1st August next, which Cruel decree will throw many families into the utmost distress. – and to add to our

grief, none of us are to be allowed to go to Carolina to the Assistance of our Dear familys there, but must proceed directly for Virginia or Philadelphia.[38]

A second removal

William Brown conveyed Colonel Glazier's message to the exiles that they and their servants should be ready on Sunday evening to proceed to Georgia, then march to the St Johns River, where boats would be provided for them to travel to Savannah 'by way of St. Marys. A schooner was ready to take their baggage on board'. Much alarmed by this 'extraordinary Order', they drafted a response to the Commandant. When they were removed to St Augustine on the orders of Lord Cornwallis, they wrote, they insisted they had received assurances from the Commandant at Charleston since they had been removed, not for breaches of parole, but for reasons of policy, they should not 'be subjected to any unnecessary difficulties or sufferings'. They interpreted the orders to be ready to march by land to St Johns, 'from thence to be convey'd by boats to Savanah', since they were not aware of having breached their parole, that this was a 'Second removal' and adopted again 'from motives of policy'. They asked for changes.

> There are many among us Aged and Infirm, and all of us since our Captivity, more or less enervated by an inactive & sedentary life, in such circumstances, a fatiguing March in this Sultry Season, through a Wilderness destitute of every accommodation, and at this dry season, even of the necessary refreshment of Water; and then to be confined for near a fortnight on board Small Boats, exposed to every inclemency of the weather, will probably to many of us, be attended with fatal consequences.

If they were unable to reach an accommodation over a route, they would prefer to stay where they were. So, they remained where they were.[39]

In July, the exiles were declared free and sent not to Charleston, but to Philadelphia, by which time their wives and families had been ordered to leave the town and the state before 1 August by Colonel Balfour. There was no reason for the government to be responsible for their support. The financial position of the exiles was poor. News of the release of 'Rutledge, Gadsden & Middleton' was known in Congress in July and they were expected in Philadelphia 'in a Flag . . . every day'. But by the end of July, the city, according to Elias Boudinot, was 'so filled with the distressed Georgia and Carolina refugees that I was afraid I should be prevented getting any Quarters out of a Tavern'.[40] Massachusetts delegate George Partridge wrote to Samuel Holten, Member of the Council, that four or five cartels had recently arrived from Charleston and St Augustine 'with some soldiers, but principally Citizens from Charlestown, who have been driven out by the Enemy from the city & taken from Guard ships. Many of these people are gentlemen who have lived in ease & affluence, but are now real objects of Charity & compassion; as the Enemy, contrary to the faith of the most solemn treaty, & every feeling of humanity, denyd them the smallest pittance of their own Estates'.[41]

South Carolina delegates were negotiating a loan of 30, 000 dollars from Congress as well as appealing for voluntary contributions for 'the relief of these distressed, and magnanimous people', wrote John Matthews to Nathanael Greene on 14 August 1781. Both applications met with great success and he was hopeful that the relief would 'render their situations comfortable, tho' not affluent'. 'None of them will remain here, one hour longer than is indispensably necessary; as soon as they can get their families accommodated in such a manner, as to place them beyond absolute want, they have all agreed to set out immediately for their country'. Matthews had great hopes of their impact when they returned home. 'They are mostly men of the first fortune, & influence there, & will be able to give the Governor such substantial support as will be productive of the most happy effects. The re-establishing of civil government in that country, is of the utmost consequence, in the present situation of our affairs'. He did not expect serious negotiations with the British to take place until the conclusion of the campaign. The *Pennsylvania Gazette* also noted the arrival of several flags from Charleston 'with the families of many of those virtuous citizens lately arrived from *Augustine* who were cruelly exiled from South Carolina, contrary to the articles of Capitulation'.[42]

Reunion

Josiah Smith recorded his reunion with his family in Philadelphia on 3 August, a few days after his own arrival – his wife 'and five children, Polly, Betsy, William, Edward, & Nancy together with his elderly father, and four slaves, Peggy, Tenah, Hannah, & Girl Linda', who had embarked on 25 July on board a flag from Charleston with 10 other families. Two slaves were left behind and three others refused to leave Charleston. During the whole of Smith's narrative and despite their numbers in St. Augustine, this is the first occasion when Smith identifies any slaves by name with one exception – the death of Scipio, slave of Anthony Toomer, a member of his mess who was allegedly poisoned by a fellow slave. The only time they were mentioned in St. Augustine was when they were working – removing baggage from the vessels, fishing in the harbour to supplement the exiles' diet and being badged so they could be distinguished from others in the town. Not only did Josiah Smith's slaves acquire an identity once he arrived in Philadelphia, so female refugees from Charleston acquired a reputation for outspokenness once they reached Philadelphia.[43]

Josiah Smith and his family stayed temporarily at the 'Country Seat' of Mr James Pemberton on the Banks of the River Schuylkill 'who very generously offer'd us the use of his Spacious house there, and the furniture in it, till the coming of Spring'. It was a couple of miles from the city 'and very pleasantly scituated'. His father and brother in law and his family had moved there on 7 August and Josiah Smith and his family on 31 August, but found it difficult to resume the normal rhythm of family life. Because they had no horses or carriage, it proved difficult to visit the market, attend public worship and take their children regularly to school. Smith and his family and relatives resolved to get back into the city as soon as they could find suitable housing 'at a moderate Rent, our Finances being small, and no hope of doing anything here to gain a penny, will oblige us to live very savingly'. In August, Smith learnt that his house in Charleston had been taken over by Commandant Balfour for use as a hospital for British soldiers. Although Balfour promised to pay a reasonable rent, Smith did not expect to receive anything for it. In August, 'a Friend, Neighbour, and Companion in Exile', John Edwards, died shortly before the arrival of his wife and ten children. Smith's own father died two months later. On 30 November in snow, sleet and rain, Smith began moving his goods from Mr Pemberton's farm to the three storey brick house he had rented in Sixth Street between Arch and Market Streets. When Smith did return to Charleston, he resumed a successful career as a merchant.[44]

Led by Christopher Gadsden, a committee formed from those banished to St Augustine sent an address to Thomas McKean, then President of Congress, congratulating Congress on the recovery of their state 'out of the hands of the Enemy' while, at the same time, they wished to hold up to public view 'the conduct of that perfidious, that faithless Nation; which during the whole course of the American War, but more especially since the reduction of Charlestown, has been trampling on all laws human and divine'. Though Congress knew of their detention, the committee they did not think they were fully acquainted 'with all the circumstances attending that iniquitous and despotic procedure' – how they had been taken in 'the most instantaneous manner so as to leave us no opportunity of making provision for our support in a distant Country', how soon after their arrival at St Augustine, most of them learnt of the sequestration of their estates and 'the few who had their estates secured by the Capitulation, found it extremely difficult to derive any means of subsistence from them, as every difficulty was thrown in the way by the British, by extravagant freights and otherwise; and the scanty supplies which were sent, were repeatedly intercepted by American Privateers'. Their fellow citizens who have arrived from Charlestown 'were taken up in the same sudden and unexpected manner, were equally affected by the sequestrations, and were indeed positively prohibited the bringing any money with them. . . . the Finances of all are in a state greatly exhausted and that many are reduced to the greatest straits'. They solicited the aid of Congress on behalf of their 'fellow-citizens and fellow sufferers'.[45] Unlike the 'Virginia Exiles', those of St Augustine and Charleston were welcomed to Philadelphia, but like them, they had exchanged one set of problems for another.

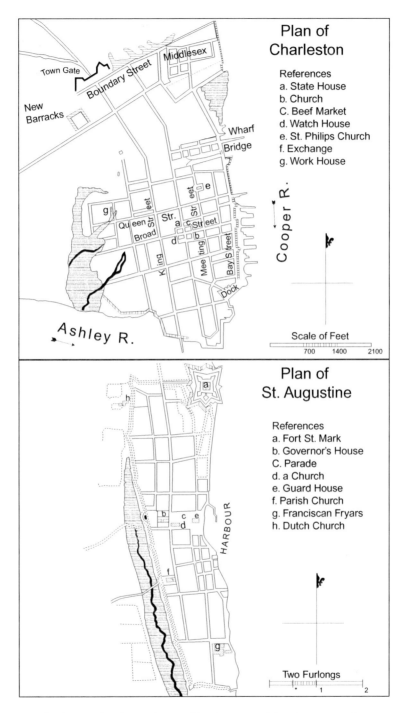

Plan of Charleston

Town Gate

Middlesex

Boundary Street

New Barracks

Wharf

Bridge

Cooper R.

References
a. State House
b. Church
C. Beef Market
d. Watch House
e. St. Philips Church
f. Exchange
g. Work House

g

Queen Str.

Str.

Broad

Str.

Street

King

Meeting

Bay Street

Dock

Ashley R.

Scale of Feet

700   1400   2100

Plan of St. Augustine

References
a. Fort St. Mark
b. Governor's House
C. Parade
d. a Church
e. Guard House
f. Parish Church
g. Franciscan Fryars
h. Dutch Church

HARBOUR

Two Furlongs

1   2

MAP 7 Charleston, South Carolina and *St. Augustine, Florida – street plans* [*details from de Brahm et al.,* A General Map of the Southern British Colonies in America (*1776*)].

10

The transported beggars
of St Eustatius

When news of the capture of St Eustatius reached London on 13 March 1781, it was an occasion of great public rejoicing. Lady Rodney, wife of the victorious admiral, wrote to her husband about how visitors came constantly to their house to congratulate her on her husband's great victory over the Dutch and how she was fêted at court, while on the streets of Amsterdam, a hostile public protested against the action of the British and the failures of their own government. Yet, within a few weeks, the reputation of Admiral George Brydges Rodney was sullied and, despite his subsequent victory over the French in the Battle of the Saints, it never fully recovered. Tainted by charges of stripping the islanders of their goods for personal gain, reducing its Jewish inhabitants to beggary and banishing many of its merchants, Rodney, according to Edmund Burke, one of his sternest critics, brought shame and dishonour upon the nation.[1]

Burke, who took up the cause of some of the victims of Rodney's and Vaughan's assault on St Eustatius, described the island as unlike any other. It was 'rocky and barren', and he compared it to 'the chimney of a volcano' for '[i]t seemed to have been shot up from the ocean by some convulsion'. The Scottish traveller Janet Schaw who visited St Eustatius just before the Revolution described the island as 'the only ugly one' she had seen on her travels in the Caribbean. She would not have spent any time there at all, but for the fact it was 'an instance of Dutch industry little inferior to their dykes'. One resident of the neighbouring island of St Christopher (otherwise known as St Kitts) put it less elliptically. It was 'but a rock' and 'without its trade, a mere rock – and without its trade, neither of real nor relative importance'.[2]

The golden rock

St Eustatius enjoyed a special status as a free port serving as a depot for trade between England, parts of continental Europe, North and South

America and the Caribbean. Jameson described it as 'a small rocky island near the north-east corner of the West Indian chain'. Neither large nor fertile, it was less than seven square miles in area. It had one landing place and was poorly defended. At the time of the Revolution, it did not produce more than 600 barrels of sugar a year, but it was its location that gave it 'in the hands of the Dutch, exceptional advantages', attracting merchants from around the globe. Schaw painted a vivid picture of the inhabitants in her journal. The low town was one long street, about a mile in length. It was 'very narrow and most disagreeable, as every one smokes tobacco, and the whiffs are constantly blown in your face'. Even so, the island was mesmerizing. It was 'a place of vast traffick' where fine ships 'of various nations' rode at anchor in the bay. She could hear goods being sold in Dutch, French and Spanish and all wore 'the habit of their country'. The first people she encountered were Jewish, a people whom she had never before met so attired, among whom there were tragic victims of the Inquisition.[3]

> From one end to the town to the other was a continuous market where goods of the most different uses and qualities are displayed before the shop-doors. Here hang rich embroideries, painted silks, flowered Muslins, with all the Manufactures of the Indies. Just by hang Sailor's Jackets, trousers, shoes, hats etc.[The] Next stall contains most exquisite silver plate, the most beautiful indeed I ever saw, and close by these, iron-pots, kettles and shovels. Perhaps the next presents you with French and English Millinary-wares.

It was pointless to enumerate all the types of goods found there 'for in every store you find everything', though their quality might differ.[4]

What Schaw did not mention, however, was the large slave population on St Eustatius, which outnumbered its free population though not substantially. Active in the slave trade since the mid-seventeenth century, the island supplied labour to nearby sugar and tobacco producing islands.[5]

An American lifeline

For the rebellious American colonies, St Eustatius was a lifeline. Cut off from imports from Britain, first by their own non-importation agreements and then by the war, the Americans found in the neutral islands of the West Indies a source of European goods and a market for American exports. St Eustatius became the principal channel through which the Americans purchased war materials, its significance being further enhanced when France entered the war on the American side. If Schaw provides a picture of the bustling economic life and range of goods available on St Eustatius before the American Revolution, historian Andrew O'Shaughnessy offers one of its economic importance once the war had commenced. According to O'Shaughnessy, it was not unusual 'to see two hundred ships at anchor on any day there. Storehouses were rented for as much as £1,200 sterling a year. An armed convoy of forty to fifty French merchant ships visited the island every other week to buy provisions for Martinique and Guadeloupe'. The North American patriots exported 94,000 pounds of indigo and 12,000 hogsheads of tobacco to St Eustatius to buy military and naval supplies. The American trade was 'immense' with between seven and ten ships arriving every night and regular fleets of 10 to 30 sail. The French similarly obtained vital supplies for their navy and their island colonies in the Caribbean.[6]

Writing to his wife after the successful capture of the island, Admiral Rodney claims that St Eustatius 'has done England more harm than all the arms of her most potent enemies, and alone supported the infamous American rebellion'. Rather than the colourful melee of people and goods perceived by Schaw, Rodney regarded the island 'as an asylum for men guilty of every crime, and a receptacle for the outcast of every nation'. He raged against the island in which trade was openly carried on with the rebellious colonies in guns, powder, rifles, and ammunition, often purchased by Dutch firms from France and Belgium. Some of the colonies in rebellion even had their own agents on St Eustatius.[7]

'Not properly a colony'

From the British perspective, Dutch-owned St Eustatius was 'not properly a colony but a nest of outlaws, or at best Adventurers'. Initially, the British tried diplomacy to contain the threat posed by the island, protesting that supplying the American rebels was inconsistent with the status of the Dutch as neutrals and a breach of existing treaty obligations. Following the capture of Henry Laurens, the prospective American ambassador to the Netherlands and a former president of Congress, and the discovery among his papers of a draft treaty between the Americans and the Dutch, the long serving British ambassador to the Hague, Sir Joseph Yorke, sent two memorials to the States General, the one demanding 'a formal disavowal of the conduct of the magistrates of Amsterdam' and the second, the punishment of principals engaged in the trade, such as Engebert Francis Van Berkel, Councellor and Pensionary of Amsterdam and his accomplices who were denounced 'as disturbers of the public peace and violators of the law of nations'. The Dutch response was feeble and on 20 December 1780, the British issued a manifesto declaring war between these former allies and long-term friends.[8]

Rodney's orders

On the same day that the manifesto declaring war on the Dutch was issued, instructions were sent to Rodney, Admiral in the East Caribbean, regarding the neutral islands:

> as the enemy have derived great advantages from those islands, and it is highly probable considerable quantities of provisions and other stores are laid up there, or are on their way thither, which may fall into our hands if we get possession speedily, it is his Majesty's pleas[ure] that we should, and we do hereby accordingly, recommend to you the immediate attack and reduction of those islands, as of very great importance to his Majesty's service.

Edmund Burke, leading member of the opposition, protested the decision to go to war for 'however light a war with the states of Holland might be in the opinions of some men, he had not forgotten the old fashioned idea, that going to war, at all events, [was] a very serious matter; a matter which nothing but great necessity could justify'. Speaking for the government, Lord George Germain responded that he also considered war a matter of great seriousness, 'but Holland was in open violation of its treaty obligations. It had refused to give Great Britain that assistance to which she was entitled when attacked by the House of Bourbon, who had in direct violation of the law of nations, for a long time persisted in furnishing France with warlike stores and was now entering into a treaty with the rebellious colonies in North America'.[9]

Writing to Philip Stephens, Secretary of the Admiralty, from on board the *Sandwich,* the day after the assault, Rodney reported the great surprise and astonishment of the governor and inhabitants of St Eustatius at the appearance of the fleet and his demand for the 'instant surrender' of the island and its dependencies, 'with every thing in and belonging thereto, for the use of his said Majesty'. He congratulated their Lordships 'on the severe blow' that had been dealt to the Dutch West India Company and the perfidious magistrates of Amsterdam. 'Upwards of one hundred and fifty sail of ships of all denominations are taken in the bay, exclusive of the Mars, which I have commissioned and manned, and in a few days she will cruize against the enemy as a British ship of war'. After detailing the ships taken, Rodney then described the magazines and stores, all of which were full and even the beach was 'covered with tobacco and sugar'. All this would be shipped 'on board the vessels now in the bay . . . and sent under a proper convoy to Great Britain to abide his Majesty's pleasure'. It was no small irony that most of these vessels and the goods with which they were laden were later recaptured by a French squadron at the mouth of the English channel.[10]

Lambert Blair on the assault on St Eustatius

Born in Newry, Ireland, merchant and successful slave trader Lambert Blair, who had been resident on the island for two years, provides a graphic account of the appearance of the English fleet off St Eustatius and the subsequent treatment of the islanders. He reported how, on the third day of February 1781, 'the British Fleet under the command of Sir George Rodney appeared off the Island of St Eustatius'. He counted 17 ships of the line as well as frigates and tenders. On board were three or four thousand Troops under the Command of Major General Vaughan. About noon, 'several of the Ships of the Line having come to an anchor close to the Town with the Springs on their Cables so as to bring their Broad Sides to bear upon it. Lt Colonel Cockburn came on Shore with a Flag and demanded a Surrender of the Island, giving the Governor but one Hour to determine. The defenceless Situation of the Island was such as prevented every Idea of resistance'.[11] Such defences as there were 'were manned by about Sixty wretched Soldiers of whom some were people of Colour'. There was 'no Regular Militia of any kind on the Island'. In this situation, the Governor surrendered the island at discretion and 'about 4 o'clock the British Troops took possession'. Guards were immediately put into position from one end of the bay to the other, where the merchants' warehouses were located. They were all locked and nothing was to be removed without an order from an officer to the guard on duty. Blair related how he himself was frequently refused admittance to his own warehouses. Dutch merchants were never permitted to go to their stores, 'not even to take an Inventory of their Effects agreeable to the public orders, altho every person was threatened with Military Execution if an Inventory was not given in to the Quarter Master General by a Certain day' .... 'the disturbed Situation of almost any Class of the Inhabitants can hardly be conceived. There was a Stop to all business even the common necessaries of Life Such as Flour, Salt, Groceries, Liquors, Cloathing, in Short every thing that, could in any degree be Merchandize was prohibited from being Sold .... Soldiers and Officers quartered in every House, in many instances the Inhabitants turn'd out to make Room for them. Proclamations were every day issued out of such a nature as to continue or increase the consternation which every rank of people were thrown into by such extraordinary proceedings. Many of the most respectable Merchants were torn from their families and sent on board the Kings Ships on pretence that their having traded & corresponded with the Enemies of Great Britain was an act of Treason'.[12]

Proclamations

The new masters of St Eustatius signalled their demands to the islanders in a series of proclamations. There were some 38 of these, printed in English and Dutch, and 'posted in a variety of locations and brought to the notice of the residents by the role of a drum'. They were issued every two to three days though on some days there would be more than one. Eight of the proclamations were signed by the Quarter Master General Colonel J. Cockburn. The very first proclamation issued on 6 February 1781 reveals the primary concern of the Commander in Chief, who declared 'that every inhabitant of this island (without exception) do forthwith render a full and just account of all his effects to the quarter-master-general, of every description, namely plantations, houses, furniture, plate, merchandize, slaves, horses, horned cattle, and all other four footed beasts'. The order was to be strictly complied with 'on pain of confiscation and banishment'. Measures relating to the pacification of the island followed five days later, when there were two orders, one requiring 'all strangers whatsoever, do immediately prepare to quit the island, till such time as order and a regular police can be established'. The other ordered that 'All arms, without exception, belonging to the inhabitants' be handed in at Fort George (formerly Fort Orange) by the 15th of the month. The pecuniary concern of the commanders was still evident in the proclamation of 13 February 1781, when 'all persons that have any property or cash belonging to any Americans, that have either been sent on board ship, or have absconded, are forthwith to give up the same to the quarter-master-general'. Those failing to do so were threatened with 'military execution'.[13]

So busy were Rodney and Vaughan in compiling an inventory of disposable merchandize on the island and who owned it, that they paid little attention to issues of subsistence until their proclamation of 16 February 1781, two weeks after the invasion of the island. On that day, an urgent proclamation required 'all merchants and others, do with the utmost expedition give in returns of all provisions they are possessed of, to Mr Texier's, specifying the quantity and how long they have been imported'. Details were wanted of flour, biscuit, beef, pork, oatmeal, pease, butter, rice, oats, beans, vinegar, rum and wine. All returns were to be given in by 12 o'clock the next day. Two further proclamations were issued on 17 February 1781, dealing with slaves and horses. The first of these wanted a list of all slaves and their owners to be given to the Marshall so that 'proper numbers required for the king's service' may be furnished. Second, 'all horses belonging to every inhabitant of this island, without exception, were to be brought to the quarter-master general's quarters by 8 o'clock on Monday morning to be disposed of, agreeable to the orders of his excellency the commander in chief'. The next batch of proclamations dealt with the banishment of traders on St Eustatius. On 22 February 1781, it was proclaimed that 'The commander in chief orders that all Americans do quit this island forthwith' and that 'boats will be ready to receive them this afternoon at 5 o'clock, at Gallows Bay'. Two days later, 'All merchants residing at present in this place, who are inhabitants of the city of Amsterdam, are to prepare to leave this island forthwith, and to return to Holland; they are to give their names at Mr Brooks's, secretary to the island, at Mr Henricus Godets, between the hours of 9 and 12 o'clock tomorrow morning'. Two further proclamations issued on 5 March 1781 dealt with the French and remaining Dutch residents. The first addressed 'all natives of France, or other subjects of the French king, residing at present on this island'. They should 'prepare to quit the same, as soon as vessels can be got ready to receive them' and to leave behind them 'all sorts of merchandize and other stores'. On the same day, it was also ordered 'that all natives of Holland, and others who were in any degree subjects of the States General, residing at present on the island, do prepare to quit the same, as soon as vessels can be got ready to receive them'. They were to leave behind them all their wealth and merchandize and take with them only those effects for which they could obtain a licence.[14]

In chronicling the banishment of these groups, Lambert Blair provided details that contributed to the notoriety associated with the British capture of St Eustatius.[15] 'In several instances', he wrote, 'where it was supposed Money was secreted by the people, Soldiers & Negroes were employed to dig up the Earth in their Yards & Gardens; the Floors of Houses were taken up & in one instance a Tomb in the Church Yard was broke open in order to look for Moneys which was supposed to be hid therein'. Blair also noted that though the French were ordered to leave the island abandoning their wealth, things did not go according to plan. The Marquis De Bruille, Governor of Martinique, threatened retaliation against the population of four recently conquered British islands in the Caribbean, if the French on St Eustatius were deprived of their possessions. As a consequence of this threat, the French achieved a protected status or as Lambert Blair put it, 'they became people the most favoured of any other Class'. They were permitted to hire flags of truce to carry them to any of the French islands and to take with them their money, plate and household furniture. That large quantities of goods were shipped in this way 'was a matter of public Notoriety' according to Blair who also claimed 'that at one time a small Fleet consisting of I think Seventeen Sails of these Flags of Truce were conveyed from St Eustatius to Guadaloup & Martinique by an English Frigate'.

The sale of the confiscated property was scheduled to start on 15 March. All manner of people were invited to attend the sales except those whose property was being sold. Vessels flying flags of truce carried large sums of money from the French islands returning with 'considerable Quantities of Merchandize which had been purchased at the Sales'. Blair claimed that '[t]he most extraordinary partiality was shown during the Sales'. In some cases, 'the property of Merchants residing in Great Britain was sold with out Hesitation' but in other instances, it was surrendered 'when sufficient Interest cou'd be made with the Commander in Chief or their Agents'.

Blair's own experience was unfortunate. His refusal to deliver up the keys of his warehouse and stores 'exasperated both the Commanders & their Agents'. On 24 March, 'my Warehouse [and stores] were broke open by order & in the presence of Capt Young & Mr Forster, the principal agents'. When he wanted to know why, he was told that they were suspicious that part of his property 'belonged to People in America as a Consequence of which they intended to proceed immediately to the Sale of the Whole'. When Blair produced books, papers and clerks to provide evidence that everything was his property, they backed off. 'I now thought my property Safe', he wrote, but he was mistaken. On 29 March, his property was repossessed. On inquiring why, Captain Young informed him that he had intercepted letters on board an American vessel addressed to his brother and partner James Blair, which 'proved that he had been concerned in Trade with the Rebellious part of the Continent & that in consequence thereof the whole of the property in my Stores without destination was confiscated & was then going to be exposed to public Sale'. Although '[i]n the fullest & plainest manner', Lambert Blair 'proved to every unprejudiced person that the Letters in Question were not intended for my Partner who for three Years before had never been in St Eustatia but resided wholly in New York & Charles Town I pointed out the person they were intended for a Gentleman, an inhabitant of Philadelphia who was in St Eustatia at the time of the Capture & had been banished with the rest of the Americans. . . . every thing I said was in vain'. Captain Young told him that he had laid the matter before the Commanders in Chief and 'that it was their orders that my property should at all events be Sold'. When he applied for redress in a British court, he understood that the letters which condemned his property would be produced instantly. He petitioned 'the Commanders in Chief informing them of the Circumstances & requesting they wou'd put a Stop to the Sale till they coud satisfy themselves of the Justness' of his case, but he could not obtain any orders and was told that 'neither the General or the Admiral woud receive any petition'. He could do nothing further, but 'protest against the Sale of any part of the Merchandize in my Stores which the Agents proceeded immediately to dispose of. Some part of the Merchandize was the property of Mr Stratford Canning & Mr Hugh Johnston of London'. When Blair protested against the sale of his goods, Captain Young publicly declared that that morning, he had received orders from Admiral Rodney to make no distinction, but sell property of every kind belonging to British subjects as well as of others. Blair left for St Kitts a few days later to attend to business and could not speak of subsequent events, but all the things he had mentioned 'were matters of public Notoriety'.[16]

Another claimant and critic was Richard Downing Jennings, who first defended himself against accusations of being a British spy and double-dealing in a pamphlet published in 1784 and republished in 1790. He wrote that he would:

> not enlarge upon the particular severities, which were exercised upon the inhabitants of St. Eustatius, by the military parade, with which they were kept in perpetual terror, while every necessary of life, for the space of twenty-seven days, before the retail shops were permitted to be opened, was withheld; and that from the same cause the sick soldiers died for want of nourishment,

but he could not 'lightly pass over the 13th of February, a day of desolation to the community at large, and the Jews in particular'. He had remonstrated with General Vaughan and pointed out how 'the French had behaved differently to those who had fallen into their power', but to no effect. . . . 'these poor wretches, without respect to age, infirmity, or attachment to the British interests, had been driven like cattle into boats, and transported, nobody knew where'. Lambert Blair did not observe what happened to the Jews himself and would not therefore speak of 'the Scandalous affairs of the Jews', but referred his readers to his clerk Mr Shipton, He 'was present when these people were plundered of their Money' and was then in London and 'willing to appear to prove the transaction if necessary'.[17]

The Jewish community on St Eustatius

The origins of the Jewish community and congregation on St Eustatius are unknown, but it is unlikely that its founders came directly from Brazil when the Portuguese expelled the Dutch colony there in 1646. More likely migration was directly from Europe – from Holland, Portugal and Spain, judging by the surnames. In the second half of the seventeenth century, writes Jacob Marcus, Jews could be found on Barbados, Nevis and Jamaica as well as on the mainland in English Surinam. In the second half of the eighteenth century, there were Dutch and French Sephardic Jews living on St Eustatius and plans for a synagogue were approved in 1737. Based on the analysis of three lists of the island's inhabitants, Norman Barka argues that 'Statian society was composed of a small core of long-term residents and a majority of burghers who were more recent immigrants from North America, England, Ireland, the West Indian islands, and Bermuda' and that Jewish society most likely conformed to this pattern. In 1781, 20 per cent of the white male population had arrived within the past six months'.[18] When Admiral Rodney and Major General Vaughan made their infamous attack on the island, there were more Jews living together in one place on St Eustatius than anywhere else in North America. Marcus put their number at about 400, though O'Shaughnessy and Barka revise this figure downwards to about 350.[19]

The Jews

The Jews were the first victims. The process of expropriation and banishment began with them, 'the people', declared Edmund Burke in his speech in the House of Commons on 14 May 1781, 'whom of all others it ought to be the care and the wish of human nations to protect . . . ' but those living on St Eustatius 'were treated in a worse manner, if possible, than all the other inhabitants; they were stripped of all their money and eight of them put on board a ship to be carried out of the island'. Burke depicted them as follows:

> Having no fixed settlement in any part of the world, no kingdom nor country in which they have a government, a community, and a system of laws, they are thrown upon the benevolence of nations, and claim protection and civility from their weakness, as well as from their utility. They were a people, who by shunning the profession of any, could give no well-founded jealousy to any state. . . . Their abandoned state, and their defenceless situation calls most forcibly for the protection of civilized nations. If Dutchmen are injured and attacked, the Dutch have a nation, a government and armies to redress or revenge their cause. If Britons are injured, Britons have armies and laws, the laws of nations, (or at least they once had the laws of nations,) to fly to for protection and justice. But the Jews have no such power, and no such friend to depend on. Humanity then must become their protector and ally. Did they find it in the British conquerors of St. Eustatius? No: – On the contrary, a resolution was taken to banish this unhappy people from the island.[20]

Unlike subsequent proclamations regarding the Dutch, French, British and Americans, there was no public proclamation regarding the Jews. However, on 13 February 1781, as highlighted by Richard Downing Jennings, 20 to 30 Jewish men were banished from St Eustatius, at least 20 of them to the island of St Christopher, possibly others to Antigua. A list of these men appeared in the muster roll of HMS *Shrewsbury* (Captain Robertson). Among those listed were Samuel Hoheb, Soloman Levy, Levy Abraham, Jacob Robeless, Lyon Kann, Jacob Almeida, Nathn Samuel, Elias Penna, Elizah Ab Levy, Ben Cortiosos, Sl. D. Hehob, Gomez Ware, Danl Levy, Abm Demarza, Barnet Levy, Rh Benjamin, David Porto, Ben Meirs and J. J. Courlanda. In Burke's notes on the case, it seems that Mr Hoheb and others received a verbal message from the Assistant Quarter Master General Mr Ford to depart from the island, leaving all their effects and wives and children behind them. When challenged, the Quarter Master General Colonel Cockburn, maintained that he had the order 'in writing'.[21]

Among those caught in the net was Myer Pollock. He had already been banished from mainland America as a Tory being 'stripped of all his worth' in Rhode Island for importing East India tea. According to Marcus, 'After the Hart clan left the city (Newport), their estates were confiscated and they were declared banished. Some of the Harts and Pollocks moved to the New York area and settled on Long Island, on land given them by Sir William Howe, but in an attack on a Tory-held fort there, Isaac Hart, a civilian, was bayoneted and clubbed to death. The burden of looking after the surviving members of the Hart-Pollock clan fell to the lot of one of the Pollocks, who fled to Dutch St Eustatius. He lost a brother and brother in law in the British cause in New York and was left to care for their surviving families as well as a mother and sister. Attempting to conceal some money from his captors, he was singled out from the others for additional punishment. Samson Myers, the secretary of the synagogue and a loyalist refugee from Norwalk, Connecticut, suffered a similar fate'.[22]

Samuel Hoheb

Samuel Hoheb who was banished to St. Kitts on the *Shrewsbury*, was described by Burke in his 4 December 1781 speech to members of the House of Commons as 'a venerable old gentleman of near 70 years of age, [who] had even his cloaths searched'. Burke displayed a piece of linen 'which was sewed in the poor man's coat' from which 'were taken 36 shillings, which he had the consummate audacity to endeavour to conceal for the purpose of buying victuals'. Burke could produce the coat 'from which it was taken, and the man who wore it'. 'Mr Hoheb was treated in the most harsh manner, as were all his brethren for this concealment'. . . . 'ill-treated because he had endeavoured to carry away some of his own money'. Clearly one of Burke's informants, Hoheb had come to London to seek restitution for his losses. On 4 February 1782, Burke presented Hoheb's petition complaining of hardships and losses sustained by the capture of St Eustatius. It was brought up and read. It stated that he was 'of the Hebrew Nation' and a native of Amsterdam,

> that he had been a resident of St. Eustatius for 25 years; that when that island had submitted to his Majesty's government, he and all the others of his nation had been forced to quit the island, though no crime whatever had been proved against them; nay, though not as much as a charge of a crime had been made, unless it was, that after he had received orders to depart, it had been discovered that he had sewed up a few shillings of his own money, in the lining of his coat; that afterwards he had been permitted to return to St. Eustatius, but it was only to see the whole of his stock in trade sold for one-third of its value, and appropriated to the use of his Britannic Majesty; that he had got out of all his property one small bag of money, which was in his bureau, when he was banished from the island; and afterwards he obtained leave to come to England, where he could expect redress only from that House: because if he should be referred for his remedy to the courts of law, it would be totally out of his power to avail himself of that remedy; and, stripped of his whole fortune, to contend with Sir George Rodney and General Vaughan, who by the very means that had put it out of his power to see lawyers, had secured to themselves the means of withholding from him that property which he had been his whole life in acquiring. He therefore prayed for such relief as the House in their wisdom should think proper to grant him.[23]

In reply, the Secretary of War warned the House that if they were inclined to be charitable, they should be careful about whose money they would be giving away though he did not object to the petition going to a committee. Mr Byng suggested 'that as Mr Hoheb was poor, the House might, if it was found that he should have redress in law, order the Attorney and Solicitor General to carry on his suit for him gratis. Lord Mahon thought that the petitioner had been so ill-treated, that the Attorney General should be ordered to prosecute at the King's expence, the plunderers who had so shamefully robbed a respectable merchant, and put it out of his power of doing himself justice'. The motion to refer the petition to a committee passed. Among Burke's papers on the St Eustatius affair was a testimonial from a former employer dated the following day – 5 February. Jacob Jesurun Barrelay wrote that Hoheb had gone with Abraham Mendes to St Eustatius, where he worked as a factor for the firm of Aron Jesurun and Son for seven years. He had 'behaved with the Integrity required of him', after which he remained on the island, where he carried 'on his business as a Merchant'. The committee did prepare a report on the petition, but since the matter was not finalized before it was necessary for Hoheb to return to the West Indies, he applied to the Treasury for an advance payment to fund his return. Before the report was presented to the House – Vaughan's brother Lord Lisburne was one of its members – news of Rodney's victory at the battle of the Saints precluded further action. In a letter dated 13 February 1784 Hoheb wrote to Burke from Curaçao that he despaired of recovering 'the cruel losses' that he had suffered by the surrender of St Eustatius and describing his current state as 'deplorable'. He inquired whether his personal appearance in London would be of service to him.[24]

The reaction

Four days after the expulsion of the first Jews to St Christopher, some of the remaining Jewish men addressed a petition to Admiral Rodney and General Vaughan on behalf of themselves and others 'of the Hebrew nation, residents in the island of St Eustatius', expressing their 'utmost concern and astonishment' that:

> we have already, not only received your Excellencies afflicting order and sentence, to give up the keys of our stores, with an inventory thereof, and of our household plate and furniture, and to hold ourselves in readiness to depart this island: ignorant of our destination, and leaving our Beloved wives and helpless children behind us, and our property and effects liable to seizure and confiscation; but also find that those orders are for the major part carried into execution, a number of our brethren having on Tuesday the thirteenth instant, been sent on board of a ship and have not since been heard of.[25]

The petitioners stated that it was 'beyond their comprehension' that British commanders who were usually known for their 'mercy and humanity' should issue orders such as these with the result that 'numbers of families [were] now helpless, disconsolate, and in an absolute state of indigence and despair'. Such 'horrid and melancholy scenes' as they were witnessing were usually associated with a very different type of warfare, what they termed 'a rigid war'. Like many other people caught in similar circumstances, they did not know'[f]or what reason, or from what motive', they were 'to be banished [from] this island'. If a member or members of their faith were guilty of some offence, let them be charged with it, but 'if nothing can be alleged against them 'but the religion of our forefathers', they hoped that it would 'not be considered a crime; or that a religion, which preaches peace and recommends obedience to government, should point out its sectaries as objects of your Excellencies rigour, and merit exclusion from a British island by the express orders of a British commander'.[26]

The backlash

The petition of the Jews dated 16 February found its way into the press on both sides of the Atlantic. On the nearby Dutch island of St Martin, the population observed a day of fasting and prayer. The exiles in St Augustine learnt of the capture of St Eustatius when a vessel from New Providence called in at the port. (See Chapter 9) Within days of the news reaching London, the committee of West India Planters and Merchants were at work, drafting a petition to the King, which made clear their concerns relating to events in the West Indies. Dated 6 April 1781, they pointed out that they had considerable property and debts due to them in the islands subject to the crown of Great Britain, but also on those islands that had lately fallen to the French. They then stated their conviction that it was 'a maxim among civilized Nations, established in humanity and sound policy, 'that war should be carried on with the least possible injury to private property, found in any countries or towns, which may be invaded or conquered'. Having been the beneficiaries of such policies in the West Indies, they were 'seriously alarmed at the general Seizure, made by the Commanders of your Majesty's Sea and Land Forces, of Goods, Merchandise, and Specie, found in the *Dutch* Islands of *Saint Eustatius* and *Saint Martin*' that had surrendered '*without resistance, and at discretion*' in the belief 'that the inhabitants of places, which submit to the will, and surrender themselves to the discretion of an invading enemy, immediately upon such Submission, become the Subjects of that Sovereign, or State, to whom the victorious army belongs, and, consequently, by their allegiance, are entitled to Security in their persons and Property; it being as repugnant to policy as humanity, to permit one Class of subjects to plunder another, the Trader having an equal claim with the Soldier to the protection of Government'. They protested vehemently at the loss of St Eustatius as a

free port, pointing out how only earlier in the year, supplies from the island
had sustained the population of some of Britain's Caribbean islands. What
was more, Parliament had passed legislation in 1780, sanctioning trade in
tobacco with the island for the sake 'of the Consumption and Revenue of
Great-Britain'.[27]

Speeches made in the assembly of the nearby island, St Christopher (St
Kitts) also registered disapproval. One speech made on 6 November 1781
was published in London in 1782. It complained of:

> the oppressive, illegal and unwarrantable proceedings of the commanders
> of the expedition against St. Eustatius towards Dutch, Americans, Jews, and
> British merchants, resident there at the time of the capture; and likewise
> setting forth the indiscriminate confiscation and sale of the greater part of
> the property seized there, and the subsequent sales and direct exportation
> from St. Eustatius, and transportation to the French islands of great
> quantities of the goods, wares and merchandizes sold at public sales, and
> likewise setting forth the great and imminent danger of his Majesty's West
> India islands, and praying our most gracious sovereign to grant effectual
> protection to his loyal and faithful subjects of the Leeward Islands.

The St Christopher protest not only described the 'proceedings of the
commanders' against the resident Dutch, American, Jewish and British
merchants as 'oppressive, illegal and unwarrantable', but the confiscation
of their property was indiscriminate, as was the greater part of its sale.
Great quantities of the 'goods, wares and merchandizes' went to the French
islands. The safety of his Majesty's 'loyal and faithful subjects in the Leeward
Islands' was at risk.[28]

The publication then addressed the defence that the commanders were
making of their actions. The facts of the case were not in dispute, but it was
said that the commanders 'disclaimed all knowledge of them'. The speaker
pointed out that even 'in the most relaxed state of military discipline, the
faults of inferior officers and soldiery are attributed to the commanders,
unless prevented or enquired into and punished'. He continued,

> If then, Americans of every denomination – loyalist or rebel, have been
> stripped of their effects, if the Dutch have been despoiled of their property,
> – if something more than military discretion has been let loose upon British
> subjects, – if the afflicted Jews have not been spared, – if the persons of
> women have been ransacked with indecent search, – if the earth has been
> dug up, if the tombs of the dead have been opened to seek for hidden
> treasure, let the friends of the honourable commanders . . . promote the
> discovery and punishment of the perpetrators of such violence. If they
> refuse, I call upon the House to proceed with the enquiry and address: if
> I am yet unsuccessful . . . forgetting our own calamitous situation, let us
> weep over the dishonour of our country.

Having examined the case of the Americans and the Dutch, the speaker turned once more to the subject of 'the afflicted Jews'.

> Again we see that miserable nation despoiled of their property, banished from St. Eustatius, and truly speaking, not knowing where to hide their heads. For ages has that wandering people been scattered over the face of the earth, pursued by divine providence, harrassed and persecuted by almost every nation with whom they have attempted to incorporate themselves.

Were the Jews still the object of divine displeasure, and were 'the arms of my country to find a miserable justification for violated honour and humanity, in being considered as the instruments of divine vengeance upon the outcasts of mankind'?

On the subject of 'the law of conquest', while in the past, it was 'understood in its most unlimited and cruel sense', its meaning had changed.

> Without resorting to great writers on this subject, conquest is now generally understood (and to the praise of our enemies be it said) used as an incorporation of the conquered subjects into the body of the conquering state.

The *Amsterdam Gazette* of 27 April added further details of the treatment of the Jews. 'The Jews established in the island have been treated in a manner that cries for vengeance. They had notice to quit the island; they were compelled to assemble on a certain day, under pretence of embarking them; they were all driven into the Custom-house, where every one was unmercifully stripped of his all. There was taken from them about 8000 pounds sterling in specie. After this act of violence, they were told they might return to their habitations'.[29]

The pursuit of Rodney's instructions

What probably injured Admiral Rodney's reputation most was the manner in which the affair of St Eustatius was raised in the House of Commons and reported in the press. On 14 May 1781, Edmund Burke introduced a motion in the House of Commons intended to secure the instructions given to Admiral Rodney regarding St Eustatius. In his speech of three and a half hours, Burke first drew attention to Britain's isolation in an international war where she had no friends and many enemies and where the tactics employed in the recent campaign in the West Indies were likely to alienate neutrals and make Britain's position worse. Second, Burke examined the policies of confiscation and deportation visited upon the inhabitants of St Eustatius, with a particular emphasis on the plight of the Jews. Third, he argued that the tactics employed by Rodney and Vaughan were violations of the law of nations and constructed a lengthy argument on the viability of the law of nations and its applicability to St Eustatius. What Burke sought was the release of the instructions given to Rodney, which would reveal to what extent, or otherwise, he had followed or strayed from them in expropriating the property of the island's inhabitants. The motion was lost. Rodney was still in the Caribbean, but that was not the end of the affair.

Burke's speech in the House of Commons, 14 May 1781

When Edmund Burke addressed the House of Commons on 14 May 1781, he sought to 'draw the attention of the House to the very important question of the Seizure and Confiscation of Private Property on the late capture of the Island of St Eustatius'. It was a matter of great consequence and the 'eyes of Europe would be on the conduct of the British legislature in the present instance'. He pointed out that Britain 'stood in a new situation: we were engaged in a most calamitous war'. The speed with which the expedition against St Eustatius had been undertaken was a matter of suspicion. The declaration of hostilities had not yet reached that part of the world that had just suffered 'a most melancholy and general disaster' when all the islands had been hit by a hurricane, 'the scourge of providence' and endured 'common suffering and common distress'.[30] Following the capture of St Eustatius, a 'general confiscation of all the property found upon the island, public and private, Dutch and British; without discrimination, without regard to friend or foe, to the subjects of neutral powers, or to the subjects of our own state: the wealth of the opulent; the goods of the merchant; the utensils of the artisan; the necessaries of the poor were seized on; and a sentence of general beggary pronounced in one moment upon a whole people'. It was a cruelty 'unheard of in Europe for many years, and such as he would venture to proclaim was a most unjustifiable, outrageous, and unprincipled violation of the laws of nations'. When the *Whitehall Evening Post* reported Burke's speech the following day, it was rather more apocalyptic. 'We were standing on the brink of a dreadful precipice; and instead of deserving, or endeavouring to deserve assistance of those who were not already our enemies, we were provoking them by the most flagrant acts of violation of the laws of nations, to put forth their hand and push us headlong to destruction'.[31]

Having cautioned the House on the vulnerability of the kingdom, Burke argued that the commanders were mistaken in their actions on St Eustatius and invoked the laws of nations as his authority on the sanctity of the property of a conquered people. He declared 'that the general confiscation of property found upon the island was contrary to the law of nations, and to that system of war which civilized states had of late, by the consent and practice, thought proper to introduce', in which statement he appeared to be echoing the sentiments expressed in the West India petition issued a month earlier. Burke was willing to agree there was no positive law of nations – no general laws framed and settled by acts in which every nation had a voice. They were 'not like the laws of Britain in black letter, by statute and record; but there was a law of nations as firm, as clear, as manifest, as obligatory, as indispensible'. He started from the premise that it was 'generally established' and agreed 'that the rights of war were not unlimited' and he could demonstrate that there were certain limited and defined rights of war practised in enlightened Europe.[32]

First, he could prove that they were established by reason, in which they had their origin and rise; next, by the convention of parties; third, by the authority of writers, who took the laws and maxims not from their own invention and ideas, but from the content and sense of past ages; and lastly, from the guidance of precedent.

> The basis of the Law of Nations lies in reason, precedent and the Authority of the Grave and Learned. If founded in Reason and Nature it wants no Legislative Sanction for it is the Law of God. If it has precedent in the reciprocal practice of men it has all the force of a tacit universal convention, and if it has the latest, the most learned, and best . . . authorities – it has united all that can make a Law binding on Mankind.

Burke went on to argue that the Law of Nations established that 'the moment any Governour abandons his Government, and surrenders over his people with their consent to another sovereign – the new sovereign succeeds not only to all the rights of the old, but to all his Duties, to all Trusts to all his Cares, and even all his affections . . . there can be no lawful power over men which for a single moment can be freed from a relative Duty of Protection nor does it signifye whether the origin of this power be force or Custom or even actual consent, for no force nor custom can give a destructive power to the Governour over the Governd (sic) . . .'. 'The origin of this principle lies in the practical experience of soldiers and merchants. The sword taught the rules of humanity to the Gown, the compting houses of mercantile men gave new and enlightened and liberal rules of Jurisprudence to the Bench'. The principle had been accepted by Princes and finally by Gownsmen – notably by Vattel. The latest precedent – French conduct in Grenada – supported it.' 'You cannot like Sir G R [Rodney] and Genl V [aughan] sort and select Enemies – The Rule is general – So far as regards the Effects of War all parties are presumd (sic) to have justice on their Side'.

In O'Shaughnessy's view, the commanders had exceeded their instructions which, although giving them discretion over seizures, did not permit a general confiscation. Germain clarified his original instructions when he ordered the commanders not to mistreat the inhabitants and 'not to take the Property of English subjects lawfully exported to St Eustatius'. These orders were disobeyed.[33]

Aftermath

Rodney and Vaughan had interpreted their instructions in the widest possible manner and were vulnerable in legal actions against them. Unlike the Acadians, those deprived of their property on St Eustatius used remonstrances, petitions, the press, the legislatures, and most especially the courts to seek redress, though not necessarily successfully. In something of a panic, Vaughan and Rodney wrote to Lord George Germain to complain about the campaign being mounted against them. They sought assurances that the crown lawyers would assist them in their defence 'against the Persecution already commenced, by these disappointed Miscreants, who pursue every means to harass us, and who we are assured, will employ every Engine of Litigation against us'. Lamely, the British officers pleaded that, as military men, they could not be expected to be familiar with the Laws of Nations and, with even less conviction since both men were members of Parliament, the particular law of their own country. Initially, Germain seems to have supported them, but regretted that 'their business' had delayed them for so long in the islands. In the opinion of historians O'Shaughnessy and Hurst as well as Lord Shelburne, the consequence of Rodney's delay meant that the English fleet failed to prevent De Grasse from reaching the Chesapeake and so cutting off any escape Cornwallis and his troops might have had before the battle of Yorktown sealed their doom.[34]

Burke's speech, 4 December 1781

When Burke made his second speech in Parliament on 4 December on the St Eustatius affair, he covered much the same ground as previously, moving a motion that the house would resolve itself into a committee of the whole,

> to examine into the confiscation of the effects, wares, and merchandize, belonging to his Majesty's new subjects, as well as the British Subjects, on the island of St. Eustatius; and further, that the House would resolve itself into a Committee of the whole House, to enquire into the sale, distribution, and mode of conveyance, of the great part of the said effects, wares, and merchandize, to the islands belonging to France, and to other parts of the dominions of his Majesty's enemies.

Lord George Germain protested. 'With respect to the confiscation, that it was a matter to be discussed in another place; the legality or illegality of the measure was properly cognizable in a court of law: the parties concerned had resorted to the law of the land, and by that law the legality or illegality of the confiscation was to be ascertained. The matter being at issue, did the Honourable Gentleman wish to interfere'? Germain did not think it was the right time 'for Parliament to come to decisions, which, *pendent lite*, must be injurious to one party or the other'. Turning to St Eustatius, Burke argued that since 'Our Commanders' had 'miscarried before St. Vincent's, directed their arms against St Eustatius', which they knew to be lightly defended. [T]here, 'stout privateers well manned might have taken the place', but they 'appeared before it with fifteen ships of the line, a proportionable number of frigates and 3000, or at least 2500, of the best troops in the world'. Ranged against them were 'a few pieces of useless artillery, and about 36 soldiers, who might be assisted with some invalids, etc. to the amount of about 24 more; in all about sixty men.' Burke continued 'The place, being incapable of defence, surrendered at discretion; but it seems that our commanders interpreted discretion' to mean '*destruction*, for they did not leave the conquered a shilling.'[35]

When Dodsley's *Annual Register* for 1782 summarized Burke's speech the language was more colourful and the points more pithy, a difference that has been noted by Burke scholars, but not convincingly explained. After stating that the island was surrendered *at discretion*, the next paragraph engages in a discussion of how Burke interpreted discretion. From the authority of the most celebrated writers on the laws of nations, he demonstrated that it did not warrant 'the arbitrary exercise of any species of rapine or cruelty', and that '*discretion* was universally agreed to be, not *arbitrium cujus libet pravi*; but, *equi bonique viri*'.[36]

Burke also raised the case of Mr Isaac Gouverneur, who 'had traded solely in dry goods, and no naval or military stores whatsoever had passed through his hands; but he acted upon commission from the Congress. This gentleman was seized, his property confiscated, and he himself hurried on board, to be carried to England; while his wife was unable to obtain even a bed from her own house, for her husband and herself'. Carried to England, he spent five months in close confinement 'in a gaol, with the meanest and most depraved malefactors'. His English captors showed none of the consideration made to status and class, which was evident in the cases of the Virginia exiles and those banished to St Augustine. Burke continued with observations on the treatment of the French on St Eustatius. They were also banished, 'but they were indeed treated with a degree of politeness which the other nations had not experienced: the Americans our subjects, and the Dutch our natural allies were treated with uncommon severity; while the French, our natural enemies, met with some respect and politeness; probably because they were the subjects of a polite nation, or rather because a retaliation was apprehended'. 'With respect to the confiscation in general, the Commanders were without the shadow of an excuse; for they had very able assistance at hand, if they had thought proper to resort to it'. They could have consulted the King's Attorney and Solicitor General of St Kitts 'on the point of law', but they did not. Burke declared that he would not abandon the cause of those he had taken up. Though 'the character of an accuser, it was true, was odious . . . . it was not odious to accuse guilt in stars and ribbons; guilt rewarded and countenanced by the official and the opulent'. That Samuel

Hoheb's petition going to a committee of the house was a source of anxiety to Vaughan is apparent from the correspondence that passed between him and Burke. Vaughan wanted to know whether Hoheb had made any particular accusation about his behaviour, to which Burke replied that it was only in connection with his failure to gain access to the general with his complaint. 'Poor Hoheb is very anxious to depart', wrote Burke and on 26 April, a memorial from Hoheb was read to the Treasury. It stated 'that he has presented a Petition to the House of Commons, praying Indemnification for the Losses he sustained by the Capture of Saint Eustatius; that he has been examined, and has verified the Allegations of his Petition before a Committee of the said House, but who have not yet made any Report; and praying that, as he is obliged to return to the West Indies, My Lords would order the payment of his Losses, out of any Monies due to Sir George Rodney And General Vaughan, or afford him such other Relief as they may think fit'. On 18 May came news of Rodney's great victory at the Battle of the Saints, after which it became impractical to pursue the St Eustatius affair any further.[37]

Reflections

A few days later, on 25 May 1782, Burke wrote to the Duke of Portland ' . . . one must admire the ways of Providence which has hung all these Trophies on such a Post, as we know this Rodney to be, a perfect fool, a compleat Rascal, and (as many think) a Poltroon into the Bargain. Rodney, it appeares', has done us a more brilliant, and all circumstances considered, a more effectual Service, than the best, wisest, and bravest commanders have ever performed to this Country'. For that, they must be thankful 'without considering whether the Cup that holds it be of gold or of Clay'. Before the end of 1782, the French captured St Eustatius and after the peace, the Dutch title to the island was restored. Although Jewish merchants continued to live there, their numbers fell rapidly in the early nineteenth century. The trade of the island revived, but relations with the independent United States were no longer the same. Patterns of trade changed as the young republic looked to the Pacific to develop new trade links. Though Barka concludes that the:

> British occupation of Statia resulted in its looting as well as a loss of livelihood and harsh conditions for some citizens, especially Jewish merchants. Yet in the long run Rodney's actions amounted to little more than an interruption of normal trade patterns. After a period of political instability, the Dutch regained St. Eustatius; and by the 1790s, it was once again a thriving port with an even larger population and expansive mercantile activity.[38]

It was not to last.

National honour

Burke linked the violation of the laws of nations to national dishonour when he first raised the matter in his speech on 14 May 1781. He raised it again in his speech on 4 December, but he dwelt on this characterization most fully when he presented Samuel Hoheb's petition to the house on 4 February 1782 in response to the Secretary of War's dismissal of his earlier arguments.

> The fortune of war might wrest victory from us, without disgracing us; or robbing us of our virtue, which was beyond the reach of fortune: but our commanders had robbed us of character.; they had committed acts which had robbed the nation of that high name which it was accustomed to bear in Europe, for its liberality and justice

At St Eustatius, the commander may have been negligent but his negligence 'did not dishonour the nation; it was when private property was ransacked; when innocent people were robbed stripped of all they were worth, and banished from the island, that such acts of barbarity would remain stains upon the national honour, if the nation did not, by some public declaration, express its abhorrence of them . . . '. Here, the character of England was a stake.[39]

The British attack on St Eustatius and the treatment of those they found there constituted one of the most notorious incidents of the war between Britain and the rebel colonies. Early histories of the American Revolution contrasted the generosity of spirit demonstrated by the French commanders operating in the Caribbean with the inhumanity displayed by the British. David Ramsay (1789) and Mercy Otis Warren (1805), who arguably wrote the two best contemporary studies of the Revolution and who were themselves major players in the conflict, both drew attention to the questionable behaviour of the British in the Caribbean, and especially St Eustatius.[40] Modern historians have tended to ignore it, but in terms of simple rapacity and the displacement of a population, it is a sordid finale to the series of such expulsions undertaken by the British in their transatlantic empire.

CONCLUSION

This has been a study in the exercise of imperial power in the early modern period, and the way that authorities at all levels moved, expelled or transported people within the empire. At this time, no place in the British Atlantic could be unaffected by events and relationships in what was an increasingly interconnected social and economic society.[1] Moreover, domestic British policies were affected by the development of an overseas empire, and the lives of people in the colonies were, in their turn, affected by what authorities were doing in Britain. The forced movements of people had different origins, and involved different processes and consequences. Sometimes, individuals and groups were driven out by pressure on the authorities from below, for example, by a community's urge to expel the unwanted criminals or aliens in their midst. On other occasions, expulsion was instigated and managed from above as an expedient way of dealing with troublesome groups or an entire people. Whatever the driving force, these practices shaped many communities, both the ones losing people and the ones receiving them. The results at the individual level were extraordinary. A petty criminal from an obscure village in England could end up at the western frontier of British America. A Native American might end up in the West Indies. Refugee Acadians might find themselves on the streets of Liverpool. It is almost impossible to equate some of these experiences and what they meant to those enduring them, or fit them into a neat explanatory framework. The transportation of small numbers of gypsies from England or Scotland is hard to compare with the wholesale displacement of thousands in Ireland in the 1650s or in Nova Scotia a century later. Yet, they were all the outcomes of a series of disparate processes under the British Empire.

What these actions have in common, and this is perhaps their most extraordinary feature, is that the authorities were able to get away with them at all. That might be an exaggeration, perhaps, with the case of criminals from England and Scotland, for whom the gallows was the only alternative. But these were not the majority, for most transported criminals were relatively minor offenders. Public support for this kind of punishment was equivocal, partly because pamphlets and newspapers reported that hardened criminals could easily return. In the case of most offenders sent from the local courts of English counties, little was heard of them after the newspapers recorded their safe arrival.[2] With regard to rebels and those deemed potentially rebellious, however, the legal foundation of banishment was more uncertain. Some expulsions were so extreme that political leaders found it hard to legitimize them, even in retrospect. Power and legitimacy were rarely neatly associated, and the law was often an afterthought, rather than at the start of the process. At the personal level of those taking the actions, some leaders felt the need for justification, as the self-defensive letters of Oliver Cromwell from Drogheda, or Admiral Rodney's replies to the coruscating attacks by Edmund Burke on the treatment of the Jews in St Eustatius, show. Their reputations were sullied at the time, and ever since, by their responsibility. Yet, with regard to groups such as the Jacobite prisoners, a fig leaf of law was constructed to cover the transportations to the colonies. The legal alternative, if it had been possible, would have been mass trials and executions for treason and rebellion, but severity with regard to rebels, as with convicted criminals, had unfortunate repercussions if taken too far. The state needed mercy as much as severity, and its legitimacy would have been under question if gratuitous cruelties had been inflicted in Britain. The story was different in the colonies, where military authorities in particular could disguise their actions.

The British Empire kept discovering that having power was not necessarily the same as having the law on your side, even if retrospective justification was found. So the administrators, the royal governors, British commanders and even the secretaries of state, all had to be concerned with the lawfulness of what they wanted to do. These were, if not trained lawyers, certainly men of the law. It is deeply implausible that Admiral Rodney knew nothing at all about the laws of his own country as well as of the laws of nations. Yet, his example suggests that in the British Atlantic, it was possible to be out of control and beyond the law. Though it was less and less possible in Britain or Ireland, in the colonies, the military authorities particularly could evade immediate legal or even political accountability. Partly, this was simply a matter of distance and the time taken for letters to go to and from London. Their evasion of accountability, however, was aided considerably if the banishments could be hidden behind the expediency of war. Thus, both Governor Lawrence and Admiral Rodney could be sure that there would be no legal challenges to their actions at the time, though it is significant that civil suits involving the seizure of property were directed at Rodney and the British government for years after the forcible evacuations in St Eustatius. Property mattered in the eighteenth century, and the propertied could make it count through a civil law whose processes were both more time-consuming, and more expensive, than the authorities could withstand.

The fact we know so much about some of these expulsions is a tribute to the power of the printing press as much as anything else. Most of the banished resorted, if they could, to resistance within the law. Legal and political-administrative records have, therefore, formed the key sources for this chapter, often providing rare glimpses of how people reacted to plans for their expulsion. Just as law became more diverse in this period, proliferating in the British Atlantic, so claims against the over-mighty actions of authority had to take different forms. Victims of banishment used the legal weapons available to them. Jacobite captives refused to sign petitions asking for mercy (since that was admitting guilt) or, if they did sign, refused to sign indentures for their own servitude. The Quakers refused to swear oaths and, like Jacobite petitioners on ships in the Chesapeake, seemingly read their law books and demanded to know by what right – or law – they were being banished from their homeland. Acadians petitioned in Massachusetts, and had a sympathetic press in England. Monmouth's and Argyll's rebels managed to write their interpretation into British history – to the annoyance even of their supporters. These were people intensely aware of their rights in some ways, and possessed a strong sense that the legal traditions of England and Scotland and its associated colonies, did not allow arbitrary transportation of people without due process of law. Legalism was, therefore, not just a convenient device for the state's managers, but deeply embedded in popular culture.

The diversity of these processes of banishment though, makes it hard to generalize about the consequences. Throughout the period, forced labour, exile, judicial banishment, and ethnic cleansing thrown in for good measure, mingled uneasily together. The niches into which the banished were to fit were just as various. The losers in the political struggle saw themselves as different from criminals or ordinary prisoners. But there was never a clear definition of 'political' banishment. Generally, political prisoners after 1800 escaped penal labour, though this was never clearly recognized in the British system, despite campaigns in the nineteenth and early twentieth centuries on behalf of Chartists organizers in the 1840s, Irish nationalists and female suffragists. To British law before that period, there were no 'political' crimes, just crimes, and strenuous efforts were made in times of rebellion to make sure that the captured confessed their treasons so that they could be graciously forgiven and transported. The Jacobite prisoners were the poorest sort, and were sold as such.[3] Though they saw that as unjust, it was not that different a service than that endured by voluntary migrants. Even where convicts were reduced to servant status, as happened to British transportees, they were treated like the servants in husbandry in English farming, only on much longer contracts of indenture, and much more severe penalties for their breach. The labour was not clearly specified in law, but the time spans of it were. The most common period, usually seven years, had become established by custom in the 1600s. Things were not so clear with some ethnic or cultural groups expelled simply for being in the wrong place in the eyes of authority, such as some Native Americans, the Acadians, or the Jews of St Eustatius – these were given no destination or any intended role after they had been removed. In these instances, the political urge to expel sometimes overrode any forward planning. There were some exceptions – though some Native Americans were formally exported into slavery in the bitter aftermath of King Philip's War in the 1670s, the Nanziatticos of Virginia were exported into indentured service. Most forced migration, apart from that from Africa, did not result in formal chattel slavery. The acquisition of what were, to Europeans, empty lands, provided both the means and the justification for different forms of forced migration. 'The creation of empires brought banishment and forced labour together in the eighteenth century'.[4] The need to ensure the 'better peopling' of new territory provided a framework in which the operations of the judicial system could work to fill a need through the criminal conviction and transportation of the convicted. Colonial interests did not always extend to interfering with the selection of those banished and shipped, as long as a steady supply of labour was maintained. The official drives to expel and the colonial need to import, what might be called the push and the pull factors in banishment, operated sometimes together, sometimes in conflict, first in an Atlantic, and eventually in a global context.

The consequences of these human movements are not always clear to historians. Were Ireland or Northern England full of minor criminals banished 'furth the kingdom' of Scotland? If so, they are scarcely visible for most of the early modern period. In the case of British and Irish convicts transported to the North American colonies, their destinies as individuals can sometimes be traced, often in the records of further crimes and punishments. In their service – or rather, in their attempts to escape service – they emerge in the newspapers as runaways. In the mid-Atlantic colonies of Virginia, Maryland and Pennsylvania, in particular, slaves and indentured servants are often found running away to find freedom. In the often vivid descriptions of clothing and appearance can be seen evidence of defiance, individualism and self-fashioning among the poorest and most subordinated groups in colonial America. But a generation afterwards, white convict servants are almost invisible. They did not write their history, but their example is suggestive of the new framework of eighteenth-, compared with seventeenth-century society. Increasingly, in the period from 1600 to 1800, what appeared in print shaped the final judgement on the actions of the powerful and the weak alike, both locally and internationally. When American General Horatio Gates wrote to his opposite number Burgoyne in 1777 in the Saratoga campaign, complaining of the employment of British-led Indians committing what the twentieth century would call 'war crimes', Burgoyne accused him of threatening him with the 'gazettes', that is, the newspapers:

> You seem to threaten me with European publications, which affects me as little as any other threats you could make; but in regard to American publications, whether your charge against me, which I acquaint you of believing, was penned *from* a Gazette, or *for* a Gazette, I and demand of you as a man of honour, that should it appear in print at all, this answer may follow it.[5]

Making sure your version of history was published became a necessity in this period, and not for nothing did Edmund Burke make sure that printers received details of his speeches personally from himself. Quakers always wrote and printed, and distributed their experiences through their writings to what was already by the 1660s one of the best organized and networked communities in the Atlantic. Wherever a printing press was available, and protests could reach it, publicity and accountability would follow. This was, however, outside the law, and most of the expulsions explored in this chapter were best known through the retrospective collections of memoirs, often collated years later – sometimes in the nineteenth century, as memory and national identity were combined to invent, or reinvent, the histories of the Jacobites or Acadians. The latter seem to have evoked the guilty conscience of Victorian politicians, who sponsored the publication in Nova Scotia of many of the official records. Robert Forbes's collection of oral testimonies and letters from the '45, *The Lyon in Mourning,* was only fully published by the end of the 1800s, but had achieved canonical status in the earlier part of the century. The books of Quaker sufferings were never as full again after the early part of the eighteenth century, but they managed to offend most governments with their pacificism from the Seven Years War to the American Revolution, to the 1916 introduction of conscription in Britain in World War I. Most of the victims of banishment, though, left few textual memorials outside the official records, nor did they define a collective identity. Only now do we trace the ancestry of the great artist of the period just before and during the Revolutionary War, Charles Willson Peale, to his convict father.[6] There were no communities of convicts that can be detected, and, unlike in Australia, the documentation of their descendants is difficult. Elsewhere, the effects of the processes described in this book can only be faintly traced. 'Cajan' music and food are internationally known, though few enjoying the culture trace it back to the forcible expulsion of Acadians from Nova Scotia – significantly, their experience is part of *their* historical memory and those of both Canada and Louisiana. With a few exceptions, therefore, it seems that many of the forcibly exiled disappeared into the surrounding population, and few retained an identity based on the memory of their expulsion.

The Atlantic has been the main focus of this chapter, as it was the primary arena for the forcible movements of people before 1800. If we are to take Atlantic history seriously, we need to ask what difference such a perspective has made to the history of banishment. As Joyce Chaplin has put it, 'The term Atlantic has spread throughout studies of early America – into syllabi, articles, monographs, and now textbooks – but it is not clear whether it has yet fulfilled its genuinely exciting promise to change the field'.[7] For the study of banishment, an Atlantic perspective allows us to examine the levels of integration, diversity or divergence in the British Empire. It was not a political unity, or subject to the same law code everywhere. This is reflected in the different modes of banishment adopted at different times in different places. There were many diasporas in the British Atlantic, not all of them the responsibility of the British authorities, and there were therefore many different responses to the experience of being scattered. Perhaps the most important aspect of taking an Atlantic view is that it, to some extent, mirrors that of the imperial managers of the early modern period who, whether in London or Jamaica, Dublin or New York, clearly saw their actions in the wider framework of British zones of control in the Atlantic. They became accustomed to moving people around either by inducements or force, and made few preparations for the consequences. Most of those displaced from Britain had, perhaps, been defined by authority as having lost their right to a place in society, through crime, religious dissent or rebellion. The same could not be said of conquered peoples on the other side of the Atlantic who belonged to the territories from which they were expelled. Yet, both were mingled and intertwined in these centuries of imperial movement. Like Cromwell's 'settlement' of Ireland, it is sometimes difficult to distinguish between plantation and transplantation, resettlement or transportation. The forced and the free ended up in much the same places, and, with the exception of African slaves, were often in much the same situation. These processes did not stop at 1800. Convicts were still shipped to Australia for more than 50 years after that, and indentured servitude was reinvented after the abolition of slavery through the recruitment of millions of people from the Indian subcontinent to work within the British Empire. Assisted migration sent children from Britain to Australia and Canada as late as the 1950s. Most of these later movements were not banishment in the sense of the examples taken in this chapter, but they stem from a similar and enduring urge among imperial administrators to redraw the map of the world's labour force. Migration and exile were fundamental aspects of the traditions of Empire.

NOTES

Introduction

1 Aaron S. Fogleman, 'From Slaves, Convicts, and Servants to Free Passengers: the Transformation of Immigration in the Era of the American Revolution', *Journal of American History*, 85 (1998), 43–76.

2 *Minutes of the Court of Rensselaerswyck, 1648–52*, Translated and edited by A. J. F. Van Laer (Albany, NY: University of New York, 1922), p. 51.

3 William R. Jones, 'Sanctuary, Exile and the Law: The Fugitive and Public Authority in Medieval England and Modern America' in Elisabeth A. Cawthon and David e. Narrett eds, *Essays on English Law and the American Experience* (Arlington, Texas: Texas A & M University Press, 1994), pp. 19–41.

4 Gwenda Morgan and Peter Rushton, *Eighteenth-Century Criminal Transportation: The Formation of the Criminal Atlantic* (Houndmills, Basingstoke: Palgrave Macmillan, 2004).

5 *Puritanism and Liberty, Being the Army debates from the Clarke Manuscripts*, selected and edited by A. S. P. Woodhouse (London: J. M. Dent and Sons, 1938), p. 54.

6 Robin Cohen, 'Diasporas and the Nation-State: From Victims to Challengers', *International Affairs*, 12(3) (1996), pp. 507–20.

Chapter 1

1 35 Henry VIII c.2, *Statutes at Large from the First Year of King James the First to the Tenth Year of the Reign of King William the Third*, 1543 (London: Mark Basket, 1763) Vol. 2, p. 361.

2 Richard Burn, *The History of the Poor Laws, with Observations* (London: H. Woodfall and W. Strahan, 1764), pp. 22–59; W. J. Chambliss, 'A Sociological Analysis of the Law of Vagrancy', *Social Problems*, 12(1) (1964), 67–77. *The Annalls of Ipswiche: The Laws, Customs and Government of that Towne, Collected from the Records Bookes and Writings of that Towne by Nathaniell Bacon*, ed. W. H. Richardson (originally 1654, Ipswich: S. H. Cowell, 1884). p. 135, ordered 25 February, to leave by St David's Day, and p. 181, Thomas Gardner, 1508; see also pp. 319, 398 a foreigner, his wife and children 'ordered to depart the town' (1599), and 441.

3 On poverty, vagrancy and social policies, see Paul Slack, *Poverty and Policy in Tudor and Stuart England* (London: Longman, 1988); A. L. Beier, *Masterless Men: The Vagrancy Problem in England, 1560–1640* (London: Methuen, 1985). For modern comparisons, see Mark Rathbone, 'Vagabond!', *History Today*, 51 (2005), pp. 8–13.

4 *The Statutes at Large of England and of Great-Britain*, ed. T. E. Tomlins (London: George Eyre and Andrew Strahan, 1811, Vol. 2, p. 763; Slack, *Poverty and Policy*, pp. 122–7; Patricia Fumerton, *Unsettled: The Culture of Mobility and the Working Poor in Early Modern England* (Chicago, IL: University of Chicago Press, 2006).

5 *The Statutes at Large of England and Great Britain*, 20 Volumes, ed. John Raithby (London: George Eyre and Andrew Strahan, 1811) Vol. 4, pp. 331–9 for 1572 and 504–9 for the 14 Eliz. I c.5 and 39 Eliz.I c.4.

6 Basket, *Statutes at Large* ,Vol. 2, p. 687, with fuller text in Raithby *Statutes at Large*, Vol. 4, pp. 504–9; *A Proclamation for the due and speedy execution of the Statute against Rogues, Vagabonds, Idle and Dissolute Persons* (London: Robert Barker, 1603), EEBO and STC 1875:10; renewal, for example, in 1627 under Charles I, Basket, *Statutes at Large*, Vol. 3, p. 128, and p. 243.

7 Basket, *Statutes at Large*, Vol. 3, pp. 36 (1604) and 77 (1609).

8 Adam Hansen, 'Realizing Rogues: Theory, Organization, Dialogue', *Ephemera*, 4(4) (2004), pp. 328–46, p. 333, quoting Craig Dionne and Steve Mentz, eds, *Rogues and Early Modern English Culture* (Ann Arbor, MI: University of Michigan Press, 2004) as claiming an origin in the 1560s.

9 See Adam Hansen, 'Realizing Rogues', who stresses the carnivalesque usage of the image; quotation from p. 334; Craig Dionne and Steve Mentz, eds, *Rogues and Early Modern English Culture* (Ann Arbor, MI: University of Michigan Press, 2004); Gāmini Salgādo, *Cony-catchers and Bawdy Baskets: An Anthology of Elizabethan Low Life* (Harmondsworth: Penguin, 1972); for plays, see Rebecca Ann Bach, 'Ben Jonson's "Civil Savages"', *Studies in English Literature, 1500–1900*, 37(2) (1997), pp. 277–93.

10 A. Fraser, *The Gypsies* 2nd ed. (Oxford: Blackwell, 1995), pp. 132–3, and 171.

11 See Peter Bakker, 'An Early Vocabulary of British Romani (1616): A Linguistic Analysis', *Romani Studies 5*, 12(2) (2002), pp. 75–101, derived from a 1616 Winchester confession of a man arrested because he was associating with gypsies, whom he had met in London; Joad Raymond, *Pamphlets and Pamphleteering in Early Modern England* (Cambridge: Cambridge University Press, 2003), pp. 18, Salgādo, *Cony-Catchers*; B. E. Bent, *A New Dictionary of the Terms Ancient and Modern of the Canting Crew . . .* (London: W. Hawes, 1699), and Janet Sorensen, 'Vulgar Tongues: Canting Dictionaries and the Language of the People in Eighteenth-Century Britain', *Eighteenth-Century Studies*, 37(3) (2004), pp. 435–54. On disguises, see Patricia Fumerton, 'Making Vagrancy (In)Visible: The Economics of Disguise in Early Modern Rogue Pamphlets', *English Literary Renaissance*, 33(2) (2003), pp. 211–27; on counterfeit Egyptians in print, Mark Netzloff, *England's Internal Colonies: Class, Capital,and the Literature of Early Modern English Colonialism* (Palgrave Macmillan, 2004), pp. 135–70; Tobias B. Hug, *Impostures in Early Modern England: Representations and Perceptions of Fraudulent Identities*

(Manchester: Manchester University Press, 2009), pp. 112–15; Deborah
Epstein Nord, *Gypsies and the British Imagination, 1807–1930* (New York:
Columbia University Press, 2006).

12 22 Henry VIII. c.10, (1530); H. T. Crofton, 'Early Annals of the Gypsies in
England,' *Journal of the Gypsy Lore Society*, 1st ser, 1(1) (1888), pp. 5–24,
pp. 10–11.

13 Act of 5 Elizabeth, c. 20, Basket, *Statutes at Large*, Vol. 2, pp. 560–1, and
C. S. L. Davies, 'Slavery and Protector Somerset; The Vagrancy Act of 1547',
The Economic History Review, N.S. 19(3) (1966), pp. 533–49, p. 538, note 6.

14 Crofton, 'Early Annals', p. 17; David Mayall, *English Gypsies and State
Policies* (University of Hertfordshire Press, 1995), p. 45; A. L. Beier, 'Vagrants
and the Social Order in Elizabethan England', *Past and Present*, 64 (1974),
pp. 3–29, pp. 7–8; Davies, 'Slavery and Protector Somerset'.

15 *Middlesex County Records*, ed. John Cordy Jeaffreson (Clerkenwell: 1886),
Vol. 1, pp. 221, 253 and pp. 266–7 (20 January 43 Eliz 1); Peter Bakker, 'An
Early Vocabulary of British Romani (1616)'.

16 Bryan Belton, *Questioning Gypsy Identity: Ethnic Narratives in Britain and
America* (Lanham, MD: Altamira, Rowman and Littlefield, 2004), p. 70, Joan
Scot of Henrico County in 1695; *Maryland Gazette*, 24 September 1767, three
convict servants, gypsies called Smith, ran away from the Patuxent Ironworks.
They had been imported in the *Thornton*, 'lately'.

17 Northumberland Archives, henceforth NLA QSO, 5, p. 60 Michaelmas 171.

18 Burn, *History of the Poor Laws*, p. 50, 12 Anne c.23; A. E. Smith, *Colonists in
Bondage: White Servitude and Convict Labour in America, 1607–1776* (NY:
Norton, 1971, originally University of North Carolina Press, 1947), p. 138
regards this Act as preventing transportation just for vagabondage, but he
misses the useful category of 'incorrigible rogue' which is how some vagrants,
found to be such by two magistrates, could be bound to servitude in the
colonies; NLA QSO, 5, pp. 64, 74 and 110 Michaelmas 1771 and Epiphany
and Michaelmas 1712; pp. 120, 124, 340, 341, 354.

19 Bill M. Donovan, 'Changing Perceptions of Social Deviance: Gypsies in
Early Modern Portugal and Brazil', *Journal of Social History*, 26(1) (1992),
pp. 33–53, p. 33; Pieter Spierenburg, 'Deviance and Repression in the
Netherlands. Historical Evidence and Contemporary Problems', *Historical
Social Research*, 11(1) (1986), pp. 4–16, p. 12; Gwenda Morgan and Peter
Rushton, *Eighteenth-Century Criminal Transportation: The Formation of
the Criminal Atlantic* (Houndmills, Basingstoke: Palgrave Macmillan, 2004),
pp. 80–5. See also Micheál Hayes, 'Indigenous Otherness: Some Aspects of
Irish Traveller Social History', *Éire-Ireland*, 41(3&4) (2006), pp. 33–161;
David Mayall, 'The Making of British Gypsy Identities, c.1500–1800',
Immigrants and Minorities, 11(1) (1992), pp. 21–41; Jim MacLaughlin,
'European Gypsies and the Historical Geography of Loathing', *Review
(Fernand Braudel Center)*, 22(1) (1999), pp. 31–59.

20 *Proclamation for the speedie sending away of the Irish Beggars out of this
Kingdome into their owne Countrey and for the Suppressing of English
Rogues and Vagabonds according to Our Lawes* (London: Robert Barker,
1633, EEBO 1813: 38). See Mary Ann Lyons, '"Vagabonds", "Mendiants",

"Gueux": French Reaction to Irish Immigration in the Early Seventeenth Century', *French History*, 14(4) (2000), pp. 363–82, p. 363, and Éamon Ò Ciosáin, '*Voloumous Deamboulare*: The Wandering Irish in French Literature, 1600–1789', in Anthony Coulson ed., *Exiles and Emigrants: Crossing Thresholds in European Culture and Society* (Brighton: Sussex Academic Press, 1997), pp. 32–42.

21 Paul A. Slack, 'Vagrants and Vagrancy in England, 1598–1664', *The Economic History Review*, N.S. 27(3) (1974), pp. 360–79, p. 365.

22 Durham Record Office, EP/Ga.SM 4/1, pp. 28–9 and 119 (1641–2, poor from Ireland) 149, 164, and even later such as p. 149, 24 April 1647/8.

23 Smith, *Colonists*, pp. 138–9; see Middlesex Vol. 2, p. 140, 3 September 16, James I; p. 225, 6 August 16, James I; p. 305 for undateable case of reprieve from branding on these grounds.

24 Barry M. Coldrey, '". . . A Place to Which Idle Vagrants May Be Sent". The First Phase of Child Migration during the Seventeenth and Eighteenth Centuries', *Children and Society*, 13 (1999), pp. 32–47, pp. 35–8; see *The Records of the Virginia Company of London: The Court Book*, Vol. 1, eds, S. M. Kingsbury and H. L. Osgood (Washington, DC: 1906), pp. 270–1, 293, 304–8; R. C. Johnson, 'The Transportation of Vagrant Children from London to Virginia, 1618–22', in H. S. Reinmuth ed., *Early Stuart Studies* (Minneapolis, MN: University of Minnesota Press, 1970), pp. 137–51.

25 A. L. Beier, 'Social Problems in Elizabethan London', *The Journal of Interdisciplinary History*, 9(2) (1978), pp. 203–21, p. 219.

26 *Calendar of State Papers, Domestic Series of the Reign of Charles I. 1631–33*, ed. John Bruce (London: Longman, Green, Longman and Roberts, 1862), p. 433, October 1631.

27 *Acts of the Privy Council of England, Colonial Series*, Vol. 1, eds, W. L. Grant and James Munro (Hereford: for HMSO, 1908), p. 310 [henceforth, Acts PCC].

28 SP CI, 1633–4, p. 457, 7 March 1634; CI, 1637–8, p. 467.

29 For Middlesex cases, see Peter Wilson Coldham, 'The "Spiriting" of London Children to Virginia, 1648–85', *The Virginia Magazine of History and Biography*, 8(3) (1975), 280–7; Coldrey, '". . . A Place to Which Idle Vagrants May be Sent"', 'dark underside', p. 38; J. Harry Bennett, 'William Whaley, Planter of Seventeenth-Century Jamaica', *Agricultural History*, 40(2) (1966), pp. 113–24, pp. 120–1. See also David Souden, '"Rogues, Whores and Vagabonds"? Indentured Servant Emigrants to North Anmerica and the Case of Mid-Seventeenth-Century Bristol', *Social History*, 3(1) (1978), pp. 23–41, and John Wareing, '"Violently Taken Away or Cheatingly Duckoyed": The Illicit Recruitment in London of Indentured Servants for the American Colonies', *The London Journal*, 26(2) (2001), pp. 1–22.

30 See Netzloff, *England's Internal Colonies*, who argues the necessity of a simultaneous view of both domestic and external colonialism for this period.

31 J. M. Beattie, 'The Criminality of Women in Eighteenth-Century England', *Journal of Social History*, 8(4) (1975), pp. 80–116, p. 112, n.44; Basket, *Statutes at Large*, Vol. 4, pp. 222–3 for 1706 Act.

32 J. M. Beattie, 'The Royal Pardon and Criminal Procedure in Early Modern England', *Historical Papers/Communications Historiques*, 22(1) (1987), pp. 9–22, pp. 11 and 13; J. M. Beattie, *Policing and Punishment in London, 1660–1750: Urban Crime and the Limits of Terror* (Oxford, Oxford University Press, 2001), p. 293.

33 Radzinowicz, Vol. I, ch. 8 pp. 231ff; *Hanging Not Punishment Enough* (London: A. Baldwin, 1701), William Paley, *Principles of Moral and Political Philosophy* (1785), pp. 411–12, cited by Radzinowicz, p. 254.

34 See J. M. Beattie, *Crime and the Courts in England, 1660–1800* (Princeton, NJ: Princeton University Press, 1986), p. 143 for the Tudor removals from benefit such as burglary, highway robbery, horse stealing and pickpocketing, and p. 144 for the late seventeenth- and early eighteenth-century modifications, involving shops, warehouses, stables and outhouses.

35 Smith, *Colonists in Bondage*, p. 92, quoted in Morgan and Rushton, *Eighteenth-Century Criminal Transportation*, pp. 9–10; Barbara Shapiro, 'Law Reform in Seventeenth Century England', *The American Journal of Legal History*, 19(4) (1975), pp. 280–312, p. 286.

36 Richard S. Dunn, *Sugar and Slaves: The Rise of the Planter Class in the British West Indies* (New York: W. W. Norton and Company, 1973), p.xiv.

37 TNA PRO Chancery Patent Rolls (list and Index Society, Vol. 157), p. 30, 21 Jan 1615; Chancery Patent Rolls Index, C66, Vol. 24, 1–2 CAR. I, f.12, 6 March (Commission about priests, quoted); and Index 3 & 4 CAR. I, f.97, 20 September (Commission for reprieves, quoted).

38 *Calendar of the Patent Rolls, Edward I, 1281–92* (London: HMSO, 1893), p. 3 and *passim*.

39 *Calendar of State Papers Colonial* [henceforth CSP Col.], Vol. 9, p. 56, 13 June 1618, Ambrose Smith, and p. 57, 3 February 1619, Harry Reade.

40 *Acts PCC*, Vol. 1, pp. 10–12.

41 *Acts PCC*, p. 13, 1617, George Harrison, horse stealing; and p. 288, 15 November 1633.

42 *Acts PCC*, I, pp. 10–12; Middlesex Records, Vol. 2, pp. 224 and 226, 1618 and 1620.

43 *State Papers Colonial*, 1637–8; 1661, p. 203; and p. 370, 1663; 1631–2, p. 433; 1635–6, p. 56; Basket, *Statutes at Large*, Vol. 3, p. 7, 2 James c.7, *An Act to Take away the Benefit of Clergy for some Kind of Manslaughter*.

44 *State Papers Charles I*, 1637, p. 208, 3 June 1637.

45 *State Papers Charles I*, 1631–2, pp. 119–20, and p. 184, 18 November.

46 *Acts PCC*, Vol. I, pp. 12 licence, and p. 52, warrants.

47 Smith, *Colonists in Bondage*, p. 94. Cases involving 31 people between 1635 and 1639 *Calendar State Papers Colonial* (CSP Col.) Vol. 9, pp. 75, 76, 78–9, 79, 81 and 82.

48 CSP Col., Vol. 9, p. 75, 27 July 1635.

49 CSP Col., Vol. 9, p. 75: case of Thomas Brice, 27 July 1635; Ingram, p. 76, 8 March 1635.

50 CSP Col., Vol. 9, p. 82, 5 February 1639.

51 CSP Col., Vol. 9, p. 75, 27 July 1635.

52 CSP Col., Vol. 9, pp. 78–9, 18 June 1635.

53 *State Papers Charles I*, 1637, pp. 214, 403, 422; *State Papers Charles I*, 1637–8, pp. 149, 299, 220; they were initially supposed to be held in Lostwithiel, Cornwall (Bastwick), Lancaster (Burton), and Caernarvon (Prynne); Lilburne, *State Trials*, Vol. 5, pp. 407–60, particularly p. 415; Pauline Gregg, *Free-Born John: A Biography of John Lilburne* (London: J. M. Dent and Sons, 1961), pp. 293–302, 312–33.

54 F. A. Inderwick, *The Interregnum (A.D. 1648–60): Studies of the Commonwealth, Legislative, Social and Legal* (London: Sampson Low, Marston, Searle and Rivington, 1891), p. 231; Mary Cotterell, 'Interregnum Law Reform: The Hale Commission of 1652', *The English Historical Review*, 83(329) (1968), pp. 689–704; Robert Zaller, 'The Debate on Capital Punishment during the English Revolution', *The American Journal of Legal History*, 31(2) (1987), pp. 126–44; Michael Rogers, 'Gerrard Winstanley on Crime and Punishment', *The Sixteenth Century Journal*, 27(3) (1996), pp. 735–47.

55 9 August 1650, in *Acts and Ordinances of the Interregnum, 1642–60*, eds C. H. Firth and R. S. Tait (London: HMSO, 1911), Vol. 2, pp. 409–12; there were some time limits involved in prosecution, in that the person had to be indicted within six months of the alleged offence (again, the parallels with treasonable words and practices are significant).

56 Firth and Rait, *Acts and Ordinances*, Vol. 2, pp. 425–9, p. 425, 3 October 1650.

57 26 June 1657, Firth and Rait, *Acts and Ordinances*, Vol. 2, pp. 1250–62, quotation from p. 1258 and 1251.

58 Thomas Burton, *The Diary of Thomas Burton* . . . ed John Towill Rutt (London: Henry Colburn, 1828), 4 Vols, Vol. 2, p. 142: the Irish attainder law was a month after this proposal, suggesting that the measure was only included there.

59 Burton, *Diary*, Vol. 1, pp. 38–9, 6 December 1656, p, 57 and pp. 88–9, 9 December 1656.

60 Beattie, *Policing and Punishment*, p. 29, ftn 84; 19 Chas II, c.3 (1666); pp. 291–2; rural incendiarism was also punishable by death or seven years transportation (again, in 1670). See also the table of failed and successful legislation, p. 292.

61 Beattie, *Policing and Punishment*, pp. 288, 295 and (quotation), 303; undated letter but seems to be 1666 from the surrounding documents; SP 44/14 p. 94 reports.

62 Beattie, *Policing and Punishment*, pp. 296, 297 and 302.

63 P. W. Coldham, *The Complete Book of Emigrants in Bondage*, including the supplement, *More Emigrants in Bondage*, (from Genealogical Publishing Co, Maryland, 1988 and 2002). There were 490 transportees in the eighteenth century from assizes and Berwick, 1718–1800, 218 of them reprieved for transportation: G. Morgan and P. Rushton, *Rogues, Thieves and the Rule of Law: the Problem of Law Enforcement in North-East England* (London: UCL

Press, 1998), p. 158. Note that Coldham also has evidence of frequent voyages by northeast ships to America before 1700 in the CD-ROM version of *The Complete Book of Emigrants in Bondage*; A. E. Smith, 'The Transportation of Convicts in the American Colonies in the Seventeenth Century', *American Historical Review*, 39(1934), pp. 232–49 (1934), p. 238.

64 *The Newgate Calendar*, ed. Donal Ó Danachair, 6 Volumes (Published by the Ex-classics Project, 2009, http://www.exclassics.com) Vol. 1, pp. 180–90.

65 http://www.Oldbaileyonline.com, accessed 20 March 2012; Elizabeth Longman, Ordinary's Account, 17 May 1676, Reference Number: 16760517; also Ordinary's Account, 19 December 1684, Jane Voss; Anne Savery, transportee returning to England, 13 October 1680. Anne Savery, transportee returning to England, London Metropolitan Archives, LSP/1680/1; Mary Defoe, transportee returning to England, 12 December 1683, t16840227–28; Peter Barker, transportee returning to England, 10 October 1688, t16881010–15; Dr Best, transportee returning to England, 22 February 1693; LMA LSP/1693/2; Mary Pynes, transportee returning to England, 6 December 1699, t16991213–22.

66 *SP Col.*, Vol. 7, 1669–74, pp. 63–4, 29 April 1670; *APC*, Vol. 1, p. 553, 21 October 1670; *SP Col.*, Vol 7, p. 242, 17 July 1672.

67 See Morgan and Rushton, *Eighteenth-Century Transportation*, pp. 127–51.

Chapter 2

1 Pieter Spierenburg, 'Close to the Edge: Criminals and Marginals in Dutch Cities', *Eighteenth-Century Studies*, 31(3) (1998), pp. 355–9, p. 355.

2 *Calendar of the State Papers Relating to Scotland*, I, 1509–89, ed. M. J. Thorpe (London: Longman, Brown, Green, Longmans and Roberts, 1858) – the 'banished lords', including the Earls of Marr, Angus and Glamis, pp. 479, 491, 508, 510, wandering around England in 1584–5 (including time in Cambridge) are all trying to overthrow the Earl of Arran's control of the young James VI in the years before Mary, Queen of Scot's execution.

3 David M. Walker, *A Legal History of Scotland*, 6 Vols (Edinburgh: T. and T. Clark, 1998), Vol. 3, pp. 300 and 338. Michael F. Graham, *The Uses of Reform: 'Godly Discipline' and Popular Behavior in Scotland and Beyond, 1560–1610* (Leiden: E. J. Brill, 1996), pp. 75, 85, 96.

4 Henry Grey Graham, *The Social Life of Scotland in the Eighteenth Century* 4th ed. (London: Adam and Charles Black, 1937, 1950 repr), p. 493.

5 *The Records of the Proceedings of the Justiciary court, Edinburgh, 1661–78*, 3 Vols, ed. William George Scott-Moncrieff (Edinburgh: 1905), Vol. 1, pp. 1661–9, p. xvii.

6 *The Laws and Acts of Parliament made by King James the First . . . . of Scotland*, ed. Thomas Murray Lord Glendook (Edinburgh: David Lindsay, 1681), pp. 209–11, 304, 312–13, 357, 405, 422, 423, and also *Records of the*

Parliament of Scotland, http://www.rps.sc.uk for all statutes (search under 'vagabond' or 'Egyptian'); Stanley Horsfall Turner, *The History of Local Taxation in Scotland* (Edinburgh and London: William Blackwood and Sons, 1908), pp. 15–16.

7   Graham, *Social Life*, pp. 490, n. 2, notes three Acts of Parliament, in 1607, 1611 and 1665, and p. 491, involving lifelong servitude.

8   W. J. Watson, 'Cliar Sheanchain', *The Celtic Review*, 4(13) (July, 1907), pp. 80–8, pp. 87–8, 'In 1407 the Scottish Parliament enacted "that in all justice ayres the kingis justice tak inquisicione of sornaris, bardis, maisterfull beggars or fenziet fulys, and other naysh them the cunrtre or send them to kingis presone"'; John Shaw, 'What Alexander Carmichael Did Not Print: The "Cliar Sheanchain", "Clanranald's Fool" and Related Traditions', *Béaloideas*, 70 (2002), pp. 99–126.

9   Colin Clark, 'Defining ethnicity in a cultural and socio-legal context: the case of Scottish Gypsy-Travellers', *Scottish Affairs*, 54 (2006), available online unpaginated at http://strathprints.strath.ac.uk.

10 H. T. Crofton, 'Early Annals of the Gypsies in England', *Journal of the Gypsy Lore Society*, 1st ser, 1(1) (1888), pp. 5–24, pp. 6–7, and p. 42 for the 1579 Scottish Act, with *The Laws and Acts of Parliament*, pp. 209–11; David Macritchie, *Scottish Gypsies under the Stewarts* (Edinburgh: David Douglas, 1894), pp. 62–74, 80–1.

11 *Memorabilia of the City of Glasgow, selected from the Minute Books of the Burgh, 1588–1750* (Glasgow: Printed for Private Circulation, 1835), pp. 424–6; William Chambers, *Exploits and Anecdotes of the Scottish Gypsies, with Traits of their Origin, Character, and Manners* (Edinburgh: William Brown, 1886, originally, 1821), pp. 13–14.

12 *The Justiciary Records of Argyll and the Isles*, 2 Vols, Vol. 2, 1705–42, ed. John Imrie (Edinburgh: The Stair Society, 1969), p. 404; *The Poetical Works of John Keats*, ed. H. Buxton Forman (New York: Thomas Y. Crowell and Co, 1895), pp. 404–6.

13 A. Cathcart, 'The Statutes of Iona: The Archipelagic Context', *Journal of British Studies* 49(1) (2009), pp. 4–27, pp. 7, 15.

14 Alan Douglas Kennedy, 'The Civic Government of the Scottish Highlands during the Restoration, 1660–88' (Unpublished PhD, University of Sterling, 2011), p. 256.

15 Graham, *Social Life*, p. 493, note 2, 1707 case in Lanark, and 1775 in the Gorbals 'village and barony'. *Report to the House of Commons, (1) 'A Return of the Individuals Prosecuted for Political Libel and Seditious Conduct in England and Scotland, since 1807, with the Sentences passed on them (2) A Return of the Number of Convictions throughout the Kingdoms from the 1st January 1820 the 1st January 1821 for the Offences of Blasphemy and Sedition; distinguishing each; (3) A Return of the Number of Informations filed by the Attorney General, from the 1st January 1820, to the 1st of January 1821, against Persons accused of Blasphemy and Sedition, distinguishing each'* (H. Hobhouse; Printed by the House of Commons, 5 April 1821), p. 4, where, of 15 prosecutions that resulted in 11 convictions, 8 were outlawed.

16 J. R. D. Falconer, '"Mony Utheris Divars Odious Crymes": Women, Petty
Crime and Power in Later Sixteenth-Century Aberdeen', *Crimes and
Misdemeanours*, 4(1) (2010), online, pp. 1–36, pp. 17, 22 and 30.

17 Graham, *The Uses of Reform*, pp. 1–2.

18 Elizabeth Ewan, 'Crime or Culture? Women and Daily Life in Late Medieval
Scotland', in Yvonne Galloway Brown and Rona Ferguson, eds, *Twisted
Sisters: Women, Crime and Deviance in Scotland since 1400* (East Linton:
Tuckwell Press, 2002), pp. 117–36, p. 127.

19 *Register of the Ministers, Elders and Deacons of the Christian Congregation
of St. Andrews*, ed. David Hay Fleming, Part 1, 1559–1600 (Edinburgh:
Edinburgh University Press, T. and A. Constable, for the Scottish Historical
Society, 1889), pp.liv, 44, 55, 173, 420, 475; *Selections from the Records of
the Kirk Session, Presbytery and Synod of Aberdeen*, ed. and introduction
John Stuart (Aberdeen: The Spalding Club, 1846), pp. 23, 24, 27, 146;
Inverness Kirk Session Records, 1661–1800, ed. Alexander Mitchell
(Inverness: Robert Carruthers and Son, 1902), pp. 62, 180–1, 183. Leah
Leneman, '"Disregarding the Matrimonial Vows": Divorce in Eighteenth- and
Early Nineteenth-Century Scotland', *Journal of Social History*, 30(2) (1996),
pp. 465–82, p. 466.

20 *Memorabilia of the City of Glasgow*, pp. 216–17, 24 December 1660; *The
Court Book of the Barony and Regality of Falkirk and Callendar, Vol. 1,
1638–56*, ed. Doreen M. Hunter (Edinburgh: Stair Society, 1991), pp. 1, 3
and 108; on the legislation, see David Hume, *Commentaries on the Laws
of Scotland Respecting the Description and Punishment of Crimes*, 2
Vols (Edinburgh: Bell and Bradfute, 1797), Vol. 2, pp. 302–14, who notes
transportation as one of the more lenient outcomes in the late seventeenth
century.

21 *Records of the Sheriff Court of Aberdeenshire*, ed. David Littlejohn, 3 Vols,
Vol. 2, Records, 1598–1649 (Aberdeen: Printed for the University, 1906),
pp. 37, 38 and 129 (Elspet Forbes).

22 *Records of the Sheriff Court of Aberdeenshire*, Vol. 3, pp.xvi and 49, 52,
55 (James Scott, 1655 from the three kingdoms), 62 'Britane'. C. H. Firth,
*Scotland and the Protectorate: Letters and Papers Relating to the Military
Government of Scotland, from January 1654 to June 1660* (Edinburgh: T. and
A. Constable, for the Scottish History Society, 1899), pp. xxx and 80.

23 *State Papers Colonial*, Vol. 10, p. 311, 17 December 1678.

24 David Armitage, 'The Scottish Diaspora', in Jenny Wormald, ed., *Scotland:
A History* (Oxford: Oxford University Press, 2005), pp. 225–49, p. 232.

25 Brian P. Levack, 'The Great Scottish Witch-Hunt of 1661–2', *Journal of
British Studies*, 20(1) (1980), pp. 90–108, p. 91; *The Justiciary Records of
Argyll and the Isles*, 2 Vols, Vol. 2, 1705–42, ed. John Imrie (Edinburgh:
The Stair Society, 1969), pp. 105–6, 1679; 201–4 and 204 and 298–9 for
horse thefts, 1705 and 1712; 364 (1721); p. 384 (1726); Basket, *Statutes
at Large*, Vol. 5, p. 176, 14 Geo. II, c.11; Lindsay Farmer, *Criminal Law,
Tradition and Legal Order: Crime and the Genius of Scots Law, 1747 to
the Present* (Cambridge: Cambridge University Press, 1997); John Louthian,
The Form of Process before the Court of Justiciary in Scotland, 2nd ed.

(Edinburgh: Hamilton, Balfour and Neill, 1752), p. 239; A. Roger Ekirch, 'The Transportation of Scottish Criminals to America during the Eighteenth Century', *Journal of British Studies*, 24(3) (1985), pp. 366–74, p. 374.

26   *The Justiciary Records of Argyll and the Isles*, Vol. 2, pp. 259–60, John McColl, 1711; p. 314, John McArthur, 1715.

27   *Selected Justiciary Cases, 1624–50*, 3 Vols, Vol. 1, ed. S. A. Gillon (Edinburgh: The Stair Society, J. Skinner and Co, 1953) pp. 92 and 225; Vol. 2, ed. J. Irvine Smith (Edinburgh: The Stair Society, 1972), pp. 322–3 and pp. 538–42 for Thomas McKie who had returned: his execution is not recorded; Vol. 3, ed. J. Irvine Smith (Edinburgh: The Stair Society, 1974), pp. 740–2.

28   *Justiciary*, Vol. 2, pp. 323, 371 and 373; see I. R. Bartlett, 'Scottish Mercenaries in Europe, 1570–1640: A Study in Attitudes and Policies', *International Review of Scottish Studies*, 13 (1985), pp. 15–24, pp. 20–1 for the background and a table of recruiters.

29   Brian P. Levack, 'The Prosecution of Sexual Crimes in Early Eighteenth-Century Scotland, *The Scottish Historical Review*, 89(2) (228) (2010), pp. 172–93, p. 175; *Justiciary*, Vol. 1, p. 164; Vol. 3, pp. 837–8; Vol. 2, p. 518 for attempted rape, a case criticized by David Hume, *Commentaries*, Vol. 1, p. 302 and Vol. 2, p. 406; *Justiciary*, Vol. 3, pp. 77–8; this was also the outcome of an inquisitorial process.

30   *Justiciary*, Vol. 3, pp. 731–2, 1646.

31   Lizanne Henderson, 'The Survival of Witchcraft Prosecutions and Witch Belief in South West Scotland, *The Scottish Historical Review*, 85(1) (2006), pp. 52–74, p. 66; another case p. 61. Elizabeth Ewan, 'Disorderly Damsels? Women and Interpersonal Violence in Pre-Reformation Scotland', *The Scottish Historical Review*, 89, 2(228) (2010), pp. 153–71, p. 155.

32   The data in this section is heavily reliant on the work of Roger Ekirch, 'The Transportation of Scottish Criminals', pp. 369–72; p. 374. Patrick Colquhoun had the contract for Scottish convicts in 1771, p. 374; *Calendar of Home Office Papers of the Reign of George III*, 4 Vols, Vol. 1, 1760 (25 October) to 1765, ed. Joseph Redington (London: Longman and Co, 1878), p. 256 and Vol. 2, 1766–9 (London: Longman and Co, 1879), p. 112.

33   George Tait, *A Summary of the Powers and Duties of a Justice of the Peace in Scotland* (Edinburgh and London: John Anderson and Co, and Longman, Rees, Orme, Brown and Green, 1828), p. 425; Archibald Alison, *Principles of the Criminal Law of Scotland* (Edinburgh: William Blackwood, 1832), p. 561; *The Scots Magazine*, Vol. 51 (Edinburgh: Murray and Cochrane, no date but referring to 1789), p. 255.

34   Hume, *Commentaries*, Vol. 2, pp. 81–2, 90 and 95; Howell, *State Trials*, Vol. 23, pp. 774, 786, 789, 798, trials of Maurice Margarot and Charles Sinclair; *The Parliamentary Register*, Vol. 38 (London: J. Debrett, 1794), pp. 491–2, 497, 498, Adam's emphasis; *A Biographical Dictionary of Living Authors of Great Britain and Ireland* (London: Henry Colburn, 1816), p. 2 for Adam's career; *The Parliamentary History of England, from the Earliest Period to the Year 1803*, Vol. 31, 1794–5 (London: T. C. Hansard, 1818), pp. 269 and 279. For the complex details of these cases and the general debate they provoked, see John Barrell, *Imagining the King's Death: Figurative Treason, Fantasies*

of Regicide 1793–96 (Oxford: Oxford University Press, 2000), pp. 155–7
(Margarot case); pp. 186–7 and 488–9 for Adam's political background and
involvement as defence counsel.

35 Anne-Marie Kilday, *Women and Violent Crime in Enlightenment Scotland*
(Woodbridge: The Boydell Press for the Royal Historical Society, 2007),
p. 109.

36 *London Evening Post*, 20 July 1751; 1819 Returns at Dundee Gaol, 1819 –
Lamb Collection, http://www.dundeecity.gov.uk/lamb/images/jail1919.jpg.

37 http://hansard.millbanksystems.com/commons/1828/mar/11/criminal-trials-in-
scotland-justiciary, debate on 11 March 1828, Vol. 18. Cc 1115–19, Sir M. W.
Ridley.

Chapter 3

1 See Ian Green, *Print and Protestantism in Early Modern England* (Oxford:
Oxford University Press, 2000); Christopher Higley, 'Exile and Religious
Identity in Early Modern England', *Reformation*, 15 (2010), pp. 51–61; Peter
Marshall, 'Religious Exiles and the Tudor State', in Kate Cooper and Jeremy
Gregory, eds, *Discipline and Diversity: Studies in Church History*, Vol. 43
(Woodbridge: Boydell, 2007), pp. 263–84; the situation in Ireland was very
different, as most of the reformed church was imported, and English settlers
dominated the official personnel – Alan Ford, Ch. 1 of his *James Ussher:
Theology, History, and Politics in Early-Modern Ireland and England* (Oxford:
Oxford University Press, 2007), 'Controversy and Religious Identity in
Sixteenth-Century Ireland', pp. 11–31.

2 Ann Hughes, 'Religious Diversity in Revolutionary London', in Nicholas
Tyacke ed., *The English Revolution, c1590–1720: Politics, Religion and
Communities* (Manchester: Manchester University Press, 2007), pp. 123–4.

3 John Coffey, *Persecution and Toleration in Protestant England, 1558–1689*
(Harlow: Pearson Education Limited, 2000), p. 169.

4 Craig W. Horle, *Quakers and the English Legal System, 1660–68* (Philadelphia,
PA: University of Pennsylvania Press, 1988), p. 36; Joseph Besse, *A Collection
of the Sufferings of the People Called Quakers . . .* 3 vols (London: Luke
Hindle, 1753), Vol. 1, pp. 84–5; James Raine, *Depositions from the Castle
at York Relating to Offences committed in the Northern Counties in the
Seventeenth Century*, Surtees Society Vol. 40 (Durham: Frances Andrews,
1861), note p.xxii; Coffey, *Persecution and Toleration*, pp. 52–5.

5 *State Papers Colonial*, Vol. 5, p. 245.

6 *Records of the Governor and Colony of the Massachusetts Bay in New
England*, Vol. 4, 1664–74, pt. 1, day of humiliation, Vol. 4, pt. 1, 276;
punishments, pp. 278–9; Charles II in part 2 (Boston, MA: William White,
1854) pp. 164–6, 'sharpe', p. 166; Kenneth L. Carroll, 'Persecution and
Persecutors of Maryland Quakers, 1658–61', *Quaker History* 99 (2010),
pp. 18, 15–31. On New England, see the work of Carla Gardina Pestana, 'The
Quaker Executions as Myth and History', *The Journal of American History*

80 (1993), pp. 441–69, and 'The City upon a Hill under Siege: The Puritan Perception of the Quaker Threat to Massachusetts Bay', *The New England Quarterly* 56 (1983), pp. 323–53.

7   *Records of the Governor and Company*, Vol. 4, pt.1, pp. 308–9, 14 October 1657; p. 321, 19 May 1658; pp. 346–7, 19 October 1658. The last was immediately, on the same date, applied to the prisoners in prison in Ipswich, Suffolk County, p. 349.

8   Pestana, 'The Quaker Executions', p. 441, and *Records of the Governor and Company*, Vol. 4, pt. 1, pp. 383–5, 18 October 1659, quotation on p. 385, and the authorities' theological justifications, pp. 386–90; Mary Dyer and Nicholas and Jane Nicholson, p. 419, 30 May 1660; the latter wished to go to England, p. 433, 16 October 1660; see also Pestana, 'The City upon a Hill under Siege'.

9   *Records of the Governor and Company*, Vol. 4, pt. 1, p. 366, 11 May 1659; p. 391, 18 October 1659; pp. 403 and 407, 12 November 1659; pp. 426–7 for entertaining Quakers; whole group of ten Quakers 12 November 1659, pp. 410–11, whipped and ordered to 'depart this jurisdiction'.

10 *Records of the Governor and Company*, Vol. 4, pt. 1, p. 433, 16 October 1660.

11 Pestana, 'Quaker Executions', pp. 446–7; *Records of the Governor and Company*,Vol. 4, pt. 1, pp. 453–6, 16 December 1660.

12 Edward Burroughs, *A Declaration of the Sad and Great Persecution and Martyrdom of the People of God, called Quakers, in New England* (London: Robert Wilson, 1661); Pestana, 'Quaker Executions', p. 448.

13 Coffey, *Persecution and Toleration*, pp. 21 and 155; John R. Knott, 'Joseph Besse and the Quaker Culture of Suffering', *Prose Studies*, 17(3) (December, 1994), pp. 126–41.

14 *Records of the Governor and Colony*, Vol. 4, pt. 2, pp. 2–40 and 59, and Vol. 5 pt. 2, p. 34, 27 November 1661; Besse, *Sufferings*, Vol. 2, p. 225.

15 Charles II in *Records of the Governor and Colony*, Vol. 4, pt 1, pp. 164–6, indulgence p. 165, 'sharpe', p. 166; *Records of the Governor and Colony*, Vol. 5, pp. 198–9, 2 October 1678 and pp. 287 and 322, 11 June 1680.

16 *The Colonial Laws of Massachusetts, Reprinted from the Edition of 1672, with the supplements through 1686*, ed. William H. Whitmore (Boston, MA: Rockwell and Churchill, 1890) pp. 61–2 for the revised general laws of 1658; Carroll, 'Persecution and Persecutors', p. 18; William Waller Hening, *The Statutes at Large, being a Collection of the Laws of Virginia, from the First Session of the Legislature in the Year 1619, Statutes*, Vol. 3, pp. 180–3; Owen Ruffhead, *The Statutes at Large from the Fifth Year of King James the First to the Tenth Year of the Reign of William the Third*, 3 Vols (London: Mark Basket, 1763), 3: pp. 217–18, 295–6.

17 See Horle, *Quakers and the Engish Legal System*; Besse, *Sufferings*, on Cromwell's attitudes, Vol. 1: pp.vi–vii; William Waller Hening, *The Statutes at Large*, Vol. 2, pp. 180–3; Owen Ruffhead, *The Statutes at Large from the Fifth Year of King James the First to the Tenth Year of the Reign of William the Third*, 3 Vols (London: Mark Basket, 1763), Vol. 3: pp. 217–18, 295–6 on laws; David T. Konig, 'Regionalism in Early American Law', in Michael

Grossberg and Christopher L. Tomlins, eds, *The Cambridge History of Law in America* (Cambridge: Cambridge University Press, 2008), pp. 144–77; on 'legal culture' as a concept, see Richard J. Ross, 'The Legal Past of Early New England: Notes for the Study of Law, Legal Culture, and Intellectual History', *The William and Mary Quarterly*, 3rd ser, 50 (1993): pp. 28–41 and 'Puritan Godly Discipline in Comparative Perspective: Legal Pluralism and the Sources of "Intensity"', *American Historical Review* 113 (2008), pp. 975–1002.

18   Horle, *Quakers and the English Legal System*, p. 36 and pp. 36–43 for established possibilities in law before the legislation of the 1660s from misdemeanours to heresy; Anthony Fletcher, 'The Enforcement of the Conventicle Acts, 1664–79', in W. J. Sheils, ed., *Persecution and Toleration* (Oxford: Blackwell Publishing, 1984), pp. 234–46.

19   Thomas Ellwood, *A Discourse Concerning Riots (London, 1683) and also A Caution to Constables and Other Inferior Officers concerned in the execution of the Conventicle Act with some observations thereupon, humbly offered by way of advice to such well-meaning and moderate justices of the peace, as would not willingly ruine their peaceable neighbours but act (in relation to that act) rather by restraint than by choice* (London, 1683) p. 8; Thomas Gibson, *Something offered to the Consideration of all those who have had a hand in putting the late made Act (entituled, An Act to Prevent and Suppress Seditious Conventicles) in execution* . . . (London: 1665), p. 3.

20   Justin Champion, '"My Kingdom is not of this World": The Politics of Religion after the Revolution', in Tyacke, *English Revolution*, pp. 185–202, p. 187, commenting on Ellwood and imprisonment for 'riot'; Richard L. Greaves, 'Seditious Sectaries or "Sober and Useful Inhabitants"? Changing Conceptions of the Quakers in Early Modern Britain', *Albion*, 33(1) (2001), pp. 24–50.

21   C.II. 13–14, c. 1 (1661), *An Act for Preventing the Mischief and Dangers that may arise by certain Persons called Quakers and others, refusing to take lawful oaths*, in *The Statutes at Large from the First Year of King James the First to the Tenth Year of the Reign of William the Third*, 3 Vols, (London: Mark Masket, 1758), Vol. 1, pp. 217–18; The 'Conventicle Act' of 1664 (16 CII, c. 4) , see Besse, *Sufferings*, Vol. 1, pp.xiv–xvi; in 1665, there was legislation excluding the Quakers from 'corporations' such as guilds and town councils, Besse, pp.xx–xxii, (17 CII. c. 2).

22   TNA SP 44/22/48, 7 March 1664/5, Order to the Lord Chief Justice from Henry Bennett, King's Secretary (also in *State Papers Colonial*, V, p. 287), and 25 February 1664–5.

23   *An Abstract of the Sufferings of the People Called Quakers for the Testimony of a Good Conscience, from the time of their being first distinguished by that name, taken from original records and authentick accounts* 3 Vols (London: printed by J. Sowle, 1733–8), Vol. 1, 1733, 'From the Year 1650 to 1660', Vol. 2, 1738, 'From the Year 1660 to 1666'; Vol. 3, 1738, 'From the Year 1660 to 1666', favours statistical tables; see also Besse, *A Collection of the Sufferings*; Knott, 'Joseph Besse'. Some local studies, such as that of the fate of Quakers persecuted in the Isle of Man, confirm the accuracy of these sources, which can be checked in some instances also against the central government, such as the Privy Council records, see Conal F. Carswell, 'Man and the

Quakers: Quakers in the Isle of Man, 1655–1735', http://www.isle-of-man.
com/manxnotebook/parishes/nc/quakerp.htm. *The Cry of the Innocent and
Oppressed for Justice or A Brief Relation of the late Proceedings against the
Prisoners called Quakers in London . . . Hick's Hall and Old Bailey on the
14th, 15th and 17th day of October 1664 . . .* (London: 1664); *The Norffs
President of Persecution (unto Banishment) against some of the innocent
People called Quakers* (n.d. 1665), referring to the trials in Norfolk on
20 February 1665, with four men sentenced to transportation, and EEBO
attributes to one of them, Henry Kittle; George Bishop, *Manifesto Declaring
what George Bishope hath been to the City of Bristoll . . ., Occasioned by the
late Sentence of Banishment Pronounced upon him . . .* (1665) – 'I am Banisht
my Native City, and Country to Barbados (with many more of my Brethren)
for my Conscience to God' (27).

24   Horle, *Quakers*, p. 268; Besse, *A Collection of the Sufferings*, Vol. 1, pp. 52,
     402 and 406; by my counting, Sowle listed 137 by name and Besse 141 from
     London; 120 were still in jail in June 1665; see also *The Cry of the Innocent
     and Oppressed*, on London, and Bishop, *Manifesto*, on Bristol.

25   Horle, *Quakers*, pp. 267–8; he emotively confuses indentured servitude for
     seven years with slavery.

26   TNA PC 2/58, ff.37 (10 March 1664–5), 39v (15 March 1664–5), and 100v (5
     July 1665); *Privy Council, Colonial*, pp. 388–9.

27   Besse, *Sufferings*, Vol. 1, pp. 245–8; *State Papers Colonial*, Vol. 5, p. 256, 19
     November 1664; *Extracts from State Papers Relating to Friends, 1654–72*, ed.
     Norman Penney, with an introduction by R. A. Roberts, Supplements 8–11
     to the *Journal of the Friends Historical Society* (London: Friends Historical
     Society/Headley Brothers, 1913), p. 219; Acts *Privy Council Colonial*, Vol.
     1, p. 388, 7 December 1664; *Acts of the Privy Council Colonial*, Vol. 1,
     pp. 414–15, 30 May and 8 June 1666; 417, 11 July 1666.

28   *State Papers Colonial*, 5, p. 269, 7 Jan 1665 and in Penney, *Extracts from State
     Papers*, pp. 230–1; note that this is also accurately transcribed in Besse, *A
     Collection of the Sufferings*, pp. 51–2; TNA PC 2/58 fol. 100v.

29   Besse, *Sufferings*, Vol. 1, pp. 406–7; the authorities had already had to
     provide a security for the crew against being impressed into the navy, TNA
     PC 2/58, f. 39v.

30   Greaves, 'Seditious Sectaries'; for similar patterns of local arrest in Gateshead
     in north-east England in 1683, see Peter Rushton, 'Gateshead 1550–1700 –
     Independence against all the Odds?', *Newcastle and Gateshead before 1700*,
     edited by Diana Newton and A. J. Pollard (Chichester: Phillimore, 2009),
     pp. 295–322, p. 316; Ned C. Landsman, *Scotland and Its First American
     Colony, 1683–1765* (Princeton, NJ: Princeton University Press, 1985),
     pp. 145–6; John Miller, '"A Suffering People": English Quakers and Their
     Neighbours c.1650–c1700', *Past and Present*, 188(1) (2005), pp. 71–103;
     Richard S. Dunn, *Sugar and Slaves: The Rise of the Planter Class in the English
     West Indies, 1624–1713* (Chapel Hill, NC: University of North Carolina
     Press, 1972), pp. 103–4 on problems in Barbados; Larry Gragg, *The Quaker
     Community on Barbados: Challenging the Culture of the Planter Class*
     (Colombia, MO: University of Missouri Press, 2009).

Chapter 4

1   Sean O'Callaghan, *From Hell to Barbados: The Ethnic Cleansing of Ireland* (Dingle, Co. Kerry: Brandon Publishing, 2001).

2   Thomas Carlyle ed., *Oliver Cromwell's Letters and Speeches*, 5 Vols (New York and London: The Continental Press/John Wiley, 1845), Vol. 1, p. 461, 17 September 1649, to William Lenthall, the Speaker of the House of Commons, pp. 457–8, 16 September 1649 to John Bradshaw, Sec to Council of State to Lenthall, p. 461; Micheál ó Siochrú, *God's Executioner: Oliver Cromwell and the Conquest of Ireland* (London: Faber and Faber, 2008), pp. 83–4 for comments on these letters and p. 85 for his noting that most scholars have neglected the expressions of remorse, and p. 92; Barbara Donagan, *War In England, 1642–49* (Oxford: Oxford University Press, 2008), and 'Atrocity, War Crime, and Treason in the English Civil War', *The American Historical Review*, 99(4) (1994), pp. 1137–66, and, with regard to the treatment of Irish in England, see her 'Codes and Conduct in the English Civil War', *Past and Present*, 188 (1988), pp. 65–95.

3   Intercepted letters, originally from Thurloe, quoted by Carlyle, *Cromwell's Letters*, Vol. 1, pt. 9. p. 487; General Monk (in Scotland) to Secretary Thurloe papers, 21 August 1654, *A Collection of the State Papers of John Thurloe*, Volume 2: 1654 (1742), pp. 549–62. http://www.british-history.ac.uk/report.as px?compid=55339&strquery=barbadoes.

4   John P. Prendergast, *The Cromwellian Settlement of Ireland* (New York: P.M. Haverty, 1868), pp. 244 and 246.

5   Ó Siochrú, *God's Executioner*, pp. 232–3; S. J. Connelly, *Divided Kingdom: Ireland, 1630–1800* (Oxford: Oxford University Press, 2008), p. 100.

6   Thurloe, Vol. 4, p. 23 Henry Cromwell to Thurloe, 11 September 1655; p. 40, 18 September 1655; Connelly, *Divided Kingdom*, pp. 115 and 121; John Blake, 'Transportation from Ireland to America, 1653–60', *Irish Historical Studies*, 3(11) (1943), pp. 267–81, p. 270–1 for evidence of young children to New England and Virginia in 1653–4.

7   Aubrey Gwynn, 'Cromwell's Policy of Transportation', *Studies: An Irish Quarterly Review*, 19(76) (1930), pp. 607–23; O'Callaghan, *From Hell to Barbados*.

8   Richard Flatman, 'Transported to Barbados, 1655', *Irish Family History*, 12 (1996), pp. 46–8, and O'Callaghan, *To Hell or Barbados*, pp. 59–60; Prendergast, *Cromwellian Settlement*, pp. 72, orders for 80–100 people to be sent, following the assizes in Connaught, and pp. 185–6; Connelly, *Divided Kingdom*, p. 116 on the effects of transportation on the Catholic Church; Aubrey Gwynn, 'Cromwell's Policy of Transportation: Part II', *Studies: An Irish Quarterly Review* 20(78) (1931), pp. 291–305, p. 293; Kevin MacGrath, 'Irish Priests Transported under the Commonwealth'. *Archivium Hibernicum*, 14 (1949), pp. 92–5.

9   Ó Siochrú, *God's Executioner*, p. 233; *State Papers Colonial*, Vol. 5, 1667, p. 529.

10 Gwynn, 'Cromwell's Policy of Transportation: Part II', pp. 296–8.

11   Richard Ligon, *A True and Exact History of the Island of Barbadoes* (London: Peter Parker, 1673), pp. 45–6; Hilary Beckles, 'A "Riotous and Unruly Lot": Irish Indentured Servants and Freemen in the West Indies, 1644–1713', *William and Mary Quarterly*, 3rd ser, 47 (1990), pp. 503–22.

12   6 November 1655, in Aubrey Gwynn, 'Documents Relating to the Irish in the West Indies', *Analecta Hibernica*, 4 (1932), pp. 139–286, particularly extracts from the Minute Books of Council of Barbados, item 19, pp. 234 and 237–8.

13   Kristen Block and Jenny Shaw, 'Subjects without an Empire: The Irish in the Early Modern Caribbean', *Past and Present*, 210 (2010), 33–60; Howard A. Fergus, 'Montserrat "Colony of Ireland": The Myth and the Reality', *Studies: An Irish Quarterly Review* 70(280) (1981), pp. 325–40; Jill Sheppard, 'A Historical Sketch of the Poor Whites of Barbados: From Indentured Servants to "Redlegs"', *Caribbean Studies*, 14(3) (1974), pp. 71–94.

14   Nini Rodgers, 'The Irish in the Caribbean, 1641–1837: An Overview', *Irish Migration Studies in Latin America*, 5(3) (2007), pp. 145–56, and Thomas Byrne, 'Banished by Cromwell? John Hooks and the Caribbean', pp. 215–19.

15   *A Collection of the State Papers of John Thurloe*, Volume 6: January 1657– March 1658 (1742), pp. 797–810. http://www.british-history.ac.uk/report.asp x?compid=55638&strquery=barbados; originally Vol. l vii. p. 349. This was intercepted and translated by the Cromwellian spy network.

16   *Records and Fines of the Quarterly Courts of Essex County, Massachusetts*, Vol. 2, 1656–2 (Salem, MA: The Essex Institute, 1912), pp. 293–5; Gwynn, 'Cromwell's Policy', p. 612.

17   Unton Croke, 'Cromwell and the Insurrection of 1655', *English Historical Review*, 4(14) (1889), pp. 313–38, p. 322; C. H. Firth, 'Cromwell and the Insurrection of 1655', *English Historical Review*, 3(10) (1888), pp. 323–50, pp. 326 (quotation), 330, 341; see also Reginald F. D. Palgrave, 'Cromwell and the Insurrection of 1655: A Reply to Mr Firth', *English Historical Review*, 3(11)(1888), pp. 521–39, 'Cromwell and the Insurrection of 1655: A Reply to Mr Firth (Continued)', *English Historical Review*, 3(12)(1888), pp. 722–51, and 'Cromwell and the Insurrection of 1655: A Reply to Mr Firth (Continued)', *English Historical Review*, 4(13)(1889), pp. 110–31.

18   Andrea Button, 'Royalist Women Petitioners in South-West England, 1655–62', *Seventeenth Century*, 15 (2000), pp. 53–66, quotation p. 54, who also looks at the women left behind when men were exiled (including one who died in the East, not West, Indies); Croke, 'Cromwell and the Insurrection of 1655', slightly different figures on pp. 334–6; Penruddock in *State Trials*, Vol. 5, pp. 767–91, with verdicts 790–1.

19   British History Online - http://www.british-history.ac.uk, 'Letters from Mr Corker: 4 of 5', *A Collection of the State Papers of John Thurloe*, Volume 1: 1638–53 (1742), pp. 745–54, and 'state Papers, 1655: April (4 of 6)', *A Collection of the State Papers of John Thurloe*, Volume 3: December 1654–August 1655 (1742), pp. 380–95.

20   'A German Indentured Servant Servant in Barbados in 1652: The Account of Heinrich von Uchteritz', translated by Alexander Gunkel and Jerome S. Handler, *Journal of the Barbados Museum and Historical Society*, 33 (1970), pp. 91–100, pp. 92–5; the number of Native American (Indian) slaves is

regarded by Jerome Handler as a unique record, Jerome S. Handler, 'Aspects of Amerindian Ethnography in 17th-Century Barbados', *Caribbean Studies*, 9(4) (1970), pp. 50–72, p. 51; see also his 'The Amerindian Slave Population of Barbados in the Seventeenth and Early Eighteenth Centuries', *Caribbean Studies*, 8(4) (1969), pp. 38–64.

21 *England's Slavery or Barbados Merchandize represented in a Petition to the High and Honourable Court of Parliament by Marcellus Rivers and Oxenbridge Foyle* (London: printed in the eleventh year of England's Liberty, 1659), pp. 4–7; first letter, pp. 8–10; the second letter seems to be a version of the petition preserved in Thurloe, above, with very much better spelling; p. 18 (men-stealers).

22 Larry Gragg, *Englishmen Transplanted: The English Colonization of Barbados, 1627–60* (Oxford: Oxford University Press, 2003), pp. 126 and 129.

23 P. H. Hardacre, 'The Royalists in Exile during the Puritan Revolution, 1642–60', *Huntington Library Quarterly*, 16(4) (1953), pp. 353–70, p. 363; intercepted letter, 'State Papers, 1655: May (5 of 5)', *A collection of the State Papers of John Thurloe*, Volume 3: December 1654–August 1655 (1742), pp. 480–98. http://www.british-history.ac.uk/report. aspx?compid=55386&strquery=intercepted; Richard Ligon, *A True and Exact History of the Island of Barbadoes* (London, 1657, repr. Peter Parker, 1673), pp. 43–6.

24 Roger A. Mason, 'Usable Pasts: History and Identity in Reformation Scotland', *The Scottish Historical Review*, 76(1), no. 201 (1997), pp. 54–68; Janette Currie, 'History, Hagiography, and Fakestory: Representations of the Scottish Covenanters in Non-Fictional and Fictional Texts from 1638 to 1835', (Unpublished PhD, Department of English, University of Stirling, 1999) A. M. Starkey, 'Robert Wodrow and the History of the Sufferings of the Church of Scotland', *Church History*, 43(4) (1974), pp. 488–98. For some of the books published in the nineteenth century, see Archibald Stewart, *History Vindicated in the Case of the Wigtown Martyrs* 2nd ed. (Edinburgh: Edmonston and Douglas, 1870), and Mark Napier, *History Rescued, in Answer to 'History Vindicated'* . . . (Edinburgh: Edmonston and Douglas, 1870); Sir George Mackenzie, *A Vindication of the Government in Scotland during the Reign of Charles II against Mis-Representation made in Several Scandalous Pamphlets* (London, 1691 and Edinburgh: James Watson, 1712), p. 11; George Gilfillan, *Martyrs, Heroes and Bards of the Scottish Covenant* (New York: Robert Carter and Brothers, 1853); Alexander Smelie, *Men of the Covenant: The Story of the Scottish Church in the Years of the Persecution* (Edinburgh: Fleming H. Revell Co, no date).

25 Walter Scott, *Minstrelsy of the Scottish Border: Historical and Romantic Ballads*, 3 Vols (Edinburgh: Longman, Hurst, Rees, Orme and Brown, 1812), Vol. 2, pp. 78–99, p. 78, noting that Cameronians were at the success at Loudon Hill, while other more 'moderate' preachers and others consequently joined Hamilton and ended in Bothwell Bridge (p. 79); for the ballad, see pp. 89–92; for the twists and turns of the political problems after the death of Richard Cromwell to the early years of the Restoration, see Ian B. Cowan, *The Scottish Covenanters, 1660–88*, (London: Victor Gollancz Ltd, 1976), pp. 35–52.

26 Cowan, *Scottish Covenanters*, p. 57, and quotation from p. 72; Alasdair J. N.
    Raffe, 'Religious Controversy and Scottish Society,c.1679–1714' (Unpublished
    PhD, The University of Edinburgh, 2007), p. 37 (Act of 1670). Raffe helpfully
    includes many individual cases such as that of George Ridpath, p. 106 and
    generally ch. 5, pp. 101–29. See also many cases of banishment in Mark
    Jardine, 'The United Societies: Militancy, Martyrdom and the Presbyterian
    Movement in Late-Restoration Scotland,1679 to 1688' (Unpublished PhD
    Thesis, University of Edinburgh, 2009). *The Laws and Acts of Parliament
    made by King James the First . . . . of Scotland*, ed. Thomas Murray Lord
    Glendook (Edinburgh: David Lindsay, 1681), 2nd session of the second
    Parliament, Charles II, pp. 134–6, two Acts, the second against house and
    field conventicles; 8 May 1685, 'An Act brought in ordaining that preachers
    at house and field conventicles and those present at field conventicles shall be
    punished with death, being read, was appointed to be considered by the lords
    of the clergy until the next meeting.', Records of the Parliament of Scotland,
    http://www.rps.ac.uk.

27 Robert Wodrow, *The History of the Sufferings of the Church of Scotland
    from the Restoration to the Rebellion*, 4 Vols edited and introduced by
    Robert Burns (Glasgow: Blackie and Son, 1830–35),Vol. 2 (1830), p. 476;
    Williamson had been authorised to transport them by royal order, *State Papers
    Colonial*, Vol. 10, p. 311, 17 December 1678. See Chapter 2. Patrick Walker,
    Some Remarkable Passages of the Life and Death of Mr Alexander Peden
    (Glasgow: J. and J. Robertson, 1781, originally 1724), pp. 7–9; see also Peter
    H. Denton, 'At the Banquet in Hell: Sir George Mackenzie and Narratives of
    Religious Conflict in 17th Century Scotland', in his edited collection, *Believers
    in the Battlespace: Religion, Ideology and War* (Kingston, Ontario: Canadian
    Defence Academy Press, 2011), pp. 3–21.

28 Alexander S. Morton, *Galloway and the Covenanters: or, The Struggle for
    Religious Liberty in the South-West of Scotland* (Paisley: Alexander Gardner,
    1904), pp. 319–28.

29 *A Further Account of the Proceedings against the Rebels since the Arrival
    of His Grace the Duke of Monmouth* (London: 1679); P. Coertzen and
    David Osborne Christie, 'Bible and Sword: The Cameronian Contribution
    to Freedom of Religion', *Dutch Reformed Theological Journal*, 49(1 and 2)
    (2008), pp. 16–27.

30 Wodrow, *History*, Vol. 3, p. 41; p. 116 – King's letter to the (Scottish) Council,
    29 June 1679; p. 114 ('the rabble'); pp. 130–1.

31 Catherine B. H. Cant, 'The Archpriest Avvakum and his Scottish
    Contemporaries', *The Slavonic and East European Review*, 44(103) (1966),
    pp. 381–402, pp. 394–5, who notes that Walker was writing against Robert
    Wodrow's account; R. M. Young, 'News from Ireland: Being the Examination
    and Confession of William Kelso, etc., 1679', *Ulster Journal of Archaeology*,
    2nd ser. 2(4) (1896), pp. 274–9, pp. 276–7.

32 Robert Wodrow, *History*, Vol. 4, pp. 7–8, order 24 April 1684, p. 7; see also
    William Crookshank, *The History of the State and Sufferings of the Church of
    Scotland from the Restoration to the Revolution* (London: J. Oswald, 1749),
    2 Vols, Vol. 2, pp. 261 (West Flanders) and pp. 272–3 who has used different
    words, 'harbouring rebels', p. 273.

33 Wodrow, *History*, Vol. 4, pp. 9 and 11; George Howe, *The History of the Presbyterian Church in South Carolina* (Columbia, SC: Duffie and Chapman, 1870), p. 85.

34 Sir John Lauder of Fountainhall, *Historical Notices of Scotish [sic] Affairs* . . . 2 Vols, vol. 2, ed. David Laing (Edinburgh: T. Constable,1848), p. 627, 12 March 1685, 'One of his Majestie's yauchts arrived at Leith, with 7 or 8 Scots prisoners, taen at a Conventicle in London'; pp. 641–2; Cowan, *The Scottish Covenanters*, pp. 123–4, suggests that 274 were sent to Dunnottar, and that about 100 were transported. See description of the castle in the official online guide for the Whigs' Vault.

35 Cowan, *The Scottish Covenanters*, pp. 124–6; *The Register of the Privy Council of Scotland*, ed. and abridged by Henry Paton, intro by Robert Kerr Hannay, 3rd series, Vol. 11, 1685–6 (HM General Register House, Edinburgh, 1929), pp. 117–19; lists, pp. 329–31, summation, p. 331. Wodrow's lists of the banished are in *History* Vol. 4, p. 221, and he also gives earlier cases of branding in Vol. 1, p. 181.

36 Sir John Lauder of Fountainhall, *The Decisions of the Lords of Council and Session, from June 6th 1678 to July 30th, 1712*, 2 Vols (Edinburgh: G. Hamilton and J. Balfour, 1759), Vol. 1, pp. 303 and 367; *Register of the Privy Council*, Vol. 11, p. 330; Lauder, *Historical Notes*, Vol. 2, p. 664, 5 September 1685.

37 Fraser, as memorialized in *The Original Secession Magazine*, 19 (1889–90), pp. 578–86; Ned C. Landsman, *Scotland and its First American Colony, 1683–1765* (Princeton, NJ: Princeton University Press, 1985), pp. 145 and 190; Gilbert Milroy in Wodrow, *History*, Vol. 4, pp. 185–7, and Smith, *Colonists in Bondage*, pp. 186–7 – John Menzies was transported to Barbados. For other experiences of exile in the colonies, see Ruth Richens, 'The Stewarts in Underbank: Two Decades in the Life of a Covenanting Family', *The Scottish Historical Review*, 64(178) pt. 2 (1985), pp. 107–27.

38 See Allan I. MacInnes, 'Repression and Conciliation: The Highland Dimension 1660–88', *The Scottish Historical Review*, 65(180) pt. 2 (1986), pp. 167–95.

39 Melinda Zook, '"The Bloody Assizes": Whig Martyrdom and Memory after the Glorious Revolution', *Albion*, 27(3) (1995), pp. 373–96.

40 Thomas Babington Macaulay, *History of England from the Accession of James II*, 4 Vols, Vol 1, Introduction by Douglas Jerrold (London: J.M. Dent and Sons, Everyman Library,1906), p. 484; see pp. 476–7 for the legend of Col. Kirke, sexual exploitation of a wife's plea, 'unsupported by proof', p. 467, and pp. 292–3 for the Maids of Taunton.

41 Lois G. Schwoerer, 'William, Lord Russell: The Making of a Martyr, 1683–1983', *Journal of British Studies*, 24 (1985), pp. 41–71.

42 Tim Harris, *Revolution: The Great Crisis of the British Monarchy, 1685–1720* (London: Penguin, 2007), pp. 75 and 81; at least a 100 were summarily executed, compared with fewer than 200 in the actual battle, p. 88; see Stephen A. Timmons, 'Executions Following Monmouth's Rebellion: A Missing Link', *Historical Research*, 76(192) (2003), pp. 286–91, pp. 287–8.

43 Peter Earle, *Monmouth's Rebels: The Road to Sedgemoor 1685* (London: Weidenfeld and Nicolson, 1977), p. 175; the evidence for confirmed executions is good for Devon and Dorset, but weaker for Somerset cases, p. 174. But, see views from E. S. De Beer, 'Executions Following the "Bloody Assize"', *Bulletin of the Institute of Historical Research*, 4 (1926–7), pp. 36–9; Markus Eder, '*At the Instigation of the Devil*': *Capital Punishment and the Assize in Early Modern England* (Hilgertshausen-Tandern, Germany: 2009), pp. 70–1 throws doubt that the number of executions in the Western Circuit was much higher than the 52 marked for execution in the jail book; Robin Clifton, *The Last Popular Rebellion: The Western Rising of 1685* (London: Maurice Temple Smith, St. Martin's Press, 1984), endorses John Tutchin's account, p. 238; John Tutchin, *The Western Martyrology or Bloody Assize* . . . 5th edition (London: John Marshall, 1705).

44 See orders to Lord Lieutenants, SP 31/2 Monmouth's Rebellion 'Letterbook', f.10v and following, identical letters to arrest 'all disaffected and suspicious persons, and particularly all non-conformist ministers, and such persons as have served against our Royal Father and late Royal Brother of Blessed Memory', 20 June 1685; 'Entry Book: November 1685, 11–15', *Calendar of Treasury Books*, Volume 8: 1685–9, ed. William A Shaw (London: HMSO, 1923), pp. 413–26. http://www.british-history.ac.uk/report.aspx?compid=82513.

45 W. Macdonald Wigfield, *The Monmouth Rebels, 1685* (Taunton: Somerset Record Society, 1985), pp.vii–viii; John Coad, *A Memorandum of the Wonderful Providences of God to a Poor Unworthy Creature during the Time of the Duke of Monmouth's Rebellion and to the Revolution in 1688* (London: Longman, Brown, Green and Longmans, 1849), p. 17.

46 Robin Clifton, *The Last Popular Rebellion: The Western Rising of 1685* (London: Maurice Temple Smith, St. Martin's Press, 1984), pp. 241, 253–4; 'Entry Books', Somerset (Wells). The sentences in the assize records are also not entirely helpful, see TNA PRO ASSI/23, which F. A. Inderwick, *Side-Lights on the Stuarts*, 2nd ed. (London, Sampson Low, Marston, Searle and Rivington, 1891), transcribed, pp. 365–97, Monmouth's Rebellion, Appendix, pp. 398–427; Wigfield, *Monmouth Rebels*, pp.viii–ix; see also *The Proceeedings of the Government against the Rebels, compared with Persecutions of the late Reigns* (1716, attributed to Daniel Defoe), pp. 1–2, sentenced to be executed 334, of which 23 were, and transported 854, and James Bent, *The Bloody Assizes, or a Complete History of the Life of George Lord Jefferies* . . . (London: J. Dunton, 1690).

47 See *An Account of the Proceedings against the Rebels at Dorchester at an Assize holden there on Friday and Saturday 4th and 5th September* (London: 1685), *A Further Account of the Proceedings against the Rebels in the West of England* . . . *on 10 September 1685* (London: 1685), and *An Account of the Proceedings against the Rebels at an Assize holden at Exeter on the 14th* . . . *September 1685* (London: 1685).

48 *A Relation of the Great Sufferings and Strange Adventures of Henry Pitman, Chyrurgion to the late Duke of Monmouth* . . . . (London: Andrew Sowle, 1689), pp. 4–5, 11–15 and passim; Earle, *Monmouth's Rebels*, 180.

49 Coad, *Memorandum*, pp. 23–5, 26, 30, 35–9; Macaulay, *History*, Vol. 1, 647; despite this support, there is only a 'Thomas Coad' in the *Entry Books*, and this may be the same man (his son, a dissenting minister, was also called Thomas).

50 Clifton, *The Last Popular Rebellion*, pp. 273–4; Zook, 'Bloody Assizes'.

Chapter 5

1 *The Proceeedings of the Government against the Rebels, compared with Persecutions of the late Reigns* (1716, attributed to Defoe), p. 2; see also *The Mercy of the Government Vindicated, to which are added Remarks upon a late Pamphlet entituled An Argument to prove the Affections of the People the best Security of the Government* (London: James Roberts, 1716), also attributed to Defoe.

2 David Armitage, 'The Scottish Diaspora', in Jenny Wormald ed., *Scotland: A History* (Oxford University Press, 2005), pp. 225–49, p. 239 notes precedents.

3 Daniel Szechi, *1715: The Great Jacobite Rebellion* (New Haven, CT: Yale University Press, 2006), p. 199.

4 Defoe, *The Mercy of Government Vindicated*, p. 27; *Remarks on the Speeches of William Paul, Clerk, and John Hall of Otterburn Esq., Executed at Tyburn for Rebellion, the 13th of July, 1716* (London: J. Baker and T. Warner, 1716), pp. 3, 4 and 26. His petition to the government is TNA SP 53/33, where he 'prostrates himself' and relies on 'his Majesty's Clemency' for his actions in 'having readily and inconsiderately joined the rebels at Preston'.

5 Richard B. Scher, 'Scotland Transformed: The Eighteenth Century', in Wormald ed., *Scotland*, pp. 150–75, p. 152, notes that Episcopalian bishops remained pro-Jacobite until the death of Charles Edward Stuart.

6 Murray G. H. Pittock, 'Jacobite Culture', in *1745: Charles Edward Stuart and the Jacobites*, ed. Robert C. Woosnam-Savage (Edinburgh: HMSO, 1995, for Glasgow Museums), pp. 72–86.

7 Bruce Lenman, *The Jacobite Risings in Britain, 1689–1746* (Aberdeen: Scottish Cultural Press, 1995), p. 273.

8 TNA SP 54/12/16, 35 and 40 – the last expresses their delight that the King had ordered the release of the prisoners.

9 The phrase is Neil Davidson's, *Discovering the Scottish Revolution, 1692–1746* (London: Pluto Press, 2003), p. 236; see his discussion pp. 236–9; note Christopher Sinclair-Stevenson, *Inglorious Rebellion: The Jacobite Risings of 1708, 1715 and 1719* (London: Hamish Hamilton, 1971), p. 110, local Lancashire Catholics joining the rebel army under Mackintosh. Note earlier attempts to guarantee the tenants' children renewed leases if they died in King James's service, 1690 – *Jacobite Trials in Manchester*, ed. William Beamont (Manchester: Chetham Society, 1853), pp. xxiii–xxiv.

10 Note attitudes and prescriptive policies for 'regulating' the Highlands at various times after the flight of James II: *A Letter to an English Member of Parliament from a Gentleman in Scotland, concerning the Slavish*

*Dependencies which a great part of that Nation is still kept under by
Superiorities, Wards, Reliefs and other Remains of Feudal Law, and by
Clanships first printed in Edinburgh in 1721* (London: M. Cooper, 1746);
*Culloden Papers: comprising an Extensive and Interesting Correspondence
from the year 1625 to 1746 . . . from the originals in the possession of
Duncan George Forbes of Culloden* (London: T. Cadell and W. Davies,
1815), item no 20(XX), pp. 14–18, 'Memoir of a Plan for Preserving the
Peace of the Highlands: written a short time after the Revolution', which
blames Charles II and James II for introducing Popery and 'setting up
Superiors and Chiefs again' (15); *Historical Papers Relating to the Jacobite
Period, 1699–1750*, ed. Col. J. Allardyce (Aberdeen: The New Spalding
Club, 1895), 2 Vols, Vol. 1, both General Wade's reports on the state of the
Highlands; pp. 131–48, item XV, 'Report etc. Relating to the Highlands,
1724'; item XVI, pp. 150–65, 'Report etc. Relating to the Highlands,
1727'; also item XVII, pp. 166–76, 'Memoriall anent the True State of the
Highlands . . .' undated; see Neil Davidson, 'The Scottish Path to Capitalist
Agriculture 2: The Capitalist Offensive (1747–1815)', *Journal of Agrarian
Change*, 4(4) (2004), pp. 411–60.

11   TNA SP 54/3/168, which may be the report mentioned earlier at SP54/3/35,
letter dated 8 May 1746, 'Mr Morris's Paper for the future Regulation of
the Highlands, 8 May 1746'. See also *An Act for the more effectual securing
the Peace of the Highlands of Scotland* (1716) and the printed report of
the commission to establish the schools, in 1724, SP 54/12/229–33, and
the parallel activities of the Society for Scotland for Propagating Christian
Knowledge, established in 1709 by Royal Proclamation, accompanying it in
SP 54/12/234. On legal reforms of 1747, see Lindsay Farmer, *Criminal Law,
Tradition and Legal Order: Crime and the Genius of Scots Law, 1747 to the
Present* (Cambridge: Cambridge University Press, 1997); Scher, 'Scotland
Transformed', in Wormald, *Scotland*, p. 164, on attacks on the clan system.
On similar attitudes to traditional Ireland, see Kerby A. Miller, *Emigrants
and Exiles: Ireland and the Irish Exodus to North America* (NY and Oxford:
Oxford University Press, 1985), p. 23. Note that intellectual and academic
problems with the Highlands and the 'Celtic' fringe of Britain continued from
the late eighteenth into the nineteenth and twentieth centuries. See Ian Carter,
'The Highlands of Scotland as an Underdeveloped Region', in E. de Kadt and
G. Williams eds, *Sociology and Development* (London: Tavistock, for the
British Sociological Association, 1974), pp. 279–307; Neil Davidson, 'The
Scottish Path to Capitalist Agriculture 1: From the Crisis of Feudal Agriculture
to the Origins of Agrarian Transformation (1688–1746)', *Journal of Agrarian
Change*, 4(3) (1994), pp. 227–68, and 'Marx and Engels on the Scottish
Highlands', *Science and Society* 63(3) (2001), pp. 286–326; T. M. Devine,
'Landlordism and Highland Emigration', in *Scottish Emigration and Scottish
Society*, ed. T. M. Devine (Edinburgh: John Donald, 1992), pp. 84–103;
Terence J. Byres, *Capitalism From Above and Capitalism From Below*
(Basingstoke: Macmillan, 1996). In the North American colonies, says one
historian, Highlanders were 'products of cultures of violence and much else
that was undesirable besides, they made "hard neighbours" to the Indians':
Colin G. Calloway, *The Revolution in Indian Country: Crisis and Diversity
in Indian Communities* (New York, 1995), pp. 19–20, quoted in Gwenda

Morgan, *The Debate on the American Revolution* (Manchester: Manchester University Press, 2007), p. 288.

12 Pittock, 'Jacobite Culture'; Kieran German, 'Jacobite Politics in Aberdeen and the '15', in pp. 82–97, and Daniel Szechi, 'Retrieving Captain Le Cocq's Plunder: Plebeian Scots and the Aftermath of the 1715 Rebellion', pp. 98–119, in Paul Monod, Murray Pittock, and Daniel Szechi eds, *Loyalty and Identity: Jacobites at Home and Abroad* (Basingstoke: Palgrave Macmillan, 2010); TNA TS 20/80/13 listings.

13 Pittock, 'Jacobite Culture', pp. 72, 83 and 85.

14 TS 20/47/1–5, Thomas Waite to John Sharpe, 8 September, 1746, 'enclosing 3 extracts of 1715–17 precedents'.

15 Geoffrey Plank, *Rebellion and Savagery: The Jacobite Rising of 1745 and the British Empire,* (Philadelphia, PA: University of Pennsylvania Press, 2006), p. 95.

16 Margaret Sankey, *Jacobite Prisoners of the 1715 Rebellion: Preventing and Punishing Insurrection in Early Hanoverian Britain* (Burlington: Ashgate, 2005), note 66, p. 74; Gwenda Morgan and Peter Rushton, *Eighteenth-Century Criminal Transportation: The Formation of the Criminal Atlantic* (Houndmills, Basingstoke: Palgrave Macmillan, 2004).

17 See above, and *Remarks on the Speeches of William Paul, Clerk, and John Hall of Otterburn, Esq., Executed at Tyburn for Rebellion, the 13th of July 1716* (London: J. Baker and T. Warner, 1716).

18 TS 20/47/2, 26 and 29 December 1715.

19 TS 20/47/2, 18 April 1716, to Col Rapin.

20 Robert Forbes, *The Lyon in Mourning, or a Collection of Speeches, Letters Journals etc Relative to the Affairs of Prince Charles Edward Stuart, by the Rev. Robert Forbes MA, Bishop of Ross and Caithness, 1746–75*, 3 Vols, with a preface by Henry Paton (Edinburgh: University Press, 1895 for The Scottish Historical Society, Vol. 21), pp. 231–43, selectively reprinted in *Maryland Historical Magazine*, Vol. 1, March 1905.

21 Francis Douglas, *The History of the Rebellion in 1745 and 1746, Extracted from the Scots Magazine; with an Appendix, Containing an Account of the Trials of the Rebels; the Pretender and His Son's Declarations etc* (Aberdeen: F. Douglass and W. Murray, 1755), pp. 266–7, Ogilvy of Coul against one Captain Hamilton.

22 *Gentleman's Magazine* 16 (1746), p. 261, From the *Westminster Journal*, 24 May, 'On Punishing the Rebels'; and see pp. 416–17, for and against mercy (from the *General Evening Post*).

23 See Szechi, *1715*, pp. 138–69, for the most recent and clearest analysis of the campaigning, which was largely over before the Pretender himself arrived in Scotland.

24 See Szechi, *1715*, p. 200; Sankey, *Jacobite Prisoners*, pp. 4–5; 118, 120, 124–5. *Habeas Corpus* had been suspended for one year in July 1715 by Act of Parliament. The Scottish law was the 1701 Act against Wrongful Imprisonment.

25 *Jacobite Trials at Manchester in 1694, from an Unpublished Manuscript,* ed. William Beaumont (Manchester: The Chetham Society, Vol. 28, 1853);

Jane Garrett, *The Triumphs of Providence: The Assassination Plot, 1696* (Cambridge: Cambridge University Press, 1980), pp. 237–46. Note that the laws also introduced time limits after which it was not possible to bring a prosecution for things allegedly done years before.

26 A. Francis Stewart, ed. *News-Letters of 1715–16* (London and Edinburgh: W. R. Chambers, 1910), pp.xiv, 152; *News-Letter*, 21 January 1716, Lord Louden and 15 other Scottish nobles arrived in London.

27 SP 44/118/143, 30 November 1715; TS 20/47/2, 15 December 1715 a copy of the Order in Council of the 13th authorizing the lottery; SP 44/118/153–153v, 15 December 1715.

28 SP 44/118/190v, copied in TS 20/47/2, 7 February 1716.

29 TNA PRO KB 33/1/5/14–14v gives the figure at the end of a much shorter list of names; SP 44/118/190v, 7 February 1716 copied in TS 20/47/2, 17 January 1716, and order to governors copied, 16 and 18 April 1716.

30 Sankey, *Jacobite Prisoners*, p. 69.

31 'Gentlemen' KB 33/1/5/19–19v; SP 54/12/19 Rutherford's plea for mercy; Sankey, *Jacobite Prisoners*, pp. 62–3; evidence from ship listings suggest that nearly half of these were in fact transported: 53 of the 113, traced in David Dobson, *Directory of Scots Banished to the American Plantations, 1650–1775* (Baltimore, MD: Genealogical Publishing Co, 1984).

32 Successful plea by Richard Withington and Richard Birches, SP 44/118/255 (17 May 1716) and 287 (2 August 1716); and SP 44/118/204v, order about indentures.

33 *Newsletter*, 11 February 1716; *Weekly Remarks and Political Reflections*, 18 February 1716; Sankey, *Jacobite Prisoners*, pp. 50–1, the executions began on 28 January, eight days after the trials started; and p. 51, quoting SP 44/118/188 Townsend 2 February 1716; see p. 56, more than half of those executed had been selected by lot; 638 were transported.

34 *The Postman*, 8 March 1716; *The Statutes at Large from the first year of the Reign of George the First to the third year of the Reign of King George the second*, 5 Vols, Vol. 5 (London: Mark Basket, 1763), pp. 74–5.

35 Sankey, *Jacobite Prisoners*, pp. 70–2; Lenman, *Jacobite Risings*, pp. 158 and p. 271; there were 639 in all, according to the shipping lists in TNA TS 20/47/3, 340 intended for the North American colonies, 173 for the Caribbean, and 126 for either Virginia or Jamaica on the *Friendship*, which went to the Chesapeake.

36 Szechi, *1715*, pp. 206–8, p. 208 (quotation).

37 *Executive Journals of the Council of Colonial Virginia*, ed. H. R. McIlwaine, Vol. 3, (Richmond, VA: D. Bottom, 1938), pp. 428–31; petition 430–1, and *Calendar of Virginia State Papers, 1652–1781*, Vol. 1, ed. W. P. Palmer (Richmond, VA: R. F. Walker, 1875), pp. 187–8; Plank, *Rebellion and Savagery*, p. 95.

38 *Archives of Maryland*, Vol. 25, pp. 347–51, and Vol. 426, pp. 245–6; Thomas Scharf, *A History of Maryland*, 3 Vols (Baltimore, MD: John B. Piet, 1879), Vol. 1, pp. 385–9.

39 See TNA TS 20/33/190–1, petition of Alexander Kinlock, 29 October 1746; Francis Douglas, *The History of the Rebellion*, p. 342.

40   TNA SP 54/31/138, Cumberland to Newcastle, 27 May 1746.

41   Figures as summarized by Davidson, *Discovering the Scottish Revolution*,
     p. 258, *following The Prisoners of the '45, edited from the State Papers*, Sir
     Bruce Gordon Seton and Jean Gordon Arnot, 3 Vols, Vol. 1 (Edinburgh:
     Edinburgh University Press, for the Scottish History Society, 1928), Vols 2 and
     3, 1929, Vols 13–15 of *Publications of the Scottish History Society*, 3rd series,
     Vol. 1, pp. 4, 8, 10, 16–17, 22, 143, 152–3.

42   Daniel Szechi, '"Cam Ye O'er Frae France?" Exile and the Mind of Scottish
     Jacobitism', *Journal of British Studies*, 37(4) (1998), pp. 357–90, p. 364; TNA
     TS 20/80/1–17 'Prisoners in Transports', piece 14 for the *Liberty and Property*,
     136 listed; Davidson, *Discovering the Scottish Revolution*, p. 239. On the
     policy towards the members of the Manchester regiment, see TNA TS 11/179
     Treasury Solicitor's Papers piece 787.

43   TNA TS 20/80/15 'The Report of Mr Minshaw who was sent to Woolwich to
     Examine into the State of the Rebel Prisoners on board the Transport there',
     20 August 1746.

44   TNA TS 20/35/4 (i) Samuel Smith in Liverpool to John Sharpe, 4 (i) 11
     September 1746, and /7, 18 November 1746; TS 20/33/217, to Gildart and
     Smith, undated; T1/325/178–9 – 'Memorial of Samuel Smith Merchant for
     transporting 453 Rebel Prisoners. Cateaton Street 10 Decr 1747. 15 Decr
     1747', final demand on 179 after list of deliveries; the law was 20 Geo.II
     c.46, in J. Macbeth Forbes, *Jacobite Gleanings from State Manuscripts: Short
     Sketches of Jacobites, the Transportations in 1745* (Edinburgh: O. Anderson
     and Ferrier, 1903), p. 41.

45   TNA T1/325/178–9, he claimed £1132 10s for transporting the prisoners;
     CO 28/49, list of the 128 prisoners landed in Barbados; Geoffrey Plank,
     Rebellion and Savagery: The Jacobite Rising of 1745 and the British Empire
     (Philadelphia, PA: University of Pennsylvania Press, 2006), p. 95. On the men
     on the *Veteran*, see David Dobson, *Scottish Emigration to Colonial America,
     1607–1785* (Athens, GA: University of Georgia Press, 2004), pp. 125–6.

46   Scharf, *History of Maryland*, Vol. 1, p. 435.

47   *The Lyon in Mourning*, Vol. 2, pp. 231–43, reprinted in part in *Maryland
     Hist. Mag.* 1 (1906), pp. 346–52; Morgan and Rushton, *Eighteenth-Century
     Criminal Transportation*, on rich convicts to the colonies.

48   *Virginia Gazette* (Hunter), Williamsburg, 7 March, 1750–1, advertised by
     Jacob Andrew Minitree, Virginia Runaways Project online.

49   *Pennsylvania Gazette*, 5 June 1755, also in *Boston Gazette*, 16 June 1755.

50   Donna J. Spindell, 'The Law of Words: Verbal Abuse in North Carolina
     to 1730', *American Journal of Legal History*, 39 (1995), pp. 5–42; Duane
     Meyer, *The Highland Scots of North Carolina, 1732–76* (Chapel Hill, NC:
     University of North Carolina Press, 1957 and 1961), pp. 28–9. See career
     of former Jacobite and revolutionary war general Hugh Mercer, *New York
     Gazette Revived in the Weekly Post-Boy*, 28 September 1747, also *Pennsylvania
     Gazette*, 1 October, *New York Evening Post*, 5 Oct 1747; *Norwich Packet*, 17
     March 1777; *Archives of Maryland*, Vol. 50, pp. 181–2 (1753); (no author),
     'Jacobitism in Virginia: Charges against Captain Jacob Lumpkin', *The Virginia
     Magazine of History and Biography*, 6(4) (1899), pp. 389–96 (accused in 1690).

51 See also Edgar Erskine Hume, 'A Colonial Scottish Jacobite Family:
    Establishment in Virginia of a Branch of the Humes of Wedderburn', *The
    Virginia Magazine of History and Biography*, 38(1) (1930), pp. 1–37 and
    (Continued), 38(4) (1930), pp. 293–346; Paul Monod, Murray Pittock and
    Daniel Szechi, eds, *Loyalty and Identity: Jacobites at Home and Abroad*
    (Houndmills, Basingstoke: Palgrave Macmillan, 2010).

Chapter 6

1   T. M. Devine, *Scotland's Empire, 1600–1815* (London: Allen Lane, 2003),
    pp. 40–8; Patricia Seed, *Ceremonies of Posssession: Europe's Conquest of the
    New World, 1492–1640* (Cambridge: Cambridge University Press, 1995);
    Karen O. Kupperman, *Roanoke: The Abandoned Colony* (Totowa, NJ: Rowen
    and Allenhead, 1984); Edmund S. Morgan, *American Slavery, American
    Freedom: The Ordeal of Colonial Virginia* (New York: Norton, 1975).

2   Lauren Benton, *A Search for Sovereignty: Law and Geography in European
    Empire, 1400–1900* (Cambridge: Cambridge University Press, 2010); Richard
    Hakluyt, *A Discourse on Western Planting* (1584); A. L. Beier, *Masterless
    Men: The Vagrancy Problem in England, 1560–1640* (London: Methuen,
    1985); G. R. Taylor, ed., *The Original Writings and Correspondence of the
    Two Richard Hakluyts*, Hakluyt Society, 2nd ser, LXXVI, LXXVII (London,
    1935), pp. 142–3; Francis Bacon, 'Of Plantations' (1625) in Jack P. Greene,
    ed., *Settlements to Society: 1584–1763* (New York: McGraw Hill, 1966),
    pp. 9–11.

3   Yasuhide Kawashima, *Puritan Justice and the Indian: White Man's Law in
    Massachusetts, 1630–1763* (Middleton, CT: Wesleyan University Press, 1986),
    p. 135; Nan Goodman, 'Banishment, Jurisdiction, and Identity in Seventeenth-
    Century New England', *Early American Studies* (Spring, 2009), pp. 109–39,
    pp. 109–10.

4   Warren M. Billings, 'A Quaker in Seventeenth-Century Virginia: Four
    Remonstrances by George Wilson', *WMQ*, 3d ser., 33(1) (1976), pp. 127–40,
    pp. 129–30.

5   W. W. Hening, ed., *Statutes at Large of Virginia* (Charlottesville, VA: University
    Press of Virginia, (1969) [1823], Vol. 1, pp. 532–3, Vol. 2, pp. 48, 180–3, 198;
    James Horn, *Adapting to a New World: English Society in the Seventeenth-
    Century Chesapeake* (Chapel Hill, NC: University of North Carolina Press,
    1994), p. 394.

6   Horn, *Adapting to a New World*, p. 395.

7   Kenneth L. Carroll, 'Persecution and Persecutors of Maryland Quakers,
    1658–61', *Quaker History*, 99 (Spring, 2010), pp. 15–31, p. 17; Kenneth L.
    Carroll, 'Thomas Thurston, Renegade Maryland Quaker', *Maryland Historical
    Magazine*, 62 (June, 1967), pp. 170–92.

8   TNA PRO SP 44/14, pp. 57–8. 1 March 1664; Herbert Friedenwald,
    'Material for the History of the Jews in the British West Indies', *Publications
    of the American Jewish Historical Society*, 5 (1897), pp. 45–68; N. Darnell
    Davis, 'Notes on the History of the Jews in Barbados', *Publications of the*

American Jewish Historical Society, 18 (1909), pp. 129–81. On later changes in attitudes, see Bryan Edwards, *The History, Civil and Commericial, of the British Colonies in the West Indies*, 2 Vols (Dublin: Luke White, 1793), Vol. 2, pp. 4–5.

9   Michael Leroy Oberg, ed., Samuel Wiseman's, *Book of Record: The Official Account of Bacon's Rebellion in Virginia, 1676–77* (Lanham, MD: Rowman and Littlefield Publishers, 2005), pp. 9–10; Charles M. Andrews, *Narratives of the Insurrections, 1675–90* (New York, Barnes & Noble, 1956) [1915]; Edmund S. Morgan, *American Slavery, American Freedom. The Ordeal of Colonial Virginia* (New York: Norton, 1975), pp. 215–70; Warren M. Billings, *Sir William Berkeley and the Forging of Colonial Virginia* (Baton Rouge, LA: Louisiana State University Press, 2004), p. 248.

10 Lyon G. Tyler, 'Isle of Wight Papers Relating to Bacon's Rebellion', *WMQ*, 4(2) (1895), pp. 111–15, pp. 113–14; *WMQ*, 7(4) (1899), pp. 229–30.

11 Hening, ed., *Statutes*, Vol. 2, p. 378.

12 Ibid., pp. 547–8, p. 555.

13 TNA PRO CO 1/41/f.258.

14 Edward Waterhouse, 'A Declaration of the State of the Colony and Affairs in Virginia' in Susan Kingsbury, ed., *Records of the Virginia Company*, Vol. 3, pp. 556–7; Karen O. Kupperman, 'English Perceptions of Treachery, 1583–1640: The Case of the American 'Savages', *Historical Journal*, 20(2) (1977), pp. 263–87; Gary B. Nash, 'The Image of the Indian in the Southern Colonial Mind', *WMQ*, 3d ser, Vol. 29(2) (1972), pp. 197–230.

15 Nicholas P. Canny, 'The Ideology of English Colonization: From Ireland to America', *WMQ*, 3d ser, 30 (1972), pp. 575–98; Barbara Donagan, 'Atrocity, War Crime and Treason in the English Civil War', *American Historical Review*, 99(4) (1994), pp. 1137–66.

16 On the earlier Pequot War, see Alfred A. Cave, *The Pequot War* (Amherst, MA: University of Massachusetts Press, 1996), pp. 161–3; Seventeen Pequot boys and women were carried to Providence Island in 1638. Karen Kupperman, Providence Island 1630–1641 (Cambridge: University of Cambridge Press, 1993), p. 172; James Drake, 'Restraining Atrocity: The Conduct of King Philip's War', *New England Quarterly*, 70(1) (1997), pp. 33–56, pp. 36–7; Kawashima, *Puritan Justice*, p. 135, also p. 164, p. 165, p. 170; Jill Lepore, *The Name of War: King Philip's War and the Origins of American Identity* (New York: Knopf, 1998), pp. 150–70, p. 154; James P. Ronda, 'Red and White at the Bench: Indians and the Law in Plymouth Colony, 1620–91', *Essex Institute Historical Collections in Early America*, 110 (1974), pp. 200–15; Alan Taylor, *American Colonies: The Settling of North America* (Harmondsworth, Middlesex: Viking Penguin, 2002), pp. 199–203.

17 TNA PRO, CO 1/39, ff.200–1; Hening, ed., *Statutes*, Vol. 2, p. 215; Rappahannock County Deeds, 1663–8, p. 57; Lepore, *The Name of War*, pp. 108–13.

18 John Demos, ed. *Remarkable Providences*, 2nd ed. (Boston, MA: Northeastern University Press, 1991), pp. 372–4; John Demos, *The Unredeemed Captive: A Family Story from Early America* (New York: Knopf, 1994), p. 112.

19 Hening, ed., *Statutes*, 2, pp. 193–4, pp. 218–19, pp. 237–8, p. 484.

20 Abstract of Proceedings of the Commission of Oyer and Terminer, TNA PRO, CO. 5/1314, ff.31–3; although C. S. Everett discusses the case of the Nanziatticos in '"They shal be slaves for their lives": Indian Slavery in Colonial Virginia', in Alan Gallay, ed. *Indian Slavery in Colonial America* (Lincoln, NE: University of Nebraska Press, 2009), pp. 67–108, pp. 96–7, for a fuller and earlier account, see Gwenda Morgan, *The Hegemony of the Law: Richmond County, Virginia, 1692–1776* (New York: Garland, 1989), pp. 32–8.

21 H. R. McLlwaine and W. L. Hall, eds, *Executive Journals of the Council of Colonial Virginia*, 5 Vols (Richmond, 1924–5), Vol. 2, pp. 396, 397–8, 458; J. P. Kennedy and H. R. McLlwaine, eds, *Journals of the House of Burgesses of Virginia, 1619–1776*, 13 Vols (Richmond, VA: Colonial Press, 1905–15), 1702–12, p. 97; An Act Concerning the Nansiattico and Other Indians', W. W. Winfree, comp., *The Laws of Virginia: Being A Supplement of Hening's The Statutes at Large, 1700–50* (Richmond, VA: Virginia State Library, 1971), pp. 41–3; *EJC*, Vol. 3, pp. 5–6; H. R. McLlwaine, ed., *Legislative Journals of the Council of Colonial Virginia*, 3 Vols (Richmond, 1918–19), Vol. 1, p. 414, p. 420; Morgan, *Hegemony of the Law*, pp. 35–6.

22 An Act Concerning the Nansiattico and Other Indians, p. 42.

23 Verner W. Crane, *The Southern Frontier, 1670–1732* (Ann Arbor, MI: University of Michigan,1956 [1928]), pp. 162–86; Gary B. Nash, *Red, White and Black: The Peoples of Early North America*, 4th ed. (Upper Saddle River, NJ: Prentice Hall, 2000), p. 122, pp. 123–6; Alan Taylor, *American Colonies: The Settling of North America* (New York: Penguin, 2001), pp. 224–40; Alan Gallay, 'South Carolina's Entrance into the Indian Slave Trade', in *Indian Slavery in Colonial America*, pp. 109–45.

24 Frank Tannenbaum, *Slave and Citizen: The Negro in the Americas* (New York: Knopf, 1946; republished by Beacon Press, 1992 with an introduction by Franklin W. Knight), pp. 116–18.

25 Jerome S. Handler, 'Slave Revolts and Conspiracies in Seventeenth-Century Barbados', *New West Indian Guide*, 56 (1982), 1–2, Leiden, pp. 5–42, pp. 5–6, 18, 28, 35.

26 Hening, ed., *Statutes*, Vol. 3, pp. 87–8; Hening, ed., *Statutes*, Vol. 4, p. 132; H. N. Sherwood, 'Early Negro Deportation Projects', *Mississippi Valley Historical Review*, 2, 4 (March, 1916), pp. 484–508, pp. 484–5.

27 David J. McCord and Thomas Cooper, eds, *Statutes at Large of South Carolina*, 10 Vols (Columbia, SC, 1834–41), Vol. 7, no. 344, 365–8; no. 388, 368–70, and no. 476, 371–84.

28 An Act for the Transportation of Dick and other Negroe Slaves, in Winfree, *The Laws of Virginia: A Supplement*, pp. 257–9; Philip J. Schwarz, 'The Transportation of Slaves from Virginia, 1801–65', *Slavery and Abolition*, 7 (1986), pp. 215–40.

29 Philip J. Schwartz, *Twice Condemned, Slaves and the Criminal Laws in Virginia, 1705–1865* (Baton Rouge, LA: Louisiana State University Press, 1988), pp. 27–9 and 194–9; Philip J. Schwartz, *Slave Laws in Virginia* (Athens and London: University of Georgia Press, 1996), p. 103.

30 Peter Linebaugh and Marcus Rediker, *The Many-Headed Hydra: Sailors, Slaves, Commoners and the Hidden History of the Revolutionary Atlantic* (London and New York: Verso, 2000), p. 200.

31 Council Minutes, 17 March, 12 April, 13, 25, 1737, TNA PRO, CO 9/11;
    Assembly Minutes, 15 February, 16 March, 1738, TNA PRO, CO 9/12;
    Calendar of State Papers, Colonial Series, America and West Indies (London:
    H. M. Stationary Office, 1963), pp. 10–14. For reports in the colonial press,
    see *Pennsylvania Gazette*, 2 December, 16, 1736, 31 March, 1737, *Virginia
    Gazette*, 8 April, 1737, *South Carolina Gazette*, 30 April, 1737; David B.
    Gaspar, *Bondsmen and Rebels: A Study of Master-Slave Relations in Antigua*
    (Durham and London: Duke University Press, 1993 [1984]), pp. 35–7.

32 Daniel Horsmanden, *Journal of the Proceedings in the Detection of the
    Conspiracy Found by Some Ehite People in Conjunction with Negroes and
    Other Slaves for the Burning of the City of New York in America* (New
    York, 1744); Peter Charles Hoffer, *The Great New York Conspiracy of 1741:
    Slavery, Crime, and Colonial Law* (Lawrence, KS: University Press of Kansas,
    2003); Jill Lepore, *New York Burning: Liberty, Slavery, and Conspiracy
    in Eighteenth-Century Manhattan* (New York: Knopf, 2005), pp.xvi–xx,
    pp. 122–8; Peter Linebaugh and Marcus Rediker, *The Many-Headed Hydra*,
    pp. 174–210.

33 Naval Office Records for New York, TNA PRO, CO 5/1226, pp. 176–80;
    Lepore, *New York Burning*, p. 175.

34 Richard Price, ed., *Maroon Societies: Rebel Slave Communities in the
    Americas* (Garden City, NY: Anchor, 1973); James D. Lockett, 'The
    Deportation of the Maroons of Trelawny Town to Nova Scotia, Then Back to
    Africa', *Journal of Black Studies*, 30(1), pp. 5–14, pp. 6–8.

35 Bryan Edwards, *The Proceedings of the Governor and Assembly of Jamaica
    in regard to the Maroon Negroes* (Piccadilly: Stockdale, 1796), p. 50; John
    N. Grant, *The Maroons in Nova Scotia* (Halifax: Formac Publishing, 2002);
    Robin W. Winks, *The Blacks in Canada: A History* (New Haven, CT: Yale
    University Press,1971), 1st ed., pp. 78–95; Miles Ogburn, 'A War of Words·
    Speech, Script and Print in the Maroon War of 1795–96', *Journal of Historical
    Geography*, 37 (2011), pp. 203–15.

36 Sir John Wentworth to Duke of Portland, 7 May 1797, *Papers relative to the
    Settling of the Maroons in His Majesty's Province of Nova Scotia* (1798).

37 Debrett, *Parliamentary Register*, V, 26 February 1796, 115.

38 Debrett, *Parliamentary Register*, VI, 1 May 1797, 84–95.

39 *Extracts and Copies of Letters from Sir John Wentworth, Lieutenant Governor
    of Nova Scotia, to his Grace the Duke of Portland; Respecting the Settlement
    of the Maroons in that Province* (1797), and *Papers Relative to the Settling
    of the Maroons in His Majesty's Province of Nova Scotia* (1798); Debrett,
    Parliamentary Register, VI (1798); Lockhart; 'The Deportation of the Maroons,'
    pp. 9–10, p. 12; Edwards, *Proceedings*, pp.lxvii–ix, lxxiii, lxxix–lxxxi.

40 Bradley J. Nicholson, 'Legal Borrowing and the Origins of Slave Law in
    the British Colonies', *American Journal of Legal History*, 38 (1994) (1),
    pp. 38–54, p. 48.

41 Court Minutes of New Amsterdam, *Records of New Amsterdam from 1653
    to 1674* (New York, 1897), Vol. 2, pp. 130–1, 142–3, 300–1; Linda Biemer,
    'Criminal Law and Women in New Amsterdam and Early New York', *Selected*

Rensselaerswick Seminar Papers. pp. 73–82, p. 79, p. 82, fn. 31; on the New Netherland and cases of political banishment, see Jaap Jacobs, *The Colony of New Netherland: A Dutch Settlement in Seventeenth-Century America* (Ithaca and London: Cornell University Press, 2009), pp. 80–1.

42 J. M. Beattie, *Policing and Punishment in London, 1660–1750: Urban Crime and the Limits of Terror* (Oxford: Oxford University Press, 2001); Gwenda Morgan and Peter Rushton, *Eighteenth-Century Criminal Transportation: the Formation of the Criminal Atlantic* (Basingstoke: Palgrave Macmillan, 2004), pp. 33–8; despite recent revisionism, Abbot E. Smith's *Colonists in Bondage: White Servitude and Convict Labor in America, 1607–1776* (NY: Norton, 1971, originally University of North Carolina Press, 1947) remains a useful study, especially for the seventeenth century; for a more sceptical note on the figures for Irish transportation, see James Kelly, 'Transportation from Ireland to North America, 1703–89', in David Dickson and Cormac Ó Gráda, eds, *Refiguring Ireland: Essays in Honour of L. M. Cullen* (Dublin: Lilliput Press, 2003), pp. 112–35.

43 A. Roger Ekirch, *Bound for America: the Transportation of British Convicts to the Colonies, 1718–75* (Oxford: Clarendon Press, 1987), p. 38.

44 Jack D. Marietta and G. S. Rowe, *Troubled Experiment: Crime and Justice in Pennsylvania, 1682–1600* (Philadelphia, PA: University of Pennsylvania Press, 2006), pp. 77–8.

45 Morgan and Rushton, *Eighteenth-Century Criminal Transportation*, Chapter 5 particularly.

46 *London Evening Post*, 11 May 1736, p. 1; *Old Bailey Sessions Papers*, 5 and 11 May 1736; *London Evening Post*, 20 May 1736, p. 2; *Gentleman's Magazine* 6 (1736), p. 290; *Old Bailey Sessions Papers*, December 1735 for the trial of William Wreathock, Peter Chamberlain, James Ruffett alias Rufhead, George Bird the Younger, and Gilbert Campbell for highway robbery of Dr Nathaniel Lancaster the previous June; also trial of Thomas Cray or MacCray or MacCreagh, *Old Bailey Sessions Papers*, 3 July 1735; *Virginia Gazette*, 26 November 1737; 28 January 1737; TNA PRO, T.53/38/337.

47 David Waldstreicher, 'Reading the Runaways: Self-Fashioning, Print Culture, and Confidence in Slavery in the Eighteenth-Century Mid-Atlantic', *WMQ*, 3rd ser, 56(2) (1999), pp. 243–72; Morgan and Rushton, *Eighteenth-Century Criminal Transportation*, Ch. 5, and 'Running Away and Returning Home: the Fate of English Convicts in the American Colonies', *Crime, Histoire & Sociétés/Crime, History & Societies* 7(2) (2003), pp. 61–80, and 'Visible Bodies: Power, Subordination and Identity in the Eighteenth-Century Atlantic World', *Journal of Social History* 39(1) (Fall, 2005), pp. 39–64.

48 Morgan and Rushton, *Eighteenth-Century Criminal Transportation*, p. 155; A. Roger Ekirch, 'Great Britain's Secret Convict Trade to America, 1783–4', *American Historical Review*, 89(5) (1984), pp. 1285–91. On the disastrous attempt to locate a convict base in West Africa during the war, see Emma Christopher, *A Merciless Place: The Lost Story of Britain's Convict Disaster in Africa* (Oxford: Oxford University Press, 2010).

49 Carla Gardina Pestana, *The English Atlantic in an Age of Revolution 1640–51* (Cambridge, MA: University of Cambridge Press, 2004), p. 188.

Chapter 7

1 John Mack Faragher, *A Great and Noble Scheme: The Tragic Story of the Expulsions of the French Acadians from their American Homeland* (New York and London: Norton, 2005), p. 336.

2 Christopher Hodson, 'Exile on Spruce Street: An Acadian History', *WMQ*, 3d ser. 67(2) (2010), pp. 249–78; Christopher Hodson, *The Acadian Diaspora: An Eighteenth-Century History* (Oxford and New York: Oxford University Press, 2012); Emma Rothschild, 'A Horrible Tragedy in the French Atlantic', *Past and Present*, 192 (Spring, 2006), pp. 67–108.

3 Lieutenant Governor Lawrence to Colonel Monckton, 31 July 1755, British Library, Add Mss 19, 173, f.36; N. E. S. Griffiths, *From Migrant to Acadian: A North American Border People, 1604–1755* (Montreal and Kingston: McGill-Queen's University Press, 2005), p. 88; Naomi E. S. Griffiths, *The Contexts of Acadian History, 1686–1784*, (Montreal and Kingston: McGill-Queen's University Press, 1992), p. 63.

4 *Histoire philosophique et politique de l'établissment des Européenes du Commerce dans les deux Indes*, 1766 ed., 7 Vols; Thomas Haliburton, *An Historical and Statistical Account of Nova Scotia*, 2 Vols (Halifax: J. Howe, 1829); Geoffrey Plank, *An Unsettled Conquest: The British Campaign Against the Peoples of Acadia* (Philadelphia, PA: University of Pennsylvania Press, 2001); Faragher, *A Great and Noble Scheme*; N. E. S. Griffiths, *From Migrant to Acadian*; A. J. B. Johnston, 'The Call of the Archetype and the Challenge of Acadian History', *French Colonial History*, 5 (2004), pp. 63–92.

5 Naomi E. S. Griffiths, *The Contexts of Acadian History, 1686–1784*; Placide Gaudet, *Le Grand Derangement: sur qui Retombe la Responsibilité de l'Expulsion des Acadiens?* (Ottawa: Ottawa Print, 1922); Griffiths, *From Migrant to Acadian*, pp. 419–30; George A. Rawlyk, *Nova Scotia's Massachusetts: A Study of Massachusetts-Nova Scotia Relations, 1630 to 1784* (Montreal and London: McGill-Queen's University Press, 1973), pp. 193–216.

6 Matthew Ward, 'Fighting the "Old Women": Indian Strategy on the Virginia and Pennsylvania Frontier, 1754–58', *Virginia Magazine of History and Biography*, 103(3) (1995), pp. 297–320, p. 298, Hodson, *The Acadian Diaspora*, pp. 52–61.

7 Faragher, *A Great and Noble Scheme*, p. 338; N. E. S. Griffiths, 'Petitions of Acadian Exiles, 1755–85: a Neglected Source', *Histoire Sociale/Social History*, 11 (1978), pp. 213–23.

8 See J. B. Brebner, *New England's Outpost: Acadia before the Conquest of Canada* (New York: Columbia University Press, 1927), pp. 199–202, pp. 212–13; Griffiths, *From Migrant to Acadian*, p. 88, p. 457, fn. 134, fn. 135. For the history of the Acadians before their removal, see Plank, *An Unsettled Conquest*, pp. 1–105.

9 Jonathan Belcher to Thomas Pownall, 28 July 1755, TNA PRO, CO 217/16/24–7; it was stamped 'received 26 March 1756, read 7 April 1756'.

10 'Journal of Colonel John Winslow', *Report and Collections of the Nova Scotia Historical Society*, Vol. 3 (Halifax, N. S., 1883), pp. 94–5; Jedidiah Preble to Colonel Winslow, 5 September 1755, p. 100.

11 TNA PRO, CO 217/15/f.351–54. Governor Lawrence's circular letter to the colonial governors.

12 *Journals of the House of Representatives of Massachusetts*, Vol. 32, pt. 1, 1 October 1755, pp. 182–3, 218, 220–1, 224 and 226.

13 Faragher, *A Great and Noble Scheme*, pp. 374–5; Richard G. Lowe, 'Massachusetts and the Acadians', *WMQ*, 3d ser, 25(2) (1968), pp. 212–29; for further details of the removals from Charlestown and the role of Jacques Vigneau, see Plank, *An Unsettled Conquest*, p. 153.

14 *Journals of the House of Representatives of Massachusetts*, Vol. 32, pt. 1, pp. 226, 235, 237, 249, and 250.

15 *Journals of the House of Representatives of Massachusetts*, Vol. 32, pt. 1, 27 December 1755, pp. 265–6, pp. 266–7.

16 *Journals of the House of Representatives*, Vol. 33, pt. 1, p. 68, p. 108, pp. 112–13, pp. 118–19, p. 120, p. 121, p. 164, p. 165; Charles Lawrence to the Board of Trade, 5 August 1756, alerts London that the Acadians are returning, TNA PRO CO 217/16, ff.43–7.

17 *Journals of the House of Representatives of Massachusetts*, Vol. 33, pt. 1, pp. 126, 163–5, 187, 189, 196, 218.

18 Ibid., p. 186.

19 Faragher, *A Great and Noble Scheme*, p. 378.

20 Faragher, *A Great and Noble Scheme*, p. 378, fn. 20; Gaudet, *Appendix E*, pp. 114–15, pp. 117–18, p. 124.

21 Faragher, *A Great and Noble Scheme*, pp. 378–9; fn. 21; Gaudet, *Appendix E*, pp. 100–4.

22 Faragher, *A Great and Noble Scheme*, pp. 379–80; Gaudet, *Appendix E*, pp. 88–9, p. 107, pp. 110–11, pp. 190–1.

23 Circular Letter to the Governors, 11 August 1755, f.351; Faragher, *A Great and Noble Scheme*, pp. 373–4, p. 528.

24 *Governor Morris to Governor Belcher*, 22 November 1755, *Pennsylvania Archives*, Vol. 2 (Philadelphia, 1853), p. 509; Wilton Paul Ledet, 'Acadian Exiles in Pennsylvania', *Pennsylvania History*, 9(2) (1942), pp. 118–28.

25 Governor Belcher to Governor Morris, n.d, *Pennsylvania Archives*, II, p. 513.

26 Faragher, *A Great and Noble Scheme*, p. 375, fn. 13, General Court to William Shirley, 7 February 1756, Lowe, 'Massachusetts and the Acadians', pp. 214–15; Naomi Griffiths, 'Acadians in Exile: the Experiences of the Acadians in the British Seaports', *Acadiensis*, 4, pt. 1 (1974), 67–84.

27 Faragher, *A Great and Noble Scheme*, p. 375, fn. 14, Basil Sollers, 'The Acadians (French Neutrals) Transported to Maryland', *Maryland Historical Magazine*, 3(1) (1908), pp. 1–21, pp. 19–20.

28 William D. Hoyt, Jr., 'A Contemporary View of the Acadian Arrival in Maryland, 1755', *WMQ*, 3d ser., 5(4) (1948), pp. 571–5, p. 572, p. 575.

29 Faragher, *A Great and Noble Scheme*, 381; Governor Dinwiddie to General Shirley, 31 October 1755, Dinwiddie to the Lords of the Treasury, 24 November 1755, R. A. Brock, ed., *The Official Records of Robert Dinwiddie*, 2 Vols (Richmond, VA: Virginia Historical Society, 1884), Vol. 2, p. 258, p. 286.

30 Adam Stephen to George Washington, Winchester, 4 October 1755, W. W. Abbot, ed., *The Papers of George Washington, Colonial Series*, Vol. 2, August 1755–April 1756 (Charlottesville, VA: University Press of Virginia, 1983), p. 72; George Washington to Governor Dinwiddie, Winchester, 17 October 1755, *Dinwiddie Papers*, Vol. 2, p. 20.

31 Governor Dinwiddie to James Abercromby, 24 November 1755, *Dinwiddie Papers*, Vol. 2, p 287; Governor Dinwiddie to the Earl of Halifax, 15 November 1755, *Dinwiddie Papers*, Vol 2, p. 273.

32 Governor Dinwiddie to the Earl of Halifax, 24 February 1756, *Dinwiddie Papers*, Vol. 2, p. 346.

33 Governor Dinwiddie to the Earl of Halifax, 15 November 1755, Governor Dinwiddie to General Shirley, 31 October 1755, *Dinwiddie Papers*, Vol. 2, p. 273, p. 258.

34 Governor Dinwiddie, postscript 17 November 1755, *Dinwiddie Papers*, Vol. 2, p. 268.

35 Governor Dinwiddie to the Lords of Trade, 15 November 1755, *Dinwiddie Papers*, Vol. 2, p. 270, p. 282.

36 Governor Dinwiddie to Governor Sharpe, 22 November 1755, *Dinwiddie Papers*, Vol. 2, p. 279.

37 Governor Dinwiddie to Sir Thomas Robinson, 24 November 1755, *Dinwiddie Papers*, Vol. 2, pp. 281–3.

38 Governor Dinwiddie to the Lords of Trade, 24 November 1755, Governor Dinwiddie to the Earl of Halifax, 24 November 1755, *Dinwiddie Papers*, Vol. 2, p. 284.

39 Clifford Millard, 'The Acadians in Virginia', *Virginia Magazine of History and Biography*, 40(3) (July, 1932), pp. 241–58; Governor Dinwiddie to Sir Thomas Robinson, 24 Novenber 1755, *Dinwiddie Papers*, Vol. 2, pp. 281–3.

40 *Pennsylvania Gazette*, 5 February 1756; Faragher, *A Great and Noble Scheme*, p. 382, fn. 2; Dinwiddie to Henry Fox, 9 November 1755; Millard, 'Acadians in Virginia', pp. 250–1.

41 *South Carolina Gazette*, 22 July 1756, 6 October and 3 November 1758.

42 *South Carolina Gazette*, 5, 19 February, 1 April, 7 May, 1756; *Pennsylvania Gazette*, 4 March and 27 May 1756.

43 *South Carolina Gazette*, 5 and 24, 5 June, 1756; *Pennsylvania Gazette*, 1 July 1756.

44 *The Colonial Records of the State of Georgia*, Vol. 1, *Proceedings and Minutes of the Governor and Council*, 30 October 1754 to 13 February 1782 (Atlanta, GA: The Franklin –Turner Co, 1907), ed. Allen D Candler, pp. 302, 304, 506, 507.

45 Charles Lawrence to the Board of Trade, 5 August 1756, TNA PRO CO 217/16/ff.43–7.

46 *Gazetteer and London Daily Advertiser*, 22 June 1756, *British Spy*, 26 June 1756, 10 July 1756; *Public Advertiser*, 29 June 1756, 15 July 1756.

47 Griffiths, 'Acadians in Exile', pp. 69–70.

48 *Public Advertiser*, 29 June 1756; *Gazetteer and London Daily Advertiser*, 22 June 1756, *British Spy*, 26 June 1756.

49 JM/JB to Hon John Cleveland, 28 June 1756, TNA PRO, ADM 98/5, f.176.

50 Eddowes to the Medical Department, 3 July 1756, ADM 98/5, f.178.

51 JM/JB to Cleveland, 30 June 1756, TNA PRO, ADM 98/5, f.177.

52 2 July 1756, ADM 98/5, f.178, p. 360; See also letter of 6 July 1756, written by Crawgay and Kingston which reported they had 'distributed the said Neutrals in several Houses in those parts 'and agreed to pay 6d per week for each of their lodging.

53 L. G., J. M., J. B. to John Cleveland, 31 July 1756, TNA PRO, ADM 98/5, f.184.

54 Minutes of the Committee, 16 July 1756, TNA PRO, ADM 99/30/610.

55 L. G, J. B, to John Cleveland, 13 April 1757, TNA PRO, ADM 98/6, ff.129–30.

56 L. G., J. M., J. B., H. J. to John Cleveland, 18 July 1757, TNA PRO, ADM 98/6, f.193.

57 TNA PRO, ADM 98/8/67; J. B., H. J. to John Cleveland 27 November 1759, ADM 98/8 ff.52–3.

58 CSHS to John Cleveland, 3 July 1756, TNA PRO, ADM 98/5/f.178; TNA PRO, ADM 98/5, f.188; CSHS to John Cleveland, 17 September 1756, TNA PRO, ADM 98/5, f.207; TNA PRO, ADM 98/5, f.208.

59 L. G., J. B., H. G. to John Cleveland, 19 July 1756/7, TNA PRO, ADM 98/7, f.108.

60 CSHS to John Cleveland, 21 May 1761, TNA PRO, ADM 98/8, f.200.

61 TNA PRO, ADM 98/5, ff.208–90; TNA PRO, ADM 98/5, f.209.

62 *London Chronicle*, 11–14 August 1759.

63 Ibid.

64 Hodson, *The Acadian Diaspora*.

65 *Lloyd's Evening Post*, 20 May 1763. It was also reported in the *Gazetteer and London Daily Advertiser*, 24 May 1763; *London Evening Post*, 11 June 1763; *London Evening Chronicle*, 11 June 1763; Griffiths, 'Acadians in Exile', p. 74; see also Christopher Hodson. *The Acadian Diaspora*.

66 Griffiths, 'Acadians in Exile', pp. 82–4.

67 Hodson, *The Acadian Diaspora*, pp. 79–116 and 197–212.

Chapter 8

1 *An Address to the Inhabitants of Pennsylvania* (Philadelphia, PA: Robert Bell, 1777); *An Address to the Inhabitants of Pennsylvania* (Dublin: Robert

Jackson, 1778). These pamphlets contain the major public statements made by the detainees in the Free Mason's Lodge along with those of the Council and Congress together with brief commentaries.

2 Theodore Thayer, *Pennsylvania Politics and the Growth of Democracy, 1740–76* (Harrisburg, PA: Pennsylvania Historical and Museum Commission, 1953), pp. 172–3.

3 Richard Bauman, *For the Reputation of Truth: Politics, Religion, and Conflict Among the Pennsylvania Quakers 1750–1800* (Baltimore and London: Johns Hopkins University Press, 1971), pp. 163–4; Pemberton Papers, XXVIII, 75; Minutes of the Meeting for Sufferings, II, 30 November 1775; *Pennsylvania Gazette*, 18 February 1768; Thayer, *Pennsylvania Politics and the Growth of Democracy 1740–76*, pp. 172–3.

4 Gary B. Nash, *First City: Philadelphia and the Forging of Historical Memory* (Philadelphia, PA: University of Pennsylvania Press, 2002).

5 Thomas Gilpin, *Exiles in Virginia: with Observations on the Conduct of the Society of Friends during the Revolutionary War* (Philadelphia, 1848, published for the subscribers), Appendix pp. 294–9; Judith Van Buskirk, 'They Didn't Join the Band: Disaffected Women in Revolutionary Philadelphia', *Pennsylvania History*, 62 (1995), pp. 306–29, pp. 310–11; Nicholas B. Wainwright and Sarah Logan Fisher, '"A Diary of Trifling Occurrences"; Philadelphia, 1776–78', *Pennsylvania Magazine of History and Biography*, 82(4) (1958), pp. 411–65, pp. 437–8.

6 Thomas Gilpin, *Exiles*, Appendix, p. 299; Wainwright and Fisher, '"A Diary of Trifling Occurrences"', p. 446.

7 *Pennsylvania Packet*, 9 September 1777; Theodore Thayer, *Israel Pemberton: King of the Quakers* (Philadelphia, PA: Historical Society of Pennsylvania, 1943), pp. 215–16.

8 L. H. Butterfield, ed., *The Adams Papers: Diary and Autobiography of John Adams*, Vol. 3 Diary 1782–1804, Autobiography Through 1776 (Belknap Press of Harvard University Press, 1961), p. 310; Jack D. Marietta, *The Reformation of American Quakerism 1748–53* (Philadelphia, PA: University of Pennsylvania Press, 1984), pp. 240–1.

9 Richard Henry Lee to Patrick Henry, *Letters of Delegates to Congress*, Vol. 7, 8 September 1777, pp. 636–8.

10 Gilpin, *Exiles*, p. 292.

11 *Pennsylvania Packet*, 6 September 1777.

12 Minutes of the Supreme Executive Council, 31 August 1777, *Pennsylvania Colonial Records*, XI, pp. 283–4.

13 *Pennsylvania Colonial Records*, XI, p. 284.

14 *Minutes of the Supreme Executive Council*, 3 September 1777, pp. 287–9, p. 288.

15 *Minutes of the Supreme Executive Council*, pp. 288–90.

16 Wainwright and Fisher, '"A Diary of Trifling Occurrences"', p. 444.

17 Gilpin, *Exiles*, pp. 67–8.

18 Ibid., p. 266.

19 Ibid., p. 267.

20 'Remonstrance of Israel Pemberton, John Hunt, and Samuel Pleasants' in *An Address to The Inhabitants of Pennsylvania* (Philadelphia, PA: Robert Bell, 1777), pp. 13–14.

21 To the President and Council, remonstrance of the subscribers, freemen and inhabitants of the city of Philadelphia, now confined in the Free Masons Lodge in *An Address to the Inhabitants of Pennsylvania* (Philadelphia, PA: Robert Bell, 1777), pp. 18–20.

22 Remonstrance of the subscribers, pp. 22, 24.

23 *Address to the Inhabitants of Pennsylvania*, pp. 1–4.

24 Remonstrance (no 3) of the Subscribers, Freemen, and Inhabitants of the City of Philadelphia, now confined in the Mason's Lodge in *Address to the Inhabitants of Pennsylvania*, pp. 38–45, pp. 39–40; Gilpin, *Exiles*, pp. 103, 107.

25 Remonstrance no 3, pp. 41–2.

26 Ibid., pp. 43–5.

27 In Council, 9 September 1777, *An Address to the Inhabitants of Pennsylvania*, pp. 46–8.

28 Remonstrance and Protest, pp. 49–50.

29 Supreme Executive Council to Col. Wm Bradford, 4 September 1777, *Pennsylvania Archives 1777*, pp. 582, 584, 586, 590–1, 593, 604–5 (quotations), 608–10, 612, 632.

30 Thomas Wharton to Rachel Wharton, 20 September 1777, Willing–Wharton Collection (hereafter WWC), Historical Society of Pennsylvania, Philadelphia, PA (hereafter HSP); James Pemberton's Journal cited in Thayer, *Israel Pemberton*, p. 221.

31 James Donald Anderson, 'Thomas Wharton, Exile in Virginia, 1777–78', *Virginia Magazine of History and Biography*, 89(4) (1981), pp. 425–47, p. 436.

32 *Pennsylvania Packet*, 30 October 1775; Thayer, *Pennsylvania Politics*, pp. 171–2.

33 Gilpin, *Exiles*, pp. 135–6; Thayer, *Israel Pemberton*, p. 222; Paul D. Halliday, *Habeas Corpus: From England to Empire* (Cambridge, MA: Harvard University Press, 2010), pp. 1–2.

34 Thomas McKean Papers, Box 1, folder 8, Historical Society of Pennsylvania.

35 Diary of James Pemberton 1777–8, 30 September.

36 Gilpin, *Exiles*, pp. 162–3.

37 Ibid., pp. 165–71.

38 Wainwright and Fisher, '"A Diary of Trifling Occurrences"'; Catherine La Courreye Blecki and Karin A. Wulf, eds, *Milcah Martha Moore's Book: A Commonplace Book from Revolutionary America* (University Park: Pennsylvania State University Press, 1997), pp. 1–37.

39 Wendy Lucas Castro, '"Being Separated from my Dearest Husband, in This Cruel Manner:" Elizabeth Drinker and the Seven-Month Exile of Philadelphia Quakers', *Quaker History*, 100(1) (2011), pp. 40–63, p. 44.

40 Gilpin, *Exiles*, pp. 173, 181.

41 Ibid., pp. 173–4, 178.

42 Ibid., pp. 175, 180.

43 James Pemberton, *Memoirs* (1835), pp. 73–4; Anderson, 'Thomas Wharton', pp. 440–1, 445; James Pemberton's Diary, HSP entry for 2 March 1778.

44 Wainwright and Fisher, '"A Diary of Trifling Occurrences"', p. 459; Anderson, 'Thomas Wharton', p. 429.

45 T. Wharton to Rachel Wharton, 28 December 1777, WWC, HSP; Anderson, pp. 441–2.

46 To the Congress and Executive Council of Pennsylvania, 19 December 1777, Papers of the Continental Congress, reel 51; Meirs Fisher to Alexander White, 20 December 1777, 'Exiles' Journal,' Gilpin, *Exiles*, pp. 194–6; *JCC*, Vol. 10, p. 8; *Pennsylvania Colonial Records*, Vol. 11, p. 395; Council to Congress, 5 January 1778, RG 27, Pennsylvania State Archives; Timothy Matlock to Owen Jones, Jr., 5 January 1778, *Pennsylvania Archives*, 2nd series (Harrisburg, 1874–90), Vol. 3, p. 160.

47 T. Wharton to T. Wharton, Jr., 20 January 1778, WWC, HSP.

48 Biddle, *Journal of Elizabeth Drinker*, p. 89, entry for 28 March 1778; Anderson, 'Thomas Wharton', p. 444, T. Wharton to Rachel Wharton, 26 January 1778, WWC, HSP.

49 Wainwright and Fisher, '"A Diary of Trifling Occurrences"', p. 461.

50 Gilpin, *Exiles*, p. 216.

51 Ibid., pp. 222–3.

52 Anderson, 'Thomas Wharton', 444; T. Wharton to Robert Pleasants, 2 February 1778, and to Rachel Wharton, 8 February 1778, WWC, HSP; 'Observations Concerning the Memorial of Israel Pemberton and Others', 31 January 1778, *Pa. Archives*, 2nd ser, Vol. 3, pp. 144–6; *Pennsylvania Colonial Records*, Vol. 11, pp. 426–7; Council to George Washington, 6 April 1778, *Pa. Archives*, 1st ser, Vol. 6, p. 401.

53 Anderson, 'Thomas Wharton', pp. 444–5; T. Wharton, Jr., to Bailey and Lang, 10 April 1778, Committee of Safety Collection, HSP.

54 Anderson, 'Thomas Wharton', p. 445; James Pemberton's Diary, HSP, entries for 16 April, 18, 21, 24, 1778; receipt to T. Wharton 18 April 1778, pass from Bailey and Lang to T. Wharton 18 April, correspondence, WP, HSP.

55 Anderson, 'Thomas Wharton', p. 446; 'Life of John Pemberton', *Friends Library*, 6, p. 297; James Pemberton Diary, HSP, entries for 25–7 April 1778; Supreme Executive Council Minutes, 27 April 1778, *Pennsylvania Colonial Records*, Vol. 11, pp. 472–3.

56 James Pemberton, *Memoirs* (1835), p. 77.

57 Eliphalet Dyer to Joseph Trumbull, Lancaster, 28 September 1777, *Letters of Delegates to Congress*, Vol. 8, p. 24.

58 Samuel Adams to Peter Thacher, 11 August 1778, *Letters of Delegates to Congress*, Vol. 10, pp. 420–1.

59 Josiah Bartlett to William Whipple, Philadelphia, 18 August 1778, *Letters of Delegates to Congress*, Vol. 10, pp. 471–2.

60 Oaks, 'Philadelphians in Exile', p. 300; Bauman, *For the Reputation of Truth*, p. 164.

61 Leonard W. Levy, *Original Intent and the Framers' Constitution* (New York: Macmillan, 1988), p. 240 cited in Jack D. Marietta and G. S. Rowe, *Troubled Experiment: Crime and Justice in Pennsylvania, 1682–1800* (Philadelphia, PA: University of Pennsylvania Press, 2006), pp. 186–7.

Chapter 9

1 Wayne E. Lee, *Crowds and Soldiers in Revolutionary North Carolina: The Culture of Violence in Riot and War* (Gainesville, FL: University Press of Florida, 2001), pp. 176–211; John S. Pancake, *This Destructive War: The British Campaign in the Carolinas, 1780–82* (Tuscaloosa, AL: University of Alabama Press, 2003), pp. 78–90; Ronald Hoffman, Thad W. Tate and Peter J, Albert, eds, *An Uncivil War: The Southern Backcountry during the American Revolution* (Charlottesville, VA: University Press of Virginia, 1985); for the cruelties of partisan warfare in Georgia, see the apologies of Georgia Delegates to Nathanael Greene, 27 July 1781, *Letters of Delegates to Congress*, Vol. 17, ed. Paul H. Smith (Washington, D.C.: Library of Congress, 1976–2000), p. 450.

2 On the siege of Charleston and discussions over the terms of capitulation, see William Moultrie, *Memoirs of the American Revolution*, 2 Vols (New York: New York Times and Arno Press, 1968 [1802], Vol. 2, pp. 61–106; Alexander R. Stoesen, 'The British Occupation of Charleston, 1780–82', *South Carolina Historical and Genealogical Magazine*, 63(2) (1963), pp. 71–82, pp. 71–2. The articles of capitulation were drafted and redrafted several times, Moultrie, *Memoirs*, Vol. 2, pp. 68–105.

3 *Journals of the Continental Congress, 1774–89* (Washington: Government Printing Office, 1910), Vol. 17, pp. 697–8.

4 Moultrie, *Memoirs*, Vol. 2, pp. 126–7.

5 Ibid., pp. 128–9.

6 Josiah Smith and Mabel L. Webber, 'Josiah Smith's Diary, 1780–81', *South Carolina Historical and Geneaological Magazine [SCHGM]*, 33(1) (January, 1932), pp. 1–28, pp. 2–3; the seizure of these men was reported in the London press, see *London Courant*, 12 October 1780, 6 November 1780.

7 Moultrie, *Memoirs*, Vol. 2, pp. 5–6; Smith and Webber, 'Josiah Smith's Diary', 33(1) (January, 1932), pp. 3–4; David Ramsay, *History of South Carolina*, 2 Vols (Charleston, 1809), Vol. 2, p. 370. John Sansum's widow Mary petitioned the South Carolina Assembly in 1788 for money she believed was owed her late husband for the support of herself and her three children. Cynthia A. Kierner, *Southern Women in Revolution, 1776–1800: Personal and Political Narratives* (Columbia, SC: University of South Carolina Press, 1998), pp. 39–41.

8 David Ramsay, *The History of the Revolution in South Carolina*, 2 Vols (Trenton, NJ: Isaac Collins, 1785), Vol. 2, p. 162.

9 Moultrie, *Memoirs*, Vol. 2, p. 252; Smith and Webber, 'Josiah Smith's Diary', 33(1) (January, 1932), pp. 5–6, pp. 7–8.

10   Moultrie to Balfour, 1 September 1780, Benson to Moultrie, 4 September
     1780, Moultrie, *Memoirs*, Vol. 2, pp. 138–9.

11   Smith and Webber, 'Josiah Smith's Diary', 33(1) (January, 1932), pp. 6–7.

12   Ibid., p. 7, pp. 7–9.

13   Smith and Webber, 'Josiah Smith's Diary', 33(1) (January, 1932), pp. 9–10;
     Richard Walsh, ed., *The Writings of Christopher Gadsden 1746–1805*
     (Columbia, SC: University of South Carolina, 1966), pp. 170–1; Thomas Bee
     to John Laurens, 28 March 1781, Paul H. Smith, ed., *Letters of Delegates to
     Congress*, Vol. 17, pp. 101–2.

14   Smith and Webber, 'Josiah Smith's Diary', p. 10.

15   Smith and Webber, 'Josiah Smith's Diary', 33(1) (January, 1932), pp. 13–14.

16   Balfour to Cornwallis, 15 November 1780, TNA PRO 30/11/12, f.64.

17   Josiah Smith and Mabel L. Webber, 'Josiah Smith's Diary', *SCHGM*, 33(2)
     (April, 1932), pp. 79–116, p. 100; *Journals of the Continental Congress*, Vol.
     16, p. 499; Ramsay, *History of South Carolina*, Vol. 1, p. 370. The wife of Dr
     Noble W. Jones, Sarah, petitioned the South Carolina in 1783 to rescind the
     banishment imposed on her son-in-law, John Glen. She and her husband who
     had returned to Georgia were the sole support of their daughter and her six
     small children, but her husband's fortunes had been 'already ruined by the
     Enemies invasion of Georgia, by his long Captivity in the hands of the British
     and by his attention to Publick business, in total Neglect of his own'. Kierner,
     Southern Women in Revolution, pp. 34–5.

18   Thomas Bee to John Laurens, 28 March 1781, *Letters of Delegates to
     Congress*, Vol. 17, pp. 102.

19   Smith and Webber, 'Josiah Smith's Diary', 33(1) (January, 1932), pp. 11–12.

20   Ibid., pp. 19–21, pp. 26–8; 33(2) (April, 1932), p. 93.

21   Smith and Webber, 'Josiah Smith's Diary', 33(2) (April, 1932), p. 103, p. 115;
     33(3) (July, 1932), pp. 197–207, p. 198.

22   David Ramsay, *History of American Revolution*, ed. Lester H. Cohen, 2 Vols
     (Indianapolis, IN: 1990 [1789]), Vol. 2, p. 496; Smith and Webber, 'Josiah
     Smith's Diary', 33(2) (April, 1732), p. 112, p. 115.

23   Smith and Webber, 'Josiah Smith's Diary', 33(1) (January, 1932), p. 13, p. 23, p. 24.

24   Ibid., p. 20.

25   Ibid., pp. 24–5.

26   Ibid., p. 12, p. 20.

27   Smith and Webber, 'Josiah Smith's Diary', 33(2) (April, 1932), p. 83, p. 105,
     p. 108, pp. 111–12.

28   Smith and Webber, 'Josiah Smith's Diary', 33 (2) (April, 1932), p. 84.

29   Ibid., p. 85.

30   Ibid., p. 98.

31   Ibid., pp. 98–100. See Penelope J. Corfield, 'Dress for Deference and Dissent:
     Hats and the Decline of Hat Honour', *Costume*, 23 (1989), 64–79.

32   Ibid., pp. 79–116, pp. 109–10.

33 George Washington to Sir Henry Clinton, 6 October 1780, in Jared Sparks, ed., *The Writings of George Washington*, 12 Vols (Boston, MA: Little, Brown, and Company, 1858), Vol. 7, pp. 234–5; Sir Henry Clinton to General Washington, 9 October 1780, Appendix 8, pp. 552–3, p. 553. See also letters and footnotes of the correspondence in question, Sparks, *Writings*, Vol. 7, Appendix 8, pp. 554–6, especially fn, p. 555, 'It had its effect on the Irish'. Mss Letter to Sir Henry Clinton and fn, p. 556.

34 Cornwallis to Clinton, 3 September 1780, PRO 30/11/72, ff.51–2; 'James Simpson's Reports on the Carolina Loyalists, 1779 and 1780', ed., Alan S. Brown, *Journal of Southern History*, 21(4) (1955), pp. 513–19.

35 Washington to the President of Congress, 7 November 1780, Sparks, ed. *Writings of George Washington*, Vol. 7, 286–8; Washington to John Matthews 26 February 1781, Sparks, ed., *Writings of George Washington*, Vol. 7, p. 437; Washington to Matthews, 23 March 1781, http:/etext.virginia.edu, accessed 13/09/12.

36 William Moultrie to General Greene, 30 January 1781, Moultrie, *Memoirs*, Vol. 2, p. 153; John Matthews to George Washington, 15 February 1781, *Journals of the Continental Congress*, Vol. 16, p. 167.

37 Balfour to Moultrie, March 1781, in Moultrie, *Memoirs*, Vol. 2, pp. 1–2.

38 Smith and Webber,'Josiah Smith's Diary', 33(3) (July, 1932), p. 199.

39 Smith and Webber, 'Josiah Smith's Diary', *SCHGM*, 33(3) (July, 1932), pp. 199–201.

40 Stoesen,'The British Occcupation of Charleston', pp. 73–4; Daniel of St. Thomas Jenifer to Thomas Stone, 23 July 1781, to Charles Carroll, 24 July 1781, to John Hall, 24 July 1781, *Letters of Delegates to Congress*, Vol. 17, p. 426, p. 434, p. 436; Elias Boudinot to Hannah Boudinot, 29 July 1781, *Letters of Delegates to Congress*, Vol. 17, p. 456.

41 George Partridge to Samuel Holten, 31 July 1781, *Letters of Delegates to Congress*, Vol. 17, p. 460.

42 John Matthews to Nathanael Greene, 14 August 1781, *Letters of Delegates to Congress*, Vol. 17, pp. 518–20; *Pennsylvania Gazette*, 15 August 1781.

43 Judith Van Buskirk, 'They Didn't Join the Band: Disaffected Women in Revolutionary Philadelphia', *Pennsylvania History* 62(3) (1995), pp. 306–29, p. 321; Ramsey, *History of the American Revolution*, Vol. 2, p. 96.

44 Smith and Webber, 'Josiah Smith's Diary', *SCHGM*, 34(2) (April, 1933), pp. 67–84, p. 70; Stoesen, 'The British Occupation of Charleston', p. 78.

45 Walsh, ed., *The Writings of Christopher Gadsden*, pp. 171–3.

Chapter 10

1 Lady Rodney to Admiral Rodney, 17 March 1781 in Godfrey Basil Mundy, *The Life and Correspondence of the Late Admiral Rodney*, 2 Vols (London: 1830) II, pp. 50–1; J. Franklin Jameson, 'St Eustatius and the American Revolution', *American Historical Review*, 8 (July, 1903), pp. 683–708, p. 701; Jan Willem Schulte Nordholt trans. Herbert H. Rowen, *The Dutch Republic*

and American Independence (Chapel Hill & London: University of North Carolina Press, 1982), p. 46; Barbara W. Tuchman, *The First Salute* (New York: Knopf, 1988).

2 *History of Parliament* (Cobbett), Vol. 22, p. 220; Janet Schaw, *Journal of a Lady of Quality*, ed. Evangeline W. Andrews and Charles M. Andrews (New Haven, CT: Yale University Press, 1921), 136; *Speech Which was Spoken in the Assembly of St Christopher* (London: Debrett,1782), p. 11.

3 Jameson, 'St Eustatius and the American Revolution', p. 683; Schaw, *Journal of a Lady of Quality*, pp. 135–7.

4 Schaw, *Journal of a Lady of Quality*, pp. 136–7.

5 Guido Abbattista, 'Edmund Burke, the Atlantic American War and the 'Poor Jews at St. Eustatius': Empire and the Law of Nations', *Cromohs*, 13 (2008), pp. 1–39, pp. 9–10.

6 Jameson, 'St Eustatius in the American Revolution', p. 685; Andrew Jackson O'Shaughnessy, *An Empire Divided: The American Revolution and the British Caribbean* (Philadelphia, PA: University of Pennsylvania, 2000), p. 216.

7 Admiral Rodney to Lady Rodney, 23 April 1781, Major General G. B. Mundy, *The Life and Correspondence of the late Lord Rodney* (London: Murray, 1830), 2 Vols, Vol. 1, p. 97; Rodney to Philip Stephens, 6 March 1781, Mundy, *Life and Correspondence of Lord Rodney*, Vol. 2, pp. 41–6.

8 Jameson, 'St Eustatius in the American Revolution', pp. 696–7; Ronald Hurst, *The Golden Rock: An Episode of the American War of Independence 1775–83* (London: Leo Cooper, 1996), pp. 55–9; on the complexity of Dutch politics and policies, see F. C. Van Oosten, 'Some Notes Concerning the Dutch West Indies during the American Revolutionary War', *American Neptune* 36 (1976), pp. 155–69.

9 Copy of his Majesty's Instructions to Sir George Brydges Rodney, 20 December 1780, Mundy, *Life and Correspondence of Lord Rodney*, Vol. 2, pp. 6–8; *Annual Register*, 25 January 1781, pp. 164–5.

10 To his Excellency the Governor of St. Eustatius, 'Summons' signed G. B. Rodney and J. Vaughan, 3 February 1781, Mundy, *Life and Correspondence of Lord Rodney*, Vol. 2, pp. 12–13.

11 Burke Papers Reel 18, Book 7/9b.

12 Ibid.

13 Hurst, *The Golden Rock*, p. 134.

14 *Pennsylvania Packet*, 12 June 1781.

15 Burke Papers, Reel 18. Book 7/9d.

16 Burke Papers, Reel 18, Book 7/9f.

17 Richard Downing Jennings, *The Case of Richard Downing Jennings, an English Subject* (London: J. W. Galabin, 1790), pp. 18–19, ECCO reprint.

18 Jacob R. Marcus, *The Colonial American Jew, 1492–1776*, 3 Vols (Detroit, MI: Wayne State University Press, 1970), Vol. 1, p. 95, p. 141; Norman F. Barca, 'Citizens of St Eustatius, 1781: A Historical and Archaeological Study' in *The Lesser Antilles in the Age of European Expansion*, eds,

Robert L. Paquette and Stanley L. Engerman (Gainesville, FL: University of Florida Press, 1996), pp. 223–38, p. 223, p. 228, p. 235.

19 Marcus, *The Colonial American Jew*, Vol. 1, p. 142; O'Shaughnessy, *An Empire Divided*, p. 218; based on the three documents to be found in CO 318/8. Barka hypothesizes that the 73 burghers, listed in document number two, were Jews. Extrapolating from this to the general population of burghers, he postulates that many were recent arrivals 'at least within several years before 1781'.

20 Speech of Edmund Burke to the House of Commons, 14 May 1781, *Parliamentary History of England*, Vol. 22, pp. 223–4 and 4 December 1781, p. 775. Burke's figure of eight transproted Jews is far too low.

21 A copy of this list was published in Hurst's *The Golden Rock*, pp. 144–5, but the reference appears to be incorrect; Burke Papers, Reel 18, Book 7.

22 O'Shaughnessy, *An Empire Divided*, p. 219; Jennings, *Case of an English Subject*; Speech of Edmund Burke, *St James's Chronicle*, 14 May 1781.

23 *Parliamentary History of England*, Vol. 22, pp. 1023–6.

24 *Parliamentary History of England*, Vol. 22, p. 1026; Burke Papers, Reel 18, Book/7/11; TNA PRO, T 29/52/8; F. P. Lock, *Edmund Burke*, Vol. 1, 1730–84 (Oxford: Clarendon Press, 1998), p. 495.

25 *Annual Register*, Vol. 11, pp. 344–5.

26 *Annual Register*, Vol. 11, pp. 308–10; *Freeman's Journal*, 25 April 1781.

27 *Copy of the Petition of the West-India Planters and Merchants to the King*, 6 April 1781, pp. 1–2; on the earlier organization of the West India interests, see Andrew J. O'Shaughnessy, 'The Formation of a Commercial Lobby: The West India Interest, British Colonial Policy and the American Revolution', *Historical Journal*, 40(1), March (1997), pp. 71–95.

28 *A Speech in the House of Assembly of St Christopher* (London: Debrett, 1782), pp. 1–2.

29 *A Speech in the House of Assembly*, pp. 13–14, pp. 16–17; *Annual Register*, XI, pp. 344–5, 346.

30 *Parliamentary History of England*, Vol. 22, p. 216, p. 218, pp. 219–20.

31 *Historical Register*, Vol. 4, pp. 302–3; *Whitehall Evening Post*, 15 May 1781.

32 *Parliamentary Register*, Vol. 4, p. 308; *Parliamentary History of England*, Vol. 22, p. 229.

33 *Parliamentary Register*, Vol. 4, pp. 309–11; *Parliamentary History of England*, Vol. 22, pp. 228–31; Vattel's *Le Droit des gens* (1758) and the English translation (*Law of Nations*, 1760); Francis Stephen Ruddy, *International Law in the Enlightenment: The Background of Emmerich de Vattel's 'Le Droit des gens'* (Dobbs Ferry, NY, 1975); F. P. Lock, *Edmund Burke*, 1, 1730–84, p. 496; O'Shaughnessy, *An Empire Divided*, p. 220; Speech of Edmund Burke, 14 May 1781, *St. James's Chronicle*, 12–14 May 1781; *A Speech Which was Spoken in the House of the Assembly of St Christopher*, p. 16; Richard Neave to Germain, 26 April 1781; Germain to Vaughan, 30 March 1781, TNA PRO, CO, 318/8/ f.89.

34 Vaughan and Rodney to Germain, 3 July 1781, TNA PRO, CO 318/7,
    f.119; Germain to Rodney and Vaughan, 30 March 1781, CO 318/8, f.89;
    O'Shaughnessy, *An Empire Divided*, p. 232; Hurst, *The Golden Rock*,
    pp. 126–7; Kenneth Breen, 'General Rodney and St Eustatius in the American
    War: A Commercial and Naval Distraction, 1775–81', *The Mariner's Mirror*,
    84(2), 1998, pp. 193–203, pp. 200–2; Jameson, 'St Eustatius and the American
    Revolution', pp. 706–7.

35 *Parliamentary Register*, Vol. 5, pp. 82–5.

36 Christopher Reid, *Edmund Burke and the Practice of Political Writing*
    (Dublin: Gill and Macmillan/St Martin's Press, 1985); *Annual Register, 1782*
    (London, 1783), pp. 137–8.

37 *Parliamentary Register*, Vol. 5, pp. 85–7, 90; Wilmot Vaughan, 1st Earl of
    Lisburne, was General Vaughan's brother, *Correspondence*, Vol. 4, ed. Woods,
    p. 403; TNA PRO, T 29/52, p. 81.

38 *The Correspondence of Edmund Burke*, Vol. 5, July 1778–June 1782, ed.,
    John A. Woods (Cambridge and Chicago, IL: Cambridge University Press,
    1963), p. 456; Barca, 'Citizens of St Eustatius, 1781', p. 236.

39 *Parliamentary History of England*, Vol. 22, pp. 1024–5.

40 David Ramsay, *The History of the American Revolution*, 2 Vols [Philadelphia,
    1789], ed. Lester H. Cohen (Indianapolis, IN: Liberty Classics, 1990), p. 11,
    pp. 535–8; Mercy Otis Warren, *History of the Rise, Progress and Termination
    of the American Revolution*, 2 Vols [Boston, 1805], ed. Lester H. Cohen
    (Indianapolis, IN: Liberty Classics, 1988), II, pp. 532–44.

Conclusion

1 David Armitage, 'Three Concepts of Atlantic History', in David Armitage
   and Michael J. Braddick eds, *The British Atlantic World* (London: Palgrave
   Macmilan, 2002), pp. 11–27.

2 Gwenda Morgan and Peter Rushton, *Eighteenth-Century Criminal
   Transportation: The Formation of the Criminal Atlantic* (Houndmills,
   Basingstoke: Palgrave Macmillan, 2004).

3 Sir Leon Radzinowicz and Roger Hood, 'The Status of Political Prisoner in
   England: The Struggle for Recognition', *Virginia Law Review*, 65(8) (1979),
   pp. 1421–91.

4 Gwenda Morgan, 'Convict Labor and Migration', in Immanuel Ness ed., *The
   Encyclopedia of Global Human Migration* (Oxford: Blackwell Publishers, 2013).

5 *The Virginia Gazette*, 3 October 1777, letter from Burgoyne dated 6
   September (this was about the Jane McCrae murder).

6 Morgan and Rushton, *Eighteenth-Century Criminal Transportation*, pp. 64–5,
   and 'Visible Bodies: Power, Subordination and Identity in the Eighteenth-Century
   Atlantic World', *Journal of Social History*, 39(1) (Fall, 2005), pp. 39–64.

7 Joyce E. Chaplin, 'Expansion and Exceptionalism in Early American History'
   The Journal of American History, 89(4) (2003), pp. 1431–55, p. 1439.

BIBLIOGRAPHY

Archives

British Library
British Library, Add Mss 19

County Durham Record Office
EP/Ga.SM 4/1

The National Archives:
ADM 98/5
ADM 98/6
ADM 98/7
ADM 98/8
ADM 99/30/610
ASSI/23
Chancery Patent Rolls (List and Index Society, Vol. 157)
Chancery Patent Rolls Index, C66 Vol. 24,1–2 CAR. I
CO 1/39
CO 5/1226
CO 5/1314
CO 9/11
CO 9/12
CO 28/49
CO 217/16/24–7
CO 318/7 and 8
KB 33/1/5
PC 2/58
PRO 30/11/12
SP 31/2
SP 44/14, pp. 57–8. 1 March 1664
SP 44/22/48
SP 44/118
SP 53/33
SP 54/3/35
SP 54/3/168
SP 54/12
SP 54/31/138
T1/325/178–9

T 29/52
TS 20/47/1–5
TS 20/33/190–1
TS 20/35/4
TS 20/80/1–17

Historical Society of Pennsylvania
Thomas McKean Papers
Minutes of the Meeting for Sufferings, II
Pemberton Papers, XXVIII
Willing-Wharton Collection

Published primary sources

An Abstract of the Sufferings of the People Called Quakers for the Testimony of a Good Conscience, from the time of their being first distinguished by that name, taken from original records and authentick accounts, 3 Vols (London: printed by J. Sowle, 1733–8).

An Account of the Proceedings against the Rebels at Dorchester at an Assize holden there on Friday and Saturday 4th and 5th September (London: s.n., 1685).

Acts and Ordinances of the Interregnum, 1642–1660, Vol. 2, eds C. H. Firth and R. S. Tait (London: HMSO, 1911).

Acts of the Privy Council of England, Colonial Series, Vol. 1, ed. W. L. Grant and James Munro (Hereford: for HMSO, 1908).

Adams, John, *The Adams Papers: Diary and Autobiography of John Adams*, Vol. 3 Diary 1782–1804, Autobiography Through 1776, ed. L. H. Butterfield (Belknap Press of Harvard University Press, 1961).

A Further Account of the Proceedings against the Rebels since the Arrival of His Grace the Duke of Monmouth (London: s.n., 1679).

A Further Account of the Proceedings against the Rebels in the West of England . . . on 10 September 1685 (London: 1685), and *An Account of the Proceedings against the Rebels at an Assize holden at Exeter on the 14th . . . September* 1685 (London: s.n., 1685).

'A German Indentured Servant Servant in Barbados in 1652: The Account of Heinrich von Uchteritz', translated by Alexander Gunkel and Jerome S. Handler, *Journal of the Barbados Museum and Historical Society*, 33 (1970), 91–100.

An Address to the Inhabitants of Pennsylvania (Philadelphia, PA: Robert Bell, 1777).

An Address to the Inhabitants of Pennsylvania (Dublin: Robert Jackson, 1778).

The Annalls of Ipswiche: The Laws, Customs and Government of that Towne, Collected from the Records Bookes and Writings of that Towne by Nathaniell Bacon, ed. W. H. Richardson (Ipswich: S. H. Cowell, 1884; originally 1654).

Archives of Maryland, Vol. 25, ed. William H. Browne (Baltimore, MD: Isaac Fiedenwald Co for Maryland Historical Society, 1905).

Bacon, Francis, 'Of Plantations' (1625), in *Settlements to Society: 1584–1763*, ed. Jack P. Greene (New York: McGraw Hill, 1966), pp. 9–11.

James Bent, *The Bloody Assizes, or a Complete History of the Life of George Lord Jefferies . . .* (London: J. Dunton, 1690).

A Biographical Dictionary of Living Authors of Great Britain and Ireland
  (London: Henry Colburn, 1816).

Bishop, George, *Manifesto Declaring what George Bishope hath been to the City
  of Bristoll* . . . , *Occasioned by the late Sentence of Banishment Pronounced
  upon him* . . . (1665).

Burke, Edmund, *The Correspondence of Edmund Burke*, Vol. 5, July 1778 to June
  1782, ed., John A. Woods (Cambridge and Chicago: Cambridge University
  Press, 1963).

Burroughs, Edward, *A Declaration of the Sad and Great Persecution and
  Martyrdom of the People of God, called Quakers, in New England* (London:
  Robert Wilson, 1661).

Burton, Thomas, *The Diary of Thomas Burton* . . ., 4 Vols, ed. John Towill Rutt
  (London: Henry Colburn, 1828).

Calendar of Home Office Papers of the Reign of George III, 4 Vols, ed. Joseph
  Redington and Vols 3 and 4, ed. R. A. Roberts (London: Longman and Co,
  1878, 1879, 1881, 1889).

Calendar of the Patent Rolls, Edward I, 1281–1292 (London: HMSO, 1893).

Calendar of State Papers Colonial, Vols 5, 1637–8 and Vol. 9, 1764–5, ed. W. Noel
  Sainsbury (London: HMSO, 1880 and 1893).

Calendar of State Papers, Domestic Series of the Reign of Charles I. 1631 — 1633,
  ed. John Bruce (London: Longman, Green, Longman and Roberts, 1862).

Calendar of the State Papers Relating to Scotland, Vol. I, 1509–89, ed. M. J. Thorpe
  (London: Longman, Brown, Green, Longmans and Roberts, 1858).

Calendar of Treasury Books, Vol. 8: 1685–1689, ed. William A Shaw (London:
  HMSO, 1923).

Calendar of Virginia State Papers, 1652–1781, Vol. 1, ed. W. P. Palmer (Richmond,
  VA: R. F. Walker, 1875).

Coad, John, *A Memorandum of the Wonderful Providences of God to a Poor
  Unworthy Creature during the Time of the Duke of Monmouth's Rebellion and
  to the Revolution in 1688* (London: Longman, Brown, Green and Longmans,
  1849).

*The Colonial Laws of Massachusetts, Reprinted from the Edition of 1672, with the
  supplements through 1686*, ed. William H. Whitmore (Boston, MA: Rockwell
  and Churchill, 1890).

Copy of the Petition of the West India Planters and Merchants to the King, 6 April,
  1781.

The Court Book of the Barony and Regality of Falkirk and Callendar, Vol. 1,
  1638–56, ed. Doreen M. Hunter (Edinburgh: Stair Society, 1991).

Cromwell, Oliver, *Oliver Cromwell's Letters and Speeches*, 5 Vols, ed. Thomas
  Carlyle (New York and London: The Continental Press/John Wiley, 1845).

*The Cry of the Innocent and Oppressed for Justice or A Brief Relation of the late
  Proceedings against the Prisoners called Quakers in London* . . . *Hick's Hall
  and Old Bailey on the 14th, 15th and 17th day of October 1664* . . . (London:
  1664).

*Culloden Papers: Comprising an Extensive and Interesting Correspondence from
  the Year 1625 to 1746* . . . *from the Originals in the Possession of Duncan
  George Forbes of Culloden* (London: T. Cadell and W. Davies, 1815).

Dinwiddie, Governor Robert, *The Official Records of Robert Dinwiddie*, 2 Vols,
  ed. R. A. Brock (Richmond, VA: Virginia Historical Society, 1884).

Douglas, Francis, *The History of the Rebellion in 1745 and 1746, Extracted from the Scots Magazine; with an Appendix, Containing an Account of the Trials of the Rebels; the Pretender and His Son's Declarations etc* (Aberdeen: F. Douglass and W. Murray, 1755).

Edwards, Bryan, *The History, Civil and Commericial, of the British Colonies in the West Indies*, 2 Vols (Dublin: Luke White, 1793).

— *The Proceedings of the Governor and Assembly of Jamaica in Regard to the Maroon Negroes* (Piccadilly: Stockdale, 1796).

Ellwood, Thomas, *A Discourse Concerning Riots* (London, 1683).

— *A Caution to Constables and Other Inferior Officers concerned in the execution of the Conventicle Act with some observations thereupon, humbly offered by way of advice to such well-meaning and moderate justices of the peace, as would not willingly ruine their peaceable neighbours but act (in relation to that act) rather by restraint than by choice* (London: printed for Thomas Hoskins, 1683).

Executive Journals of the Council of Colonial Virginia, ed. H. R. McIlwaine, Vol. 3, (Richmond, VA: D. Bottom, 1938).

Extracts and Copies of Letters from Sir John Wentworth, Lieutenant Governor of Nova Scotia, to his Grace the Duke of Portland; respecting the Settlement of the Maroons in that Province (1797).

Extracts from State Papers Relating to Friends, 1654–1672, ed. Norman Penney, with an introduction by R. A. Roberts, Supplements 8–11 to the *Journal of the Friends Historical Society* (London: Friends Historical Society/Headley Brothers, 1913).

Firth, C. Harding, *Scotland and the Protectorate: Letters and Papers Relating to the Military Government of Scotland, from January 1654 to June 1660* (Edinburgh: T. and A. Constable, for the Scottish History Society, 1899).

Forbes, Robert, *The Lyon in Mourning, or a Collection of Speeches, Letters Journals etc Relative to the Affairs of Prince Charles Edward Stuart, by the Rev. Robert Forbes MA, Bishop of Ross and Caithness, 1746–1775*, 3 Vols (Edinburgh: University Press, 1895 for The Scottish Historical Society).

Forbes, J. Macbeth, *Jacobite Gleanings from State Manuscripts: Short Sketches of Jacobites, the Transportations in 1745* (Edinburgh: O. Anderson and Ferrier, 1903).

Gadsden, Christopher, *The Writings of Christopher Gadsden, 1746–1805*, ed. Richard Walsh, (Columbia, SC: University of South Carolina, 1966).

Gibson, Thomas, *Something offered to the Consideration of all those who have had a hand in putting the late made Act (entituled, An Act to Prevent and Suppress Seditious Conventicles) in execution . .* (London: s.n., 1665).

— *Exiles in Virginia: with Observations on the Conduct of the Society of Friends during the Revolutionary War* (Philadelphia, PA: published for the subscribers, 1848).

Gwynn, Aubrey, 'Documents Relating to the Irish in the West Indies', *Analecta Hibernica*, 4 (1932), 139–286.

Hakluyt, Richard, *A Discourse on Western Planting* (Cambridge, MA: John Wilson and Son, 1877, printed for Maine Historical Society; Originally 1584).

— *The Original Writings and Correspondence of the Two Richard Hakluyts*, ed. G. R. Taylor, Hakluyt Society, 2nd ser, LXXVI, LXXVII (London: 1935).

Haliburton, Thomas, *An Historical and Statistical Account of Nova Scotia*, 2 Vols (Halifax: J. Howe, 1829).

Histoire philosophique et politique de l'établissment des Européenes du Commerce dans les deux Indes, 1766 edn, 7 Vols.

Historical Papers Relating to the Jacobite Period, 1699–1750, 2 Vols, ed. Col. J. Allardyce (Aberdeen: The New Spalding Club, 1895).

Horsmanden, Daniel, *Journal of the Proceedings in the Detection of the Conspiracy found by some White People in Conjunction with Negroes and other Slaves for the burning of the City of New York in America* (New York: James Parker, 1744).

Inverness Kirk Session Records, 1661–1800, ed. Alexander Mitchell (Inverness: Robert Carruthers and Son, 1902).

'Jacobitism in Virginia: Charges against Captain Jacob Lumpkin', *The Virginia Magazine of History and Biography*, 6(4) (1899), 389–96.

Jacobite Trials in Manchester, ed. William Beamont (Manchester: Chetham Society, 1853).

Jennings, Richard Downing, *The Case of Richard Downing Jennings, an English Subject* (London: J. W. Galabin, 1790).

The Justiciary Records of Argyll and the Isles, 2 Vols, ed. John Imrie (Edinburgh: The Stair Society, 1969).

Journals of the Continental Congress, 1774–1789, Vol. 17 (Washington: Government Printing Office, 1910).

Journals of the House of Burgesses of Virginia, 1619–1776, 13 Vols, eds J. P. Kennedy and H. R. McLlwaine (Richmond, VA: Colonial Press, 1905–15).

Journals of the House of Representatives of Massachusetts, Vol. 32, pt. 1 (Boston, MA: Massachusetts Historical Society, 1957).

Lauder, Sir John of Fountainhall, *The Decisions of the Lords of Council and Session, from June 6th 1678 to July 30th, 1712*, 2 Vols (Edinburgh: G. Hamilton and J. Balfour, 1759).

— *Historical Notices of Scotish [sic] Affairs . . .*, 2 Vols, ed. David Laing (Edinburgh: T. Constable, 1848).

The Laws and Acts of Parliament made by King James the First . . . . of Scotland, ed. Thomas Murray Lord Glendook (Edinburgh: David Lindsay, 1681).

The Laws of Virginia: Being A Supplement of Hening's The Statutes at Large, 1700–1750, W. W. Winfree, comp (Richmond, VA: Virginia State Library, 1971).

Legislative Journals of the Council of Colonial Virginia, 3 Vols, ed. H. R. McLlwaine, (Richmond, VA: Virginia State Library, 1918–19).

A Letter to an English Member of Parliament from a Gentleman in Scotland, concerning the Slavish Dependencies which a great part of that Nation is still kept under by Superiorities, Wards, Reliefs and other Remains of Feudal Law, and by Clanships first printed in Edinburgh in 1721 (London: M. Cooper, 1746).

Letters of Delegates to Congress, 1774–1789, ed. Paul H. Smith (Washington, DC: Library of Congress, 1976–2000), Vols 7, 8, 10 and 17.

Ligon, Richard, *A True and Exact History of the Island of Barbadoes* (London: Peter Parker, 1673).

Mackenzie, Sir George, *A Vindication of the Government in Scotland during the Reign of Charles II against Mis-Representation made in Several Scandalous Pamphlets* (London, 1691 and Edinburgh: James Watson, 1712).

The Mercy of the Government Vindicated, to which are added Remarks upon a late Pamphlet entituled An Argument to prove the Affections of the People the best Security of the Government, attributed to Daniel Defoe (London: James Roberts, 1716).

Memorabilia of the City of Glasgow, selected from the Minute Books of the Burgh, 1588–1750 (Glasgow: Printed for Private Circulation, 1835).

Middlesex County Records, Vol. 1, ed. John Cordy Jeaffreson (Clerkenwell: Middlesex County Records Society, at the Clerkenwell Sessions House, 1886).

Minutes of the Court of Rensselaerswyck, 1648–1652, trans. and ed. A. J. F. Van Laer (Albany, NY: University of New York, 1922).

Minutes of the Supreme Executive Council (Harrisburg, PA: State of Pennsylvania).

Moore, Milcah Martha, *Milcah Martha Moore's Book: A Commonplace Book from Revolutionary America*, eds Catherine La Courreye Blecki and Karin A. Wulf (University Park, PA: Pennsylvania State University Press, 1997).

Moultrie, William, *Memoirs of the American Revolution*, 2 Vols (New York: New York Times and Arno Press, 1968 [1802]).

The Newgate Calendar, ed. Donal Ó Danachair, 6 Volumes (Published by the Ex-classics Project, 2009, http://www.exclassics.com).

The Norffs President of Persecution (unto Banishment) against some of the innocent People called Quakers (n.d. 1665).

Papers relative to the Settling of the Maroons in His Majesty's Province of Nova Scotia (1798).

The Parliamentary History of England, from the Earliest Period to the Year 1803 (London: T. C. Hansard, 1815–18).

The Parliamentary Register, or History of the Proceedings and Debates of the House of Commons, 5 Vols (London: J. Almon, 1775–81; J. Debrett, 1782).

Pennsylvania Archives, 1st ser, ed. Samuel Hazard (Philadelphia, PA: J. Severns, 1851–70).

Pennsylvania Colonial Records, 16 Vols (Harrisburg: PA: State of Pennsylvania, 1838–53).

Pitman, Henry, *A Relation of the Great Sufferings and Strange Adventures of Henry Pitman, Chyrurgion to the late Duke of Monmouth . . . .* (London: Andrew Sowle, 1689).

The Proceeedings of the Government against the Rebels, compared with Persecutions of the late Reigns (1716, attributed to Daniel Defoe).

The Prisoners of the '45, edited from the State Papers, Sir Bruce Gordon Seton and Jean Gordon Arnot, 3 Vols (Edinburgh: Edinburgh University Press, for the Scottish History Society, 1928 and 1929).

A Proclamation for the due and speedy execution of the Statute against Rogues, Vagabonds, Idle and Dissolute Persons (London: Robert Barker, 1603, EEBO and STC 1875:10).

Proclamation for the speedie sending away of the Irish Beggars out of this Kingdome into their owne Countrey and for the Suppressing of English Rogues and Vagabonds according to Our Lawes (London: Robert Barker, 1633, EEBO 1813:38).

Puritanism and Liberty, Being the Army debates from the Clarke Manuscripts, selected and ed. A. S. P.Woodhouse (London: J. M. Dent and Sons, 1938).

Raine, James, *Depositions from the Castle at York Relating to Offences committed in the Northern Counties in the Seventeenth Century*, Surtees Society, Vol. 40 (Durham: Frances Andrews, 1861).

Ramsay, David, *The History of the Revolution in South Carolina*, 2 Vols (Trenton: Isaac Collins, 1785).

— *History of American Revolution*, ed. Lester H. Cohen, 2 Vols (Indianapolis, IN: Liberty Fund, 1990 [1789]).

— *History of South Carolina*, 2 Vols (Charleston, SC: David Longworth, 1809).

Records and Fines of the Quarterly Courts of Essex County, Massachusetts, Vol. 2, 1656–62 (Salem, MA: The Essex Institute, 1912).

Records of New Amsterdam from 1653 to 1674, Vol. 2, ed. Berthold Fernow (New York: The Knickerbocker Press, 1897).

Records of the Governor and Colony of the Massachusetts Bay in New England, 4 Vols (Boston, MA: William White, 1853–4).

The Records of the Proceedings of the Justiciary court, Edinburgh, 1661–1678, 3 Vols, ed. William George Scott-Moncrieff (Edinburgh: Printed at the University Press, 1905).

Records of the Sheriff Court of Aberdeenshire, 3 Vols, Vol. 2, Records, 1598–1649, ed. David Littlejohn (Aberdeen: Printed for the University, 1906).

The Records of the Virginia Company of London: The Court Book, Vol. 1, eds S. M. Kingsbury and H. L. Osgood (Washington, DC: The Government Printing Office, 1906).

Register of the Ministers, Elders and Deacons of the Christian Congregation of St. Andrews, ed. David Hay Fleming, Part 1, 1559–1600 (Edinburgh: Edinburgh University Press, T. and A. Constable, for the Scottish History Society, 1889).

The Register of the Privy Council of Scotland, ed. and abridged by Henry Paton, intro by Robert Kerr Hannay, 3rd series, Vol. 11, 1685–6 (Edinburgh: HM General Register House, 1929).

Remarks on the Speeches of William Paul, Clerk, and John Hall of Otterburn Esq., Executed at Tyburn for Rebellion, the 13th of July, 1716 (London: J. Baker and T. Warner, 1716).

Report to the House of Commons, (1) 'A Return of the Individuals Prosecuted for Political Libel and Seditious Conduct in England and Scotland, since 1807, with the Sentences passed on them (2) A Return of the Number of Convictions throughout the Kingdoms from the 1st January 1820 the 1st January 1821 for the Offences of Blasphemy and Sedition; distinguishing each; (3) A Return of the Number of Informations filed by the Attorney General, from the 1st January 1820, to the 1st of January 1821, against Persons accused of Blasphemy and Sedition, distinguishing each' (H. Hobhouse; Printed by the House of Commons, 5 April 1821).

Rivers, Marcellus, *England's Slavery or Barbados Merchandize represented in a Petition to the High and Honourable Court of Parliament by Marcellus Rivers and Oxenbridge Foyle* (London: printed in the eleventh year of England's Liberty, 1659).

Rodney, Admiral George, Godfrey Basil Mundy, *Life and Correspondence of George Brydges Rodney*, 2 Vols (London: John Murray, 1830).

Ruffhead, Owen, *The Statutes at Large from the Fifth Year of King James the First to the Tenth Year of the Reign of William the Third*, 3 Vols (London: Mark Basket, 1763).

Janet Schaw, *Journal of a Lady of Quality*, eds Evangeline Andrews and Charles M. Andrews (New Haven, CT: Yale University Press, 1921).

Scott, Walter, *Minstrelsy of the Scottish Border: Historical and Romantic Ballads*, 3 Vols (Edinburgh: Longman, Hurst, Rees, Orme and Brown, 1812).

Selections from the Records of the Kirk Session, Presbytery and Synod of Aberdeen, ed. and introduction John Stuart (Aberdeen: The Spalding Club, 1846).

Selected Justiciary Cases, 1624–1650, 3 Vols, Vol. 1, ed. S. A. Gillon (Edinburgh: The Stair Society, J. Skinner and Co, 1953); Vol. 2, ed. J. Irvine Smith (Edinburgh: The Stair Society, 1972); Vol.3, ed. J. Irvine Smith (Edinburgh: The Stair Society, 1974).

Simpson, James, 'James Simpson's Reports on the Carolina Loyalists, 1779 and 1780', ed. Alan S. Brown, *Journal of Southern History*, 21(4) (1955), 513–19.

Smith, Josiah, and Mabel L. Webber, 'Josiah Smith's Diary, 1780–1', *South Carolina Historical and Genealogical Magazine*, 33(1) (January, 1932), 1–28; 33(2) (April, 1932), 79–116; 33(3) (July, 1932), 197–207; 34(2) (April, 1933), 67–84; 33(4), 281–9.

Speech which was spoken in the Assembly of St Christopher (London: Debrett, 1782).

Statutes at Large from the First Year of King James the First to the tenth year of the Reign of King William the Third (London: Mark Basket, 1763).

The Statutes at Large of England and of Great-Britain, ed. T. E.Tomlins (London: George Eyre and Andrew Strahan, 1811).

The Statutes at Large, being a Collection of the Laws of Virginia, from the First Session of the Legislature in the Year 1619, 13 Vols, ed. William Waller Hening (Charlottesville, VA: University of Virginia Press, 1969—; Originally New York, 1819–33).

The Statutes at Large of England and Great Britain, 20 Volumes, ed. John Raithby (London: George Eyre and Andrew Strahan, 1811).

Statutes at Large of South Carolina, 10 Vols, eds David J. McCord and Thomas Cooper (Columbia, SC: A. S. Johnston, 1834–41).

Stewart, A. Francis, ed., *News-Letters of 1715–16* (London and Edinburgh: W. R. Chambers, 1910).

Thurloe, John, *A Collection of the State Papers of John Thurloe*, 7 Vols, ed. Thomas Birch (London: for the late Fletcher Gyles, Thomas Woodward, 1742).

— *The Western Martyrology or Bloody Assize . . .* 5th edition (London: John Marshall, 1705).

The Virginia Company, *Records of the Virginia Company*, Vol. 3, ed. Susan M. Kingsbury (Washington, DC: The Government Printing Office, 1933).

Walker, Patrick, *Some Remarkable Passages of the Life and Death of Mr Alexander Peden* (Glasgow: J. and J. Robertson, 1781; originally 1724).

Warren, Mercy Otis, *History of the Rise, Progress and Termination of the American Revolution*, 2 Vols [Boston: 1805], ed. Lester H. Cohen (Indianapolis, IN: Liberty Classics, 1988).

Washington, George, *The Writings of George Washington*, 12 Vols, ed. Jared Sparks (Boston, MA: Little, Brown, and Company, 1858).

— *The Papers of George Washington, Colonial Series*, Vol. 2, August 1755 to April 1756, ed. W. W. Abbot (Charlottesville, VA: University Press of Virginia, 1983).

Winslow, John, 'Journal of Colonel John Winslow', *Report and Collections of the Nova Scotia Historical Society*, Vol. 3 (Halifax, N.S.: Nova Scotia Historical Society, 1883).

Wisemans, Samuel, *Samuel Wiseman's Book of Record: The Official Account of Bacon's Rebellion in Virginia, 1676–1677*, ed. Michael Leroy Oberg (Lanham: MD: Rowman and Littlefield Publishers, 2005).

Young, R. M., 'News from Ireland: Being the Examination and Confession of William Kelso, etc., 1679', *Ulster Journal of Archaeology*, 2nd ser, 2(4) (1896), 274–9.

Secondary sources

Abbattista, Guido, 'Edmund Burke, the Atlantic American War and the 'Poor Jews at St. Eustatius': Empire and the Law of Nations', *Cromohs*, 13 (2008), 1–39.
Alison, Archibald, *Principles of the Criminal Law of Scotland* (Edinburgh: William Blackwood, 1832).
Anderson, James Donald, 'Thomas Wharton, Exile in Virginia, 1777–8', *Virginia Magazine of History and Biography*, 89(4) (1981), 425–47.
Andrews, Charles M., *Narratives of the Insurrections, 1675–1690* (New York: Barnes & Noble, 1956) [1915].
Anon., *Hanging Not Punishment Enough* (London: A. Baldwin, 1701).
Armitage, David, 'The Scottish Diaspora', in *Scotland: A History*, ed. Jenny Wormald, (Oxford: Oxford University Press, 2005), pp. 225–49.
Bach, Rebecca Ann, 'Ben Jonson's "Civil Savages"', *Studies in English Literature, 1500–1900*, 37(2) (1997), 277–93.
Bakker, Peter, 'An Early Vocabulary of British Romani (1616): A Linguistic Analysis', *Romani Studies*, 5, 12(2) (2002), 75–101.
Barca, Norman F., 'Citizens of St Eustatius, 1781: A Historical and Archaeological Study', in *The Lesser Antilles in the Age of European Expansion*, eds Robert L. Paquette and Stanley L. Engerman (Gainesville: University of Florida Press, 1996), pp. 223–38.
Barrell, John, *Imagining the King's Death: Figurative Treason, Fantasies of Regicide 1793–1796* (Oxford: Oxford University Press, 2000).
Bartlett, I. Ross, 'Scottish Mercenaries in Europe, 1570–1640: A Study in Attitudes and Policies', *International Review of Scottish Studies*, 13 (1985), 15–24.
Bauman, Richard, *For the Reputation of Truth: Politics, Religion, and Conflict Among the Pennsylvania Quakers 1750–1800* (Baltimore and London: Johns Hopkins University Press, 1971).
Beattie, John M., 'The Criminality of Women in Eighteenth-Century England', *Journal of Social History*, 8(4) (1975), 80–116.
— *Crime and the Courts in England, 1660–1800* (Princeton, NJ: Princeton University Press, 1986).
— 'The Royal Pardon and Criminal Procedure in Early Modern England', *Historical Papers/Communications Historiques*, 22(1) (1987), 9–22.
— *Policing and Punishment in London, 1660–1750: Urban Crime and the Limits of Terror* (Oxford: Oxford University Press, 2001).
Beckles, Hilary, 'A "Riotous and Unruly Lot": Irish Indentured Servants and Freemen in the West Indies, 1644–1713', *WMQ*, 3rd ser, 47 (1990), 503–22.
Beier, A. L., 'Vagrants and the Social Order in Elizabethan England', *Past and Present*, 64 (1974), 3–29.
— 'Social Problems in Elizabethan London', *The Journal of Interdisciplinary History*, 9(2) (1978), 203–21.
— *Masterless Men: The Vagrancy Problem in England, 1560–1640* (London: Methuen, 1985).
Belton, Bryan, *Questioning Gypsy Identity: Ethnic Narratives in Britain and America* (Lanham, MD: Altamira, Rowman and Littlefield, 2004).
Bennett, J. Harry, 'William Whaley, Planter of Seventeenth-Century Jamaica', *Agricultural History*, 40(2) (1966), 113–24.

B. E., *A New Dictionary of the Terms Ancient and Modern of the Canting Crew* . . . (London: W. Hawes, 1699).

Benton, Lauren, *A Search for Sovereignty: Law and Geography in European Empire, 1400–1900* (Cambridge: Cambridge University Press, 2010).

Biemer, Linda, 'Criminal Law and Women in New Amsterdam and Early New York', *Rensselaerswijk Seminar Papers* (1991, online at http://www.nnp.org/nnp/publications/ABAFB/3.1.pdf).

Billings, Warren M., 'A Quaker in Seventeenth-Century Virginia: Four Remonstrances by George Wilson', *WMQ*, 33(1) (1976), 127–40.

— *Sir William Berkeley and the Forging of Colonial Virginia* (Baton Rouge, LA: Louisiana State University Press, 2004).

Blake, John, 'Transportation from Ireland to America, 1653–60', *Irish Historical Studies*, 3(11) (1943), 267–81.

Block, Kristen and Jenny Shaw, 'Subjects without an Empire: The Irish in the Early Modern Caribbean', *Past and Present*, 210 (2010), 33–60.

Brebner, J. B., *New England's Outpost: Acadia before the Conquest of Canada* (New York: Columbia University Press, 1927).

Breen, Kenneth, 'General Rodney and St Eustatius in the American War: A Commercial and Naval Distraction, 1775–81', *The Mariner's Mirror*, 84(2), 1998, 193–203.

Burn, Richard, *The History of the Poor Laws, with Observations* (London: H. Woodfall and W. Strahan, 1764).

Button, Andrea, 'Royalist Women Petitioners in South-West England, 1655–62', *Seventeenth Century*, 15 (2000), 53–66.

Byres, Terence J., *Capitalism From Above and Capitalism From Below* (Basingstoke: Macmillan, 1996).

Byrne, Thomas, 'Banished by Cromwell? John Hooks and the Caribbean', *Irish Migration Studies in Latin America*, 5(3) (2007), 215–19.

Calloway, Colin G., *The Revolution in Indian Country: Crisis and Diversity in Indian Communities* (New York: Cambridge University Press, 1995).

Cant, Catherine B. H., 'The Archpriest Avvakum and his Scottish Contemporaries', *The Slavonic and East European Review*, 44(103) (1966), 381–402.

Canny, Nicholas P., 'The Ideology of English Colonization: From Ireland to America', *WMQ*, 3d ser, 30 (1972), 575–98.

Carroll, Kenneth L., 'Thomas Thurston, Renegade Maryland Quaker', *Maryland Historical Magazine*, 62 (June, 1967), 170–92.

— 'Persecution and Persecutors of Maryland Quakers, 1658–61', *Quaker History*, 99 (2010), 15–31.

Carter, Ian, 'The Highlands of Scotland as an Underdeveloped Region', in *Sociology and Development*, eds E. de Kadt and G. Williams (London: Tavistock, for the British Sociological Association, 1974), pp. 279–307.

Castro, Wendy Lucas, '"Being Separated from my Dearest Husband, in This Cruel Manner:" Elizabeth Drinker and the Seven-Month Exile of Philadelphia Quakers', *Quaker History*, 100(1) (2011), 40–63.

Cathcart, A., 'The Statutes of Iona: The Archipelagic Context', *Journal of British Studies*, 49(1) (2009), 4–27.

Cave, Alfred A., *The Pequot War* (Amherst, MA: University of Massachusetts Press, 1996).

Chambers, William, *Exploits and Anecdotes of the Scottish Gypsies, with Traits of their Origin, Character, and Manners* (Edinburgh: William Brown, 1886; originally, 1821).

Chambliss, William J., 'A Sociological Analysis of the Law of Vagrancy', *Social Problems*, 12(1) (1964), 67–77.

Champion, Justin, '"My Kingdom is not of this World": The Politics of Religion after the Revolution', in *English Revolution*, ed. Tyacke (Manchester: Manchester University Press), pp. 185–202.

Chaplin, Joyce E., 'Expansion and Exceptionalism in Early American History' *The Journal of American History*, 89(4) (2003), 1431–55, 1439.

Christopher, Emma, *A Merciless Place: The Lost Story of Britain's Convict Disaster in Africa* (Oxford: Oxford University Press, 2010).

Clark, Colin, 'Defining ethnicity in a cultural and socio-legal context: the case of Scottish Gypsy-Travellers', *Scottish Affairs*, 54 (2006), available online unpaginated at http://strathprints.strath.ac.uk.

Clifton, Robin, *The Last Popular Rebellion: The Western Rising of 1685* (London: Maurice Temple Smith, St. Martin's Press, 1984).

Coertzen, Pieter and David Osborne Christie 'Bible and Sword: The Cameronian Contribution to Freedom of Religion', *Dutch Reformed Theological Journal*, 49(1 and 2) (2008), 16–27.

Coffey, John, *Persecution and Toleration in Protestant England, 1558–1689* (Harlow: Pearson Education Limited, 2000)

Cohen, Robin, 'Diasporas and the Nation-State: From Victims to Challengers', *International Affairs*, 12(3) (1996), 507–20.

Coldham, Peter Wilson, 'The "Spiriting" of London Children to Virginia, 1648–85', *The Virginia Magazine of History and Biography*, 8(3) (1975), 280–7.

— *The Complete Book of Emigrants in Bondage*, including the supplement, *More Emigrants in Bondage* (Baltimore, MD: Genealogical Publishing Co, 1988 and 2002).

Coldrey, Barry M., '"A Place to which Idle Vagrants May Be Sent". The First Phase of Child Migration during the Seventeenth and Eighteenth centuries', *Children and Society*, 13 (1999), 32–47.

Connelly, Sean J., *Divided Kingdom: Ireland, 1630–1800* (Oxford: Oxford University Press, 2008).

Corfield, Penelope J., 'Dress for Deference and Dissent: Hats and the Decline of Hat Honour', *Costume*, 23 (1989), 64–79.

Cotterell, Mary, 'Interregnum Law Reform: The Hale Commission of 1652', *The English Historical Review*, 83(329) (1968), 689–704.

Cowan, Ian B., *The Scottish Covenanters, 1660–1688*, (London: Victor Gollancz Ltd, 1976).

Crane, Verner W., *The Southern Frontier, 1670–1732* (Ann Arbor, MI: University of Michigan, 1956 [1928]).

Crofton, Henry T.,'Early Annals of the Gypsies in England,' *Journal of the Gypsy Lore Society*, 1st ser, 1(1) (1888), 5–24.

Croke, Unton, 'Cromwell and the Insurrection of 1655', *English Historical Review*, 4(14) (1889), 313–38.

Crookshank, William, *The History of the State and Sufferings of the Church of Scotland from the Restoration to the Revolution*, 2 Vols (London: J. Oswald, 1749).

Currie, Janette, 'History, Hagiography, and Fakestory: Representations of the Scottish Covenanters in Non-Fictional and Fictional Texts from 1638 to 1835', (Unpublished PhD, Department of English, University of Stirling, 1999).

Davidson, Neil, 'Marx and Engels on the Scottish Highlands', *Science and Society*, 63(3) (2001), 286–326.

— *Discovering the Scottish Revolution, 1692–1746* (London: Pluto Press, 2003).

— 'The Scottish Path to Capitalist Agriculture 1: From the Crisis of Feudal Agriculture to the Origins of Agrarian Transformation (1688–1746)', *Journal of Agrarian Change*, 4(3) (2004), 227–68.

— 'The Scottish Path to Capitalist Agriculture 2: The Capitalist Offensive (1747–1815)', *Journal of Agrarian Change*, 4(4) (2004), 411–60.

Davies, C. S. L., 'Slavery and Protector Somerset; The Vagrancy Act of 1547', *The Economic History Review*, N. S. 19(3) (1966), 533–49.

Davis, N. Darnell, 'Notes on the History of the Jews in Barbados', *Publications of the American Jewish Historical Society*, 18 (1909), 129–81.

De Beer, Esmond S., 'Executions Following the "Bloody Assize"', *Bulletin of the Institute of Historical Research*, 4 (1926–7), 36–9.

Demos, John, ed. *Remarkable Providences*, 2nd edn (Boston, MA: Northeastern University Press, 1991).

— *The Unredeemed Captive: a Family Story from Early America* (New York: Knopf, 1994).

Denton, Peter H., 'At the Banquet in Hell: Sir George Mackenzie and Narratives of Religious Conflict in 17th Century Scotland', in *Believers in the Battlespace: Religion, Ideology and War*, ed. Peter H. Denton (Kingston, Ontario: Canadian Defence Academy Press, 2011), pp. 3–21.

Devine, T. M., 'Landlordism and Highland Emigration', in *Scottish Emigration and Scottish Society*, ed. T. M. Devine (Edinburgh: John Donald, 1992), pp. 84–103.

— *Scotland's Empire, 1600–1815* (London: Allen Lane, 2003).

Dionne, Craig and Steve Mentz, eds, *Rogues and Early Modern English Culture* (Ann Arbor, MI: University of Michigan Press, 2004).

Dobson, David, *Directory of Scots Banished to the American Plantations, 1650–1775* (Baltimore, MD: Genealogical Publishing Co, 1984).

— *Scottish Emigration to Colonial America, 1607–1785* (Athens, GA: University of Georgia Press, 2004).

Donagan, Barbara, 'Codes and Conduct in the English Civil War', *Past and Present*, 188 (1988), 65–95.

— 'Atrocity, War Crime, and Treason in the English Civil War', *The American Historical Review*, 99(4) (1994),1137–66.

— *War In England, 1642–1649* (Oxford: Oxford University Press, 2008).

Donovan, Bill M.,'Changing Perceptions of Social Deviance: Gypsies in Early Modern Portugal and Brazil', *Journal of Social History*, 26(1) (1992), 33–53.

Drake, James, 'Restraining Atrocity: The Conduct of King Philip's War', *New England Quarterly*, 70(1) (1997), 33–56.

Dunn, Richard S., *Sugar and Slaves: The Rise of the Planter Class in the British West Indies* (Chapel Hill, NC: University of North Carolina Press, 1972 and New York: W. W. Norton and Company, 1973).

Earle, Peter, *Monmouth's Rebels: The Road to Sedgemoor 1685* (London: Weidenfeld and Nicolson, 1977).

Eder, Markus, *'At the Instigation of the Devil': Capital Punishment and the Assize in Early Modern England* (Hilgertshausen-Tandern, Germany: 2009).

Ekirch, A. Roger, 'Great Britain's Secret Convict Trade to America, 1783–4', *American Historical Review*, 89(5) (1984), 1285–91.

— 'The Transportation of Scottish Criminals to America during the Eighteenth Century', *Journal of British Studies*, 24(3) (1985), 366–74.

Everett, C. S.,'"They shalbe slaves for their lives": Indian Slavery in Colonial Virginia', in *Indian Slavery in Colonial America*, ed. Alan Gallay (Lincoln, NE: University of Nebraska Press, 2009), 67–108.

Ewan, Elizabeth, 'Crime or Culture? Women and Daily Life in Late Medieval Scotland', in *Twisted Sisters: Women, Crime and Deviance in Scotland since 1400*, eds Yvonne Galloway Brown and Rona Ferguson (East Linton: Tuckwell Press, 2002), 117–36.

— 'Disorderly Damsels? Women and Interpersonal Violence in Pre-Reformation Scotland', *Scottish Historical Review*, 89, 2(228) (2010), 153–71.

Falconer, J. R. D., '"Mony Utheris Divars Odious Crymes": Women, Petty Crime and Power in Later Sixteenth-Century Aberdeen', *Crimes and Misdemeanours*, 4(1) (2010), online, 1–36.

Faragher, John Mack, *A Great and Noble Scheme: The Tragic Story of the Expulsions of the French Acadians from their American Homeland* (New York and London: Norton, 2005).

Farmer, Lindsay, *Criminal Law, Tradition and Legal Order: Crime and the Genius of Scots Law, 1747 to the Present* (Cambridge: Cambridge University Press, 1997).

Fergus, Howard A., 'Montserrat "Colony of Ireland": The Myth and the Reality', *Studies: An Irish Quarterly Review*, 70(280) (1981), 325–40.

Firth, Charles Harding, 'Cromwell and the Insurrection of 1655', *English Historical Review*, 3(10) (1888), 323–50.

Flatman, Richard, 'Transported to Barbados, 1655', *Irish Family History*, 12 (1996), 46–8.

Fletcher, Anthony, 'The Enforcement of the Conventicle Acts, 1664–79', in *Persecution and Toleration*, ed. W. J. Sheils (Oxford: Blackwell Publishing, 1984), 234–46.

Fogleman, Aaron S., 'From Slaves, Convicts, and Servants to Free Passengers: the Transformation of Immigration in the Era of the American Revolution', *Journal of American History*, 85 (1998), 43–76.

Ford, Alan, *James Ussher: Theology, History, and Politics in Early-Modern Ireland and England* (Oxford: Oxford University Press, 2007).

Fraser, A., *The Gypsies*, 2nd edn (Oxford: Blackwell, 1995).

Friedenwald, Herbert, 'Material for the History of the Jews in the British West Indies', *Publications of the American Jewish Historical Society*, 5 (1897), 45–68.

Fumerton, Patricia, 'Making Vagrancy (In)Visible: The Economics of Disguise in Early Modern Rogue Pamphlets', *English Literary Renaissance*, 33(2) (2003), 211–27.

— *Unsettled: The Culture of Mobility and the Working Poor in Early Modern England* (Chicago, IL: University of Chicago Press, 2006).

Gallay, Alan,'South Carolina's Entrance into the Indian Slave Trade', in *Indian Slavery in Colonial America* (Lincoln, NE: University of Nebraska Press, 2010), pp. 109–45.

Garrett, Jane, *The Triumphs of Providence: The Assassination Plot, 1696* (Cambridge: Cambridge University Press, 1980).

Gaspar, David B., *Bondsmen and Rebels: A Study of Master-Slave Relations in Antigua* (Durham and London: Duke University Press, 1993 [1984]).

Gaudet, Placide, *Le Grand Derangement: sur qui Retombe la Responsibilité de l'Expulsion des Acadiens?* (Ottawa: Ottawa Print, 1922).

German, Kieran, 'Jacobite Politics in Aberdeen and the '15', in *Loyalty and Identity*, eds Monod, Pittock and Szechi, 82–97.

Gilfillan, George, *Martyrs, Heroes and Bards of the Scottish Covenant* (New York: Robert Carter and Brothers, 1853).

Goodman, Nan, 'Banishment, Jurisdiction, and Identity in Seventeenth-Century New England', *Early American Studies*, 71(1), (Spring 2009), 109–39.

Gragg, Larry, *Englishmen Transplanted: The English Colonization of Barbados, 1627–1660* (Oxford: Oxford University Press, 2003).

— *The Quaker Community on Barbados: Challenging the Culture of the Planter Class* (Colombia, MO: University of Missouri Press, 2009).

Graham, Henry Grey, *The Social Life of Scotland in the Eighteenth Century*, 4th edn (London: Adam and Charles Black, 1937, 1950 repr).

Graham, Michael F., *The Uses of Reform: 'Godly Discipline' and Popular Behavior in Scotland and Beyond, 1560–1610* (Leiden: E. J. Brill, 1996).

Grant, John N., *The Maroons in Nova Scotia* (Halifax: Formac Publishing, 2002).

Greaves, Richard L., 'Seditious Sectaries or "Sober and Useful Inhabitants"? Changing Conceptions of the Quakers in Early Modern Britain', *Albion*, 33(1) (2001), 24–50.

Green, Ian, *Print and Protestantism in Early Modern England* (Oxford: Oxford University Press, 2000).

Gregg, Pauline, *Free-Born John: A Biography of John Lilburne* (London: J. M. Dent and Sons, 1961).

Griffiths, Naomi E. S., 'Acadians in Exile: the Experiences of the Acadians in the British Seaports', *Acadiensis*, 4, pt. 1 (1974), 67–84.

— 'Petitions of Acadian Exiles, 1755–1785: A Neglected Source', *Histoire Sociale/Social History*, 11 (1978), 213–23.

— *The Contexts of Acadian History, 1686–1784* (Montreal and Kingston: McGill-Queen's University Press, 1992).

— *From Migrant to Acadian: A North American Border People, 1604–1755* (Montreal and Kingston: McGill-Queen's University Press, 2005).

Gwynn, Aubrey, 'Cromwell's Policy of Transportation', *Studies: An Irish Quarterly Review*, 19(76) (1930), 607–23.

— 'Cromwell's Policy of Transportation: Part II', *Studies: An Irish Quarterly Review*, 20(78) (1931), 291–305.

Halliday, Paul D., *Habeas Corpus: From England to Empire* (Cambridge: Harvard University Press, 2010).

Handler, Jerome S., 'Aspects of Amerindian Ethnography in 17th-Century Barbados', *Caribbean Studies*, 9(4) (1970), 50–72.

— 'The Amerindian Slave Population of Barbados in the Seventeenth and Early Eighteenth Centuries', *Caribbean Studies*, 8(4) (1969), 38–64.

— 'Slave Revolts and Conspiracies in Seventeenth-Century Barbados', *New West Indian Guide*, 56 (1982), 1–2, Leiden, 5–42.

Hansen, Adam, 'Realizing Rogues: Theory, Organization, Dialogue', *Ephemera*, 4(4) (2004), 328–46.

Hardacre, Paul H., 'The Royalists in Exile during the Puritan Revolution, 1642–60', *Huntington Library Quarterly*, 16(4) (1953), 353–70.

Harris, Tim, *Revolution: The Great Crisis of the British Monarchy, 1685–1720* (London: Penguin, 2007).

Hayes, Micheál, 'Indigenous Otherness: Some Aspects of Irish Traveller Social History', *Éire-Ireland*, 41(3&4) (2006), 33–161.

Henderson, Lizanne, 'The Survival of Witchcraft Prosecutions and Witch Belief in South West Scotland, *Scottish Hist. Review*, 85(1) (2006), 52–74.

Higley, Christopher, 'Exile and Religious Identity in Early Modern England', *Reformation*, 15 (2010), 51–61.

Hodson, Christopher, 'Exile on Spruce Street: An Acadian History', *WMQ*, 67(2) (2010), 249–78.

— *The Acadian Diaspora: An Eighteenth-Century History* (Oxford and New York: Oxford University Press, 2012).

Hoffer, Peter Charles, *The Great New York Conspiracy of 1741: Slavery, Crime, and Colonial Law* (Lawrence, KS: University Press of Kansas, 2003).

Hoffman, Ronald, Thad W. Tate and Peter J, Albert, eds, *An Uncivil War: The Southern Backcountry during the American Revolution* (Charlottesville, VA: University Press of Virginia, 1985).

Horn, James, *Adapting to a New World: English Society in the Seventeenth-Century Chesapeake* (Chapel Hill, NC: University of North Carolina Press, 1994).

Howe, George, *The History of the Presbyterian Church in South Carolina* (Columbia, SC: Duffie and Chapman, 1870).

Hoyr, William D., Jr., 'A Contemporary View of the Acadian Arrival in Maryland, 1755', *WMQ*, 5(4) (1948), 571–5.

Hug, Tobias B., *Impostures in Early Modern England: Representations and Perceptions of Fraudulent Identities* (Manchester: Manchester University Press, 2009).

Hughes, Ann, 'Religious Diversity in Revolutionary London', in *The English Revolution*, ed. Tyacke, pp. 123–4.

Hume, David, *Commentaries on the Laws of Scotland Respecting the Description and Punishment of Crimes*, 2 Vols (Edinburgh: Bell and Bradfute, 1797).

Hume, Edgar Erskine, 'A Colonial Scottish Jacobite Family: Establishment in Virginia of a Branch of the Humes of Wedderburn', *The Virginia Magazine of History and Biography*, 38(1) (1930), 1–37 and (Continued), 38(4) (1930), 293–346.

Hurst, Ronald, *The Golden Rock: An Episode of the American War of Independence, 1775–1783* (London: Leo Cooper, 1996).

Inderwick, Frederick A., *The Interregnum (A.D. 1648–1660): Studies of the Commonwealth, Legislative, Social and Legal* (London: Sampson Low, Marston, Searle and Rivington, 1891).

— *Side-Lights on the Stuarts*, 2nd edn (London: Sampson Low, Marston, Searle and Rivington, 1891).

Jacobs, Jaap, *The Colony of New Netherland: A Dutch Settlement in Seventeenth-Century America* (Ithaca and London: Cornell University Press, 2009).

Jameson, J. Franklin, 'St Eustatius and the American Revolution', *American Historical Review*, 8 (July, 1903), 683–708.

Jardine, Mark, 'The United Societies: Militancy, Martyrdom and the Presbyterian Movement in Late-Restoration Scotland,1679 to 1688' (Unpublished PhD Thesis, University of Edinburgh, 2009).

Johnson, Robert C., 'The Transportation of Vagrant Children from London to Virginia, 1618–22', in *Early Stuart Studies*, ed. H. S. Reinmuth (Minneapolis, MN: University of Minnesota Press, 1970), pp. 137–51.

Johnston, Andrew J. B., 'The Call of the Archetype and the Challenge of Acadian History', *French Colonial History*, 5 (2004), 63–92.

Jones, William R., 'Sanctuary, Exile and the Law: The Fugitive and Public Authority in Medieval England and Modern America' in *Essays on English Law and the American Experience*, eds Elisabeth A. Cawthon and David E. Narrett (Arlington, TX: Texas A & M University Press, 1994), 19–41.

Kawashima, Yasuhide, *Puritan Justice and the Indian: White Man's Law in Massachusetts, 1630–1763* (Middleton, CT: Wesleyan University Press, 1986).

Keats, John, *The Poetical Works of John Keats*, ed. H. Buxton Forman (New York: Thomas Y. Crowell and Co, 1895).

Kelly, James, 'Transportation from Ireland to North America, 1703–89', in *Refiguring Ireland: Essays in Honour of L. M. Cullen*, eds David Dickson and Cormac Ó Gráda (Dublin: Lilliput Press, 2003), 112–35.

Kennedy, Alan Douglas, 'The Civic Government of the Scottish Highlands during the Restoration, 1660–88' (Unpublished PhD, University of Sterling, 2011).

Kierner, Cynthia A., *Southern Women in Revolution, 1776–1800: Personal and Political Narratives* (Columbia, SC: University of South Carolina Press, 1998).

Kilday, Anne-Marie, *Women and Violent Crime in Enlightenment Scotland* (Woodbridge: The Boydell Press for the Royal Historical Society, 2007).

Knott, John R., 'Joseph Besse and the Quaker Culture of Suffering', *Prose Studies*, 17(3) (December, 1994), 126–41.

Konig, David T., 'Regionalism in Early American Law', in *The Cambridge History of Law in America*, eds Michael Grossberg and Christopher L. Tomlins (Cambridge: Cambridge University Press, 2008), 144–77.

Kupperman, Karen O., 'English Perceptions of Treachery, 1583–1640: The Case of the American 'Savages', *Historical Journal*, 20(2) (1977), 263–87.

— *Roanoke: The Abandoned Colony* (Totowa, NJ: Rowen and Allenhead, 1984).

Landsman, Ned C., *Scotland and Its First American Colony, 1683–1765* (Princeton, NJ: Princeton University Press, 1985).

Ledet, Wilton Paul, 'Acadian Exiles in Pennsylvania', *Pennsylvania History*, 9(2) (1942), 118–28.

Lee, Wayne E., *Crowds and Soldiers in Revolutionary North Carolina: The Culture of Violence in Riot and War* (Gainesville, FL: University Press of Florida, 2001).

Leneman, Leah, '"Disregarding the Matrimonial Vows": Divorce in Eighteenth- and Early Nineteenth-Century Scotland', *Journal of Social History*, 30(2) (1996), 465–82.

Lenman, Bruce, *The Jacobite Risings in Britain, 1689–1746* (Aberdeen: Scottish Cultural Press, 1995).

Lepore, Jill, *The Name of War: King Philip's War and the Origins of American Identity* (New York: Knopf, 1998).

— *New York Burning: Liberty, Slavery, and Conspiracy in Eighteenth-Century Manhattan* (New York: Knopf, 2005).

Levack, Brian P., 'The Great Scottish Witch-Hunt of 1661–2', *Journal of British Studies*, 20(1) (1980), 90–108.

— 'The Prosecution of Sexual Crimes in Early Eighteenth-Century Scotland', *The Scottish Historical Review*, 89(2) no. 228, (2010), 172–93.

Linebaugh, Peter, and Marcus Rediker, *The Many-Headed Hydra: Sailors, Slaves, Commoners and the Hidden History of the Revolutionary Atlantic* (London and New York: Verso, 2000).

Lock, F. P., *Edmund Burke*, 1, 1730–84 (Oxford: Clarendon Press, 1998).

Lockett, James D., 'The Deportation of the Maroons of Trelawny Town to Nova
    Scotia, Then Back to Africa', *Journal of Black Studies*, 30(1) (1999), 5–14.
Louthian, John, *The Form of Process before the Court of Justiciary in Scotland*,
    2nd edn (Edinburgh: Hamilton, Balfour and Neill, 1752).
Lowe, Richard G., 'Massachusetts and the Acadians', *WMQ*, 3d ser, 25(2) (1968),
    212–29.
Lyons, Mary Ann, ' "Vagabonds", "Mendiants", "Gueux": French Reaction to
    Irish Immigration in the Early Seventeenth Century', *French History*, 14(4)
    (2000), 363–82.
Macaulay, Thomas Babington, *History of England from the Accession of James II*,
    4 Vols, Vol. 1, Introduction by Douglas Jerrold (London: J. M. Dent and Sons,
    Everyman Library, 1906).
MacGrath, Kevin, 'Irish Priests Transported under the Commonwealth'. *Archivium
    Hibernicum*, 14 (1949), 92–5.
MacInnes, Allan I., 'Repression and Conciliation: The Highland Dimension
    1660–88', *The Scottish Historical Review*, 65(180) pt. 2 (1986), 167–95.
MacLaughlin, Jim, 'European Gypsies and the Historical Geography of Loathing',
    Review (Fernand Braudel Center), 22(1) (1999), 31–59.
Macritchie, David, *Scottish Gypsies under the Stewarts* (Edinburgh: David
    Douglas, 1894).
Marcus, Jacob R., *The Colonial American Jew 1492–1776*, 3 Vols (Detroit, MI:
    Wayne State University Press, 1970).
Marietta, Jack D., *The Reform of American Quakerism 1748–1753* (Philadelphia,
    PA: University of Pennsylvania Press, 1984).
Marietta. Jack D. and G. S. Rowe, *Troubled Experiment: Crime and Justice in
    Pennsylvania, 1682–1800* (Philadelphia, PA: University of Pennsylvania Press,
    2006).
Marshall, Peter, 'Religious Exiles and the Tudor State', in *Discipline and Diversity:
    Studies in Church History*, Vol. 43, eds Kate Cooper and Jeremy Gregory
    (Woodbridge: Boydell, 2007), 263–84.
Mason, Roger A., 'Usable Pasts: History and Identity in Reformation Scotland',
    The Scottish Historical Review, 76(1), 201 (1997), 54–68.
Mayall, David, 'The Making of British Gypsy Identities, c.1500–1800', *Immigrants
    and Minorities*, 11(1) (1992), 21–41.
— *English Gypsies and State Policies* (University of Hertfordshire Press, 1995).
Millard, Clifford, 'The Acadians in Virginia', *Virginia Magazine of History and
    Biography*, 40(3) (July, 1932), 241–58.
Miller, John, '"A Suffering People": English Quakers and Their Neighbours c.1650–
    c1700', *Past and Present*, 188(1) (2005), 71–103.
Miller, Kerby A., *Emigrants and Exiles: Ireland and the Irish Exodus to North
    America* (NY and Oxford: Oxford University Press, 1985).
Meyer, Duane, *The Highland Scots of North Carolina, 1732–1776* (Chapel Hill,
    NC: University of North Carolina Press, 1957 and 1961).
Monod, Paul, Murray Pittock and Daniel Szechi, eds, *Loyalty and Identity:
    Jacobites at Home and Abroad* (Basingstoke: Palgrave Macmillan, 2010).
Morgan, Edmund S., *American Slavery, American Freedom: The Ordeal of
    Colonial Virginia* (New York: Norton, 1975).
Morgan, Gwenda, *The Hegemony of the Law: Richmond County, Virginia,
    1692–1776* (New York: Garland, 1989).

— *The Debate on the American Revolution* (Manchester: Manchester University Press, 2007).
— 'Convict Labor and Migration', in *The Encyclopedia of Global Human Migration*, ed. Immanuel Ness (Oxford: Blackwell Publishers, 2013).
Morgan Gwenda and Peter Rushton, *Rogues, Thieves and the Rule of Law: the Problem of Law Enforcement in North-East England 1718–1800* (London: UCL Press, 1998).
— *Eighteenth-Century Criminal Transportation: The Formation of the Criminal Atlantic* (Houndmills, Basingstoke: Palgrave Macmillan, 2004).
— 'Running Away and Returning Home: the Fate of English Convicts in the American Colonies', *Crime, Histoire & Sociétés/Crime, History & Societies*, 7(2) (2003), 61–80.
— 'Visible Bodies: Power, Subordination and Identity in the Eighteenth-Century Atlantic World', *Journal of Social History*, 39(1) (Fall 2005), 39–64.
Morton, Alexander S., *Galloway and the Covenanters: or, The Struggle for Religious Liberty in the South-West of Scotland* (Paisley: Alexander Gardner, 1904).
Napier, Mark, *History Rescued, in Answer to 'History Vindicated'* . . . (Edinburgh: Edmonston and Douglas, 1870).
Nash, Gary B., 'The Image of the Indian in the Southern Colonial Mind'. *WMQ*, 3d ser, Vol. 29(2) (1972), 197–230.
— *First City: Philadelphia and the Forging of Historical Memory* (Philadelphia, PA: University of Pennsylvania Press, 2002).
— *Red, White and Black: The Peoples of Early America*, 6th edn (Englewood Cliffs, NJ: Prentice Hall, 2009).
Netzloff, Mark, *England's Internal Colonies: Class, Capital, and the Literature of Early Modern English Colonialism* (Basingstoke: Palgrave Macmillan, 2004).
Nicholson, Bradley J., 'Legal Borrowing and the Origins of Slave Law in the British Colonies', *American Journal of Legal History*, 38 (1994) (1), 38–54.
Nord, Deborah Epstein, *Gypsies and the British Imagination, 1807–1930* (New York: Columbia University Press, 2006).
Nordholt, Jan Willem Schulte, *The Dutch Republic and American Independence*, trans Herbert H. Rowen (Chapel Hill & London: University of North Carolina Press, 1982).
O'Callaghan, Sean, *From Hell to Barbados: The Ethnic Cleansing of Ireland* (Dingle, Co. Kerry: Brandon Publishing, 2001).
Ò Ciosáin, Éamon, '*Voloumous Deamboulare*: The Wandering Irish in French Literature, 1600–1789', in *Exiles and Emigrants: Crossing Thresholds in European Culture and Society*, ed. Anthony Coulson (Brighton: Sussex Academic Press, 1997), pp. 32–42.
Ò Siochrú, Micheál, *God's Executioner: Oliver Cromwell and the Conquest of Ireland* (London: Faber and Faber, 2008).
Ogburn, Miles, 'A War of Words: Speech, Script and Print in the Maroon War of 1795–6', *Journal of Historical Geography*, 37 (2011), 203–15.
O'Shaughnessy, Andrew Jackson, *An Empire Divided: The American Revolution and the British Caribbean* (Philadelphia, PA: University of Pennsylvania, 2000).
Pestana, Carla Gardina, 'The Quaker Executions as Myth and History', *The Journal of American History*, 80 (1993), 441–69.

Pestana, Carla Gardina, 'The City upon a Hill under Siege: The Puritan Perception of the Quaker Threat to Massachusetts Bay', *The New England Quarterly*, 56 (1983), 323–53.

— *The English Atlantic in an Age of Revolution 1640–1651* (Cambridge, MA: University of Cambridge Press, 2004).

Palgrave, Reginald F. D., ' Cromwell and the Insurrection of 1655: A Reply to Mr Firth', *English Historical Review*, 3(11), (1888), 521–39.

— 'Cromwell and the Insurrection of 1655: A Reply to Mr Firth (Continued)', *English Historical Review*, 3(12), (1888), 722–51.

— 'Cromwell and the Insurrection of 1655: A Reply to Mr Firth (Continued)', *English Historical Review*, 4(13), (1889), 110–31.

Pancake, John S., *This Destructive War: The British Campaign in the Carolinas, 1780–1782* (Tuscaloosa, AL: University of Alabama Press, 2003).

Pittock, Murray G. H., 'Jacobite Culture', in *1745: Charles Edward Stuart and the Jacobites*, ed. Robert C. Woosnam-Savage (Edinburgh: HMSO, 1995, for Glasgow Museums), pp. 72–86.

Plank, Geoffrey, *Rebellion and Savagery: The Jacobite Rising of 1745 and the British Empire* (Philadelphia, PA: University of Pennsylvania Press, 2006).

— *An Unsettled Conquest: The British Campaign Against the Peoples of Acadia* (Philadelphia, PA: University of Pennsylvania Press, 2001).

Prendergast, John P., *The Cromwellian Settlement of Ireland* (New York: P. M. Haverty, 1868).

Price, Richard, ed., *Maroon Societies: Rebel Slave Communities in the Americas* (Garden City, N. Y.: Anchor, 1973).

Radzinowicz, Sir Leon and Roger Hood, 'The Status of Political Prisoner in England: The Struggle for Recognition', *Virginia Law Review*, 65(8) (1979), 1421–91.

Raffe, Alasdair J. N., 'Religious Controversy and Scottish Society, c.1679–1714' (Unpublished PhD, The University of Edinburgh, 2007).

Rathbone, Mark, 'Vagabond!', *History Today*, 51 (2005), 8–13.

Rawlyk, George A., *Nova Scotia's Massachusetts: A Study of Massachusetts-Nova Scotia Relations, 1630 to 1784* (Montreal and London: McGill-Queen's University Press, 1973).

Raymond, Joad, *Pamphlets and Pamphleteering in Early Modern England* (Cambridge: Cambridge University Press, 2003).

Reid, Christopher, *Edmund Burke and the Practice of Political Writing* (Dublin: Gill and Macmillan/St Martin's Press, 1985).

Richens, Ruth, 'The Stewarts in Underbank: Two Decades in the Life of a Covenant-ing Family', *The Scottish Historical Review*, 64(178) pt. 2 (1985), 107–27.

Rogers, Michael, 'Gerrard Winstanley on Crime and Punishment', *The Sixteenth Century Journal*, 27(3) (1996), 735–47.

Rodgers, Nini, 'The Irish in the Caribbean, 1641–1837: An Overview', *Irish Migration Studies in Latin America*, 5(3) (2007), 145–56.

Ronda, James P., 'Red and White at the Bench: Indians and the Law in Plymouth Colony, 1620–91', *Essex Institute Historical Collections in Early America*, 110 (1974), 200–15.

Ross, Richard J., 'The Legal Past of Early New England: Notes for the Study of Law, Legal Culture, and Intellectual History', *The WMQ*, 3rd ser, 50 (1993): 28–41.

— 'Puritan Godly Discipline in Comparative Perspective: Legal Pluralism and the Sources of "Intensity"', *American Historical Review*, 113 (2008), 975–1002.

Rothschild, Emma, 'A Horrible Tragedy in the French Atlantic', *Past and Present*, 192 (Spring, 2006), 67–108.

Ruddy, Francis Stephen, *International Law in the Enlightenment: The Background of Emmerich de Vattel's 'Le Droit des gens'* (Dobbs Ferry, NY: Oceana Publications,1975).

Rushton, Peter, 'Gateshead 1550–1700 – Independence against all the Odds?', *Newcastle and Gateshead before 1700*, eds Diana Newton and A. J. Pollard (Chichester: Phillimore, 2009), pp. 295–322.

Salgãdo, Gãmini, *Cony-catchers and Bawdy Baskets: An Anthology of Elizabethan Low Life* (Harmondsworth: Penguin, 1972).

Sankey, Margaret, *Jacobite Prisoners of the 1715 Rebellion:Preventing and Punishing Insurrection in Early Hanoverian Britain* (Burlington: Ashgate, 2005).

Scharf, Thomas, *A History of Maryland*, 3 Vols (Baltimore, MD: John B. Piet, 1879).

Scher, Richard B., 'Scotland Transformed: The Eighteenth Century', in *Scotland: A History*, ed. Jenny Wormald (Oxford: Oxford University Press, 2005), pp. 215–40.

Schwarz, Philip J., 'The Transportation of Slaves from Virginia, 1801–65', *Slavery and Abolition*, 7 (1986), 215–40.

Schwartz, Philip J., *Twice Condemned, Slaves and the Criminal Laws in Virginia, 1705–1865* (Baton Rouge, LA: Louisiana State University Press, 1988).

— *Slave Laws in Virginia* (Athens and London: University of Georgia Press, 1996).

Schwoerer, Lois G., 'William, Lord Russell: The Making of a Martyr, 1683–1983', *Journal of British Studies*, 24 (1985), 41–71.

Seed, Patricia, *Ceremonies of Posssession:Europe's Conquest of the New World 1492–1640* (Cambridge: Cambridge University Press, 1995).

Shapiro, Barbara, 'Law Reform in Seventeenth Century England', *The American Journal of Legal History*, 19(4) (1975), 280–312.

Shaw, John, 'What Alexander Carmichael Did Not Print: The "Cliar Sheanchain", "Clanranald's Fool" and Related Traditions', *Béaloideas*, 70 (2002), 99–126.

Sheppard, Jill, 'A Historical Sketch of the Poor Whites of Barbados: From Indentured Servants to "Redlegs"', *Caribbean Studies*, 14(3) (1974), 71–94.

Sherwood, H. N., 'Early Negro Deportation Projects', *Mississippi Valley Historical Review*, 2, 4 (March, 1916), 484–508.

Slack, Paul A., 'Vagrants and Vagrancy in England, 1598–1664', *The Economic History Review*, N.S. 27(3) (1974), 360–79.

Slack, Paul, *Poverty and Policy in Tudor and Stuart England* (London: Longman, 1988).

Sinclair-Stevenson, Christopher, *Inglorious Rebellion: The Jacobite Risings of 1708, 1715 and 1719* (London: Hamish Hamilton, 1971).

Smelie, Alexander, *Men of the Covenant: The Story of the Scottish Church in the Years of the Persecution* (Edinburgh: Fleming H. Revell Co, no date).

Smith, Abbot E., 'The Transportation of Convicts in the American Colonies in the Seventeenth Century', *American Historical Review*, 39 (1934), 232–49.

— *Colonists in Bondage: White Servitude and Convict Labour in America, 1607–1776* (New York: Norton, 1971; originally University of North Carolina Press, 1947).

Sollers, Basil, "The Acadians (French Neutrals) Transported to Maryland," *Maryland Historical Magazine*, 3(1) (1908), 19–20.

Sorensen, Janet, 'Vulgar Tongues: Canting Dictionaries and the Language of the People in Eighteenth-Century Britain', *Eighteenth-Century Studies*, 37(3) (2004), 435–54.

Souden, David, '"Rogues, Whores and Vagabonds"? Indentured Servant Emigrants to North America and the Case of Mid-Seventeenth-Century Bristol', *Social History*, 3(1) (1978), 23–41.

Spierenburg, Pieter, 'Deviance and Repression in the Netherlands. Historical Evidence and Contemporary Problems', *Historical Social Research*, 11(1) (1986), 4–16.

— 'Close to the Edge: Criminals and Marginals in Dutch Cities', *Eighteenth-Century Studies*, 31(3) (1998), 355–59.

Spindell, Donna J., 'The Law of Words: Verbal Abuse in North Carolina to 1730', *American Journal of Legal History*, 39 (1995), 5–42.

Starkey, A. M., 'Robert Wodrow and the History of the Sufferings of the Church of Scotland', *Church History*, 43(4) (1974), 488–98.

Stewart, Archibald, *History Vindicated in the Case of the Wigtown Martyrs*, 2nd edn (Edinburgh: Edmonston and Douglas, 1870).

Stoesen, Alexander R., 'The British Occupation of Charleston, 1780–2', *South Carolina Historical and Genealogical Magazine*, 63(2) (1963), 71–82.

Szechi, Daniel, '"Cam Ye O'er Frae France?" Exile and the Mind of Scottish Jacobitism', *Journal of British Studies*, 37(4) (1998), 357–90.

— *1715; The Great Jacobite Rebellion* (New Haven, CT: Yale University Press, 2006).

— 'Retrieving Captain Le Cocq's Plunder: Plebeian Scots and the Aftermath of the 1715 Rebellion', in *Loyalty and Identity*, eds Monod, Pittock and Szechi, pp. 98–119.

Tait, George, *A Summary of the Powers and Duties of a Justice of the Peace in Scotland* (Edinburgh and London: John Anderson and Co, and Longman, Rees, Orme, Brown and Green, 1828).

Tannenbaum, Frank, *Slave and Citizen: The Negro in the Americas* (New York: Knopf, 1946; republished by Beacon Press, 1992 with an introduction by Franklin W. Knight).

Taylor, Alan, *American Colonies: The Settling of North America* (Harmondsworth, Middlesex: Viking Penguin, 2002).

Thayer, Theodore, *Israel Pemberton: King of the Quakers* (Philadelphia, PA: Historical Society of Pennsylvania, 1943).

— *Pennsylvania Politics and the Growth of Democracy, 1740–1776* (Harrisburg, PA: Pennsylvania Historical and Museum Commission, 1953).

Timmons, Stephen A., 'Executions Following Monmouth's Rebellion: A Missing Link', *Historical Research*, 76(192) (2003), 286–91.

Tuchman, Barbara W, *The First Salute* (New York: Knopf, 1988).

Turner, Stanley Horsfall, *The History of Local Taxation in Scotland* (Edinburgh and London: William Blackwood and Sons, 1908).

Tyacke, Nicholas, ed., *The English Revolution, c1590–1720: Politics, Religion and Communities* (Manchester: Manchester University Press, 2007).

Tyler, Lyon G., 'Isle of Wight Papers Relating to Bacon's Rebellion', *WMQ*, 4(2) (1895), 111–15; *WMQ*, 7(4) (1899), 229–30.

Van Buskirk, Judith, 'They Didn't Join the Band: Disaffected Women in Revolutionary Philadelphia', *Pennsylvania History*, 62(3) (1995), 306–29.

Van Oosten, F. C., 'Some Notes Concerning the Dutch West Indies during the American Revolutionary War', *American Neptune*, 36 (1976), 155–69.

Vattel, Emerich de, *Les Droits des Gens* (1758) and the English translation (Law of Nations, 1760).

Wainwright, Nicholas B. and Sarah Logan Fisher, '"A Day of Trifling Occurrences"; Philadelphia, 1776–8', *Pennsylvania Magazine of History and Biography*, 82(4) (1958), 411–65.

Waldstreicher, David, 'Reading the Runaways: Self-Fashioning, Print Culture, and Confidence in Slavery in the Eighteenth-Century Mid-Atlantic', *WMQ*, 3rd ser, 56(2) (1999), 243–72.

Walker, David M., *A Legal History of Scotland*, 6 Vols (Edinburgh: T. and T. Clark, 1998).

Ward, Matthew, 'Fighting the "Old Women": Indian Strategy on the Virginia and Pennsylvania Frontier, 1754–8', *Virginia Magazine of History and Biography*, 103(3) (1995), 297–320.

Wareing, John, ' "Violently Taken Away or Cheatingly Duckoyed": The Illicit Recruitment in London of Indentured Servants for the American Colonies', *The London Journal*, 26(2) (2001), 1–22.

Watson, William J., 'Cliar Sheanchain', *The Celtic Review*, 4(13) (July, 1907), 80–8.

Wigfield, W. Macdonald, *The Monmouth Rebels, 1685* (Taunton: Somerset Record Society, 1985).

Winks, Robin W., *The Blacks in Canada: A History* (New Haven, CT: Yale University, 1971).

Wodrow, Robert, *The History of the Sufferings of the Church of Scotland from the Restoration to the Rebellion*, 4 Vols, ed. and introduced by Robert Burns (Glasgow: Blackie and Son, 1830–5), Vol. 2 (1830).

Zaller, Robert, 'The Debate on Capital Punishment during the English Revolution', *The American Journal of Legal History*, 31(2) (1987), 126–44.

Zook, Melinda, ' "The Bloody Assizes": Whig Martyrdom and Memory after the Glorious Revolution', *Albion*, 27(3) (1995), 373–96.

INDEX